Guitar All-in-One For Dummies®

Cheat Sheet

Relating Fingerboard Diagrams and Tablature to a Real Guitar

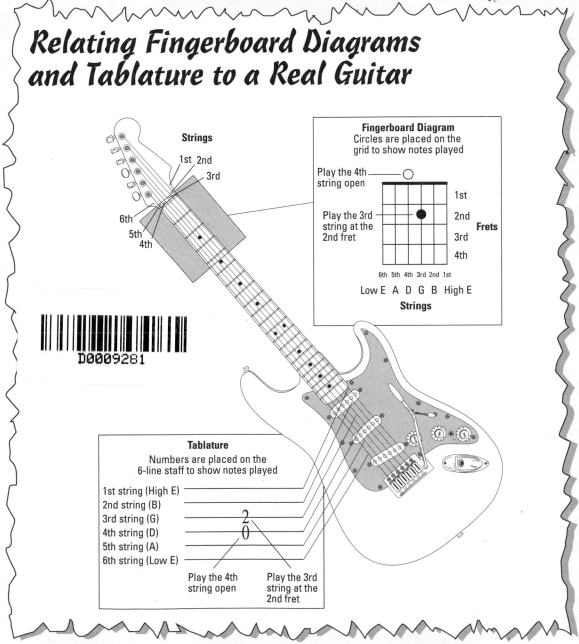

Strings

1st 2nd
3rd
6th
5th
4th

Fingerboard Diagram
Circles are placed on the grid to show notes played

Play the 4th string open

Play the 3rd string at the 2nd fret

1st
2nd
3rd
4th

Frets

6th 5th 4th 3rd 2nd 1st

Low E A D G B High E

Strings

Tablature
Numbers are placed on the 6-line staff to show notes played

1st string (High E)
2nd string (B)
3rd string (G)
4th string (D)
5th string (A)
6th string (Low E)

2
0

Play the 4th string open

Play the 3rd string at the 2nd fret

For Dummies: Bestselling Book Series for Beginners

FOR Dummies

BESTSELLING
BOOK SERIES

Guitar All-in-One
For Dummies®

Cheat
Sheet

24 Common Open-Position Chords

A	A7	Am	Am7	Amaj7	B♭
1 2 3	1 2	2 3 1	2 1	0 2 1 3	1 2 3 4
(2 1 3)	(2 3)				

B7	Bm	C	C7	Cmaj7	D
2 1 3 4	1 3 4 2	3 2 1	3 2 4 1	3 2	1 3 2

D7	Dm	Dm7	Dmaj7	E	E7
2 1 3	2 3 1	2 1 1	1 2 3	2 3 1	2 1

Em	Em7	F	Fmaj7	G	G7
2 3	2	3 2 1 1	3 2 1	2 1 3	3 2 1
				(3 2 4)	

Notes on the Neck

This 9-fret neck diagram shows the notes in letter names for all the frets on all six strings up to and including the 9th fret. This diagram helps you move any scale, arpeggio, or chord to a different starting note. For example, if you want to move an A major scale that starts on the 6th string, 5th fret, to a D♭ major scale, simply move your hand up the neck (toward the bridge) and place your starting finger on the 6th string, 9th fret.

high E	F	F#/G♭	G	G#/A♭	A	A#/B♭	B	C	C#/D♭
B	C	C#/D♭	D	D#/E♭	E	F	F#/G♭	G	G#/A♭
G	G#/A♭	A	A#/B♭	B	C	C#/D♭	D	D#/E♭	E
D	D#/E♭	E	F	F#/G♭	G	G#/A♭	A	A#/B♭	B
A	A#/B♭	B	C	C#/D♭	D	D#/E♭	E	F	F#/G♭
low E	F	F#/G♭	G	G#/A♭	A	A#/B♭	B	C	C#/D♭
		3 fr.		5 fr.		7 fr.		9 fr.

Guitar
ALL-IN-ONE

FOR
DUMMIES®

by Jon Chappell, Mark Phillips, Dave Austin, Mary Ellen Bickford, Holly Day, Scott Jarrett, Jim Peterik, and Michael Pilholfer

Wiley Publishing, Inc.

Guitar All-in-One For Dummies®

Published by
Wiley Publishing, Inc.
111 River St.
Hoboken, NJ 07030-5774
www.wiley.com

WILEY

About the Authors

Jon Chappell is a multistyle guitarist, transcriber, and arranger. He attended Carnegie-Mellon University, where he studied with Carlos Barbosa-Lima. He went on to earn his master's degree in composition from DePaul University, where he also taught theory and ear training. He was formerly editor-in-chief of *Guitar* magazine, technical editor of *Guitar Shop Magazine,* and musicologist for *Guitarra,* a classical magazine. He has played and recorded with Pat Benatar, Judy Collins, Graham Nash, and Gunther Schuller, and he has contributed numerous musical pieces to film and TV. Some of these include *Northern Exposure; Walker, Texas Ranger; Guiding Light;* and the film *Bleeding Hearts,* directed by Gregory Hines. In 1990, he became associate music director of Cherry Lane Music, where he has transcribed, edited, and arranged the music of Joe Satriani, Steve Vai, Steve Morse, Mike Stern, and Eddie Van Halen, among others.

Chappell has more than a dozen method books to his name and is the author of *The Recording Guitarist — A Guide for Home and Studio,* published by Hal Leonard. He is the author of *Rock Guitar For Dummies* and co-author of *Guitar For Dummies,* 2nd Edition, *Blues Guitar For Dummies, Classical Guitar For Dummies,* and *Guitar Exercises For Dummies* (Wiley).

Mark Phillips is a guitarist, arranger, and editor with more than 30 years in the music publishing field. He earned his bachelor's degree in music theory from Case Western Reserve University, where he received the Carolyn Neff Award for scholastic excellence, and his master's degree in music theory from Northwestern University, where he was elected to Pi Kappa Lambda, the most prestigious U.S. honor society for college music students. While working toward a doctorate in music theory at Northwestern, Phillips taught classes in theory, ear training, sight singing, counterpoint, and guitar.

During the 1970s and early 1980s, Phillips was director of popular music at Warner Bros. Publications, where he edited and arranged the songbooks of such artists as Neil Young, James Taylor, the Eagles, and Led Zeppelin. Since the mid-'80s he has served as director of music and director of publications at Cherry Lane Music, where he has edited or arranged the songbooks of such artists as John Denver, Van Halen, Guns N' Roses, and Metallica, and has been music editor of the magazines *Guitar* and *Guitar One.*

Phillips is the author of several books on musical subjects, including *Metallica Riff by Riff, Sight-Sing Any Melody Instantly,* and *Sight-Read Any Rhythm Instantly.* He is co-author of *Guitar For Dummies,* 2nd Edition, *Blues Guitar For Dummies, Classical Guitar For Dummies,* and *Guitar Exercises For Dummies* (Wiley).

Dave Austin has written the critically acclaimed book *The Unfinished Cross — Listen to the Voice Within,* published by Hampton Roads Publishing Company. He is also CEO of Transcension Music Group, a record company with a mission to bring positive music to the forefront of today's listening audience and bring together well-respected veterans in the music industry for a common cause of taking quality music to a higher level. Over the past 20 years, Dave, along with his good friend Phil Ehart (founding member of Kansas), has produced and promoted all-star concerts with some of the greatest talent in the industry. Dave lives in Camarillo, California, with his wife, Cathy, and his four sons, Jason, Shane, Chase, and Daniel. You can visit Dave at www.daveaustin.org. He is co-author of *Songwriting For Dummies* (Wiley).

Mary Ellen Bickford has been involved in writing, film production, and music for more than 20 years. She has authored two books, *The Language of Light* (co-authored with Norman B. Miller) and *Eloquence,* a book of poetry. She has also written and co-written film scripts, treatments, and corporate publications. Her work in film production includes coordinating the filming of *Hands Across America* and the unveiling of the *Statue of Liberty Celebration* for Imax producer Greg MacGillivray. She was also the director of education for the noted Imax movie *The Living Sea.* Currently, Mary Ellen serves as an officer and board member for two nonprofit organizations: the DoveSong Foundation (providing education about positive music) and Kids X-Pressions Inc. (providing opportunities for the young at heart to express themselves freely through the media). Mary Ellen currently lives in northern Georgia, where she co-writes songs with her husband, composer/musician Don Robertson. You may find out more about their work by visiting www.dovesong.com. She is co-author of *Songwriting For Dummies* (Wiley).

Holly Day is a music journalist whose articles have appeared in publications all over the world, including *Computer Music Journal, ROCKRGRL, Music Alive!, Guitar One,* and *Mixdown* magazines. Her writing has received an Isaac Asimov Award, a National Magazine Award, and two Midwest Writer's Grants. She is co-author of *Music Theory For Dummies* and *Music Composition For Dummies* (Wiley).

Scott Jarrett is a musician and producer who has worked with numerous artists, including Willie Nelson, Fiona Flanagan, Mary Klueh, and Keith Jarrett. He has served as music director for many live theatrical productions, including the Broadway production of *The Best Little Whorehouse in Texas.* He currently runs Monkey House recording studio in Hudson, Wisconsin, and has released two original albums, *Without Rhyme or Reason* and *The Gift of Thirst.* He has taught music theory, composition, production, and/or recording at the Full Sail Center for the Recording Arts in Orlando, the Acting Conservatory in Nashville, and McNally-Smith School of Music in St. Paul, Minnesota. He is co-author of *Music Composition For Dummies* (Wiley).

Jim Peterik has enjoyed a 35-year love affair with music. He has written or co-written a memorable array of top-40 hits such as "Hold On Loosely," "Caught Up In You," and "Rocking Into The Night" with Southern-rock legends 38 Special; "Heavy Metal" (theme to the award-winning animation of the same name) with Sammy Hagar; and with group co-founder Frankie Sullivan, wrote the entire catalogue for the group Survivor (of which Jim was a founding member), including smash hits like "High on You," "I Can't Hold Back," "Is This Love," "Burning Heart" (theme from *Rocky IV*), the number-one single "The Search Is Over," and the triple-platinum, Grammy-winning, Oscar-nominated theme from *Rocky III* — "Eye of the Tiger." Today, when not spending time with his wife, Karen, and son, Colin, Jim is busy discovering and producing new talent and collaborating with some of the world's best songwriters. He still plays regularly with the Ides of March and performs with his World Stage superstar lineup for special events. In his solo "Storytellers" style concerts, he tells the stories behind the songs he's written throughout the years. You can visit Jim at www.jimpeterik.com. He is co-author of *Songwriting For Dummies* (Wiley).

Michael Pilholfer teaches music theory and percussion at McNally Smith College of Music in St. Paul, Minnesota, where he serves as department head of the Ensembles Department. He has worked as a professional musician for more than 18 years and has toured and recorded with Joe Lovano, Marian McPartland, Kenny Wheeler, Dave Holland, Bill Holman, Wycliffe Gordon, Peter Erskine, and Gene Bertoncini. He is co-author of *Music Theory For Dummies* (Wiley).

Publisher's Acknowledgments

We're proud of this book; please send us your comments through our Dummies online registration form located at `http://dummies.custhelp.com`. For other comments, please contact our Customer Care Department within the U.S. at 877-762-2974, outside the U.S. at 317-572-3993, or fax 317-572-4002.

Some of the people who helped bring this book to market include the following:

Acquisitions, Editorial, and Media Development

Compilation Editor: Corbin Collins

Senior Project Editor: Georgette Beatty

Acquisitions Editor: Tracy Boggier

Senior Copy Editor: Victoria M. Adang

Assistant Editor: Erin Calligan Mooney

Editorial Program Coordinator: Joe Niesen

Technical Editor: Sandy Williams

Assistant Project Manager: Jenny Swisher

Associate Producer: Marilyn Hummel

Quality Assurance: Angie Denny

Editorial Manager: Michelle Hacker

Editorial Assistant: Jennette ElNaggar

Cover Photo: Image Source Pink

Cartoons: Rich Tennant (`www.the5thwave.com`)

Composition Services

Project Coordinator: Patrick Redmond

Layout and Graphics: Samantha K. Allen, Reuben W. Davis, Timothy Detrick, Joyce Haughey, Melissa K. Jester, Ronald Terry, Christine Williams

Special Art: W.R. Music Service

Proofreader: Melissa Cossell

Indexer: Steve Rath

Publishing and Editorial for Consumer Dummies

Diane Graves Steele, Vice President and Publisher, Consumer Dummies

Kristin Ferguson-Wagstaffe, Product Development Director, Consumer Dummies

Ensley Eikenburg, Associate Publisher, Travel

Kelly Regan, Editorial Director, Travel

Publishing for Technology Dummies

Andy Cummings, Vice President and Publisher, Dummies Technology/General User

Composition Services

Debbie Stailey, Director of Composition Services

Contents at a Glance

Table of Contents

Book IV: Blues Guitar 267

Introduction

So you want to play guitar, eh? No one can blame you. The guitar isn't just a beautiful, soulful, and versatile instrument. For about 75 years now, it has also set the standard for *coolness* in the music world. Not a bad combination!

Though the guitar as we know it is only about a century and a half old, its roots as a plucked stringed instrument go back deep into history. Many ancient folk instruments have followed the basic strings-stretched-over-fretboard-and-played-with-fingers design for thousands of years, and the guitar is in some ways the culmination of that legacy. It seems humans have always had something like the guitar in mind.

After the guitar was electrified in the 1930s — that is, when it went from soft backup instrument to a forceful and expressive vehicle for soloing — its popularity skyrocketed, and its intrinsic qualities and sound changed popular music forever. But its softer side didn't go away. When Bob Dylan famously "plugged in" at the 1965 Newport Folk Festival and was booed by outraged folk fans, it became clear that the electric guitar had entered its own universe.

Guitar All-in-One For Dummies covers both the acoustic and the electric universes — as well as the older classical guitar one, which has its own language, techniques, and musical pedigree.

About This Book

First, here's what this book is not: It's not a textbook, nor a long-winded history, nor a rote learning tool. Lots of those kinds of books are on the market, if that's what you're looking for — but beware, they are often dry and assume underlying knowledge.

Guitar All-in-One For Dummies is a generous conglomeration of material from several *For Dummies* guitar and music books. It aims to cover the guitar gamut, from what those thingies are called that wind the strings (tuning machines) to how Stevie Ray Vaughan got his incredible sound (by tuning lower, among other tricks) to which chords just plain sound good together when writing songs (depends — see Chapter 4 in Book VII).

Much of the material is relevant to any style of guitar playing. But three popular guitar genres each get their own book: rock guitar, blues guitar, and classical guitar. You also find chapters on learning to read music, on building your chord repertoire, on amps, scales, songwriting . . . let's just say there's a lot here. And don't forget the CD!

Conventions Used in This Book

Important words are defined in *italics*. Key words in lists that bring important ideas to your attention are in **bold.** And all Web addresses are in `monofont` to set them apart.

Here are a few other conventions to help you navigate this book:

- ✔ **Right hand and left hand:** Instead of using "strumming hand" and "fretting hand," this book uses "right hand" for the hand that picks or strums the strings and "left hand" for the hand that frets the strings (it's easier and shorter that way). Sincere apologies to those left-handed readers who are using this book; you folks should read "right hand" to mean "left hand" and vice versa.

- ✔ **Up and down, higher and lower, and so on:** If you're asked to move a note or chord up the guitar neck or to play it higher on the neck, it means higher in pitch, or toward the body of the guitar. If you're asked to go down or lower on the neck, it means toward the headstock, or lower in pitch. (Those of you who hold your guitar with the headstock tilted upward may need to do a bit of mental adjustment whenever you see these terms. Just remember that these terms are about pitch, not position, and you'll do just fine.)

- ✔ **Dual music notation:** Songs and exercises are arranged with the standard music staff on top and the tablature staff below. You can use either of these methods, but you don't need to look at both at the same time. In many cases, the music under scrutiny also is on the CD, so look for black boxes that point you to specific tracks on the CD and then follow along.

What You're Not to Read

There are many sidebars (in shaded gray boxes) in this book that you don't really need to read in order to follow the chapter text. They contain extra information or background stories and history that you may be interested in, or not. Feel free to skip anything marked with the Technical Stuff icon, too.

Foolish Assumptions

Guitar All-in-One For Dummies doesn't assume you know anything about playing guitar or reading music. It starts from zero and builds from the ground up — and then keeps going and going. It contains straightforward, informal explanations of how guitars work, what the different kinds are, how to get started playing, how to form chords and strum and fingerpick, and then proceeds to help deepen your knowledge in several directions.

This book is designed for just about anyone who loves guitar. It is as useful for people who have barely touched a guitar as it is for those who have fiddled around with one for years but would like to get more serious. Even advanced players — such as those who would like to try a different genre than they're used to, or who specifically need to work on, say, their outside chord inversion patterns — will find plenty of valuable information in these pages.

No matter your situation, experience, or motives, this book's goal is to give you enough information so that ultimately you can explore the guitar on your own. Discovering what the instrument can do, finding ways to make new sounds, suddenly grasping a better way to fret notes or chords that just minutes ago seemed impossible — these are tremendously exciting and satisfying experiences. Such magic awaits *you* if you're willing to put in some time and effort.

How This Book Is Organized

Guitar All-in-One For Dummies is sorted into eight books so you can find what you need to know quickly.

Book 1: Guitar 101

The first book begins with the basics by looking at how guitars are constructed, what the different parts are, and how to go about acquiring a guitar that suits your style and budget. The mechanics of getting up and running are covered here, such as stringing and tuning the instrument, and the basic how-to of playing it. A chapter in this book also tackles reading music — a skill which isn't required to play guitar, but is helpful in many ways.

Book 11: Sounds and Techniques

This book gets you going in playing guitar, starting with basic major and minor chords. Did you know you can play probably half of the most famous songs ever by knowing just three or four chords? It's true. Of course, after you get a taste of E minor, you're going to want to try E7 . . . and that's how you get hooked. This book also discusses strumming, plucking, and picking techniques. By the time you finish this book, you should have all the knowledge you need to play, in basic form, loads and loads of songs on guitar.

Book III: Rock Guitar

Nowadays, when people think of a guitar, they usually picture someone in tight pants and insufficiently trimmed hair coaxing unholy sounds out of it. That's because rock 'n' roll really brought the guitar to the forefront of popular culture, beginning in the middle of the last century. This book focuses on All Things Rock: the nitty-gritty of amplifiers, playing hot licks and sweet leads, and checking out just how the greatest guitar heroes do what they do. From Chuck Berry to Keith Richards, from Jimi Hendrix to The Edge, this book is your key to unlocking what makes rock guitar so exciting.

Book IV: Blues Guitar

A basic guitar is cheap to buy (or make), and it's perfect for strumming while you sing — which meant it was the ideal instrument for African Americans to entertain themselves and their neighbors in the rural South during hard times. The result: a unique musical genre that's as full of emotion and passion as it is easy to play. But the blues didn't stop at the porch — it migrated to various parts of the U.S. (and eventually Great Britain and elsewhere) and developed into many distinct styles. It also helped birth rock 'n' roll. This book explores all aspects of the blues, from picking styles to signature riffs, from the evolution of different song forms to the achievements of the great blues guitarists in history.

Book V: Classical Guitar

The other iconic image of a guitar player is a romantic-looking fellow, seated and holding a humble acoustic guitar, playing gorgeous and complicated instrumental music. This book makes it clear that rock and blues are the new kids on the block. Classical guitar figured out early on that the great Baroque, Classical, and Romantic compositions weren't just for violin and cello after all. This book delves into the history and development of classical guitar, both as an instrument and a style. It contains lots of music to play, too, including standards that are surprisingly easy to play and more challenging, complex pieces that vividly separate the virtuosos from the noodlers.

Book VI: Exercises: Practice, Practice, Practice

How do you get to Carnegie Hall? Practice, and lots of it, is the only way you'll ever stand on stage with confidence, poised to amaze and delight a crowd. Many guitarists find that after several months or even years of playing, their abilities plateau — they don't get worse, but they don't get better. They have reached stasis in their playing. And that may be fine, depending on commitment level. But at that point, one sure-fire way to keep improving is to repeatedly work the fingers through rigorous practice exercises. In this book you find lots and lots of moderate and advanced scales, chords, and arpeggio training designed to correct deficiencies and rev up stalled skills.

Book VII: Writing Songs and Music

Picking up a guitar and playing songs and compositions written by your favorite artists is fun, no question about it. But there may well come a point when you feel the urge to contribute something original of your own. How exactly do you go about that? Well, you could stumble around trying out random chords as you think up things that rhyme (please don't rhyme "fire" with "desire" again, okay, please?) — or you could approach the challenge armed with some wisdom from people who do it for a living. It turns out that writing songs is both an art and a science. This book is chock-full of tips and tricks to use when writing music, such as using the inherent melodies in scales and chords and putting chords together in proven progressions that evoke precisely the mood and feeling you're after.

Book VIII: Appendixes

Guitar All-in-One For Dummies ends with the Mother of All Guitar Chord Charts — a reference that should come in mighty handy when trying to recall how to form E♭dim7 — and an appendix on using the CD.

Icons Used in This Book

You'll see four icons scattered around the margins of the text. Each icon points out a certain type of information about guitars and guitar playing. They go as follows:

This icon notes something you should keep in mind. It may refer to something covered earlier in the book, or it may highlight something you ought to remember in the future.

 This icon flags the boring (but sometimes helpful) stuff. Feel free to skip text with this icon. On the other hand, you may be interested to know extra details or little-known trivia about the topic at hand, in which case by all means, read away.

 Information marked with this icon usually tells you how to play something better, faster, or easier. Sometimes it refers to especially helpful ideas and advice that can enrich your guitar experience.

 This icon points out stuff you should avoid. Guitar players often pick up bad habits that can limit their playing — watch out for this icon so you can head off trouble at the pass.

Where to Go from Here

Where to go depends on your level of skill. You may as well start with Chapter 1 in Book I if you know nothing about guitars, to lay a solid foundation for what comes later — after all, if you don't know what we're talking about later on, the book isn't of much use. If you have a little experience with guitar, try beginning with Book II for a brush-up on the basics and then move on from there. If you know guitar basics but are interested in finally trying to read music, head straight to Chapter 4 in Book I.

If you're already okay on guitar, and you know how to do things like form 7th chords and use a pick to make a controlled, bouncy rhythm, head to the chapters in the book about your favorite genre and dive in — Books III, IV, and V. We guarantee you'll learn something new and probably encounter some challenges.

If you're already a good guitar player, well . . . the thing is, you know in your heart you're not as good as you *could* be. Make for Book VI to really give those fingers a workout. And if you have the flickering of a new song in your heart, first find a voice recorder (or pen and paper if you can write music) and record your idea while it's still in your head. *Then* head to Book VII to check out a ton of ideas on how to develop your soon-to-be hit song.

All right then — it's time to get going. Good luck and much success in your playing!

Book I
Guitar 101

"Gee thanks, but I don't think a gingham neck cozy and peg board bonnet really goes with the rest of my guitar."

In this book . . .

We start by checking out how guitars are built and how to tune them so they sound just right. We go into buying a guitar (or two) that fits your wallet and lifestyle. We also wade into beginning to actually play the things — settling into position, forming simple chords, and strumming. Finally, because we are sadists, we give you a chapter on reading music, something that's not necessary but can come in handy and will help you get more out of this book.

Here are the contents of Book I at a glance.

✔ **End pin:** A metal post where the rear end of the strap connects. On *acoustic-electrics* (acoustic guitars with built-in pickups and electronics), the pin often doubles as the *output jack* where you plug in.

✔ **Fingerboard:** A flat, plank-like piece of wood that sits atop the neck, where you place your left-hand fingers to produce notes and chords. The fingerboard is also known as the *fretboard,* because the frets are embedded in it.

✔ **Frets:** Thin metal wires or bars running perpendicular to the strings that shorten the effective vibrating length of a string, enabling it to produce different pitches.

✔ **Headstock:** The section that holds the tuning machines and provides a place for the manufacturer to display its logo. Not to be confused with Woodstock, a famous upstate New York concert in 1969.

✔ **Neck:** The long, clublike wooden piece that connects the headstock to the body.

✔ **Nut:** A grooved sliver of stiff nylon, brass, bone, or other synthetic substance that stops the strings from vibrating beyond the neck. The strings pass through the grooves on their way to the tuners in the headstock. The nut is one of the two points at which the vibrating area of the string ends. (The other is the bridge.)

✔ **Output jack (electric only):** The insertion point for the cord that connects the guitar to an amplifier or other electronic device.

✔ **Pickup selector (electric only):** A switch that determines which pickups are currently active.

✔ **Pickups (electric only):** Barlike magnets that create the electrical current, which the amplifier converts into musical sound.

✔ **Sides (acoustic only):** Separate curved wooden pieces on the body that join the top to the back.

✔ **Strap pin:** Metal post where the front, or top, end of the strap connects. (Note that not all acoustics have a strap pin. If the guitar is missing one, tie the top of the strap around the headstock.)

✔ **Strings:** The six metal (for electric and steel-string acoustic guitars) or nylon (for classical guitars) wires that, drawn taut, produce the notes. Although not strictly part of the actual guitar — you attach and remove them at will on top of the guitar — strings are an integral part of the whole system, and a guitar's entire design and structure revolves around making the strings ring out with a joyful noise. (You can find out more about strings and tuning later in this chapter.)

✔ **Top:** The face of the guitar. On an acoustic, this piece is also the *sounding board,* which produces almost all the guitar's acoustic qualities. On an electric, the top is merely a cosmetic or decorative cap that overlays the rest of the body material.

✔ **Tuning machines:** Geared mechanisms that raise and lower the tension of the strings, drawing them to different pitches. The string wraps tightly around a post that sticks out through the top, or face, of the headstock. The post passes through to the back of the headstock, where gears connect it to a tuning key. Also known as tuners, tuning pegs, tuning keys, and tuning gears.

✔ **Volume and tone controls (electric only):** Knobs that vary the loudness of the guitar's sound and its bass and treble frequencies.

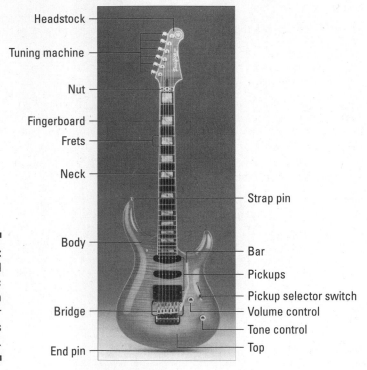

Figure 1-2:
A typical electric guitar with its major parts labeled.

Labels: Headstock, Tuning machine, Nut, Fingerboard, Frets, Neck, Body, Bridge, End pin, Strap pin, Bar, Pickups, Pickup selector switch, Volume control, Tone control, Top

How Guitars Work

After you can recognize the basic parts of the guitar, you may also want to understand how those parts work together to make sound (in case you happen to choose the "Parts of a Guitar" category on *Jeopardy!* or get into a heavy argument with another guitarist about string vibration and string length). This information is presented so you know why your guitar sounds the way it does, instead of like a kazoo or an accordion. The important thing to remember is that a guitar makes the sound, but you make the music.

String vibration and string length

Any instrument must have some part of it moving in a regular, repeated motion to produce musical sound (a sustained tone, or *pitch*). In a guitar, this part is the vibrating string. A string that you bring to a certain tension and then set in motion (by a plucking action) produces a predictable sound — for example, the note A. If you tune a string of your guitar to different tensions, you get different tones. The greater the tension of a string, the higher the pitch.

You couldn't do very much with a guitar, however, if the only way to change pitches was to frantically adjust the tension on the strings every time you pluck a string. So guitarists resort to the other way to change a string's pitch: shortening its effective vibrating length by *fretting* — pacing back and forth and mumbling to themselves. Just kidding; guitarists never do *that* kind of fretting unless they haven't held their guitars for a couple of days. In guitar-speak, *fretting* refers to pushing the string against the fretboard so it vibrates only between the fingered fret and the bridge. This way, by fretting the left hand up and down the neck (toward the bridge and the nut, respectively), you can change pitches comfortably and easily.

The fact that smaller instruments such as mandolins and violins are higher in pitch than are cellos and basses (and guitars, for that matter) is no accident. Their pitch is higher because their strings are shorter. The string tension of all of these instruments may be closely related, making them feel somewhat consistent in response to the hands and fingers, but the drastic difference in string lengths results in the wide differences of pitch among them. This principle holds true in animals, too. A Chihuahua has a higher-pitched bark than a Saint Bernard because its strings — er, vocal cords — are much shorter.

Using both hands to make a sound

The guitar normally requires two hands working together to create music. If you want to play, say, middle C on the piano, all you do is take your index finger, position it above the appropriate white key under the piano's logo, and press it down: *donnnng.* A preschooler can sound just like Vladimir Horowitz if playing only middle C, because just one finger of one hand, pressing one key, makes the sound.

The guitar is somewhat different. To play middle C on the guitar, you take your left-hand index finger and *fret* the 2nd string — that is, the 2nd string counting from the bottom as you hold the guitar — at the 1st fret. This action, however, doesn't produce a sound. You must also strike or pluck that 2nd string with your right hand to audibly produce the note middle C.

Music readers take note: The guitar sounds an octave lower than its written notes. For example, playing a written, third-space C on the guitar actually produces a middle C.

Frets and half steps

The smallest *interval* (unit of musical difference in pitch) of the musical scale is the *half step.* On the piano, every adjacent key is a half step apart, regardless of whether it's black or white. To proceed by half steps on a keyboard instrument, you move your finger up or down to the next available key. On the guitar, *frets* represent these half steps. To go up or down by half steps on a guitar means to move your left hand one fret at a time, higher or lower on the neck.

Pickups

Vibrating strings produce the different tones on a guitar. But you must be able to *hear* those tones, or you face one of those if-a-tree-falls-in-a-forest questions. For an acoustic guitar, that's no problem, because an acoustic instrument provides its own amplifier in the form of the hollow sound chamber that boosts its sound . . . well, acoustically.

But an electric guitar makes virtually no acoustic sound at all. (Well, a tiny bit, like a buzzing mosquito, but nowhere near enough to fill a stadium or anger your next-door neighbors.) An electric instrument creates its tones entirely through electronic means. The vibrating string is still the source of the sound, but a hollow wood chamber isn't what makes those vibrations audible. Instead, the vibrations disturb, or *modulate,* the magnetic field that the *pickups* — wire-wrapped magnets positioned underneath the strings — produce. As the vibrations of the strings modulate the pickup's magnetic field, the pickup produces a tiny electric current that exactly reflects that modulation.

If you remember from eighth-grade science, wrapping wire around a magnet creates a small current in the wire. If you then take any magnetic substance and disturb the magnetic field around that wire, you create fluctuations in the current itself. A taut steel string vibrating at the rate of 440 times per second creates a current that fluctuates 440 times per second. Pass that current through an amplifier and then a speaker and — *voilà* — you hear the musical tone A. More specifically, you hear the A above middle C, which is the standard absolute tuning reference in modern music — from the New York Philharmonic to the Rolling Stones to Metallica (although we've heard that Metallica sometimes uses a tuning reference of 666 — oh no, wait, that was Iron Maiden). You find out more about tuning later in this chapter.

Guitars, therefore, make sound either by amplifying string vibrations *acoustically* by passing the sound waves through a hollow chamber, or *electronically* by amplifying and outputting a current through a speaker. That's the physical process anyway. How a guitar produces *different* sounds — and the ones that you want it to make — is up to the way you control the pitches that those strings produce. Left-hand fretting is what changes these pitches. Your right-hand motions not only help produce the sound by setting the string in motion, they also determine the *rhythm* (the beat or pulse), *tempo* (the speed of the music), and *feel* (interpretation, style, spin, magic, mojo, *je ne sais quoi,* whatever) of those pitches. Put both hand motions together and they spell guitar music.

Counting Your Strings and Frets

One of the great injustices of life is that, before you can even play music on the guitar, you must endure the painstaking process of getting your instrument in tune. Fortunately for guitarists, you have only six strings as opposed to a few hundred in a piano. Before you can tune your guitar, you need to know how to refer to the two main players — strings and frets.

- **Strings:** Strings are numbered consecutively 1 through 6. The 1st string is the skinniest, located closest to the floor when you hold the guitar in playing position. (See Chapter 2 in Book 1 for details on playing positions.) Working your way up, the 6th string is the fattest, closest to the ceiling. This may seem counterintuitive, because when you look down at the strings, the first one you see is actually the 6th string, not the 1st. There's nothing to be done about this except remember it.

    It's a good idea to memorize the note names of the open strings (E, A, D, G, B, E, from 6th to 1st) so you're not limited to referring to them by number. An easy way to memorize the open strings in order is to remember the phrase "**E**ddie **A**te **D**ynamite; **G**ood-**B**ye, **E**ddie."

- **Frets:** *Frets* can refer to either the spaces where you put your left-hand finger or to the thin metal bars embedded in the fingerboard. Whenever you deal with guitar fingering, *fret* means the space in between the metal bars — where you can comfortably fit a left-hand finger.

    The 1st fret is the region between the *nut* (the thin, grooved strip that separates the headstock from the neck) and the first metal bar. The 5th fret, then, is the fifth square up from the nut — technically, the region between the fourth and fifth metal fret bars.

    Most guitars have a marker on the 5th fret, either a decorative design embedded in the fingerboard or a dot on the side of the neck, or both.

You can always check out the diagram on the Cheat Sheet at the front of the book while you get comfortable with these naming conventions.

One more point of business to square away. You'll come across the terms *open strings* and *fretted strings* from this point on in the book:

- ✔ **Open string:** A string that you play without fretting it at all.

- ✔ **Fretted string:** A string that you play while pressing down on it at a particular fret.

Everything's Relative: Tuning the Guitar to Itself

Relative tuning is so named because you don't need any outside reference to which you tune the instrument. As long as the strings are in tune in a certain relationship with each other, you can create sonorous and harmonious tones. Those same tones may turn into sounds resembling those of a catfight if you try to play along with another instrument, however; but as long as you tune the strings relative to one another, the guitar is in tune with itself.

To tune a guitar using the relative method, choose one string as the starting point — say, the 6th string. Leave the pitch of that string as is; then tune all the other strings relative to that 6th string.

The *5th-fret method* derives its name from the fact that you almost always play a string at the 5th fret and then compare the sound of that note to that of the next open string. You need to be careful, however, because the 4th fret (the 5th fret's jealous understudy) puts in a cameo appearance toward the end of the process.

Here's how to get your guitar in tune by using the 5th-fret method (check out Figure 1-3, which outlines all five steps):

1. **Play the 5th fret of the 6th (low E) string, which is the fattest one, closest to the ceiling, and then play the open 5th (A) string, the one next to it.**

   Let both notes ring together. Their pitches should match exactly. If they don't seem quite right, determine whether the 5th string is higher or lower than the fretted 6th string.

   - If the 5th string seems lower, or *flat,* turn its tuning key to raise the pitch.

   - If the 5th string seems *sharp,* or higher sounding, use its tuning key to lower the pitch.

TIP

You may go too far with the tuning key if you're not careful; if so, you need to reverse your motions. In fact, if you *can't* tell whether the 5th string is higher or lower, tune it flat intentionally (that is, tune it too low) and then come back to the desired pitch.

2. **Play the 5th fret of the 5th (A) string and then play the open 4th (D) string.**

   Let both of these notes ring together. If the 4th string seems flat or sharp relative to the fretted 5th string, use the tuning key of the 4th string to adjust its pitch accordingly. Again, if you're not sure whether the 4th string is higher or lower, "overtune" it in one direction — flat, or lower, is best — and then come back.

3. **Play the 5th fret of the 4th (D) string and then play the open 3rd (G) string.**

   Let both notes ring together again. If the 3rd string seems flat or sharp relative to the fretted 4th string, use the tuning key of the 3rd string to adjust the pitch accordingly.

4. **Play the FOURTH (*not* the 5th!) fret of the 3rd (G) string and then play the open 2nd (B) string.**

   Let both strings ring together. If the 2nd string seems flat or sharp, use its tuning key to adjust the pitch accordingly.

5. **Play the 5th (yes, back to the 5th for this one) fret of the 2nd (B) string and then play the open 1st (high E) string.**

   Let both notes ring together. If the 1st string seems flat or sharp, use its tuning key to adjust the pitch accordingly. If you're satisfied that both strings produce the same pitch, you've now tuned the upper (that is, "upper" as in higher-pitched) five strings of the guitar relative to the fixed (untuned) 6th string. Your guitar's now in tune with itself.

Figure 1-3:
Place your fingers on the frets as shown and match the pitch to the next open string.

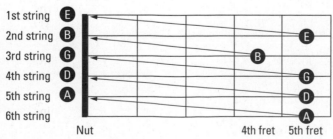

You may want to go back and repeat the process, because some strings may have slipped out of tune.

TIP

When you tune in the normal way, you use your left hand to turn the tuning peg. But after you remove your finger from the string that you're fretting, it stops ringing; therefore, you can no longer hear the string you're trying to tune to (the fretted string) as you adjust the open string. However, there's a way to tune the open string while keeping your left-hand finger on the fretted string: Simply use your right hand! After you strike the two strings in succession (the fretted string and the open string), take your right hand and reach over your left hand (which remains stationary as you fret the string) and turn the tuning key of the appropriate string until both strings sound exactly the same.

In Deference to a Reference: Tuning to a Fixed Source

Getting the guitar in tune with itself through the relative method in the preceding section is good for your ear, but isn't very practical if you need to play with other instruments or voices that are accustomed to standard tuning references. If you want to bring your guitar into the world of other people, you need to know how to tune to a fixed source, such as a piano, pitch pipe, tuning fork, or electronic tuner. Using such a source ensures that everyone is playing by the same tuning rules. Besides, your guitar and strings are built for optimal tone production if you tune to standard pitch.

The following sections describe some typical ways to tune your guitar by using fixed references. These methods not only enable you to get in tune, but also to make nice with the other instruments in the neighborhood.

Taking a turn at the piano

Because it holds its pitch so well (needing only biannual or annual tunings, depending on the conditions), a piano is a great tool for tuning a guitar. Assuming that you have an electronic keyboard or a well-tuned piano around, all you need to do is match the open strings of the guitar to the appropriate keys on the piano. Figure 1-4 shows a piano keyboard and the corresponding open guitar strings.

Tuning your guitar with a pitch pipe

Obviously, if you're off to the beach with your guitar, you're not going to want to put a piano in the back of your car, even if you're really fussy about tuning. So you need a smaller and more practical device that supplies standard-tuning reference pitches. Enter the *pitch pipe.* The pitch pipe may evoke images of stern, matronly chorus leaders who purse their prunelike lips around a circular harmonica to deliver a sharp squeak that instantly marshals together the reluctant voices of the choir — yet it does serve a worthy purpose.

For guitarists, special pitch pipes exist consisting of pipes that play only the notes of the open strings of the guitar (but sounding in a higher range) and none of the in-between notes. The advantage of a pitch pipe is that you can hold it firmly in your mouth while blowing, keeping your hands free for tuning. The disadvantage to a pitch pipe is that you sometimes take a while getting used to hearing a wind-produced pitch against a struck-string pitch. But with practice, you can tune with a pitch pipe as easily as you can with a piano.

Book I

Guitar 101

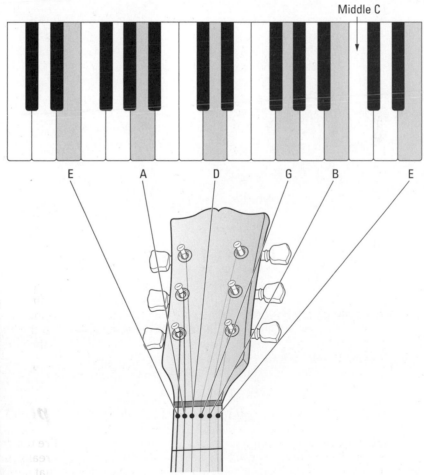

Figure 1-4:
A view of the piano keyboard, highlighting the keys that correspond to the open strings of the guitar.

Sinking your teeth into the tuning fork

After you get good enough at discerning pitches, you need only one single-pitched tuning reference to get your whole guitar in tune. The tuning fork offers only one pitch, and it usually comes in only one flavor: A (the one above middle C, which vibrates at 440 cycles per second, commonly known as A-440). But that note's really all you need. If you tune your open 5th string (A) to the tuning fork's A (although the guitar's A sounds in a lower octave), you can tune every other string to that string by using the relative tuning method outlined earlier in this chapter.

Using a tuning fork requires a little finesse. You must strike the fork against something firm, such as a tabletop or kneecap, and then hold it close to your ear or place the stem or handle — *not* the tines or fork prongs — against something that resonates. This resonator can be the tabletop again or even the top of the guitar. (You can even hold it between your teeth, which leaves your hands free! It really works!) At the same time, you must somehow play an A note and tune it to the fork's tone. The process is kinda like pulling your house keys out of your pocket while you're loaded down with an armful of groceries. The task may not be easy, but if you do it enough, you eventually become an expert.

Experiencing the electronic tuner

The quickest, most accurate way to get your guitar in tune is to employ an *electronic tuner*. This handy device seems to possess witchcraft-like powers. Newer electronic tuners made especially for guitars can usually sense what string you're playing, tell you what pitch you're nearest, and indicate whether you're flat (too low) or sharp (too high). About the only thing these devices don't do is turn the tuning keys for you (although we hear they're working on that). Some older, graph-type tuners feature a switch that selects which string you want to tune. Figure 1-5 shows a typical electronic tuner.

You can either plug your electric guitar into the tuner or use the tuner's built-in microphone to tune an acoustic. In both types of tuners — the ones where you select the strings and the ones that automatically sense the string — the display indicates two things: what note you're closest to (E, A, D, G, B, E) and whether you're flat or sharp of that note.

Electronic tuners are usually powered by 9-volt batteries or two AAs that can last for a year with regular usage (up to two or even three years with only occasional usage). Many electronic tuners are inexpensive (as low as $20 or so) and are well worth the money.

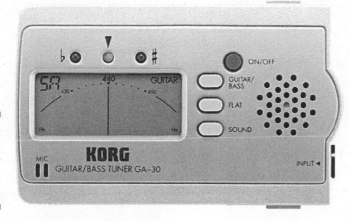

Figure 1-5:
An electronic tuner makes tuning a snap.

Using your CD

Lest we forget, you have one more fixed source as a tuning reference: your *Guitar All-in-One For Dummies* CD.

For your tuning convenience, the open strings are played on Track 1 of the audio CD that comes with this book. Listen to the tone of each open string as they sound slowly, one at a time (from the 1st to the 6th, or skinniest/highest to fattest/lowest) and tune your guitar's open strings to those on the CD. Use the track skip button on the CD player to go back to the beginning of Track 1 to repeat the tuning notes as often as necessary to get your strings exactly in tune with the strings on the CD.

Unlike a cassette tape — or any analog tape system, for that matter — a CD always plays back the exact pitch that it records and never goes sharp or flat, not even a little bit. So you can use your *For Dummies* CD on any CD player at any time to get perfectly tuned notes.

Chapter 2

Developing Basic Playing Skills

. . . .

In This Chapter

▶ Sitting and standing with the guitar

▶ Positioning the hands

▶ Reading chord diagrams and tablature

▶ Playing chords

. . . .

Guitars are user-friendly instruments. They fit comfortably into the arms of most humans, and the way your two hands fall on the strings naturally is pretty much the position in which you should play. In this chapter, you find out all about good posture techniques and how to hold your hands — just as if you were a young socialite at a finishing school.

We jest because we care. But you really do need to remember that good posture and position, at the very least, prevent strain and fatigue and, at best, help develop good concentration habits and tone. After you're positioned correctly with the guitar, you read about some basic music-deciphering skills and get the chance to play your very first chord.

Hand Position and Posture

You can either sit or stand while playing the guitar, and the position you choose makes virtually no difference whatsoever to your tone or technique. Most people prefer to practice while sitting but perform publicly while standing. The one exception to the sit or stand option is the classical guitar, which you normally play in a sitting position. This practice doesn't mean that you *can't* play a classical-style guitar or classical music while standing, but the serious pursuit of the classical guitar requires that you sit while playing. (Flip to Book V for the full scoop on playing classical guitar.)

Settling in to a sitting position

To hold the guitar in a sitting position, assuming you're right-handed, rest the waist of the guitar on your right leg. (The *waist* is the indented part between the guitar's upper and lower *bouts,* the protruding curved parts that look like shoulders and hips.) Feet slightly apart, balance the guitar by lightly resting your right forearm on the bass bout, as shown in Figure 2-1. Don't use the left hand to support the neck. You should be able to take your left hand completely off the fretboard without the guitar dipping toward the floor.

Figure 2-1: Typical sitting position for playing guitar.

Classical guitar technique, on the other hand, requires you to hold the instrument on your *left* leg, not on your right. This position puts the center of the guitar closer to the center of your body, making the instrument easier to play, especially with the left hand. That's because your wrist is straighter, so you can better execute the difficult fingerings of classical-guitar music in that position. You also elevate the classical guitar, which you can do either by raising the left leg with a specially made *guitar foot stool* (the traditional way) or by using a *support arm,* which goes between your left thigh and the guitar's lower side (the modern way). This device enables your left foot to remain on the floor and instead pushes the guitar up in the air.

Standing position

To stand and play the guitar, you need a strap that is securely fastened to both strap pins on the guitar (or otherwise tied to the guitar). Then you can stand in a normal way and check out how cool you look in the mirror with the guitar slung over your shoulder. You may need to adjust the strap to get the guitar at a comfortable playing height.

If your strap slips off a pin while you're playing in a standing position, you have about a fifty-fifty chance of catching your guitar before it hits the floor (and that's if you're quick and experienced with slipping guitars). So don't risk damaging your guitar by using an old or worn strap or one with holes that are too large for the pins to hold securely. Guitars aren't built to bounce, as Pete Townshend has demonstrated so many times.

Your body makes a natural adjustment in going from a sitting to a standing position. So don't try to overanalyze where your arms fall, relative to your sitting position. Just stay relaxed and, above all, *look cool.* (You're a guitar player now! Looking cool is just as important as knowing how to play . . . well, *almost.*) Figure 2-2 shows a typical standing position.

Figure 2-2: Typical standing position for playing guitar.

Left-hand position: Fretting made easy

To get an idea of correct left-hand positioning on the guitar, extend your left hand, palm up, and make a loose fist, placing your thumb roughly between your first and second fingers. All of your knuckles should be bent. Your hand should look about like that after you stick a guitar neck in there. The thumb glides along the back of the neck, straighter than if you were making a fist but not rigid. The finger knuckles stay bent whether they're fretting or relaxed. Again, the left hand should fall in place very naturally on the guitar neck, as if you were picking up a tool that you've been using all your life.

To *fret* a note, press the tip of your finger down on a string, keeping your knuckles bent. Try to get the fingertip to come down vertically on the string rather than at an angle. This position exerts the greatest pressure on the string and also prevents the sides of the finger from touching adjacent strings — which may cause either buzzing or *muting* (deadening the string, or preventing it from ringing). Use your thumb from its position underneath the neck to help "squeeze" the fingerboard for a tighter grip.

When playing a particular fret, you don't place your finger directly on the metal fret, but *in between* the two frets (or between the nut and 1st fret). For example, if you're playing the 5th fret, place your finger in the square between the 4th and 5th frets, not in the middle but closer to the higher fret. This gives you the clearest sound and prevents buzzing.

Left-hand fretting requires strength, but don't be tempted to try to speed up the process of strengthening your hands through artificial means. Building up the strength in your left hand takes time. You may see advertisements for hand-strengthening devices and believe that these products may expedite your left-hand endurance. Although we can't declare that these devices never work (and the same goes for the homegrown method of squeezing a racquet ball or tennis ball), one thing's for sure: Nothing helps you build your left-hand fretting strength better or faster than simply playing guitar.

Because of the strength your left hand exerts while fretting, other parts of your body may tense up to compensate. At periodic intervals, make sure you relax your left shoulder, which has a tendency to rise up as you work on your fretting. Take frequent "drop-shoulder" breaks. Make sure as well that your left elbow doesn't stick out to the side, like that of a rude dinner guest. You want to keep your upper arm and forearm parallel to the side of your body. Relax your elbow so it stays at your side.

The important thing to remember in maintaining a good left-hand position is that you need to keep it comfortable and natural. If your hand starts to hurt or ache, *stop playing and take a rest.* As with any other activity that requires muscular development, resting enables your body to catch up.

Electric endeavours

Book I

Guitar 101

Electric necks are both narrower (from the 1st string to the 6th) and shallower (from the fingerboard to the back of the neck) than acoustic necks. Electric guitars are, therefore, easier to fret. But the space between each string is smaller, so you're more likely to touch and deaden an adjacent string with your fretting finger. The biggest difference, however, between fretting on an electric and on a nylon or steel-string acoustic is the action.

A guitar's *action* refers to how high above the frets the strings ride and, to a lesser extent, how easy they are to fret. On an electric guitar, fretting strings is like passing a hot knife through butter. The easier action of an electric enables you to use a more relaxed left-hand position than you normally would on an acoustic, with the palm of the left hand facing slightly outward. Figure 2-3 shows a photo of the left hand resting on the fingerboard of an electric guitar, fretting a string.

Figure 2-3: The electric guitar neck lies comfortably between the thumb and the first finger as the first finger frets a note.

Classical conditions

Because nylon-string guitars have a wide fingerboard and are the model of choice for classical music, their necks require a slightly more (ahem) formal left-hand approach. Try to get the palm side of your knuckles (the ones that connect your fingers to your hand) to stay close to and parallel to the side of the neck. This allows the fingers to run perpendicular to the strings and puts all the fingers the same distance away from the neck. (If your hand isn't perfectly parallel, the little finger "falls away" or is farther from the neck than your index finger.) Figure 2-4 shows the correct left-hand position for nylon-string guitars.

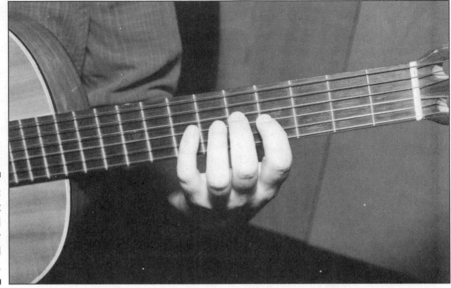

Figure 2-4:
Correct
left-hand
position for
a classical
guitar.

Right-hand position

If you hold a guitar in your lap and drape your right arm over the upper bout, your right hand, held loosely outstretched, crosses the strings at about a 60-degree angle. This position is good for playing with a pick. For fingerstyle playing, you want to turn your right hand more perpendicular to the strings. For classical guitar, you want to keep the right hand as close to a 90-degree angle as possible.

If you're using a pick

You do almost all of your electric guitar playing with a pick, whether you're belting out rock 'n' roll, blues, jazz, country, or pop. On acoustic guitar, you can play either with a pick or with your fingers. On both electric and acoustic, you play most *rhythm* (chord-based accompaniment) and virtually all *lead* (single-note melodies) by holding the pick, or *plectrum* (the old-fashioned term), between the thumb and index finger.

Figure 2-5 shows the correct way to hold a pick — with just the tip sticking out, perpendicular to the thumb.

If you're *strumming* (playing rhythm), you strike the strings with the pick by using wrist and elbow motion. The more vigorous the strum, the more elbow you must put into the mix. For playing lead, you use only the more economical wrist motion. Don't grip the pick too tightly as you play — and plan on dropping it a lot in the first few weeks that you use it.

Figure 2-5:
Correct
pick-holding
technique.

Picks come in various gauges. A pick's *gauge* indicates how stiff, or thick, it is. Thinner picks are easier to manage for the beginner. Medium picks are the most popular, because they're flexible enough for comfortable rhythm playing, yet stiff enough for leads. Heavy-gauge picks may seem unwieldy at first, but they're the choice for pros, and eventually all skilled instrumentalists graduate to them (although a few famous holdouts exist — Neil Young being a prime example).

If you're using your fingers

If you eschew such paraphernalia as picks and want to go au naturel with your right hand, you're fingerpicking (although you can fingerpick with special individual, wraparound picks that attach to your fingers — called, confusingly enough, *fingerpicks*). *Fingerpicking* means that you play the guitar by plucking the strings with the individual right-hand fingers. The thumb plays the *bass,* or low, strings, and the fingers play the *treble,* or high, strings. In fingerpicking, you use the tips of the fingers to play the strings, positioning the hand over the sound hole (if you're playing acoustic) and keeping the wrist stationary but not rigid. Maintaining a slight arch in the wrist so the fingers come down more vertically on the strings also helps.

Because of the special right-hand strokes that you use in playing classical guitar (the *free stroke* and the *rest stroke*), you must hold your fingers almost perfectly perpendicular to the strings to execute the correct technique. A perpendicular approach enables your fingers to draw against the strings with maximum strength.

Understanding Guitar Notation

Although you don't need to read music to play the guitar, musicians have developed a few simple tricks through the years that aid in communicating such basic ideas as song structure, chord construction, chord progressions, and important rhythmic figures. Pick up on the shorthand devices for *chord diagrams, rhythm slashes,* and *tablature,* and you're sure to start coppin' licks faster than Roy Clark after three cups of coffee.

You don't need to read music to play the guitar. With the help of the chord diagrams, rhythm slashes, and tablature that's explained in the following sections, plus hearing what all this stuff sounds like through the magic of CD technology, you can pick up on everything you need to understand and play the guitar, even if you can't tell a quarter note from an eighth rest. Listen closely to the CD and follow the corresponding written examples throughout the rest of this book to make sure you understand how the two relate.

Getting by with a little help from a chord diagram

Don't worry — reading a chord diagram is *not* like reading music; it's far simpler. All you need to do is understand where to put your fingers to form a chord. A *chord* is defined as the simultaneous sounding of three or more notes.

Figure 2-6 shows the anatomy of a chord chart, and the following list briefly explains what the different parts of the diagram mean:

- The grid of six vertical lines and five horizontal ones represents the guitar fretboard, as if you stood the guitar up on the floor or chair and looked straight at the upper part of the neck from the front.

- The vertical lines represent the guitar strings. The vertical line at the far left is the low 6th string, and the right-most vertical line is the high 1st string.

- The horizontal lines represent frets. The thick horizontal line at the top is the *nut* of the guitar, where the fretboard ends. So the 1st fret is actually the second vertical line from the top. (Don't let the words here confuse you; just look at the guitar.)

- The dots that appear on vertical string lines between horizontal fret lines represent notes that you fret.

✔ The numerals directly below each string line (just below the last fret line) indicate which left-hand finger you use to fret that note. On the left hand, 1 = index finger; 2 = middle finger; 3 = ring finger; and 4 = little finger. You don't use the thumb to fret, except in certain unusual circumstances.

✔ The X or O symbols directly above some string lines indicate strings that you leave open (unfretted) or that you don't play. An X (not shown in Figure 2-6) above a string means you don't pick or strike that string with your right hand. An O indicates an open string that you do play.

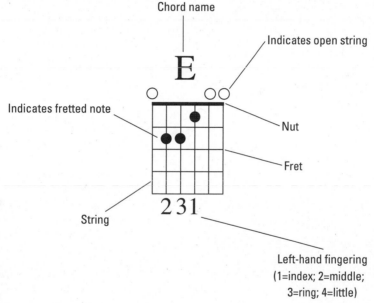

Figure 2-6:
A standard chord diagram for an E chord.

If a chord is to be played somewhere beyond the first four frets, a numeral appears to the right of the diagram, next to the top fret line, to indicate in which fret the diagram actually starts. (In such cases, the top line is *not* the nut.) In most cases, however, you deal primarily with chords that fall within only the first four frets of the guitar. Chords that fall within the first four frets typically use open strings, so they're referred to as *open* chords.

Reading rhythm slashes

Musicians use a variety of shorthand tricks to indicate certain musical directions. They use this shorthand because, although a particular musical concept itself is often simple enough, to notate that idea in standard written music form may prove unduly complicated and cumbersome. So they use a "crib sheet" or a "road map" that gets the point across yet avoids the issue of reading (or writing) music.

Rhythm slashes are slash marks (/) that simply tell you *how* to play rhythmically but not *what* to play. The chord in your left hand determines what you play. Say, for example, you see the diagram shown in Figure 2-7.

Figure 2-7:
One
measure of
an E chord.

If you see such a chord symbol with four slashes beneath it, as shown in Figure 2-7, you know to finger an E chord and strike it four times. What you don't see, however, is a number of differently pitched notes clinging to various lines of a music staff, including several hole-in-the-center half notes and a slew of solid quarter notes — in short, any of that junk you needed to memorize in grade school just to play "Mary Had a Little Lamb" on the recorder. All you need to remember on seeing this particular diagram is to "play an E chord four times." Simple, isn't it?

Taking a look at tablature

Tablature (or *tab,* for short) is a notation system that graphically represents the frets and strings of the guitar. Whereas chord diagrams do so in a static way, tablature shows how you play music over a period of time. For all the musical examples that appear in this book, you see a *tablature staff* (or *tab staff,* for short) beneath the standard notation staff. This second staff reflects exactly what's going on in the regular musical staff above it — but in *guitar language.* Tab is guitar-specific — in fact, many call it simply *guitar tab.* Tab doesn't tell you what *note* to play (such as C or F♯ or E♭). It does, however, tell you what *string* to fret and where exactly on the fingerboard to *fret* that string.

Figure 2-8 shows you the tab staff and some sample notes and a chord. The top line of the tab staff represents the 1st string of the guitar — high E. The bottom line of the tab corresponds to the 6th string on the guitar, low E. The other lines represent the other four strings in between — the second line from the bottom is the 5th string, and so on. A number appearing on any given line tells you to fret that string in that numbered fret. For example, if you see the numeral 2 on the second line from the top, you need to press down the 2nd string in the 2nd fret above the nut (actually, the space between the 1st and 2nd metal frets). A 0 on a line means you play the open string.

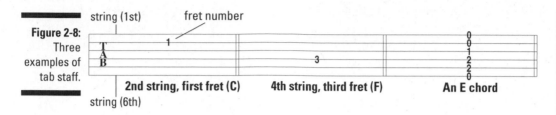

Figure 2-8:
Three examples of tab staff.

string (1st)

fret number

2nd string, first fret (C)   4th string, third fret (F)   An E chord

string (6th)

How to Play a Chord

Chords are the basic building blocks of songs. You can play a chord, which is the simultaneous sounding of three or more notes, several ways on the guitar — by *strumming* (dragging a pick or the back of your fingernails across the strings in a single, quick motion), *plucking* (with the individual right-hand fingers), or even smacking the strings with your open hand or fist. (Okay, that's rare, unless you're in a heavy metal band.) But you can't just strike *any* group of notes; you must play a group of notes organized in some musically meaningful arrangement. For the guitarist, that means learning left-hand chord forms.

Fingering a chord

After you think you understand (somewhat) the guitar notation described in the preceding sections, your best bet is to just jump right in and play your first chord. You can start with E major, because it's a particularly guitar-friendly chord and one that you use a lot.

After you get the hang of playing chords, you eventually find that you can move several fingers into position simultaneously. For now, however, just place your fingers one at a time on the frets and strings, as the following instructions indicate (you can also refer to Figure 2-6):

1. **Place your first (index) finger on the 3rd string, 1st fret (actually between the nut and 1st fret but closer to the fret).**

   Don't press down hard until you have your other fingers in place. Apply just enough pressure to keep your finger from moving off the string.

2. **Place your second (middle) finger on the 5th string (skipping over the 4th string), 2nd fret.**

   Again, apply just enough pressure to keep your fingers in place. You now have two fingers on the guitar, on the 3rd and 5th strings, with an as-yet unfretted string (the 4th) in between.

3. **Place your third (ring) finger on the 4th string, 2nd fret.**

   You may need to wriggle your ring finger a bit to get it to fit in there with the first and second fingers and below the fret wire. Figure 2-9 shows a photo of how your E chord should look after your fingers are positioned correctly.

Now that your fingers are in position, strike all six strings with your right hand to hear your first chord, E.

Figure 2-9:
Notice how the fingers curve and the knuckles bend on an E chord.

Avoiding buzzes

One of the hardest things to do in playing chords is to avoid buzzing. *Buzzing* results if you're not pressing down quite hard enough when you fret. A buzz can also result if a fretting finger accidentally comes in contact with an adjacent string, preventing that string from ringing freely. Without removing your fingers from the frets, try "rocking and rolling" your fingers around on their tips to eliminate any buzzes when you strum the chord.

Chapter 3

Buying and Stringing Guitars

*B*uying a new guitar is an exciting proposition. You go to the music store and immediately face a world of possibilities, a supermarket of tantalizing choices. Every guitar on the wall seems to scream, "Pick me! Pick me!" Should you resist, exercise restraint, and avoid the models you know you can't afford?

Heck, no. Be bold and try any model that strikes your fancy. You're not asking to test-drive a Ferrari; you're simply asking the salesperson to see how different guitars feel and sound. And you're not being frivolous either. Playing a range of guitars helps you understand the differences between high-quality, expensive guitars and acceptable but affordable guitars.

So indulge yourself. Even if you don't have enough experience to recognize the subtle differences between a good guitar and a great guitar, at least expose yourself to them. And don't wait until the day you decide to buy to pick one up for the first time. Make several visits to the music store before you're ready to buy and then take the time to absorb your experiences. Visit several different stores if you can. Some may be the exclusive dealer of a specific brand in your region; others may not be able to sell that brand of guitar. The info in this chapter can make picking out a guitar an even better experience.

After you buy a guitar (or two or three), restringing is a necessary task. Many people seem reluctant to tune their strings, let alone change them. Although you should be careful not to drop or scratch your guitar (and setting guitars afire à la Jimi Hendrix generally causes *significant* damage), you needn't worry about causing damage by changing, tuning, or overtightening guitar strings. Guitars are incredibly rugged and can deal with hundreds of pounds of string tension while enduring the playing of even the most heavy-handed guitarists. Changing strings isn't something you should be shy about: You can jump into it with both feet. It improves the sound of the guitar, helps prevent broken strings at inopportune moments, and aids you in identifying other maintenance problems. (During periodic string changing, for example, you may discover a gouged bridge slot or a loose tuning post.) This chapter explains what you need to know.

Before You Break Out Your Wallet

Before you walk into your local music store ready to plop down your hard-earned dough on a new guitar, you need to take stock of what you're doing. Ask yourself some tough questions about your pending purchase — and you need to do so *now*. Don't wait until you get to the store to develop a buying strategy. The two most important factors in making any purchasing decision — especially concerning a guitar, where passions run high — are to develop a plan and to gather all the information you need to make the best choice.

Start developing your purchasing plan by answering specific questions about exactly what you want in a guitar — and how much you can spend to attain it. Narrowing your scope doesn't mean you can't change your mind after you get to the store and see all the nifty instruments available, or that you can't let on-the-spot inspiration and whim play a significant part in your final decision. ("I just *can't* decide between these two guitars . . . oh, what the heck! Just give me *both* of them!") But you do need a point from which to depart.

Ask yourself the following questions:

- ✔ **What's my level of commitment?** Regardless of your current ability, do you realistically envision yourself practicing every day for the next five years, pursuing a dedicated program of guitar excellence? Or do you first want to see whether this whole "guitar thing" is going to stick? Just because you can *afford* a $1,000 guitar doesn't mean you should buy it. Before plunking down cash, honestly determine the importance of the guitar in your life and act responsibly according to that priority.

- ✔ **What's my spending limit?** The answer to this question is critical because, often, the more expensive the guitar, the greater its appeal. So you need to balance your level of commitment and your available resources. You don't want to have to give up food for six months and live in a cardboard box just because you got carried away at the music store. Set a limit on how much you can spend and don't exceed it.

- ✔ **Do I buy retail or online or mail order?** If you know exactly what you want — down to the color and options — you may consider buying a guitar through mail order or online; you often get the best deal and may even avoid paying sales tax (if the music company is out of state). Buying sight unseen is common with many products, such as automobiles and computers. But if you can't cotton to buying something as personal as a guitar without falling in love with it first — and you want to "date" your guitar before "marrying" it — stick with retail. A retail outlet usually comes with an official service agreement and unofficial, friendly cooperation from the staff that's worth its weight in gold. Music stores know they're competing with online and mail-order services, and they make up for it in spades with service.

✔ **Am I a "new-guitar person" or a "used-guitar person"?** You're going to have a much easier time comparing attributes among new guitars. And all the retail and discount prices of new instruments are pretty much standardized — which is not to say that all the prices are the same; stores usually discount at different rates. Expect to pay between 10 and 35 percent off the "list" price (manufacturer's suggested retail price) at a music store and even less online or via mail order. Big chains offer better discounts than smaller mom-and-pop stores because they buy in quantity and get a better price from the manufacturer.

Retail, online, and mail-order operations also offer a warranty against any manufacturer defects on new instruments. You don't find any comparable protection if you're buying a guitar from a newspaper ad (although music stores also sell used instruments, usually with warranties). But on the other hand, you *can* sometimes get a really good deal on a used instrument if you know what to look for. If you want a vintage instrument, you're looking at a used guitar by definition.

As a rule, most asking prices in newspaper ads are too high. Be ready to dicker to get a better price for such a guitar — even if it's exactly what you're looking for.

After you have satisfactory answers to the preceding questions, proceed to the second prong of your guitar-purchasing attack plan: gathering information on the specific guitar for you. The following section helps you become more knowledgeable about guitar construction, materials, and workmanship. Remember, being an informed buyer is the best defense against making a bad deal in the retail arena.

Beginner Guitars

If you're just starting out as a novice guitarist, you may ask the musical question, "What's the minimum I need to spend to avoid winding up with a piece of junk?" That's a good question, because modern manufacturing practices now enable *luthiers* (the fancy term for guitar makers) to turn out some pretty good stuff for around $200 — and even less sometimes.

If you're an adult (older than 14), and you're looking to grow with an instrument, plan to spend between $200 and $250 for an acoustic guitar and a little less for an electric. (Electric guitars are easier to build, so they usually cost a bit less than comparable acoustics.)

Consider the following criteria:

- **Appearance:** You must like the way a particular guitar looks, or you're never really happy with it. So use your eye and your aesthetic taste to select possible candidates. A red guitar isn't inherently better or worse than a green one, but you're perfectly free to base your decision to buy simply on whether you like the look of the guitar.

- **Playability:** Just because a guitar is relatively inexpensive doesn't necessarily mean it's difficult to play (although this correlation was often the case in the past). You should be able to press the strings down to the fretboard with relative ease. And you shouldn't find the up-the-neck frets unduly difficult either, although they're sometimes harder to play than the lower frets are.

  Here's a way to get some perspective on playability. Pick up a more expensive guitar and see how it plays. Then return to the more afford-able instrument you're considering. Is the playability wildly different? It shouldn't be. If it doesn't feel comfortable to you, move on.

- **Intonation:** A guitar must play in tune. Test the intonation by playing a 12th-fret harmonic (just barely touch the fret instead of pressing it down) on the 1st string and match that to the fretted note at the 12th fret. Although the notes are of a different tonal quality, the pitch should be exactly the same. Apply this test to all six strings. Listen especially to the 3rd and the 6th strings. Those strings often go out of tune first. If in doubt, enlist the aid of an experienced guitarist on this issue; it's *crucial*.

- **Solid construction:** If you're checking out an acoustic, rap gently on the top of the instrument (like your doctor does to check your ribs and chest) to make sure it's rattle-free. Peer inside the hole, looking for gobs of glue and other evidence of sloppy workmanship. Rough-sanded braces are a big tip-off to a hastily constructed instrument. On an electric, test that the metal hardware is tightly secured and rattle-free. Without plugging into an amp, strum the open strings hard and listen for rattling. Running your hand along the edge of the neck to check that the frets are smooth and filed correctly is another good test. If you're not sure what you should be feeling, consult an experienced guitarist on a "fret check."

Models for a Particular Style

Asking for a type of guitar by musical style is completely legitimate. Ask for a heavy metal guitar, for example, and the salesperson will nod knowingly and lead you to the scary-looking stuff. Ask for a jazz guitar, and you'll wind up down toward the guys with berets and "Bird lives!" buttons.

Figure 3-1 shows popular models. Note the diversity in shape and style.

Figure 3-1:
Different down-strokes for different folks.

Now, some musical styles do share guitar models. You can play both blues and rock, for example, on a Fender Stratocaster. And a Gibson Les Paul is just as capable of a wailing lead as a Strat. (As a rule, however, the tone of a Les Paul is going to be fatter and less jangly than that of a Strat.) Making your own kind of music on the guitar of your choice is part of the fun.

Following are some popular music styles and classic guitars that many people associate with those styles. This list is by no means exhaustive but does include recognized standard bearers of the respective genres:

- ✔ **Acoustic blues:** National Steel, Gibson J-200

- ✔ **Bluegrass:** Martin Dreadnought, Taylor Dreadnought, Collings Dreadnought, Santa Cruz Dreadnought, Gallagher Dreadnought

- ✔ **Classical:** Ramirez, Hopf, Khono, Humphrey, Hernandez, Alvarez

- ✔ **Country:** Fender Telecaster, Gretsch 6120, Fender Stratocaster

- ✔ **Electric blues:** Gibson ES-355, Fender Telecaster, Fender Stratocaster, Gibson Les Paul

- ✔ **Folk:** Dreadnoughts and Grand Concerts by Martin, Taylor, Collings, Larrivée, Lowden, and Guild; Gibson J-200; Ovation Adamas

- ✔ **Heavy metal:** Gibson Explorer, Flying V, and SG; Fender Stratocaster; Dean; Ibanez Iceman; Jackson Soloist

- ✔ **Jazz:** Gibson ES-175, Super 400 L-5, and Johnny Smith; archtops by D'Angelico, D'Aquisto, and Benedetto; Epiphone Emperor Regent; Ibanez signature models

- ✔ **New age, new acoustic:** Taylor Grand Concert, Ovation Balladeer, Takamine nylon-electric
- ✔ **R&B:** Fender Stratocaster, Gibson ES-335
- ✔ **Rock:** Fender Stratocaster, Gibson Les Paul and SG, Ibanez RG and signature series, Paul Reed Smith, Tom Anderson

Although the preceding list contains guitars that people generally associate with given styles, don't let that limit your creativity. Play the music you want to play on the guitar you want to play it on, no matter what some chart tells you. In other words, after you study this list, go pick out the guitar you want and play the music you want. These guitars are all super-sweet, and the price tag reflects the quality as well as the heritage of these guitars.

Choosing a Good Guitar

You may decide, if you can afford it, to start off on the right foot and pony up for a quality instrument. If you go cheap at first and fall in love with the guitar, sooner or later you *will* be back for a better one. What do you need to know when selecting a better guitar?

If you already have one guitar, consider the following three common approaches to choosing another guitar:

- ✔ **The contrasting and complementary approach:** If you own an acoustic, you may want to consider getting an electric (or vice versa), because having different guitars in your arsenal is always nice. Diversity is very healthy for a person seeking to bolster a collection.

- ✔ **The clone approach:** Some just want to acquire as many, say, Les Pauls as they can in a lifetime: old ones, new ones, red ones, blue ones . . . hey — it's *your* money. Buy as many as you want and can afford.

- ✔ **The upgrade approach:** If all you ever want to do is master the Stratocaster, just get a better version of what you had before. That way, you can use the new guitar for important occasions, such as recording and performing, and the old ax for going to the beach.

How much should you spend on your better instrument? One guideline is to go up into the next spending bracket from your old guitar. This way, you don't end up with many similar guitars. Plan on spending about $200 more than the current value (not what you paid) of the guitar you own. By doing so, you ensure that even if you stick with a certain model, you're getting a guitar that's categorically different from your initial instrument.

When should you stop? When the money runs out, of course. Actually, no hard-and-fast rules dictate how many guitars are "enough." These days, however, a reasonably well-appointed guitar arsenal includes a single-coil electric (such as a Fender Strat), a humbucker electric (such as a Gibson Les Paul), a semihollow-body electric, a hollow-body jazz (electric), an acoustic steel-string, an acoustic 12-string, and a nylon-string classical. Maybe you can add one or two more guitars in a given specialty, such as a guitar set up especially for playing slide, a 12-string electric, or an electric bass. (Then you can start collecting mandolins, banjos, ukuleles, Dobros . . .)

In upgrading, the issue again becomes one of *quality*. But instead of just making sure the instrument plays in tune, frets easily, and doesn't collapse if you breathe on it, you also need to *make informed decisions*. Don't worry — that's not as grave as it sounds. Consider the following pillars for judging quality in an instrument:

- ✔ **Construction:** How the guitar is designed and put together
- ✔ **Materials:** Mainly woods and metals (hardware, pickups, electronics)
- ✔ **Workmanship:** The quality of the building

Construction

How a guitar is built defines what type of guitar it is and (generally) what type of music it's used for. The following sections cover the three most important issues regarding guitar construction.

Solid wood versus laminated wood

A solid-wood acoustic guitar is better than a *laminated* acoustic guitar — where, instead of using a solid, thicker piece of top-wood, the guitar maker uses several layers of inexpensive wood pressed together and covered with a veneer. Guitars made completely out of solid wood cost at least $1,000.

The acoustic guitar's top is the most critical element in sound production; the back and sides primarily reflect the sound back through the top. So, if you can't pick up the tab for a solid-wood acoustic guitar, look to various configurations in which the top is solid and various other parts are laminated. A good choice is a solid-top guitar with laminated back and sides, which can cost as little as $400.

Another very popular configuration, just a step higher in quality, is a guitar with a solid top, a solid back, and laminated sides. You can find acoustics constructed this way at around the $1,200 mark or even slightly less. Because the sides have a negligible effect on the sound, and because laminates are structurally stronger than solid woods, this setup is a win-win situation for manufacturer and buyer.

If you're unsure as to whether a guitar has solid or laminated wood, ask the dealer or consult the manufacturer.

Body caps

In the electric realm, one big determinant of price is whether the top has a cap. A *cap* is a decorative layer of fine wood — usually a variety of *figured* maple (having a naturally occurring decorative grain pattern) — that sits on top of the body without affecting the sound. Popular cap woods include flame maple and quilted maple. Figured-wood tops usually come with clear, or see-through, finishes to show off the wood's attractive grain pattern.

Neck construction

The following list describes the three most common types of neck construction, from the least expensive to the most:

- ✓ **Bolt-on:** The neck attaches to the back of the guitar at the heel with four or five bolts (although a heel plate sometimes covers the bolt holes). Fender Stratocasters and Telecasters have bolt-on necks.

- ✓ **Set-in (or glued-in):** The neck joins the body with an unbroken surface covering the connection, for a seamless effect from neck to body. The joint is glued. Gibson Les Pauls and Paul Reed Smiths have set-in necks.

- ✓ **Neck through body:** A high-end construction where the neck is one long unit (although usually consisting of several pieces of wood glued together) that doesn't stop at the body but continues all the way through to the tail of the guitar. This type of neck is great for getting maximum sustain. A Jackson Soloist has a neck-through-body design.

Just because a construction technique is more advanced or expensive doesn't mean it's necessarily better. Could you "improve" the sound of Jimi Hendrix's Strat by modifying its neck to a glued-in configuration? *Sacrilege!*

Materials

A guitar isn't limited by what it's made of any more than a sculpture is. Michelangelo's *David* and your Aunt Agnes's candy dish are both made of marble, but which one would you travel to Paris to see? So don't judge a guitar *only* by its materials, but consider that a guitar with better materials (abalone inlays as opposed to plastic ones) tends to have commensurately better workmanship — and therefore be a better guitar — than a model that uses inexpensive materials.

Woods

As you may expect, the more expensive or rare a wood, the more expensive the guitar you construct from that wood. Guitar makers break woods down into categories, and each has a bearing on the guitar's overall expense.

Following are the three criteria used for classifying wood:

- ✔ **Type:** For example, mahogany, maple, or rosewood. Rosewood tends to be the most expensive wood used in the construction of acoustic-guitar bodies, followed by maple, and then mahogany.

- ✔ **Style:** You can classify woods further by looking at the wood's region or grain style. Brazilian rosewood is redder and wavier than East Indian rosewood and is also more expensive. The figured maples, such as quilted and flame, are more expensive than rock or bird's-eye maples.

- ✔ **Grade:** Guitar makers use a grading system, from A to AAA (the highest), to evaluate woods based on grain, color, and consistency. High-quality guitars get the highest-grade wood.

Hardware: Tuners and bridge assemblies

In more expensive instruments, you see upgrades on all components, including the *hardware,* or the metal parts of the guitar. Chrome-plated hardware is usually the cheapest, so if you begin looking at more expensive guitars, you start to see gold-plated and black-matte-finished knobs, switches, and tuning machines in place of chrome.

The actual hardware the manufacturer uses — not just the finishes on it — changes, too, on more expensive instruments. High-quality, name-brand hardware often replaces the guitar maker's less prestigious, generic brand of hardware on high-end axes. For example, manufacturers may use a higher-grade product for the tuning machines on an upscale guitar — such as *locking Spurzels* (a popular third-party tuner type and brand), which lock the string in place as opposed to forcing the user to tie the string off at the post.

The bridge is an important upgrade area as well. The so-called *floating bridge* (so designated because you can move it up and down by means of the whammy bar) is a complicated affair of springs, fine-tuning knobs, and anchors. The better floating assemblies, such as the Floyd Rose system or systems manufactured under a Floyd Rose license, operate much more smoothly and reliably than do the simple three-spring varieties found on low-cost guitars. (The strings spring right back to pitch on a Floyd Rose system, even after the most torturous whammy bar abuse. You can find out more about the Floyd Rose bridge later in this chapter.)

Pickups and electronics (electrics only)

Unless a guitar manufacturer is also known for making great pickups, you see more and more use of third-party pickups as you go up the quality ladder. In the electric arena, Seymour Duncan, DiMarzio, Bartolini, Bill Lawrence, Lace, and EMG are examples of high-quality pickup brands that guitar makers piggyback onto their models. Fishman and L.R. Baggs are two popular acoustic pickup systems found on many well-known guitars.

Although they're not known by name brands, the electronics in guitars also improve along with the other components as you venture into more expensive territory. You can see a greater variety, for example, in pickup manipulation. Manufacturers can provide circuitry that changes double-coil, or humbucker, pickups into single-coils, enabling them to emulate the behavior of Stratlike pickups. Having one guitar that can imitate the pickup behavior of other guitar types provides you with a tonally versatile instrument. You also see more manipulation in wiring schemes. For example, guitar makers may reverse the *polarity* of a pickup — the direction the signal flows — to make the guitar sound softer and more swirly.

With more expensive guitars, you may also encounter improved volume and tone controls, resulting in better taper. *Taper* is the gradualness or abruptness of change (also called *response*) of a signal's characteristics (in this case, volume and tone) as you turn a knob from its minimum value to its maximum. A knob exhibiting a smoother taper is evidence of a higher grade of electronics. Really cheap guitars give you no sound at all until turned up to 3; then you get a swell of sound from about 4 to about 7 and no change at all between 7 and the knob's maximum value, 10 — or, on those really rare, loud guitars, 11. (And if you don't get that last joke, go out and rent *This Is Spinal Tap*. It's required viewing for all guitarists.)

Workmanship

For more expensive guitars, you can really bring out the white glove and get fussy. We've seen prospective buyers bring in a dentist's mirror to inspect the interior of an acoustic guitar.

For acoustic guitars beyond the $600 range, you should expect to find *gapless joints* — solid wood-to-wood connections between components, especially where the neck meets the body. You should also expect clean and glob-free gluing (in the top and back bracing), a smooth and even finish application, and strings at the right height with no buzzing, the neck warp- and twist-free, and the intonation true. You can glean all of this information by simply playing the guitar and noting your impressions. Like traveling in a Rolls-Royce or Bentley, playing a quality guitar should be one smooth ride.

Buying an Ax to Grind

Buying a guitar is similar to buying a car or house (okay, it's a *little* less monumental than buying a house) in that it's lots of fun, but you must exercise caution and be a savvy customer, too. Only you know the right guitar for you, what the right price is for your budget and commitment level, and whether a deal feels right. Don't deny your natural shopping instincts, even if you're new to guitar shopping. Look, listen, consider, go have lunch before the big buy, and talk it over with your sweetie.

Bringing along an expert

A certain saying goes, "An expert is someone who knows more than you do." If you have such a friend — whose guitar knowledge and experience exceeds your own — bring the friend along, by all means. This friend not only knows about guitars, but also knows *you*. A salesperson doesn't know you, nor does he necessarily have your best interests in mind. But a friend does. And another opinion never hurts, if only to help you articulate your own.

 Enlist your guitar teacher (if you have one) to help you navigate through the guitar buyer's jungle, especially if he's been with you awhile and knows your tastes and playing style. Your teacher may know things about you that you may not even realize about yourself — for example, that you've gotten side-tracked in the steel-string section although your interests lie in nylon-string guitar music. A good teacher asks questions, listens to your answers, and gently guides you to where *you* want to go.

Your expert is also likely to bring along an electronic guitar tuner to tune potential guitars to standard pitch. This is an excellent idea. A shop may tune a guitar slightly lower to make it seem easier to play; then when you get it home and tune it properly, you find out it doesn't play like it did in the store.

Meeting the salesperson

Dealing with a salesperson doesn't need to be a stressful, adversarial affair, but some people get pretty anxious about the entire situation. If you establish your priorities before you enter the store, you don't come off as vague and unprepared as he begins his salvo of questions. A typical first question from a salesperson may be "How much do you want to spend?" In essence, the question means "What price range are you looking at so I know which end of the store to take you to?" It's a fair question, and if you can answer directly, you can save a lot of time. He may also ask about your playing ability and style preferences, so be ready for those questions, too.

 Be prepared to answer the salesperson's questions succinctly — for example, "I prefer Strat-style guitars, although not necessarily by Fender, and I'm an intermediate blues player — not a shredder — and I'd like to keep costs at less than $600." Answers such as these make you sound decisive and thoughtful, and the salesperson would have plenty to go on. But if you say, "Oh, for the right guitar, price is no object; I like the one that what's-his-name plays on MTV," you won't be taken seriously — nor are you likely to end up with the instrument you need. As the salesperson speaks, listen carefully and ask questions. You're there to observe and absorb, not impress. If you decide you're not ready to buy, tell him that. Thank him for his time and get his card. You're free to go elsewhere and investigate another store.

The art of the deal

You can find out the *retail,* or *list, price* of an instrument before you walk into the store. The manufacturer presets these numbers, and they're public knowledge (look at ads in magazines or visit the manufacturer's Web site). As of this writing, a Gibson Les Paul Standard lists for $3,899, and a Fender American Standard Stratocaster lists for $1,680 (see Figure 3-2).

Gibson Les Paul

Fender Stratocaster

Figure 3-2: Two standards by which players judge most of the electric guitars on the market.

Again, the preceding numbers are *list* prices. Music stores offer discounts, and the range can vary greatly. Big, urban-based stores that buy mass quantities of instruments can usually offer greater discounts than can smaller (mom-and-pop) stores in outlying or remote areas. Mail-order and online outlets can match and sometimes beat big-store prices, because they don't have the overhead of maintaining a retail facility.

In deciding where to buy, don't neglect the value of service. Retail and mom-and-pop stores — unlike online and mail-order houses — are in a better position to devote close, personal service to a new guitar customer. Perhaps as a result of stiff competition from the booming online and mail-order biz, many stores are upping their service incentives. Service includes anything from fixing minor problems and making adjustments to providing periodic *setups* (sort of like a tune-up and oil change for your guitar).

Remember, however, that list prices are public knowledge, and salespeople from all types of vendors must tell you their selling price with no conditions. The vendor can rightfully charge up to list price; you must wrangle the maximum discount yourself. How you do that is as old as bargaining itself, but a reasonable haggling range is somewhere between the cut-rate quote of an online or mail-order outfit and 10 percent off list.

Knowing When to Change the Strings

Old guitars improve with age, but old strings don't. The first time you play new strings is the best they ever sound. Strings gradually deteriorate until they either break or you can't take the dreary sounds they produce. Old strings sound dull and lifeless, and they lose *tensility* (ability to hold tension), becoming brittle. This condition makes them feel stiffer and harder to fret, and because the strings no longer stretch to reach the fret, they get tighter, causing your notes to go sharp, particularly up the neck.

You should replace all the strings at once, unless you break one and must replace it quickly. Strings tend to wear at the same rate, so they start the race against time on equal footing.

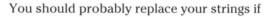

You should probably replace your strings if

- ✔ They exhibit visible signs of corrosion or caked-on dirt or grime.

- ✔ They don't play in tune or fret sharp, especially in the upper register.

- ✔ You can't remember the last time you changed them and you have an important gig (and don't want to chance any breakage).

Strings build up dirt and skin from your fingers, making them sound dull. The old boiling trick removes this gunk and can bring temporary new life to old strings. Simply fill a large pot with water, coil up your strings in it (be careful — strings tend to want to jump out of pots), and bring to boil for five minutes or so. Boiled strings really do sound better for a short time. Do this if you have a gig or jam on short notice and no way to get new strings. But then go get new strings.

Off with the Old: Removing Stressed Strings

Obviously, to put on a new string you have to remove the old one. Unless you're really in a hurry (such as in the middle of the first verse), you can take off any string by turning the tuning machine or peg to loosen the string enough that you can grab the string from the center and pull it off the post. You don't need to unwind it completely off the post using the peg. Or simply snip off the old string with wire cutters. It seems weird and brutal to snip off a string, but neither the sudden release of tension nor the cutting itself hurts the guitar.

The only reason *not* to cut a string is to save it as a spare, in case the new one breaks while putting it on (rare, but it happens). An old B string is better than no B string.

A common belief is that you should maintain constant string tension on the guitar neck at all times, and that you should replace the strings one at a time because removing all the strings at once is bad for the guitar. Every guitar expert has an opinion on this issue. Some say it's fine to remove all the strings and put new ones back on one at a time because guitars are actually tougher than you think. Others point out that changing strings one at a time is a safer way to go. Replacing strings one at a time is actually convenient for tuning, but whether it's healthier for the guitar is debated.

However you remove the old string, after it's off, you're ready to put on a new one. The methods for stringing a guitar diverge slightly, depending on whether you're stringing a steel-string acoustic, a classical, or an electric guitar. The remaining sections in this chapter describe these methods in detail.

Stringing a Steel-String Acoustic Guitar

Generally, steel-string acoustic guitars are probably easier to string than classicals or electrics (which are covered later in this chapter).

Changing strings step by step

Following are step-by-step instructions on restringing your guitar. You have two places to attach your new string: the bridge and the headstock. Start by attaching the string to the bridge, which is a pretty straightforward task.

Step 1: Attaching the string to the bridge

Acoustic guitars have a bridge with six holes leading to the inside of the guitar. To attach a new string to the bridge, follow these steps:

1. **Remove the old string and pop out the bridge pin.**

   Bridge pins sometimes stick, so you may need to use needle-nose pliers to pry them out. Always pull straight up.

2. **Place the end of the new string that has a little brass ring (called a** *ball*) **inside the hole that held the bridge pin.**

   Just stuff it down the hole a couple of inches. (How far isn't critical, because you're going to pull it up soon.)

3. **Wedge the bridge pin firmly back in the hole with the slot facing forward (toward the nut).**

   The slot provides a channel for the string to get out. Figure 3-3 shows the correct disposition for the new string and the bridge pin.

Figure 3-3:
How to
place the
new string
in the bridge
and position
the bridge
pin.

4. **Pull gently on the string until the ball rests against the bottom of the pin. Keep your thumb or finger on the pin so it doesn't pop out.**

   Be careful not to kink the string as you pull it.

5. **Test the string by gently tugging on it.**

   If you don't feel the string shift, the ball is snug against the bridge pin, and you're ready to secure the string to the tuning post.

Step 2: Securing the string to the tuning post

After securely attaching the string to the bridge pin, you can focus your attention on the headstock. The steps are slightly different for the treble strings (G, B, E) and the bass strings (E, A, D). On a typical guitar, you wind treble strings clockwise and bass strings counterclockwise.

To attach a treble string to the tuning post, follow these steps:

1. **Pass the string through the hole in the post.**

   Leave enough slack between the bridge pin and the tuning post to enable you to wind the string around the post several times.

2. **Kink (or crease) the metal wire toward the inside of the guitar.**

   Figure 3-4 shows how to kink the string to prepare it for winding.

Figure 3-4: String kinked to the inside of the head-stock, with slack for winding.

3. **While keeping the string tight against the post with one hand, wind the tuning peg clockwise with the other hand.**

   This step is a bit tricky and requires some manual dexterity. Keep your eye on the post to ensure that as the string wraps around the post, it winds *down, toward the headstock surface.* Figure 3-5 shows how the strings wrap around the posts. Be sure that the strings go into the correct slot in the nut. Don't get discouraged if you can't get your windings to look exactly like the strings shown in Figure 3-5. Getting everything to go smoothly takes a bit of practice.

Winding the string downward on the post increases what's called the *breaking angle.* The breaking angle is the angle between the post and the nut. A sharper angle brings more tension down onto the nut and creates better *sustain,* the length of time the note continues. To get the maximum angle, wind the string so it sits as low as possible on the post. (This fact is true for all guitars, not just acoustics.)

Figure 3-5:
The treble strings wrap downward around the posts in a clockwise direction; the bass strings wrap around the posts in a counter-clockwise direction.

To attach a bass string, you follow the preceding steps *except* that you wind the strings *counterclockwise* in Step 3 so the string goes up the middle and goes over the post to the left (as you face the headstock).

If you find that you've left too much slack, unwind the string and start again, kinking the string farther down. If you don't leave enough slack, your winding doesn't go all the way down the post, which may result in slipping if the string doesn't have enough length to grab firmly around the post. Neither situation is tragic. You simply undo what you've done and try again. As may happen in trying to get the two ends of a necktie the same length, you may need a couple of tries to get it right.

Tuning up

After you secure the string around the post, you can begin to hear the string come up to pitch. As the string draws tight, place it in its correct nut slot. If you're changing strings one at a time, you can just tune the new one to the old ones, which, presumably, are relatively in tune. (Check out Chapter 1 in Book I for the nuts and bolts of tuning your guitar.)

After you get the string to the correct pitch, pull on it in various places up and down its length to stretch it out a bit. Doing so can cause the string to go flat — sometimes drastically if you left any loose windings on the post — so tune it back up to pitch by winding the peg. Repeat the tune-stretch process two or three times to help the new string hold its pitch.

Using a *peg winder* to quickly turn the tuning pegs reduces your string-winding time considerably. A peg winder also features a notch in one side of the sleeve that can help you pop a stuck bridge pin. Just make sure you don't lose the pin when it comes flying out!

After the string is up to pitch and stretched out, you're ready to remove the excess length of string that sticks out from the post. You can snip this excess off with wire cutters (if you have them) or bend the string back and forth over the same crease until it breaks. Whatever you do, don't leave the straight string length protruding. It could poke you or someone standing next to you (such as the bass player) in the eye or give you a sharp jab in your fingertip.

Stringing Nylon-String Guitars

Stringing a nylon-string guitar is different from stringing a steel-string acoustic because both the bridge and the posts are different. Nylon-string guitars don't use bridge pins (strings are tied off instead) and their headstocks are slotted and have rollers, as opposed to posts.

Changing strings step by step

Nylon strings are easier to deal with than steel strings are, because nylon isn't as springy as steel. Attaching the string to the tuning post, however, can be trickier. As you do with the steel-string acoustic, begin by securing the bridge end of the string first and then turn your attention to the headstock.

Step 1: Securing the string to the bridge

Whereas steel-string acoustic strings have a ball at one end, nylon strings have no such ball: Both ends are loose. (Well, you *can* buy ball-ended nylon-string sets, but they're not what you normally use.) You can, therefore, attach either end of the string to the bridge. If the ends look different, however, use the one that looks like the middle of the string, not the one that has the loosely coiled appearance. Just follow these steps:

1. **Remove the old string, as described in the earlier section "Off with the Old: Removing Stressed Strings."**

2. **Pass one end of the new string through the hole in the top of the bridge, in the direction away from the soundhole, leaving about $1^1/_2$ inches sticking out the rear of the hole.**

3. **Secure the string by bringing the short end over the bridge and passing it under the long part of the string, as shown in Figure 3-6a. Then pass the short end under, over, and then under itself, on the top of the bridge, as shown in Figure 3-6b.**

You may need a couple of tries to get the end at just the right length, where not too much excess is dangling off the top of the bridge. (You can always cut the excess away, too.)

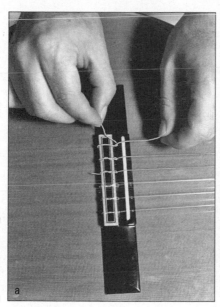

Figure 3-6:
Tying off the
bridge end
of the string.

4. **Pull on the long end of the string with one hand and move the knot with the other to remove excess slack and cause the knot to lie flat against the bridge.**

Step 2: Securing the string to the tuning post

On a nylon-string guitar, the tuning posts (called *rollers*) pass through the headstock sideways instead of perpendicularly as on a steel-string acoustic or electric guitar. This configuration is known as a *slotted headstock*.

To attach the string to the tuning post in a slotted headstock, follow these steps:

1. **Pass the string through the hole in the tuning post. Bring the end of the string back over the roller toward you; then pass the string under itself in front of the hole. Pull up on the string end so that the long part of the string (the part attached to the bridge) sits in the U-shaped loop you just formed, as shown in Figure 3-7a.**

   Make your loop come from the outside (that is, approaching from the left on the lower three bass strings, and from the right on the upper three treble strings).

2. **Pass the short end under and over itself, creating two or three wraps.**

   Doing so should hold the loose end firmly in place, as shown in Figure 3-7b, and prevent the string from slipping out of the hole.

Figure 3-7:
Creating a U-shaped loop with the short end of the string (a). Creating wraps to hold the short end of the string in place (b).

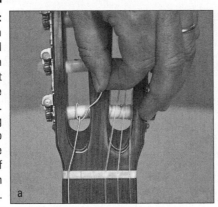
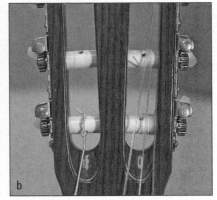

3. **Wind the peg so the string wraps on top of the loop you just formed, forcing it down against the post.**

4. **Pull the string length taut with one hand and turn the tuning peg with the other hand.**

   Wrap the windings to outside of the hole, away from the guitar's center.

Tuning up

As you continue turning the tuning peg, the string slowly comes nearer to pitch. Nylon strings, like steel strings, require quite a bit of stretching out, so after you get the string initially up to pitch, grab it at various places on its length, pull on it, and then tune it up again. Repeat this process two or three times to keep the guitar in tune longer. Snip away the excess string after you're done with all six strings. Nylon strings aren't as dangerous as steel strings if any excess protrudes, but the extra string hanging out is unsightly, and classical guitarists are extra-fussy about how their instruments look.

Stringing an Electric Guitar

Generally, electric guitarists need to change their strings more often than steel-string acoustic or classical guitarists. Because changing strings is so common on electric guitars, builders take a more progressive approach to the hardware, often making changing strings very quick and easy.

Changing strings step by step

First secure the string to the bridge and then attach the string to the headstock. Electric strings are similar to steel-string acoustic strings in that they have ball ends and are made of metal, but electric strings are usually composed of a lighter-gauge wire than steel-string acoustic strings, and the 3rd string is unwound, or plain, whereas a steel-string acoustic guitar's is wound. (A nylon-string's 3rd string also is unwound but is thicker.)

Step 1: Securing the string to the bridge

Most electric guitars use a simple method for securing the string to the bridge. You pass the string through a hole in the bridge (sometimes reinforced with a collar, or *grommet*) that's smaller than the ball at the end of the string — so the ball holds the string just as the knot at the end of a piece of thread holds a stitch in fabric. On some guitars (such as the Fender Telecaster), the collars anchor right into the body, and the strings pass through the back of the instrument, through a hole in the bridge assembly, and out the top.

Figure 3-8 shows two designs for attaching a string to an electric: from a top-mounted bridge and through the back. The following steps show how to secure the strings to the bridge.

1. **Remove the old string, as described in the section "Off with the Old: Removing Stressed Strings," earlier in this chapter.**

2. **Anchor the string at the bridge by passing the string through the hole until the ball stops the movement.**

   Then you focus on the tuning post. You do this on all but a few guitars (such as those with a Floyd Rose mechanism — see the end of this chapter).

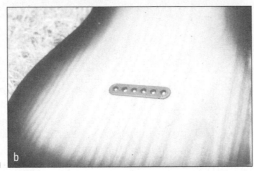

Figure 3-8: Strings pass through the bridge in the direction of the head-stock (a). Strings pass through the bridge from the back of the guitar (b).

Step 2: Securing the string to the tuning post

In most cases, the posts on an electric resemble those of a steel-string acoustic. A post protrudes through the headstock, and you pass your string through the post's hole, kink the string to the inside (toward the center of the headstock), and begin winding while holding the long part of the string with one hand for control. Refer to Figure 3-4 to see how to kink the string to prepare it for winding and about how much slack to leave.

Some electric guitars, notably Stratocasters and Telecasters, feature *string retainers,* little rollers or channels screwed into the top of the headstock that pull the top two or four strings down low onto the headstock, like a tent stake. If your guitar has string retainers, make sure you pass the strings under them.

Some tuners feature a *locking mechanism,* so you don't need to worry about winding, slack, and all that bother. Inside the post hole is a viselike device that clamps down on the string as it passes through. A *knurled* (ridge-covered) dial underneath the headstock loosens and tightens the vise. Perhaps the best-known company to make this locking device is Spurzel.

Some guitars have tuners with slotted posts instead of a hole. These also enable quick string changes, because you simply lay the string in the slot at the top of the post, kink it, and wind.

The special case of the Floyd Rose bridge

Rock music in the '80s made extensive use of the whammy bar and *floating bridge* (where the bridge isn't fixed, but floats on a spring assembly). Standard floating bridges weren't meant for the kind of abuse that creative guitarists such as Steve Vai and Joe Satriani cook up, though, so manufacturers developed better ways to make sure that bridges return to their original position and the strings remain in tune.

Floyd Rose invented the most successful of these assemblies. Rose used his own patented design to ensure a highly accurate, movable bridge system and *locking nut* (a clamplike device that replaces the standard nut).

The bridge takes the strings in a top-mounted approach, instead of through the back, but with one notable difference: Guitarists must snip the ball end off before attaching the string so the end can fit in the tiny viselike mechanism that holds the string in place. If you own a Floyd, you must carry spare strings with the balls snipped off or have wire cutters at the ready.

Because the Floyd Rose also features a locking nut, winding the string on the post isn't so critical. After you lock the nut (by using a small Allen wrench), what you do with the tuning pegs doesn't matter. You then do all tuning by using ridge-covered knobs on the bridge. These knobs are known as "fine tuners" because their movements are much smaller and more precise than are those on the headstock.

Stringing up an electric guitar fitted with a Floyd Rose system takes a little longer than it does on a regular electric, but if you plan to do a lot of whammy bar work, a Floyd Rose is well worth the effort.

Chapter 4

Deciphering Music
Notation and Tablature

In This Chapter

▶ Reading standard music notation

▶ Applying symbols to your guitar playing

▶ Decoding fingering indications and tablature

Reading music is not necessary to guitar playing, but it *is* helpful.
Plenty of great guitarists don't read a note. But then again, plenty of
great guitarists read music very well. Knowing how to read music can open
up many avenues in guitar playing and can provide a new understanding of
how it all fits together. Let's put it this way: It sure can't *hurt* to read a little
music. Plus, if you plan to write music, being able to put it down on paper is
a secure way to have it for good, without worrying about losing that demo
tape or mp3 file — and it's also satisfying.

We try in this chapter to make reading music as quick and easy as possible,
and we give you more than one way to approach the written music examples
that appear in this book. You can absorb how to play music more quickly if
you read music even a little bit, rather than not at all. So in this chapter you
can familiarize yourself with all the written symbols and notation practices
used in this book — including tablature — so you can better understand the
written exercises and pieces that appear here and elsewhere.

Knowing the Ropes of Standard
Music Notation

Standard music notation for guitar is the stuff of clefs, staves, and notes —
just as you find in music for the violin, flute, piano, trumpet, and saxophone.
So we start off by introducing the symbols you see when looking at "normal

music." In the following sections we show you the blank slate on which composers record music notation, and we cover the three main elements of music: pitch, duration (rhythm), and expression/articulation.

The composer's canvas: The staff, clef, measures, and bar lines

Our current system of writing music has evolved from centuries of different approaches, and it's come a long way since the medieval era. When composers sit down today to write music, they don't write on just any old piece of paper. The blank canvas for a composer isn't really totally blank. It's a series of horizontal grids that hold the notes and other music symbols from the composer's pen.

Figure 4-1 shows a blank staff, according to the way any musician first sees it, just waiting for a masterpiece to be written on it. The following sections explain its components.

Figure 4-1:
A blank staff with a treble clef, measures, and bar lines.

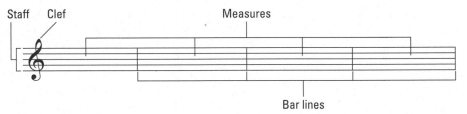

Staff

The grid of five horizontal lines and four spaces onto which all notes are placed is called a *staff.* The bottom line is the first line, and the top line is the fifth line. The space between the first and second lines is the first space. Notes can appear either on a line or in the space between two lines. The placement of a note on the staff designates the note's *pitch* (how high or low it is) and its letter name (C, D, G, and so on).

Clef

The staff appears with a *clef* (the squiggly thing at the beginning of the line), which defines what the pitches are on the lines and spaces. Guitar music uses the *treble clef,* also called the *G clef* because the curlicue of the clef symbol (which looks sort of like a fancy *G*) wraps around the second line from the bottom, which is its way of telling you, "This is G." You can then find any note on the staff by counting up or down the lines and spaces starting from G.

Measures and bar lines

Just as you need a staff and a clef to tell you the notes' pitches, you must also have some sort of context in which to place notes in time. Most music has a *beat*, or pulse, that gives the music a basic rhythmic unit that the notes play off. (If the notes go fast, it usually means they go fast in relation to the beat.)

The beat in turn is usually "felt" in larger groups of two, three, or four; you represent this division on the staff with vertical lines that separate the music into sections called *measures*, or *bars*. The section between two vertical lines is a *measure* (or *bar*), and the vertical lines themselves are called *bar lines*. Grouping music into measures is a way to keep it manageable by organizing the notes into smaller units — units that support the beat's natural emphasis. Measures allow you to keep your place in the music and to break it down into smaller chunks for easier digestion.

Pitch: The highs and lows of music

Pitch is the highness or lowness of a note. Music notation uses the staff, the clef, and the placement of a note on the staff to show pitch. Take a look at Figure 4-2 and Table 4-1 for a breakdown of the various symbols and definitions used for pitch.

Figure 4-2:
Music showing the elements of pitch.

Pitch names: G A B C   G F♯ E D   A B C A   G♯ B♭ A♭ B

Table 4-1		Symbols Used to Show Pitch
Number in Figure 4-2	*Symbol Name or Term*	*Description*
1	**Note**	A musical symbol whose position on the staff indicates its pitch and whose shape indicates its duration. The notes on the five lines of the staff (from bottom to top) are E, G, B, D, and F. You can remember these using the saying "**E**very **G**ood **B**oy **D**oes **F**ine." The notes placed on the four spaces in between the lines (from bottom to top) spell out the word *face* (F, A, C, and E).
2	**Ledger lines**	Notes can fall above or below the staff as well as within the staff. To indicate a pitch that falls higher or lower than the staff, use ledger lines, which you can think of as short, temporary staff lines. Note names progress up or down the ledger lines (and the spaces between them) the same way they do on the staff lines. So, for example, the first ledger line below the staff is C, and the first ledger line above the staff is A. Try counting down two notes from the bottom line E and up two notes from the top line F to verify this for yourself.
3	**Sharps, flats, naturals, and accidentals**	The first seven letters of the alphabet — A through G — make up the *natural* notes in music, the white keys of the piano keyboard. In between some of the natural notes (white keys) are other notes (the black keys) that don't have names of their own. These notes are known as *sharps* or *flats* and are named according to their adjacent natural notes by adding either a sharp symbol (♯) or flat symbol (♭) after the letter name. When you see F♯ in music, you play F one half step (one fret) higher than natural F. For a note with a flat symbol, such as D♭, play the note one half step lower than the natural version. A *natural sign* (♮) restores a note that's been modified by a sharp or flat to its natural state — it cancels the sharp or flat. *Accidentals* are notes outside the key (defined by the key signature) and are indicated in the music by the appearance of a sharp, flat, or natural sign modifying a note. An accidental holds for all the notes of that pitch for the rest of the measure.

Number in Figure 4-2	Symbol Name or Term	Description
4	Key signature	The listing of flats or sharps at the beginning of the staff, immediately to the right of the clef, tells you which notes to play flat or sharp for the entirety of the piece (or at least a major section of the piece), unless otherwise indicated with an accidental. For example, the music in Figure 4-2 has a *key signature* of one sharp — F♯. That means anytime you encounter any F (whether in the staff or on a ledger line), you play it a half step (one fret) higher. In other words, the key signature sends out the loud and clear message: "All Fs are hereby sharped until further notice!"

Duration: How long to hold a note and what determines rhythm

Although the placement of a note on the staff indicates its pitch, the *shape* of the note indicates its length in time, or *duration,* in relation to the beat. The longer in duration the notes are, the more slowly they move, or the more time there is between their respective starting notes. The shorter the notes' values, the faster they come. Without rhythm, notes have no motion. You need both pitch and rhythm together to make music.

Rests also pertain to duration; these symbols indicate musical silence and have specific values, just as notes do.

You can increase the length of individual notes or rests by placing a *dot* to the right of the note head or rest. You can also increase the length of a note by adding a *tie,* which connects one note to another of the same pitch immediately following it. See Table 4-2, along with other common symbols used to indicate duration — the table corresponds to Figure 4-3, which shows the symbols in the context of a musical excerpt.

Figure 4-3: Music showing duration.

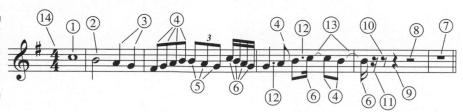

Table 4-2	Symbols Used to Indicate Duration	
Number in Figure 4-3	**Symbol Name or Term**	**Description**
1	**Whole note**	An open note head with no *stem;* receives four beats in 4/4 time.
2	**Half note**	An open note head with a stem; receives two beats in 4/4.
3	**Quarter note**	A solid note head with a stem; receives one beat in 4/4.
4	**Eighth note**	A solid note head with a stem and one *flag* or *beam;* receives half a beat in 4/4.
5	**Eighth-note triplet**	An eighth note grouped with other notes and appearing with the numeral *3,* sometimes accompanied by a bracket, to indicate three eighth notes in the space of two eighth notes' time.
6	**16th note**	A solid note head with a stem and two flags or beams; receives one quarter of a beat in 4/4.
7	**Whole rest**	A small rectangle that hangs down from a staff line indicating an entire measure's rest in any meter.
8	**Half rest**	A small rectangle that sits on a staff line indicating two beats' rest in 4/4.
9	**Quarter rest**	A symbol that indicates one beat of rest in 4/4.
10	**Eighth rest**	A symbol that indicates a half beat's rest in 4/4.
11	**16th rest**	A symbol that indicates a quarter beat's rest in 4/4.
12	**Augmentation dot**	A *dot* appearing to the right of the note head or rest that tells you to increase the note's or rest's length by half of the original value. For example, a quarter note is one beat, so a dotted quarter note equals one and a half beats.
13	**Tie**	A curved line that joins two notes of the same pitch. You play the first note for its full value, and instead of restriking the second (tied) note, you let the note sustain for the combined value of both notes.

Number in Figure 4-3	Symbol Name or Term	Description
14	Time signature	A two-digit symbol that appears at the beginning of the piece that helps you count the beats in a measure and tells you which beats to stress, or give emphasis to. The top number indicates how many beats are in each measure, and the bottom number tells you what type of note (half, quarter, eighth, and so on) gets one beat. For example, in 3/4 time, you play three beats to the measure, with the quarter note receiving one beat. In 4/4 time, you play four beats to the measure, with the quarter note receiving the pulse or beat. Knowing how to read (and play according to) the time signature helps you to capture the feel of the music.

When you tap your foot to the music on the radio, at a concert, or on your portable music player, you're tapping (or stomping or clapping) along to the *beat*. If you count to yourself 1-2-3-4, or 1-2-3 — or however many beats logically make up one measure of that song or piece — you can figure out the time signature. Most popular music is in 4/4, as is most of the music in this book. Some song forms are specifically written in a certain time signature. For example, a waltz is written in 3/4. So the next time someone says, "Do I hear a waltz?" listen and tap along in units of three to tell if that's correct.

Written high, sounding low

Guitar music is written in treble clef, but the actual sound of the pitches you play is an octave lower. For example, when you see a third-space C on the staff, you play the 2nd string, 1st fret. And you'd be playing the note correctly, according to the way guitar players play written notes on the treble clef. But just remember in the back of your mind somewhere that the note you play there actually sounds *middle* C (which is the first ledger line below the staff in music for other sound-as-written instruments, such as the piano). So the guitar is kind of a low-pitched instrument, at least compared with instruments that sound as written, such as the flute, violin, and oboe. Why is that? Writing the *actual* sounding pitches would be a little more awkward to read because it would put so many of the notes many ledger lines below the staff.

REMEMBER

The different types of note values relate to the other types of notes. For example, a whole note is equal to two half notes, and a half note equals two quarter notes. Therefore, a whole note is equal in total duration to four quarter notes. Figure 4-4 shows the relative durations of the most common note types.

REMEMBER

When "playing" a rest on the guitar, you often have to stop a string from ringing. Be careful not to get into the bad habit of looking only where to play notes rather than where to "play" or observe rests. When you see a rest, make sure that you're not only *not* striking a note during that time but also that you stop any previously struck string or strings from ringing through the rest.

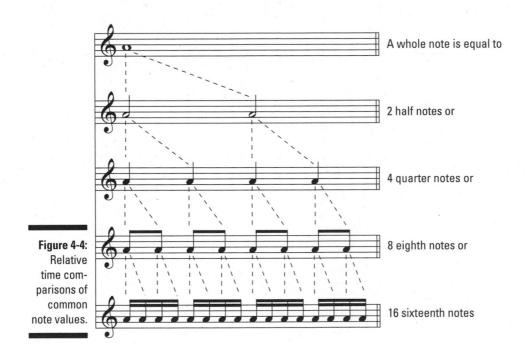

A whole note is equal to

2 half notes or

4 quarter notes or

Figure 4-4: Relative time comparisons of common note values.

8 eighth notes or

16 sixteenth notes

Expression, articulation, and other symbols

Beyond the primary elements of pitch and duration, you often see other symbols and terms in written music. These additional markings give you a range of instructions, from how to play the music more expressively to how to navigate instructions to repeat a certain passage, and so on. Figure 4-5 and Table 4-3 show just some of these expression and articulation (how notes are struck) symbols and other markings.

Book I

Guitar 101

Figure 4-5:
Expression,
articulation,
and miscel-
laneous
symbols and
terms.

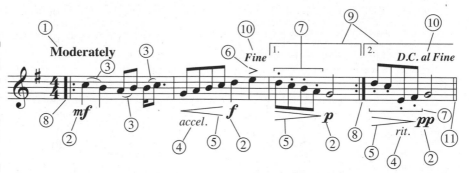

Table 4-3	Expression, Articulation, and Miscellaneous Symbols and Terms	
Number in Figure 4-5	**Symbol Name or Term**	**Description**
1	**Tempo heading**	A word or phrase that offers guidance on the speed and/or general feel of the piece. In much classical music, tempo headings are written in Italian (such as *Andante, Adagio,* or *Moderato*), but it's also common to see the words written in the composer or publisher's native language (as in Figure 4-5, with *Moderately*).
2	**Dynamic marking**	Letters that tell you how loud or soft to play. The letters are the abbreviations of Italian words and terms, such as *mf* for *mezzo-forte* (medium loud), *mp* (*mezzo-piano,* medium soft), *f* (*forte,* loud), *p* (*piano,* soft), *ff* (*fortissimo,* very loud), and *pp* (*pianissimo,* very soft).
3	**Slur**	A curved line between two notes of different pitch that tells you to connect the second note smoothly to the first. Slurs appear in music requiring a *legato* (*ligado* in Spanish) approach, where the notes blend together in a sustained, uninterrupted fashion.
4	**Accelerando and Ritardando**	Instructions that tell you to play gradually faster (*accelerando,* abbreviated *accel.*) or gradually slower (*ritardando,* abbreviated *ritard.* or *rit.*).

(continued)

Table 4-3 *(continued)*

Number in Figure 4-5	Symbol Name or Term	Description
5	**Crescendo** and **decrescendo** (**diminuendo**)	Symbols that resemble open wedges (called "hairpins" by some musicians) or the abbreviated versions *cresc.* and *decresc.* (or *dim.*) that tell you to play gradually louder *(crescendo)* or softer *(decrescendo, diminuendo).*
6	**Accent**	A small wedge-shaped or caret-like marking above or below a note that tells you to emphasize the note by striking it harder than normal.
7	**Staccato dot**	A small dot placed above or below the note head that tells you to play the note short and detached.
8	**Repeat signs**	Special bar-line-type symbols that tell you to repeat the measures between the signs.
9	**Ending brackets**	Lines that separate different endings in a repeated section. In Figure 4-5, play the measure under the first ending bracket the first time. On the repeat, play only the second ending, skipping the first ending.
10	**D.C. al Fine**	A score direction that tells you to go back to the beginning (*D.C.* stands for *Da capo,* Italian for "from the top") and play to the part marked *Fine* (Italian for "end"). **D.C. al Coda** tells you to go back to the beginning and play until you see the words *To Coda.* Then skip to the part of the music marked *Coda* (which indicates the final part of the music — *coda* is Italian for "tail") with the coda symbol (which resembles a set of crosshairs or a cross covering an oval). **D.S.** (for *dal segno,* or "from the sign") tells you to go back to the sign (a slanted, stylized *s* with two dots on either side and a slash bisecting the *s*).
11	**Double bar lines**	Two bar lines spaced close together, indicating the end of a section or, if the lines are a combination of a thick and thin pair, the end of a piece.

Relating the Notes on the Staff to the Fretboard

Guitarists are no different from other musicians when dealing with written music in that after they identify and understand the symbols of standard music notation, they have to relate them to their instrument. And by "relate," we mean *play.* At the most basic level — executing the correct pitch and rhythm — you must be able to play the note you see on the staff correctly on the guitar.

Associating a note on the staff with a string and fret location (even if the fret is zero — meaning an open string) is the first step to reading music on the guitar. A good way to begin associating notes on the staff as they relate to the guitar is to consider the pitches of the open strings, as shown in Figure 4-6.

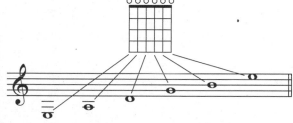

Figure 4-6:
The pitches
of the open
strings.

You can use these pitches to help tune your guitar to a piano or other fixed-pitch source. See Chapter 1 in Book I for more on tuning your guitar.

To help you correlate the notes of the treble clef with the frets on the guitar, check out Figure 4-7, which shows notes from E to F on the staff as they correspond to the fingerboard. Don't worry about playing anything yet — just get used to the idea that when you see, for example, an E on the 1st (lowest) line of the treble clef, it corresponds to the 4th string, 2nd fret.

Figure 4-7:
The notes
on the staff
correspond-
ing to the
frets on the
fingerboard.

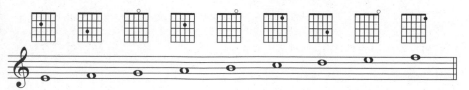

Figure 4-8 shows the entire range of notes (including sharps and flats) on the guitar on the treble clef using ledger lines above and below the staff. All 12 frets of each of the six strings are shown on the staff, which allows you to see how to play some pitches on multiple strings. The lowest possible note is the open low-E string, three ledger lines and a space below the treble staff. The highest note is E, three ledger lines above the staff.

Though the notes extend off the staff in each direction by at least three ledger lines (see "Ledger lines" in Table 4-1 for more info), in reality you rarely have to deal with notes higher than the high E that occurs three ledger lines above the staff. (You play this note on the 1st string, 12th fret.) However, the low part of the guitar's range — from the open low E on up — sees a lot of action, so be sure you get familiar with those pitches, because you'll be playing them quite a bit.

Guitar-Specific Notation

Guitarists who read standard music notation observe all symbols and practices regarding clefs, *staves* (plural of *staff*), pitches, and rhythms that other musicians do. But music written specifically for guitar also employs additional symbols that instruct you to perform the music in certain ways. If these symbols appear, observing them helps you perform the music in an easier, more efficient way, or enables you to better realize the composer or arranger's intent.

These extra symbols don't change anything regarding the pitch or rhythm; their purpose is to instruct you on how to perform the piece in the best way. In the following sections, we explore some symbols you encounter only in music written for guitar.

Fingering indications for the right and left hands

If you see little numbers and letters in the treble staff, it usually means someone (the composer or arranger, a teacher, or the editor of the music) has gone through and thoughtfully provided you with the suggested, the best, or even the *only possible* working fingering indications. *Fingering* is the term guitarists use for the choice, or assignment, of specific fingers to play a given note or passage of notes. And in classical guitar especially, the issue of fingering comes up a lot.

Book I

Guitar 101

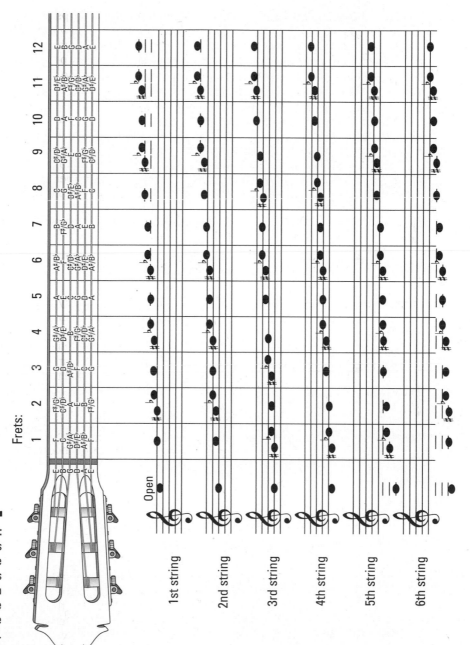

Figure 4-8:
The guitar's entire range of notes shown on the treble clef and the fretboard.

Numbers without circles appearing next to or near note heads tell you which left-hand fingers to use, as follows: 1 = index finger; 2 = middle finger; 3 = ring finger; and 4 = little finger. (You don't use the left-hand thumb in fingering.) Letters above or below notes indicate right-hand fingers, with the letters signifying the Spanish words for the thumb and the index, middle, and ring fingers: *p* = thumb *(pulgar)*; *i* = index *(índice)*; *m* = middle *(medio)*; and *a* = ring *(anular)*. Except for some special percussive techniques and in flamenco style, you don't use the right-hand little finger. Figure 4-9 shows a passage of music with some left- and right-hand fingering indications. Note that the right-hand pattern continues in both measures.

Figure 4-9:
Music with left- and right-hand fingering indications.

Sometimes you have to use the same left-hand finger to fret two consecutive notes on the same string at different frets. This requires you to actually move your left hand up or down the neck. Keeping your finger in contact with the string as you move to the new fret helps to guide your left hand. The guide finger is indicated in notation with a short, straight line appearing to the left of the second of the two finger numbers, slanting in the direction of the left-hand movement (up or down). Figure 4-10 shows the first finger acting as a guide finger moving down one fret from A to A♭.

Figure 4-10:
Notation indicating a guide finger.

Unlike the piano, where each note on the staff indicates one and only one piano key, the guitar fretboard often provides more than one place to play a given note. For example, you can play the second line G on the open 3rd string or on the 4th string at the 5th fret. If the music requires you to play a note or passage of notes on a certain string, you see a number inside a circle, which indicates the string. For example, if you must play a second-line G on the 4th string (instead of as an open 3rd string), you see a *4* inside a circle. Figure 4-11 shows a passage that's playable only if you take the downstem G on the 4th string, 5th fret, with your thumb.

Figure 4-11:
A number inside a circle tells you on which string to play a note.

Stepping up to the barre

You often have to fret more than one string at a time at the same fret, and you do this by taking a finger and flattening it out to form a "bar" — or, as it's known in guitar lingo, *barre* (Chapter 3 in Book II tells you how). You may see various ways to indicate a barre in guitar music, but here we use a capital *C* (for the Spanish *ceja* or *cejilla*) for a full barre (all six strings) and a *C* with a vertical line bisecting it for a half or partial barre (fewer than six strings). A Roman numeral tells you which fret to place the barre on, and a dotted line indicates the number of beats you must hold the barre in place to successfully execute the passage underneath it. Figure 4-12 shows how barre notation appears in guitar music.

Figure 4-12:
What a barre indication looks like.

Taking on tablature, a nice complement to standard notation

Sometimes a tablature staff (called "tab" for short) is added to the standard notation staff. *Tablature* looks kind of like normal music notation but it's not. Tablature is a six-line staff that represents the guitar fretboard (see Figure 4-13). Note that each line represents a string of the guitar, with the top line corresponding to the 1st (high-E) string and the bottom line corresponding to the 6th (low-E) string. A number on a line provides the fret location for that note. (Tablature doesn't tell you which finger to use, but you may be able to get that information from the standard music staff.)

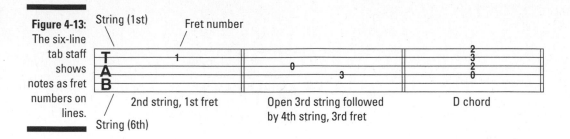

Figure 4-13:
The six-line
tab staff
shows
notes as fret
numbers on
lines.

String (1st) — Fret number — 2nd string, 1st fret — Open 3rd string followed by 4th string, 3rd fret — D chord — String (6th)

Remember when we said that all musicians have to be able to understand the symbols of standard music notation and *then* relate them to their instrument? Tablature skips that step! You can use tab right away, with no previous experience in reading music. However, tab is more limited than standard music notation. For one thing, it works only for guitar, so it doesn't teach you the more universal skill of reading music, and it doesn't indicate rhythm.

Tab does, however, work very well in conjunction with the standard music staff. All the notes in the tab staff align vertically with the notes appearing above in the standard music staff. If you're ever unsure as to where to play a note appearing in the music staff, all you need to do is shoot your eyes straight down to the corresponding string-and-fret location in the tab staff. Conversely, if you find yourself in the tab staff and you're uncertain of what's supposed to be happening with regard to rhythms or rests, take a quick trip uptown to see how that passage is displayed in the music staff. Figure 4-14 shows how the notes on the standard music notation staff relate to the tab staff and vice versa.

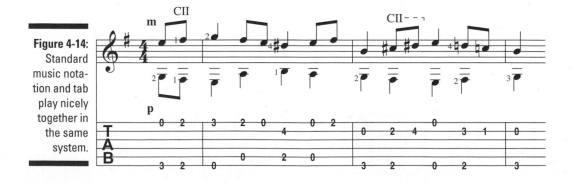

Figure 4-14:
Standard
music nota-
tion and tab
play nicely
together in
the same
system.

Book II
Sounds and Techniques

In this book . . .

We get into the meat of things — really playing guitar. We warm you up with basic major and minor chords and then add a bit of zest to the recipe: 7th chords. And we give the right hand (or left, if you're a lefty) its due in a chapter on rhythm techniques. We cover playing melodies in position in the last chapter.

Here are the contents of Book II at a glance.

Chapter 1

Basic Major and Minor Chords

* *

In This Chapter

▶ Playing the basic guitar chords

▶ Playing songs with basic major and minor chords

▶ Sweatin' to the oldies progression

* *

Accompanying yourself as you sing your favorite songs is one of the best ways to pick up basic guitar chords. If you know how to play basic chords, you can play lots of popular songs right away — from "Skip to My Lou" to "Louie Louie."

In this chapter, the major and minor chords are organized into families. A *family of chords* is simply a group of related chords. They're *related* because you often use these chords together to play songs. The concept is sort of like color-coordinating your clothing or creating a balanced meal. Chords in a family go together like peanut butter and jelly (except that chords in a family are less messy). Along the way, you expand your guitar-notation vocabulary as you start to develop your chord-playing and strumming skills.

Think of a family of chords as a plant. One of the chords — the one that feels like home base in a song (usually the chord you start and end a song with) — is the plant's root, and the other chords in the family are the different shoots rising up from that same root. Together, the root and shoots make up the family. Put 'em all together and you have a lush garden . . . er, make that a *song*. By the way, the technical term for a family is *key*. So you can say, "This song uses A-family chords," or "This song is in the key of A."

Playing Chords in the A Family

The A family is a popular one for playing songs on the guitar because, like other families in this chapter, its chords are easy to play. That's because A-family chords contain *open strings* (strings that you play without pressing down any frets). Chords that contain open strings are called *open chords,* or *open-position chords.* Listen to "Fire and Rain," by James Taylor, to hear the sound of a song that uses A-family chords.

The basic chords in the A family are A, D, and E. Each of these chords is what's known as a *major* chord. A chord that's named by a letter name alone, such as these (A, D, and E), is always major.

Fingering A-family chords

When fingering chords, you use the "ball" of your fingertip, placing it just behind the fret (on the side toward the tuning pegs). Arch your fingers so the fingertips fall perpendicular to the neck. And make sure your left-hand fingernails are short so they don't prevent you from pressing the strings all the way down to the fingerboard. Figure 1-1 shows the fingering for the A, D, and E chords — the basic chords in the A family. (If you're unclear about reading chord diagrams, check out Chapter 2 in Book I.)

Don't play any strings marked with an X (the 6th string on the A chord and the 5th and 6th strings on the D chord). Strike just the top five (5th through 1st) strings in the A chord and the top four (4th through 1st) strings in the D chord. Selectively striking strings may be awkward at first, but keep at it and you'll get the hang of it. If you play a string marked with an X and we catch you, we'll revoke your picking privileges on the spot.

Figure 1-1: Chord diagrams showing the A, D, and E chords. The diagrams graphically convey the left-hand positions in the photos.

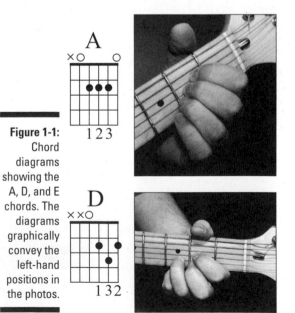

Playing callusly

Playing chords can be a little painful at first. (We mean for you, not for people within earshot; c'mon, we're not *that* cruel.) No matter how tough you are, if you've never played guitar before, your left-hand fingertips are *soft*. Fretting a guitar string, therefore, is going to hurt.

This situation isn't weird at all — in fact, it's quite normal for beginning guitarists. (Well, it's weird if you *enjoy* the pain.) You must develop nice, thick calluses on your fingertips before playing the guitar can ever feel completely comfortable. You may take weeks or even months to build up those protective layers of dead skin, depending on how much and how often you play. But after you finally earn your calluses, you never lose

them (completely, anyway). Like a Supreme Court justice, you're a guitar player *for life*.

You can develop calluses by playing the basic chords in this chapter over and over again. As you progress, you also gain strength in your hands and fingers, and become more comfortable in general while playing the guitar. Before you know it's happening, fretting a guitar becomes as natural to you as shaking hands with your best friend.

As with any physical-conditioning routine, stop and rest if you feel tenderness or soreness in your fingers or hands. Building up calluses takes time, and you can't hurry time (or love, for that matter, as Diana Ross would attest).

Book II

Sounds and Techniques

Strumming A-family chords

Use your right hand to strum these A-family chords with a pick, your thumb, or the back of your fingernails (in a brushing motion toward the floor). Start strumming from the lowest-pitched string of the chord (the top-most as you hold the guitar) and strum toward the floor.

A *chord progression* is a series of chords that you play one after the other. Figure 1-2 presents a simple progression in the key of A and instructs you to strum each chord — in the order shown (reading from left to right) — four times. Use all *downstrokes* (dragging your pick across the strings toward the floor) as you play. Listen to Track 2 to hear the rhythm of this progression and try to play along with it.

Figure 1-2:
A simple chord progression in the key of A (using only chords in the A family).

Track 2, 0:00

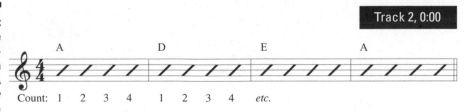

After strumming each chord four times, you come to a vertical line in the music that follows the four strum symbols. This is a *bar line.* It's not something that you play. Bar lines visually separate the music into smaller sections known as *measures,* or *bars.* (You can use these terms interchangeably; they both mean the same thing.) Measures make written music easier to grasp because they break up the music into little, digestible chunks. (See Chapter 4 in Book I for more on the basics of the musical staff.)

Don't hesitate or stop at the bar line. Keep your strumming speed the same throughout, even as you play "between the measures" — that is, in the imaginary "space" from the end of one measure to the beginning of the next that the bar line represents. Start out playing as slowly as necessary to help you keep the beat steady. You can always speed up as you become more confident and proficient in your chord fingering and switching.

By playing a progression over and over, you start to develop left-hand strength and calluses on your fingertips. If you want to play a song right away, you can. Skip to the section "Playing Songs with Basic Major and Minor Chords," at the end of this chapter. Because you now know the basic open chords in the A family, you can play "Kumbaya." Rock on!

Playing Chords in the D Family

The basic chords that make up the D family are D, Em (pronounced "E minor"), G, and A. The D family, therefore, shares two basic open chords with the A family (D and A) and introduces two new ones: Em and G. Because you already know how to play D and A from the preceding section, you need to work on only two more chords to add the entire D family to your repertoire: Em and G. Listen to "Here Comes the Sun," by the Beatles (from *Abbey Road*), to hear a song that uses D-family chords.

Minor describes the quality of a type of chord. A minor chord has a sound that's distinctly different from that of a major chord. You may characterize the sound of a minor chord as sad, mournful, scary, or even ominous.

The relationship of the notes that make up the chord determines a chord's quality. A chord that's named by a capital letter followed by a small "m" is always minor.

Chord qualities

Chords have different qualities, which has nothing to do with whether they're good or bad little chords. You can define *quality* as the *relationship* between the different notes that make up the chord — or simply, what the chord sounds like.

Besides *major,* other chord qualities include *minor, 7th, minor 7th,* and *major 7th.* The following list describes chord qualities:

- ✔ **Major chords:** These are simple chords that have a stable, positive sound.

- ✔ **Minor chords:** These are simple chords that have a soft, sometimes sad sound.

- ✔ **7th chords:** These are bluesy, funky-sounding chords.

- ✔ **Minor 7th chords:** These chords sound mellow and jazzy.

- ✔ **Major 7th chords:** These chords sound bright and jazzy.

Each type of chord, or chord quality, has a different kind of sound, and you can often distinguish the chord type just by hearing it. Listen, for example, to the sound of a major chord by strumming A, D, and E. (For more on 7th, minor 7th, and major 7th chords, check out Chapter 2 in Book II.)

Fingering D-family chords

Figure 1-3 shows you how to finger the two basic chords in the D family that aren't in the A family. You may notice that none of the strings in either chord diagram displays an X symbol, so you get to strike all the strings whenever you play a G or Em chord. Go ahead and celebrate by dragging your pick or right-hand fingers across the strings in a big *keraaaang*.

Figure 1-3: Em and G chords. You get to play all six strings in each chord.

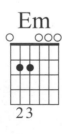

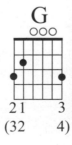

Try the following trick to quickly pick up how to play Em and to hear the difference between the major and minor chord qualities: Play E, which is a major chord, and then lift your index finger off the 3rd string. Now you're playing Em, which is the minor-chord version of E. By alternating, you can easily hear the difference in quality between a major and minor chord.

Also, notice the alternative fingering for G (2-3-4 instead of 1-2-3). As your hand gains strength and becomes more flexible, you want to switch to the 2-3-4 fingering instead of the initially easier 1-2-3 fingering. Why? You can switch to other chords faster using the 2-3-4 fingering for G.

Strumming D-family chords

In Figure 1-4, you play a simple chord progression using D-family chords. Notice the difference in the strum in this figure versus that of Figure 1-2. In Figure 1-2, you strum each chord four times per measure. Each strum is one pulse, or beat. Figure 1-4 divides the second strum of each measure (or the second beat) into two strums — up and down — both of which together take up the time of one beat, meaning that you must play each strum in beat 2 twice as quickly as you do a regular strum.

Practicing and getting good

It may sound obvious to say that the more you practice, the better you'll get, but it's true. Perhaps even better is this: *The more you practice, the faster you'll get good.* Although there's no set amount of practice time for "getting good," a good rule of thumb is to practice a minimum of 30 minutes every day. Also, it's generally agreed that practicing at regular intervals is better than jamming a week's worth of time (say, 3 1/2 hours) into one practice session.

If at first you find a new technique difficult to master, stick with it, and you'll eventually get the hang of it. To get even better on the guitar, try the following:

✔ Set aside a certain time every day for practicing.

✔ Work on one or two goals at a time, such as learning a piece and an exercise.

✔ Get together with your guitar-playing friends and get them to listen to what you're doing.

✔ Create a practice environment where you have privacy and are away from distractions (TV, conversations, your mother bugging you to come to dinner, and so on).

✔ Watch videos of guitar players who play the kind of music you like and want to learn.

Figure 1-4:
This progression contains chords commonly found in the key of D.

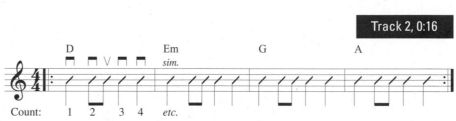

The additional symbol ⊓ with the strum symbol means that you strum down (hitting the lower strings first), and ∨ means that you strum up. The term *sim.* is an abbreviation of the Italian word *simile,* which instructs you to keep playing in a *simi*lar manner — in this case to keep strumming in a *down, down-up, down, down* pattern.

If you're playing fingerstyle (strumming with your fingers), play upstrokes with the back of your thumbnail whenever you see the symbol ∨.

Knowing the basic open chords in the D family (D, Em, G, and A) enables you to play a song in the key of D right now. If you skip to the section "Playing Songs with Basic Major and Minor Chords," later in this chapter, you can play the song "Swing Low, Sweet Chariot" right now. Go for it!

Playing Chords in the G Family

By tackling related chord families (as A, D, and G are), you carry over your knowledge from family to family in the form of chords that you already know from earlier families. The basic chords that make up the G family are G, Am, C, D, and Em. If you already know G, D, and Em (which we describe in the preceding sections on the A and D families), you can now try Am and C. Listen to "You've Got a Friend," as played by James Taylor, to hear the sound of a song that uses G-family chords.

Fingering G-family chords

In Figure 1-5, you see the fingerings for Am and C, the new chords that you need to play in the G family. Notice that the fingering of these two chords is similar: Each has finger 1 on the 2nd string, 1st fret, and finger 2 on the 4th string, 2nd fret. In moving between these chords, keep these first two fingers in place. Switching chords is always easier if you don't need to move all your fingers to new positions. The notes that different chords share are known as *common tones.* Notice the X over the 6th string in each of these chords. Don't play that string while strumming either C or Am. (We mean it!)

Figure 1-5:
The fingering for Am and C chords.

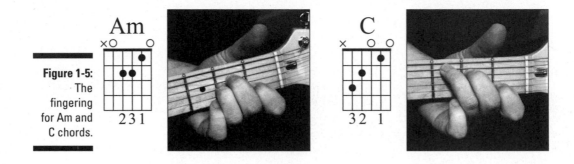

Strumming G-family chords

Figure 1-6 shows a simple chord progression that you can play by using G-family chords. Play this progression over and over to accustom yourself to switching chords and to build up those left-hand calluses. It *does* get easier after a while. Promise!

Figure 1-6:
A chord progression that you can play using only G-family chords.

Track 2, 0:43

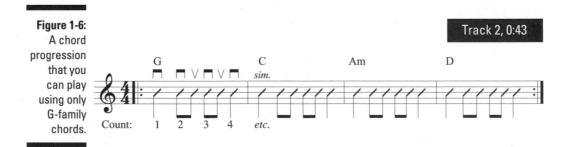

Notice that, in each measure, you play beats 2 *and* 3 as "down-up" strums. Listen to Track 2 on the CD to hear this sound.

Knowing the basic open chords in the G family (G, Am, C, D, and Em) enables you to play a song in the key of G right now. Skip to the section "Playing Songs with Basic Major and Minor Chords," later in this chapter, and you can play "Auld Lang Syne."

Playing Chords in the C Family

The last chord family we need to discuss is C. Some people say that C is the easiest key to play in. C is sort of the music-theory square one — the point at which everything (and, usually, everyone) begins in music. The C family is placed last in this chapter because it has lots of chords in its family — too many to master all at once.

The basic chords that make up the C family are C, Dm, Em, F, G, and Am. If you practice the preceding sections on the A-, D-, and G-family chords, you know C, Em, G, and Am. So in this section, you need to pick up only two more chords: Dm and F. "Dust in the Wind" by Kansas and "The Boxer" by Simon and Garfunkel use C-family chords.

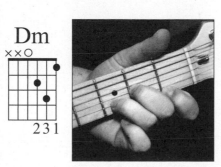
Book II

Sounds and Techniques

Fingering C-family chords

In Figure 1-7, you see the new chords that you need to play in the C family. Note that both Dm and F have the second finger on the 3rd string, 2nd fret. Hold this common tone down as you switch between these two chords.

Figure 1-7:
Dm and F
chords. The
indication
(⌒) in the
F-chord
diagram
tells you
to fret (or
barre) two
strings with
one finger.

Dm
×× O

2 3 1

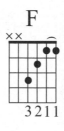

F
× ×

3 2 1 1

Many people find F the most difficult chord to play of the basic chords. That's because F uses no open strings, and it also requires a barre. A *barre* is what you're playing whenever you press down two or more strings at once with a single left-hand finger. To play the F chord, you use your first finger to press down both the 1st and 2nd strings at the 1st fret simultaneously.

You must exert extra finger pressure to play a barre. At first, you may find that, as you strum the F chord (hitting the top four strings only, as the Xs in the chord diagram indicate), you hear buzzes or muffled strings. Experiment with various placements of your index finger. Try adjusting the angle of your finger or rotating it on its side. Keep trying until you find a position for the first finger that enables all four strings to ring clearly as you strike them.

Strumming C-family chords

Figure 1-8 shows a simple chord progression using C-family chords. Play the progression over and over to get used to switching among the chords in this family and, of course, to help build up those nasty little calluses.

Figure 1-8:
A simple chord progression that you can play by using C-family chords.

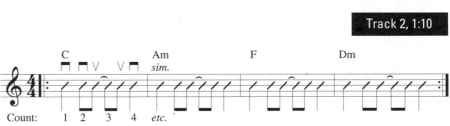

Track 2, 1:10

Look at Figure 1-8. Notice the small curved line joining the second half of beat 2 to beat 3. This line is known as a tie. A *tie* tells you not to strike the second note of the two tied notes (in this case, the one on beat 3). Instead, just keep holding the chord on that beat (letting it ring) without restriking it with your right hand.

Listen to Track 2 on the CD to hear the sound of this strumming pattern. This slightly jarring rhythmic effect is an example of syncopation. In *syncopation,* the musician either strikes a note (or chord) where you don't expect to hear it or fails to strike where you do expect to hear it.

You probably expect to strike notes on the beats (1, 2, 3, 4). In the example in Figure 1-8, however, you strike no chord on beat 3. That variation in the strumming pattern makes the chord on beat 2½ feel as if it's *accentuated* (or *accented*). This accentuation interrupts the normal (expected) pulse of the music, resulting in syncopation. *Syncopation* breaks up the regular pattern of beats and presents an element of surprise in music. The balance between expectation and surprise is what holds a listener's interest.

To play a song that uses C-family chords right now, skip to the song "Michael, Row the Boat Ashore," in the section "Playing Songs with Basic Major and Minor Chords," later in this chapter. Bon voyage!

Playing Songs with Basic Major and Minor Chords

This section is where the *real music* happens — you know, *songs*. If the titles here hark back to bygone campfire days of your youth, fear not. These songs, although seemingly simple, illustrate universal principles that carry over into the — shall we say it? — *hipper* musical genres. Pick up these songs, and you'll be playing the music of your choice in no time.

Book II

Sounds and Techniques

You may notice that all the strumming examples that we provide in this chapter are only four measures long. Must all of your exercises be limited this way? No, but songwriters do commonly write in four-measure phrases. So the length of these exercises prepares you for actual passages in real songs. You may also notice that each strumming example is in 4/4 time, which means that each measure has four beats. Most popular songs contain four beats per measure, so the 4/4 time signature in the exercises also prepares you to play actual songs. (See Chapter 4 in Book I for more on time signatures.)

In this section of actual songs, you sometimes play a single chord for more than a measure, and sometimes you change chords within a single measure. Listen to the CD to hear the rhythm of the chord changes as you follow the beat numbers (1, 2, 3, 4) that appear below the guitar staff.

After you can comfortably play your way through these songs, try to memorize them. That way, you don't need to stare into a book as you're trying to develop your rhythm.

If you get bored with these songs — or with the way *you* play these songs — have a guitar-playing friend play the same songs by using the strumming patterns and chord positions indicated. Listening to someone else play helps you hear the songs objectively, and if your friend has a little flair, you may pick up a cool little trick or two. Work on infusing a bit of *personality* into all of your playing, even if you're just strumming a simple folk song.

Here's some special information to help you play the songs in this section:

- ✔ **Kumbaya:** To play "Kumbaya" (the ultimate campfire song), you need to know how to play A, D, and E chords; how to strum using downstrokes; and how to start a fire by using only two sticks, a magnifying glass, and some dried leaves.

The first measure in this song is known as a *pickup* measure, which starts the song with one or more beats missing — in this case, the first two. During the pickup measure, the guitar part shows a *rest,* or a musical silence. Don't play during the rest; begin playing on the syllable "ya" on beat 1. Notice, too, that the last bar is missing two beats — beats 3 and 4. The missing beats in the last measure enable you to repeat the pickup measure in repeated playings of the song, and to make that measure, combined with the first incomplete one, total the requisite four beats.

✔ **Swing Low, Sweet Chariot:** To play "Swing Low, Sweet Chariot" you need to know how to play D, Em, G, and A chords; how to play down and down-up strums; and how to sing like James Earl Jones.

This song starts with a one-beat pickup, and the guitar rests for that beat. Notice that beat 2 of measures 2, 4, and 6 has two strums instead of one. Strum those beats down and then up (⊓ and ∨) with each strum twice as fast as a regular strum.

✔ **Auld Lang Syne:** To play "Auld Lang Syne" you need to know how to play G, Am, C, D, and Em chords; how to play down and down-up strums; and maybe what "Auld Lang Syne" means.

Measure 8 is a little tricky, because you play three different chords in the same measure (Em, Am, and D). In the second half of the measure, you change chords on each beat — one stroke per chord. Practice playing only measure 8 slowly, over and over. Then play the song. *Note:* In changing between G and C (bars 4–6 and 12–19), fingering G with fingers 2, 3, and 4 instead of 1, 2, and 3 makes the chord switch easier — the second and third fingers form a shape that simply moves one string.

✔ **Michael, Row the Boat Ashore:** To play "Michael, Row the Boat Ashore" you need to know how to play C, Dm, Em, F, and G chords and how to play a syncopated eighth-note strum.

The strumming pattern here is *syncopated.* The strum that normally occurs on beat 3 is *anticipated* — it comes half a beat early. This kind of syncopation gives the song a Latin feel. Listen to the CD to hear the strumming rhythm. Remember, on the Dm and F chords, you don't strum the lowest two strings (the 6th and 5th). For the C chord, don't strum the bottom string (the 6th).

Kumbaya

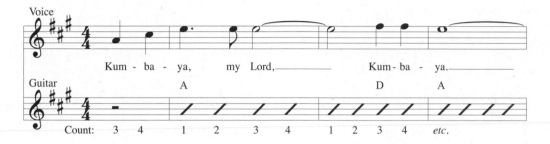

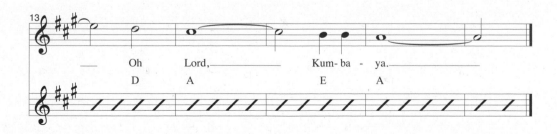

Track 4

Swing Low, Sweet Chariot

Track 5

Auld Lang Syne

Voice: Should auld ac-quaint-ance be for-got and nev-er brought to mind? Should

Guitar: G D G C
Count: 4 1 2 3 4 etc.

auld ac-quaint-ance be for-got and days of auld lang syne? For

G D Em Am D G

auld lang syne, my dear, for auld lang syne, we'll

D G C

take a cup of kind-ness yet for auld lang syne.

G D Em Am D G

Book II

Sounds and Techniques

Track 6

Michael, Row the Boat Ashore

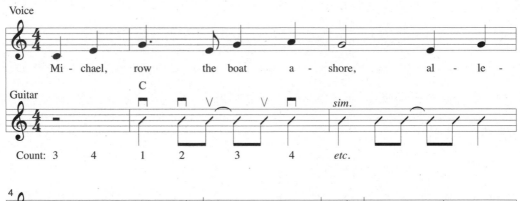

Strumming the "Oldies" Progression

One cool thing you can do right now is play *oldies* — songs from the late '50s and early '60s such as "Earth Angel" and "Duke of Earl." These songs are based on what's sometimes called the *oldies progression,* a series of four chords repeated over and over.

You can play the oldies progression in any key, but the best guitar keys for the oldies progression are C and G. In the key of C, the four chords that make up the progression are C-Am-F-G. In G, the chords are G-Em-C-D. Try strumming the progression in each key by playing four down-strums per chord. Play the four chords over and over, in the sequence given.

Book II

Sounds and Techniques

The fun begins as you sing oldies while accompanying yourself with the oldies progression. You'll find that one of the keys (C or G) better suits your vocal range, so use that key. Playing oldies can become addicting, but the good news is that you build up your calluses very quickly.

For some songs, you play four one-beat strums per chord; for others, you play eight, or two. Following are songs you can play with the oldies progression right now. How many times you strum each chord is noted next to each song title. Don't forget to sing. Have fun!

- **All I Have to Do Is Dream:** Two strums per chord.
- **Blue Moon:** Two strums per chord.
- **Breaking Up Is Hard to Do:** Two strums per chord.
- **Come Go with Me:** Two strums per chord.
- **Duke of Earl:** Four strums per chord.
- **Earth Angel:** Two strums per chord.
- **Heart and Soul:** Two strums per chord.
- **Hey Paula:** Two strums per chord.
- **In the Still of the Night:** (By the Five Satins) Four strums per chord.
- **Little Darlin':** Eight strums per chord.
- **Poor Little Fool:** Four strums per chord.
- **Runaround Sue:** Eight strums per chord.
- **Sherry:** Two strums per chord.
- **Silhouettes:** Two strums per chord.
- **Stay:** Two strums per chord.

- **Take Good Care of My Baby:** Four strums per chord.
- **Tears on My Pillow:** Two strums per chord.
- **Teenager in Love:** Four strums per chord.
- **What's Your Name:** Two strums per chord.
- **Why Do Fools Fall in Love?:** Two strums per chord.
- **You Send Me:** Two strums per chord.

Chapter 2

Adding Spice: Basic 7th Chords

*I*n this chapter, you begin to play what are known as *open-position 7th chords.* Seventh chords are no more difficult to play than the simple major or minor chords described in Chapter 1 in Book II, but their *sound* is more complex than that of major and minor chords (because they're made up of four different notes instead of three), and their usage in music is a little more specialized.

The situation's kind of like that of the knives in your kitchen. Any big, sharp knife can cut both a pizza and a pineapple, but if you spend a lot of time doing either, you figure out that you need to use the circular-bladed gizmo for the pizza and a cleaver for the pineapple. These utensils may not be as versatile or as popular as your general-purpose knives, but if you're making Hawaiian-style pizza, nothing beats 'em. The more your culinary skills develop, the more you appreciate specialized cutlery. And the more your ear skills develop, the more you understand where to substitute 7th chords for the more ordinary major and minor chords. The different 7th chords can make the blues sound "bluesy" and jazz sound "jazzy."

Seventh chords come in several varieties, and each type has a different sound, or quality. In this chapter, you meet the three most important types of 7th chords that you encounter in playing the guitar: dominant 7th, minor 7th, and major 7th.

Dominant 7th Chords

Dominant seems a funny, technical name for a chord that's called a plain "seven" if you group it with a letter-name chord symbol. If you talk about a C7 or A7 chord, for example, you're referring to a dominant 7th chord.

Actually, the term *dominant* refers to the 5th degree of a major scale — but don't worry about the theory.

The important thing is that you call the chords "dominant sevenths" merely to distinguish them from other types of 7th chords (minor 7ths and major 7ths). Note, too, that dominant has nothing whatsoever to do with leather and studded collars. You can hear the sound of dominant 7ths in such songs as Sam the Sham and the Pharaohs' "Wooly Bully" and the Beatles' "I Saw Her Standing There."

D7, G7, and C7

The D7, G7, and C7 chords are among the most common of the open dominant 7ths. Figure 2-1 shows you diagrams of these three chords that guitarists often use together to play songs.

If you already know how to play C (which is introduced in Chapter 1 in Book II), you can form C7 by simply adding your pinky on the 3rd string (at the 3rd fret).

Notice the Xs above the 5th and 6th strings on the D7 chord. Don't play those strings as you strum. Similarly, for the C7 chord, don't play the 6th string as you strum.

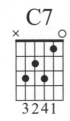

Figure 2-1: Chord diagrams for D7, G7, and C7.

Practice strumming D7, G7, and C7. You don't need written music for this exercise, so you're on the honor system to do it. Try strumming D7 four times, G7 four times, and then C7 four times. You want to accustom your left hand to the feel of the chords themselves and to switching among them.

If you want to play a song right now using these new chords, skip to the section "Playing Songs with 7th Chords," later in this chapter. You can play "Home on the Range" with the chords you know right now.

E7 and A7

Two more 7th chords that you often use together to play songs are the E7 and A7 chords. Figure 2-2 shows how you play these two open 7th chords.

If you know how to play E (check out Chapter 1 in Book II), you can form E7 by simply removing your third finger from the 4th string.

Figure 2-2: Chord diagrams for E7 and A7.

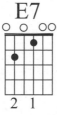   

This version of the E7 chord, as Figure 2-2 shows, uses only two fingers. You can also play an open position E7 chord with four fingers (as we describe in the following section). For now, however, play the two-finger version because it's easier to fret quickly, especially if you're just starting out.

Practice E7 and A7 by strumming each chord four times, switching back and forth between them. Remember to avoid striking the 6th string on the A7 chord.

If you want to play a song that uses these two open 7th chords right now, skip to the section "Playing Songs with 7th Chords," later in this chapter, and play "All Through the Night."

E7 (four-finger version) and B7

Two more popular open-position 7th chords are the four-finger version of E7 and the B7 chord. Figure 2-3 shows you how to finger the four-finger E7 and the B7 chords. Most people think that this E7 has a better *voicing* (vertical arrangement of notes) than does the two-finger E7. You often use the B7 chord along with E7 to play certain songs. Remember to avoid striking the 6th string on the B7 chord.

If you already know how to play E, you can form this E7 by simply adding your pinky on the 2nd string (at the 3rd fret).

Figure 2-3:
Chord diagrams for E7 (the four-finger version) and B7.

  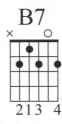 

Practice these chords by strumming each one four times, switching back and forth. As you do so, notice that your second finger plays the same note at the same fret in each chord — the one at the 2nd fret of the 5th string. This note is a *common tone* (that is, it's common to both chords). In switching back and forth between the two chords, keeping this finger down on the 5th string makes switching easier. ***Note:*** Always hold down common tones whenever you're switching chords. They provide an anchor of stability for your left hand.

To use these chords in a song right now, skip to the section "Playing Songs with 7th Chords," later in this chapter, and play "Over the River and Through the Woods."

Minor 7th Chords: Dm7, Em7, and Am7

Minor 7th chords differ from dominant 7th chords in that their character is a little softer and jazzier. Minor 7th chords are what you hear in "Moondance" by Van Morrison and the verses of "Light My Fire" by the Doors. Figure 2-4 shows diagrams for the three open-position minor 7th (m7) chords.

Notice that the Dm7 uses a two-string *barre* — that is, you press down two strings with a single finger (the first finger, in this case) at the 1st fret. Angling your finger slightly or rotating it on its side may help you fret those notes firmly and eliminate any buzzes as you play the chord. The 6th and 5th strings have Xs above them. Don't strike those strings while strumming.

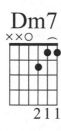

Dm7
×× O
2 1 1

Figure 2-4:
Chord
diagrams for
Dm7, Em7,
and Am7.

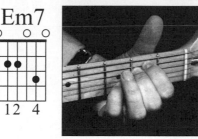

Em7
O   O O
1 2   4

Am7
× O   O   O
2 1

You finger the Am7 chord much as you do the C chord that's explained in Chapter 1 in Book II; just lift your third finger off a C chord — and you have Am7. In switching between C and Am7 chords, remember to hold down the two common tones with your first and second fingers to switch between the chords much more quickly. And if you know how to play an F chord (see Chapter 1 in Book II), you can form Dm7 simply by removing your third finger.

Major 7th Chords: Cmaj7, Fmaj7, Amaj7, and Dmaj7

Major 7th chords differ from dominant 7th chords and minor 7th chords in that their character is bright and jazzy. You can hear this kind of chord at the beginning of "Ventura Highway" by America and "Don't Let the Sun Catch You Crying" by Gerry and the Pacemakers. Figure 2-5 shows four open-position major 7th (maj7) chords. (For more major 7th chords, check out Appendix A.)

Notice that Dmaj7 uses a three-string barre with the first finger. Rotating the first finger slightly on its side makes it easier to play. Don't play the 5th or 6th strings as you strike the Dmaj7 or Fmaj7 (see the Xs in the diagrams in Figure 2-5). And don't play the 6th string on the Amaj7 or Cmaj7.

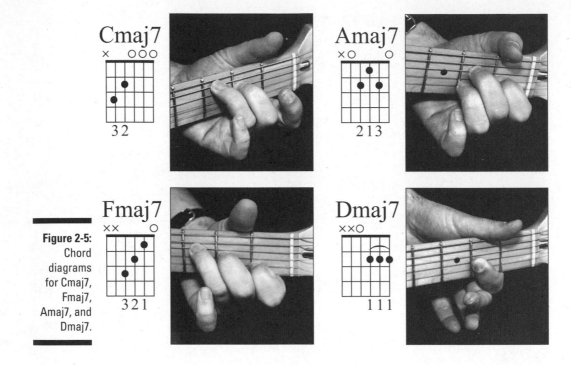

Figure 2-5:
Chord
diagrams
for Cmaj7,
Fmaj7,
Amaj7, and
Dmaj7.

In moving between Cmaj7 and Fmaj7, notice that the second and third fingers move as a fixed shape across the strings in switching between these chords. The first finger doesn't fret any string in a Cmaj7 chord, but keep it curled and poised above the 1st fret of the 2nd string so you can bring it down quickly for the switch to Fmaj7.

Practice moving back and forth (strumming four times each) between Cmaj7 and Fmaj7 and between Amaj7 and Dmaj7.

Playing Songs with 7th Chords

Listen to the CD to hear the rhythm of the strums of the songs in this section as you follow the slash notation in the guitar part. If you have difficulty remembering how to finger the chords, refer to the earlier sections in this chapter, check out the Cheat Sheet in the front of the book, or consult Appendix A. Don't try to play the vocal line. It's there only as a reference.

Here is some useful information about the songs to help you along:

  ✔ **Home on the Range:** To play "Home on the Range," you need to know how to play C, C7, F, D7, and G7 chords; how to play a "bass strum strum" pattern; and how to wail like a coyote.

In the music, you see the words *Bass strum strum* over the rhythm slashes. Instead of simply strumming the chord for three beats, play only the lowest note of the chord on the first beat and then strum the remaining notes of the chord on beats 2 and 3. The *sim.* means to keep playing this pattern throughout.

✔ **All Through the Night:** To play "All Through the Night," you need to know how to play D, G, E7, and A7 chords; how to read repeat signs; and how to stay awake during this intensely somnolent ditty. Use the two-finger E7 for this song.

In the music, you see *repeat signs* (two dots that look like a colon) that tell you to play certain measures twice. In this case, you play measures 1, 2, 3, 4, and then measures 1, 2, 3, 5.

✔ **Over the River and Through the Woods:** To play "Over the River and Through the Woods," you need to know how to play A, D, E7, and B7 chords; how to strum in 6/8 time; and the way to Grandma's house (in case your horse stumbles and you need to shoot it). Use the four-finger E7 for this song.

The 6/8 time signature has a lilting feel to it — sort of as though the music has a gallop or limp. "When Johnny Comes Marching Home Again" is another familiar song played in 6/8 time. Count only two beats per measure — not six (unless you want to sound like a rabbit that's had three cups of coffee).

✔ **It's Raining, It's Pouring:** To play "It's Raining, It's Pouring," you need to know how to play Amaj7 and Dmaj7 chords and how to sing in a really whiny, annoying voice. Use all downstrokes on the strums.

This song is a jazzed-up version of the old nursery rhyme "It's Raining, It's Pouring," also known as the childhood taunt "Billy Is a Sissy" (or whichever personal childhood nemesis you plug in to the title). The major 7th chords you play in this song sound jazzy and give any song a modern sound.

✔ **Oh, Susanna:** To play "Oh, Susanna," you need to know how to play Cmaj7, Dm7, Em7, Fmaj7, Am7, D7, Dm7, G7, and C chords and how to balance a banjo on your knee while traveling the Southern United States. Use all downstrokes on the strums.

This arrangement of "Oh, Susanna" uses three types of 7th chords: dominant 7ths (D7 and G7), minor 7ths (Dm7, Em7, and Am7), and major 7ths (Cmaj7 and Fmaj7). Using minor 7ths and major 7ths gives the song a hip sound. Lest you think this attempt to "jazz up" a simple folk song comes from out of the blue, listen to James Taylor's beautiful rendition of "Oh, Susanna" on the 1970 album *Sweet Baby James*. He actually says "banjo" without sounding corny.

Book II

Sounds and Techniques

Home on the Range

All Through the Night

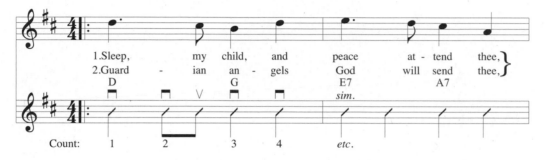

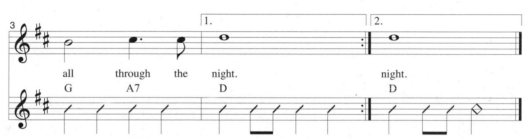

Track 9

Over the River and Through the Woods

Track 10

It's Raining, It's Pouring

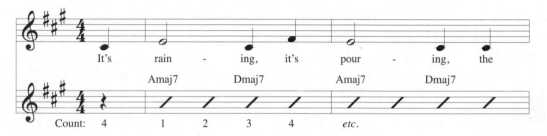

It's   rain - ing,   it's   pour - ing,   the

Amaj7   Dmaj7   Amaj7   Dmaj7

Count: 4   1   2   3   4   *etc.*

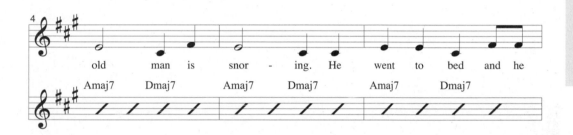

old   man   is   snor - ing.   He   went   to   bed   and   he

Amaj7   Dmaj7   Amaj7   Dmaj7   Amaj7   Dmaj7

bumped   his   head   and   he   could - n't   get   up   in   the   morn - ing.

Amaj7   Dmaj7   Amaj7   Dmaj7   Amaj7   Dmaj7

Track 11

Oh, Susanna

I____ come from Al - a - bam - a with a

Cmaj7   Dm7   Em7   Fmaj7

Count: 1   2   1   2

ban - jo on my knee.   I'm____ goin' to Lou' - si -

Am7   D7   Dm7   G7   Cmaj7   Dm7

etc.

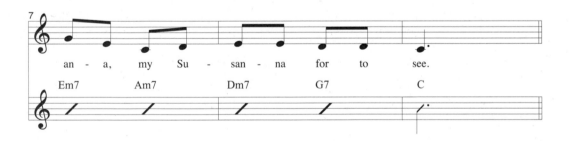

an - a, my Su - san - na for to see.

Em7   Am7   Dm7   G7   C

Chapter 3

The Left Hand: Chord Techniques

Chords are built in the left hand and realized as sound by strums from the right hand. In Chapters 1 and 2 in Book II, you start to work with chords to enable your left hand to turn the strings into a meaningful arrangement, so when you strum them it makes at least enough sense for you to check your tuning. But you don't create music on the guitar by strumming something once and letting it sit there ringing indefinitely. Music has to move. The two ways to do that are to strum cool rhythms and to play awesome-sounding chords.

For now, don't worry about what your right hand is supposed to do. You can execute the figures and rhythm charts in this chapter by playing one strum (that is, one downward stroke across the strings) per slash. Things get fancier in Chapter 4 in Book II, but playing one strum per slash allows you to concentrate on your left-hand chord work.

Of course you don't *have* to play the music here using only the one-stroke-per-beat approach. If the spirit moves you — and the musical feel allows — try throwing in some in-between, up-and-down strums to get your music moving a bit. Just don't let any right-hand fanciness get in the way of the business of switching chords.

Fingering or "grabbing" chords is the hardest thing beginning guitarists encounter — much harder than anything the right hand has to do. In this chapter, then, you tackle some chords and then focus on ways to get them memorized and under your fingers quickly. This chapter makes it easy on you, too, by including chord changes that require little more than sliding one chord form around on the neck. (Rock guitar styles are used to illustrate, but keep in mind that many of this chapter's techniques are applicable to other styles besides rock.)

Playing Open-Position Chords

Open-position chords, so named because they involve unfretted strings, are allowed to ring open, along with the fretted notes. Open-position chords have a "jangly," pleasing quality and are sometimes called "cowboy chords" — probably because you can play simple, plaintive, spur-janglin', chip-kickin' songs with them.

Figure 3-1 is a chart of 24 chords that comprise just about all the useful open chords you use to play guitar. If you've never tried your hand (pun intended!) at open-position chords, refer to Chapters 1 and 2 in Book II for in-depth lessons on how to form and play these fundamental chords.

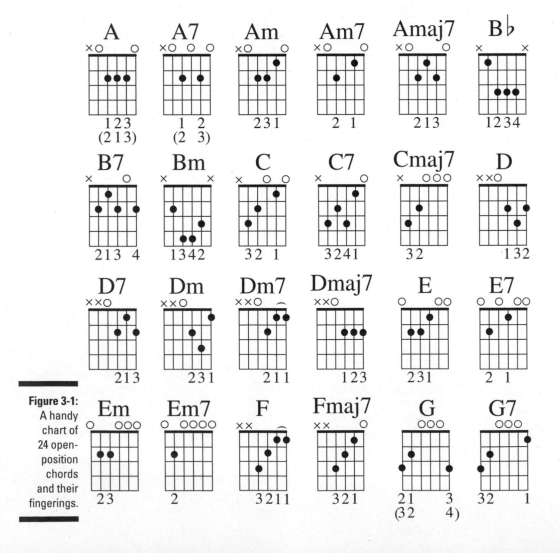

Figure 3-1: A handy chart of 24 open-position chords and their fingerings.

An X over a string means it's *not* played or sounded; an O indicates an open string that *is* sounded when strumming. (Chapter 2 in Book I introduces chord diagrams.) There's more than one way to form some chords. Note that alternate fingerings appear below the primary ones.

Putting Power Chords into Play

Now it's time to put the cowpokes out to pasture. Some guitar players, notably rock guitarists, tend to favor power chords. *Power chords* are even easier to finger than open-position chords, and they provide a simple means for moving beyond those first three frets. They represent rock guitar playing in all its raw and rugged glory, and after you understand how to use the 6th and 5th strings to name them, placing them on the neck is as easy as A-B-C♯.

A *power chord* is a two- or three-note chord that contains only the root and 5th degree of the chord. A two-note power chord contains the root on the bottom and the 5th degree on top. A three-note power chord is built from the bottom up as root, 5th, root, so it has a root at the bottom, the 5th on top of that, and then the root again, one octave higher than the chord's lowest note. (See Chapter 4 in Book I and Chapter 3 in Book VII for more about 5ths and other musical degrees and notes.) An A power chord, then, can be played either one of the two ways shown in Figure 3-2.

Book II

Sounds and Techniques

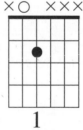 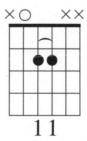

Figure 3-2: Two ways to play an A power chord.

Missing from power chords is the all-important 3rd degree. In the traditional sense, a chord is defined as three or more different notes, so a power "chord" is something of an exception. The 3rd of a chord is what determines whether the chord is major or minor. As you may have noticed from playing an open-position A chord, the *flat 3rd* (one-and-a-half steps up from the root) makes the chord minor, and the *major 3rd* (two whole steps, or four half steps, up from the root) makes the chord major. In either chord, though, the root and the 5th don't change. So take away the 3rd and you have a chord that is actually neither major nor minor: It can function as either without being "wrong." This ambiguity is precisely what makes power chords so versatile.

Power chords have another desirable quality, other than their stark construction and open sound: They sound great when played with distortion. This is because distortion imbues tones with *harmonics,* or different high-pitched notes in varying degrees of intensity, that make a sound much more harmonically rich than a nondistorted sound. Heavy distortion doesn't sound as good on full major or minor chords, because the harmonics of those closely spaced intervals (the root, 3rd, and 5th) clash in the upper registers, making the sound brittle and strident. But with just the root and 5th, the upper harmonics get close enough to dance together beautifully without stepping on each other's toes. (Book III talks more about distortion and harmonics.)

Moving power chords

Unlike their open-position brethren, most power chords don't incorporate open strings and are therefore *moveable chords.* Any chord that you can move from one position on the neck to another without rearranging your fingers is a moveable chord. Because they're moveable, not to mention minimal, you can switch from any power chord to another without twisting your fingers up like so much linguini. If you can count to 12 and recite the alphabet up to the letter G, you can find every power chord. Welcome to Easy Street.

Power chords take their name from the root note, as all chords do. In a G power chord, G is of course the root. Because power chords incorporate only the root and the 5th, they are often referred to as "5" chords. When you see a chord written "G5," it's a G power chord.

The power chord shown in Figure 3-3 has its root on the 6th string. Because the note on the 6th string at the 5th fret is A, it's an A power chord (A5). Move the whole chord up a step (two frets) and it becomes B5. Likewise, move it down a step and it's G5. Move it down one more step and it becomes — any guesses? — F5.

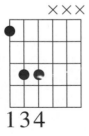

Figure 3-3:
A 6th-string-based power chord at the 5th fret, A5.

The 5th-string-based power chord looks almost exactly the same except it's shifted over a set of strings. Figure 3-4 is a 5th-string-based power chord played at the 1st fret.

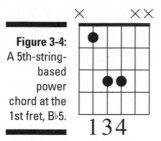

Figure 3-4:
A 5th-string-based power chord at the 1st fret, B♭5.

Book II

Sounds and Techniques

Like the 6th-string-based power chords, you can move around 5th-string-based chords with ease. Move the B♭5 up a whole step (two frets) to get C5, up another step to D5, and so on.

Pulling the power together

Position is the term used to describe where a chord is placed on the neck. A chord's position is named for the fret where you plant your first finger. It doesn't matter which string you're on, just which fret. The 5th-string-based B♭5 from the previous section is in *first position*. The first power chord you played — the 6th-string-based A5 at the 5th fret — is in 5th position.

Before you jump onstage with Aerosmith, try mixing up 6th- and 5th-string-based power chords. Because power chords have so few notes and always assume the same shape, it's a breeze to move them around the neck. Figure 3-5 is a typical power-chord progression.

Figure 3-5:
Mixing 6th- and 5th-string-based power chords in a single progression.

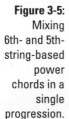

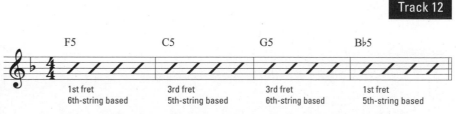

Track 12

F5	C5	G5	B♭5
1st fret	3rd fret	3rd fret	1st fret
6th-string based	5th-string based	6th-string based	5th-string based

You don't have to keep up with the performance you hear on the CD track when trying to finger and strum these chords. Just try switching the chords *in time* — that is, after every four beats.

Much like you need the individual words to form the sentences that describe thoughts and ideas, so too must you have individual chords that can be later arranged into longer musical segments, called *chord progressions.* Chord progressions form the structure, or harmonic framework, for songs.

Getting Behind the Barre

So now you're slinging power chords all over the neck, and you're thinking that all you need to be a rock god is a pair of leather pants and some friends who don't smell so good. Well, pull your Lear jet back into the hangar for a minute. Although countless songs have been written using only the chord forms covered earlier in this chapter — open-position and power chords — your musical vocabulary is about to expand a thousandfold. It's time to saddle up to barre chords.

The term *barre chord* strikes fear into the hearts of beginning guitarists everywhere. Technically, a barre chord is just a chord where your left hand's first (index) finger lies flat across the strings, forming a "bar," with the rest of the chord made up by other fingers. Nevertheless, the term usually carries with it connotations of medieval torture practices.

Beginners have trouble with barre chords because they seem to require an inordinate amount of strength. Although strength is certainly involved, you don't need quite so much of it after you become good at playing barre chords. Playing barre chords is like riding a bicycle: It's really tough at first, but then it becomes second nature.

The Barre Chord Creed

Memorize the Barre Chord Creed for the most important aspects to learning and mastering barre chords. Here are the tips to keep in mind:

- **Press firmly.** You don't need to embed the strings permanently into your flesh, but do apply strong, even pressure with your first finger. Rotate the finger slightly onto its side — the side away from the second finger.

- **Thumb it.** Keep your thumb placed directly in the center of the neck's back. This is where the strength comes from. You'll know you're doing it right when the heel of your hand gets sore. Isn't this the greatest?

- **Keep your arms in.** Try not to let your elbow stick out at your side like a chicken wing. Pull your elbow into your side if you can, and keep your left shoulder relaxed and down.

✔ **Be fat-free.** Make tiny adjustments so the fleshy parts of your fingers aren't touching adjacent strings, causing them to buzz or muffle. Keep your knuckles rounded and try to press straight down on the strings, instead of from the side. Also make sure that a string isn't running directly under the crease in the knuckle between your first and second finger joints.

Barre is the Spanish word for *bar,* and guitarists use this spelling because a lot of guitar notation uses Spanish terms (the same way other terms in music, such as *piano* for "soft," *fortissimo* for "very loud," and *scuza plisa tu pasa di pasta* for "the band is hungry" are in Italian), and because *barre* distinguishes itself from *bar,* the metal arm on the bridge of some guitars.

Book II

Sounds and Techniques

Playing E-based barre chords

Barre chords are formed as open-position-based chords with an added barre (your first finger) placed over the top. The first step is to finger an open-position E form (see Chapter 1 in Book II for a detailed explanation if you're a bit rusty). But instead of using your first three fingers, fret the chord with your second, third, and fourth fingers. This leaves your first finger free to barre.

Right now, the nut — that slotted bar between the headstock and the fret-board — is acting like a barre. You're going to move the whole chord up and take over the nut's job with your first finger.

1. **Slide all the fretted notes up (away from the headstock) exactly one fret.**

2. **Lay your index finger down in the first fret, across all six strings, parallel to the nut.**

3. **Minding the Barre Chord Creed, apply pressure and strum away.**

Congratulations. You're now playing an F barre chord (see Figure 3-6). And, in a manner of speaking, you are now the nut.

Figure 3-6: The F barre chord.

Unless you're the type weakened only by kryptonite, you'll have trouble getting the F chord to sound good and feel comfortable. In the beginning, playing an F chord strains your hand, muffles the strings, and causes you to holler at various inanimate objects. This is normal.

Barre chords are harder to play in the first few frets, where the nut offers resistance, and they're also harder way up the neck, where the action is higher and the frets are narrower. When you can form the F chord immediately, without agonizing through the steps shown above, try moving your F chord to the 5th fret (where, by the way, it becomes an A chord). It should be easier to press the strings down here than at the 1st fret.

Moving the E-form barre chord around the neck

All barre chords are moveable chords — that's the beauty of 'em. Now that you've formed a barre chord (and can play it so the strings, when strummed, ring through clearly), you're ready to move this sucker.

You've already had a glimpse of the thinking involved because you've moved power chords around the neck. (And some brave souls followed the advice in the last section to move the F chord up to the 5th fret.) Apply what you know about moving power chords to barre chords. The only difference is that you're moving *more* notes per chord.

To identify which chords you're playing on the neck as you move around, take the 6th-string shortcut. Because the lowest string of the guitar is called E, you can use the name of the notes on the 6th string to tell you where to play a given E-based form, just as you did with power chords. For example, the 5th fret of the E string is A, so the chord formed at the 5th fret using an E form is A. This shortcut enables guitarists to place chords on the fretboard by using the lowest note of the chord as the guide. (An "E-form" barre chord can also be called a 6th-string-based chord.)

Other E forms: Minor, dominant 7, minor 7, and 7sus

So far, you've built and moved only the E major barre shape. As you know from open-position chords, there are chordal varieties other than major. Chords that are given simple letter names (E, B♭, D) are majors — all others are qualified (E minor, B♭ minor7, D7sus).

Here's where your hard labor on that first barre pays off. Having successfully wrangled the E major barre-chord form, you can easily start adding other chord qualities. All of these forms can be played with small, easy changes to the E major barre. And all of them correspond directly with open-position E chords you already know. You are about to be so very happy.

To make things even easier for yourself, try these new forms at the 3rd fret, where it starts getting more reasonable to finger chords *sans* buzz and rattle.

Using the 6th-string shortcut described in the preceding section, you know that an E barre form played at the 3rd fret is a G chord. So if you play these forms in 3rd position, they'll all be G chords of one type or another. But pay attention to the shapes, which you'll move around, rather than the chords' letter names.

To change a G major into a G minor, lift your second (middle) finger. Let the newly exposed note — 3rd string, 3rd fret — ring out with the rest of the barred notes. Yeah, that's all there is to it! Figure 3-7 shows a 3rd-position G minor barre chord.

Book II

Sounds and Techniques

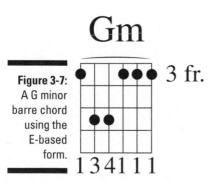

Figure 3-7:
A G minor barre chord using the E-based form.

Gm

3 fr.

1 3 4 1 1 1

To change a G major into a G7 (also known as G dominant 7; see Chapter 2 in Book II), lift the fourth finger, as shown in Figure 3-8.

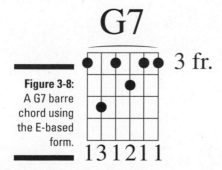

Figure 3-8:
A G7 barre chord using the E-based form.

G7

3 fr.

1 3 1 2 1 1

To change a G major into a Gm7 (G minor 7; see Chapter 2 in Book II), lift the second and fourth fingers, as shown in Figure 3-9.

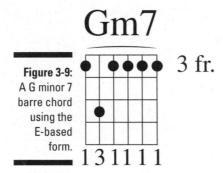

Figure 3-9:
A G minor 7 barre chord using the E-based form.

To change a G major into a G7sus (where the 3rd degree is *suspended,* or raised a half step, to the 4th degree), lift the second finger and move the fourth finger over to the 3rd string as shown in Figure 3-10.

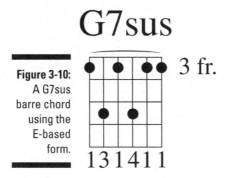

Figure 3-10:
A G7sus barre chord using the E-based form.

You've just learned four new chord forms — which, because they're applicable anywhere from 1st to 12th position, give you 48 new chords. Holy harmony. Go write a song already.

Create your own exercise by moving these forms all over the neck. Then switch between forms as you move them around: Play a major chord in 1st position, a minor in 3rd, and a dominant 7 in 8th. You may just stumble onto the next "Freebird." We could use a new "Freebird."

Playing A-based barre chords

Just as the family of E-based barres have open-position E forms (they are simply open-position shapes with a barre in front of them), A-based barres have open-position A forms. To form these chords, apply the same logic used to get from an open-position E major chord to a 1st position F major barre. No need to reinvent the wheel — save your creativity for your playing or your excuses for practicing at 2 a.m.

To create an A-based barre chord (see Figure 3-11), grab a plain ol' open A major (check Chapter 1 in Book II if you need a refresher), but use fingers 2, 3, and 4, instead of 1, 2, and 3, and then follow these steps:

Book II

Sounds and Techniques

1. **Slide all the fretted notes up exactly one fret.**

2. **Lay your index finger down in the 1st fret, across the top five strings, parallel to the nut.**

3. **Minding the Barre Chord Creed, apply pressure and strum away.**

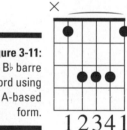

Figure 3-11:
A B♭ barre chord using the A-based form.

For A-based barre chords, the barre is shorter: Your first finger needs to span only the top five strings.

You don't have to barre all six strings for the A-based barre because its root is on the 5th string: It's a 5th-string-based form. If your index finger does lie across the 6th string (which can be hard to avoid), be careful not to strum the 6th string with your right hand. You may want to let your index finger lay limply on that bottom string, which will help mute the sound if you strum it accidentally. Be careful, because the results can be horrific when you start moving the A-based barre chord around the neck. An open low E string against a 6th-fret E♭ major chord? Ick.

TIP

The hard part about this chord is pulling up the third-finger knuckle so the barred 1st string can sound. Because most guitarists find that to be too much trouble, they just end up playing the inner four strings (2 through 5) on the A major form. When they do this, they no longer have to make a barre out of the first finger — just the third finger — which makes this a pretty easy chord to play. Try Figure 3-12, compare it with your success on the previous fingering, and choose which form works best for you.

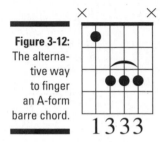

Figure 3-12:
The alternative way to finger an A-form barre chord.

Astute players who aren't yet blinded by pain may have spotted something familiar in the bottom strings of the A and E barre forms: power chords. All three lower strings of the A major and E major barres contain the same notes as their power chord counterparts. Also, you may recall that power chords don't carry a chord's 3rd degree; in keeping, the bottom three strings of the A minor and E minor barre shapes are identical not only to their power chord counterparts but to their major brethren. Wow. Full circle, dude.

Moving the A-form barre chord

Because you can play a B♭ chord as a barre chord, you can now play all 12 A-based major barre chords (the entire chromatic scale). All A-based chords are moveable and get their name from the 5th string (just as the open A chord does, and similar to how the E-chord form derives its name).

Figure 3-13 uses all A-based major barre chords. Say the names of the chords aloud as you play them at their corresponding frets. Listen to and play along with the CD to check your work. Don't worry about matching the strumming pattern you hear on the CD; just strum along at your own pace and switch between chords after every bar.

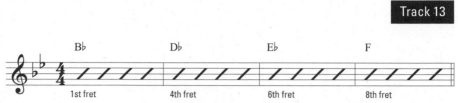

Figure 3-13:
A progres-
sion using
A-based
major barre
chords.

Track 13

Bb   Db   Eb   F

1st fret   4th fret   6th fret   8th fret

A forms: Minor, dominant 7th, minor 7, 7sus, and major 7

Everything you already know about moving chords around the neck carries over to other barre-chord forms. Playing the minor, the 7th, or the minor 7 versions is no more physically demanding than playing the major barre forms; it's just a matter of learning the fingering.

You can follow the numbered list in the section "Playing A-based barre chords" for creating the other versions of these A-based forms, or you can just try to form them after placing your first-finger barre over the appropriate fret and forming the chords from your remaining three fingers.

Figure 3-14 is a chart of five chord forms in A. The possible chord forms extend beyond these five, but these are key for playing most rock music.

You can find barre forms that directly correspond with open-position chords. For example, the 5th-string-based D minor played in 5th position has all the same notes (though some in different octaves) as the open-position D minor.

The number of chords you now can play up and down the neck is just plain incalculable. You are a veritable font of chord knowledge. Dip into the fountain and enjoy this progression, which alternates between E- (6th-string) and A-based (5th-string) forms as the chords descend the neck. The changes in Figure 3-15 fit Bob Dylan's "Lay Lady Lay."

Book II

Sounds and Techniques

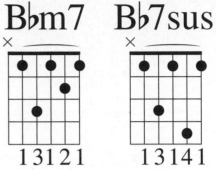

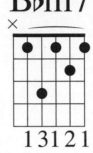

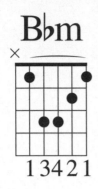

Bbm   Bb7   Bbm7   Bb7sus

1 3 4 2 1   1 3 1 4 1   1 3 1 2 1   1 3 1 4 1

Figure 3-14: The A-form versions of minor, 7, m7, 7sus, and major 7 barre chords.

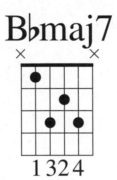

Bbmaj7

1 3 2 4

Figure 3-15: A progression with alternating E- and A-based forms.

Track 14

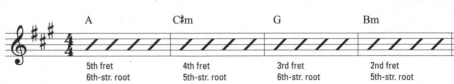

A   C#m   G   Bm

5th fret   4th fret   3rd fret   2nd fret
6th-str. root   5th-str. root   6th-str. root   5th-str. root

Chapter 4

The Right Hand: Rhythm Techniques

In This Chapter

▶ Strumming with your right hand

▶ Switching up downstrokes and upstrokes

▶ Using your palm to mute and accent

The right hand marshals the chords and notes you form in the left hand into the sounds you actually hear. The right hand of a rhythm guitarist drives the rhythm section, weaving together the bass and drums and providing the underpinning for the singer, lead guitar, or other melodic instruments. Whether it's playing in a steady eighth-note groove, a funky 16 feel, or a hard-swinging shuffle, the rhythm guitar and the right-hand strumming that propels it forge the chords and riffs that you learn into a moving musical experience.

In this chapter you discover many different ways you can strum the guitar to make the rhythm fit different styles and feels. These variations help keep your music vital sounding and help you develop your skills as a rhythm guitarist — one who provides the backing and the foundation to support the melody, and who can act as the glue between the other rhythm instruments, such as the bass and drums.

As in Chapter 3 in Book II, this chapter uses rock as a genre to illustrate guitar techniques. You can apply the skills in this chapter to other genres.

Strumming Along

Strumming is defined as dragging a pick (or your fingers) across the strings of the guitar. In Chapter 3 in Book II, you drag the pick in a downward motion (toward the floor) to sound the chords formed by the left hand, but you don't try to do anything except that. In doing even that, however, you create rhythm.

If you "pick-drag" in regular, even strokes, one per beat, adhering to a *tempo* (musical rate), you're strumming the guitar in rhythm. And that's music, whether you mean it to be or not. More specifically, you're strumming a quarter-note rhythm, which is fine for songs such as the Beatles' "Let It Be" and other ballads. For the record, strumming an E chord in quarter notes looks like the notation in Figure 4-1. Note that the figure uses rhythm slashes to show that you should play the entire chord, as opposed to note *heads* (which indicate only a single pitch).

Figure 4-1:
Playing an
E chord in
one bar of
four quarter
notes.

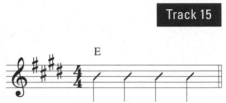

Track 15

The hardest part of learning rhythm guitar is realizing — and then maintaining — all the repetition involved. It's not what people expect when they pick up the guitar and want to learn a smorgasbord of cool licks and great riffs. But being able to play *in time* with unerring precision and rock-steady consistency is an essential skill and a hallmark of solid musicianship. Most rhythm playing in rock involves a one- or two-bar pattern repeated over and over, varying only where there are accent points that the band plays in unison.

After you learn to play consistently, you can then deviate from the established pattern you lay down and work on your own variations, as long as they're tasteful, appropriate, and not too numerous. Like a rock 'n' roll rebel once said, "You have to know the rules before you can break them."

Downstrokes

A *downstroke* (indicated by the symbol ⊓) is the motion of dragging the pick down, brushing across multiple strings on the guitar in the process. Because you execute a downstroke quickly (even on slow songs) the separate strings are sounded virtually simultaneously. If you play three or more notes this way, you produce a chord.

Strumming in eighth-note downstrokes

To get out of the somewhat plodding rhythm of a quarter-note-only strumming pattern, you turn to eighth notes. As the math implies, an eighth note is one half the value of a quarter note, but in musical terms that equates to twice as fast, or more precisely, twice as frequently.

So instead of playing one strum per beat, you now play two strums per beat. This means you must move your hand twice as fast, striking the strings two times per beat, instead of once per beat as you did to produce quarter notes. At moderate and slower tempos, you can do this easily. For faster tempos you use alternating upstrokes and downstrokes (explained later in this chapter). For playing the progression in Figure 4-1, however, simply using repeated downstrokes is easiest.

Figure 4-2 uses eighth notes for the first three beats of each bar and a quarter note for the last beat of each bar. The quarter note allows you a little more time to switch chords between the end of each bar and the beginning of the new bar. Isn't that humane?

Book II

Sounds and Techniques

Track 16

Figure 4-2:
Eighth-note progression using down-strokes.

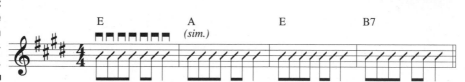

The term *sim.* in the music notation tells you to continue in a similar fashion. It's typically used for articulation directions, such as down- and upstrokes.

Reading eighth-note notation

Notice that instead of the previously used slashes, you now resort to slashes with *stems* (the vertical lines coming down from the note head) and *beams* (the thicker horizontal lines that connect the stems). Quarter notes have single stems attached to them; eighth notes have stems with beams connecting them to each other. An eighth note by itself, or separated by a rest, has a little flag instead of a beam.

Even though this newly introduced notation denotes specific rhythmic values (quarter notes, eighth notes), the note heads are still elongated and angled — not the same kind of smaller, rounded note heads used to indicate individual pitches. The symbols used in this chapter are still rhythm slashes that tell you *how* (in what rhythm) to play, but not exactly *what* (the individual pitches) to play. Your left-hand chord position determines the pitches.

Upstrokes

An upstroke (indicated by the symbol ∨) is just what it sounds like: the opposite of a downstroke. Instead of dragging your pick down toward the floor, you start from a position below the strings and drag your pick upward across the strings. Doing this comfortably may seem a little less natural than playing a downstroke. One reason for this is that you're going against gravity. Also, some beginners have a hard time holding on to their pick or preventing it from getting stuck in the strings. With practice, though, you can flow with the ups as easily as you can with the downs.

You use upstrokes for the upbeats (offbeats) in eighth-note playing, as the strokes in between the quarter-note beats.

When you start playing, don't worry about hitting all the strings in an upstroke. For example, when playing an E chord with an upstroke, you needn't strum the strings all the way through to the sixth string. Generally, in an upstroke, hitting just the top three or four strings is good enough. You may notice that your right hand naturally arcs away from the strings by that point, to an area above the center of the guitar. This is fine.

Upstrokes don't get equal time with their downwardly mobile counterparts. You typically use upstrokes only *in conjunction* with downstrokes. Whereas you can use downstrokes by themselves just fine — for entire songs, even — very rarely do you use upstrokes in isolation or without surrounding them on either side with downstrokes. (Some situations do call for just upstrokes.)

So you should first tackle upstrokes in their most natural habitat: in an eighth-note rhythm figure where they provide the in-between notes, or *off-beats,* to the on-the-beat downstrokes.

Combining downstrokes and upstrokes

The easiest way to perform an upstroke smoothly is in its reciprocal response to a downstroke. Play Figure 4-3 with a relaxed, free-swinging up-and-down arm motion, working to get equal emphasis on each stroke, and being aware that your downstrokes will naturally include more (and lower) string-strikes than your upstrokes. The time signature is 4/4, which means the measures contain four beats, and each quarter note receives one beat.

Figure 4-3:
Down-
strokes and
upstrokes
for eighth
notes.

Track 17

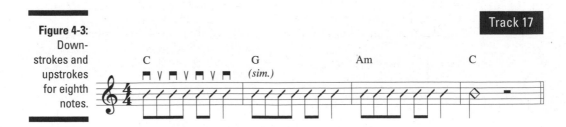

At this easygoing tempo, you can probably play Figure 4-3 with all down-strokes. If you try that, however, you discover that it introduces a tenser, more-frantic motion in your own strumming motion, which is not in character with the song's mellow feel. Frantic motion can be a very good thing in rock, though. Figure 4-12 later in this chapter, for example, shows you how an all-downstroke approach on a faster song is more appropriate than the easy back and forth of alternating downstrokes and upstrokes.

Whether an eighth-note pattern takes an all-downstroke or downstroke-upstroke approach is determined more by the feel, rather than the speed. (Although it is physically easier to play eighth notes with alternating strokes.)

Book II

Sounds and Techniques

Playing a combination figure

Quarter notes and eighth notes make up much of medium-tempo-based music, so Figure 4-4 shows how a progression might use a mixture of quarters and eighths to help convey different rhythmic intensity levels in a song.

Figure 4-4:
Strumming
in quarter
notes and
eighth
notes.

Track 18

Be aware that you not only have to control the strums in your down and up picking, but which strings you strike in each chord as well. Don't forget that you play only the top four strings in a D chord and only the top five for C.

Strumming in 16ths

Sixteenth notes come twice as fast as eighth notes, or four to the beat. That can seem pretty twitchy, so 16th notes are almost always played with alternating downstrokes and upstrokes. Some punk and metal bands play fast 16th-note-based songs with all downstrokes, but their songs are usually about pain and masochism, so it's understandable, given the circumstances. The acoustic guitar part in the Who's "Pinball Wizard" is a classic example of 16th-note strumming.

You start off with a progression played at a medium tempo, using a common 16th-note figure. Figure 4-5 is based on an R&B progression and uses a repeated 16th-note scheme. True *syncopation* (rhythms employing dots and ties) stays out of the picture until later in the chapter.

Track 19

Figure 4-5: A medium-tempo progression using 16th notes.

If the rhythmic notation seems like it's getting a little dense, don't worry too much about understanding the notation thoroughly or being able to play it at sight. What's important is to learn the figure, memorize it, and to play it correctly and with confidence. Listening to the CD repeatedly to learn this figure is okay, too. (Just don't tell your fourth-grade piano teacher we told you it was okay to memorize the recorded sound and not to read the music.)

Reading 16th-note notation

Sixteenth notes are indicated with two beams connecting their stems (or if they're by themselves, two flags).

Getting a shuffle feel

An important rhythm feel used extensively in rock is the shuffle. A *shuffle* is a lilting eighth-note sound where the beat is divided into two unbalanced halves, a long note followed by a short. Think of the riffs to such songs as Elvis Presley's "Hound Dog," the Beach Boys' "California Girls," Fleetwood Mac's "Don't Stop," and the Grateful Dead's "Truckin'." These are all based on a shuffle feel.

The shuffle is formed from triplets, where the beat is first subdivided into three equal parts. Then the first two notes are held together.

Rather than thinking about it too much, this simple exercise can help you hear the difference between straight eighth notes (equally spaced) and triplet eighth notes (the first held twice as long as the second):

1. **Tap your foot in a steady beat and say the following line, matching the bold syllables to your foot taps:**

   Twink-le **twink**-le **lit**-tle **star**.

   That's the sound of normal, equally spaced, straight eighth notes.

2. **Now in the same tempo (that is, keeping your foot tap constant), try saying this line, based in triplets:**

   Fol-low the **yel**-low brick **road**.

That's the sound of triplets. In both cases you should keep your foot tap at exactly the same tempo and change only how you subdivide the beat internally.

3. **Create shuffle eighth notes by sounding only the first and third notes of the triplet. You do this by sustaining the first note through the second or by leaving out that second note entirely.**

The new sound is a limping, uneven division that goes *l-o-n-g-short, l-o-n-g-short, l-o-n-g-short,* and so forth.

A good way to remember the sound of triplet eighth notes (the basis of a shuffle feel) is the song "When Johnny Comes Marching Home Again." If you tap your foot or snap your fingers on the beat and then try saying the lyrics in rhythm, you get:

> When **John**-ny comes **march**-ing **home** a-gain, hur-**rah**

The bold type represents the beat, where the syllables coincide with your foot tap or finger snap. The phrase "Johnny comes" is in triplets, because each syllable falls on one note of the three in between two beats. The rest of the phrase, "marching home again, hurrah," divides each beat into two-syllable pairs, the first syllable longer than the second. This is the sound of eighth notes in a shuffle feel.

Book II

Sounds and Techniques

Figure 4-6 is a shuffle feel that uses downstrokes and upstrokes. To reward you for saying "twinkle, twinkle little star" out loud while you tapped your foot, you get three new bonus chords that are easy to play and will give your shuffle progression a real lift.

Track 20

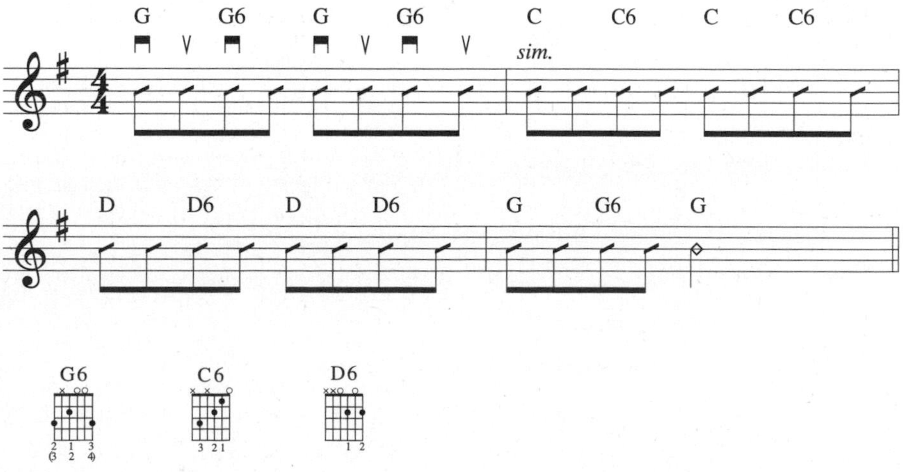

Figure 4-6: An eighth-note shuffle in G using down-strokes and upstrokes.

Dividing a band's songs by straight eighths or shuffle feel

If you've never thought of songs by your favorite band as being in a straight-eighth feel or a shuffle feel, it's fun to go down their hits and see in which category their individual songs belong. Here's how some of the Beach Boys' and the Beatles' hits break down:

The Beach Boys

Straight Eighth	Shuffle
Surfin' USA	Good Vibrations
Surfin' Safari	Barbara Ann
Kokomo	California Girls
I Get Around	Wouldn't It Be Nice
Fun, Fun, Fun	Help Me Rhonda

The Beatles

Straight Eighth	Shuffle
Hard Day's Night	Can't Buy Me Love
I Want to Hold Your Hand	Love Me Do
I Saw Her Standing There	Revolution
Yesterday	Got to Get You into My Life
Twist and Shout	Penny Lane

Actually, the chords aren't so much new as they are a one-finger variation of chords you already play. These new "chords" are easily executed by moving one and only one finger, while keeping the others anchored. It's the first step to getting both hands moving on the guitar, a really exciting accomplishment that makes you feel like a real guitar player. Have fun with this one!

The upstrokes still come at the in-between points — within the beats — but because of the unequal rhythm, it may take you a little time to adjust.

Mixing Single Notes and Strums

Rhythm guitar includes many more approaches than just simultaneously strumming the multiple strings of a chord. A piano player doesn't plunk down all of her fingers at once every time she plays an accompaniment part, and guitarists shouldn't have to strike all the strings every time they bring their pick down.

The pick-strum

Guitarists borrow a technique from their keyboard-plunking counterparts, who separate the left and right hands to play bass notes and chords, respectively. When guitarists separate out the components of a chord, they don't use separate hands, but combine both aspects in their right hand. Playing bass notes with chords is called a *pick-strum* pattern.

Separating the bass and treble so they play independently in time is a great way to provide rhythmic variety and introduce different chordal textures. Guitarists can even set up an interplay of the different parts — a bass and treble complementarity or *counterpoint.*

The boom-chick

The simplest accompaniment pattern is known by the way it sounds: *boom-chick.* The boom-chick pattern is very efficient because you don't have to play all the notes of the chord at once. Typically you play the bass note on the *boom,* and all the notes in the chord except the bass note on the *chick* — but you get sonic credit for playing twice.

Figure 4-7 shows a boom-chick, or bass-chord pattern in a bouncy country-rock progression.

Track 21

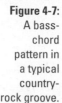

Figure 4-7:
A bass-chord pattern in a typical country-rock groove.

The symbol *C* immediately to the right of the treble clef in Figure 4-7 is a shorthand way to indicate 4/4 time. The examples in this book use *4/4* to indicate music in 4/4 time, but many examples of printed sheet music use *C* to indicate *common,* or 4/4, time.

The moving bass line

An important musical device available to you after you separate the bass from the chord is the moving bass line. Examples of songs with moving bass lines include Neil Young's "Southern Man," Led Zeppelin's "Babe, I'm Gonna Leave You," the Grateful Dead's "Friend of the Devil," and the Nitty Gritty Dirt Band's "Mr. Bojangles." A moving bass line can employ the boom-chick pattern (see the preceding section).

Figure 4-8 shows a descending bass line, made even more effective by isolating the bass line from the chords. Although this is left-hand movement within a chord form, similar to the shuffle figure in Figure 4-6, you can think of this as new chord forms entirely, if that's conceptually easier for you.

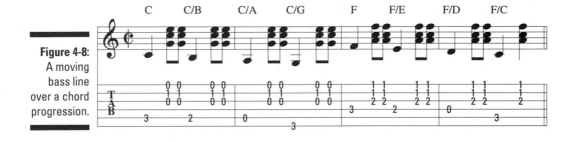

Figure 4-8:
A moving bass line over a chord progression.

When a chord symbol features two letters separated by a forward slash, it indicates the chord and the bass note over which that chord sounds. For example, C/G is a C chord with a G in the bass. In this case, the bass note is a chord member (the notes of a C chord are C, E, and G), but it doesn't always have to be that way. In the chord progression C-C/B-C/A, the bass notes B and A are not part of the chord but help to provide motion to another chord.

Disrupting Your Sound: Syncopated Strumming

After you develop a feel for strumming in different combinations of eighths, quarters, and 16ths, you can increase the rhythmic variation to these various groupings by applying syncopation. *Syncopation* is the disruption or alteration of the expected sounding of notes. In rock 'n' roll right-hand rhythm playing, you do that by staggering your strum and mixing up your up- and downstrokes to strike different parts of the beats. By doing so, you let the vehicles of syncopation — dots and ties — steer your rhythmic strumming to a more driving and interesting course.

Syncopated notation: Dots and ties

A *dot* attached to a note increases its rhythmic value by half its original value. A dot attached to a half note (two beats) makes it three beats long. A dotted quarter note is one-and-a-half beats long, or a quarter note plus an eighth note.

A *tie* is a curved line that connects two notes of the same pitch. The value of the note is the combined values of the two notes together, and only the first note is sounded.

Figure 4-9 shows some common syncopation figures employing dots and ties. The top part of the table deals with dots and shows note values, their new value with a dot and the equivalent expressed in ties, and a typical figure using a dot with that note value. The bottom part of the table deals with ties and shows note values, their new value when tied to another note, and a typical figure using a tie with that note value.

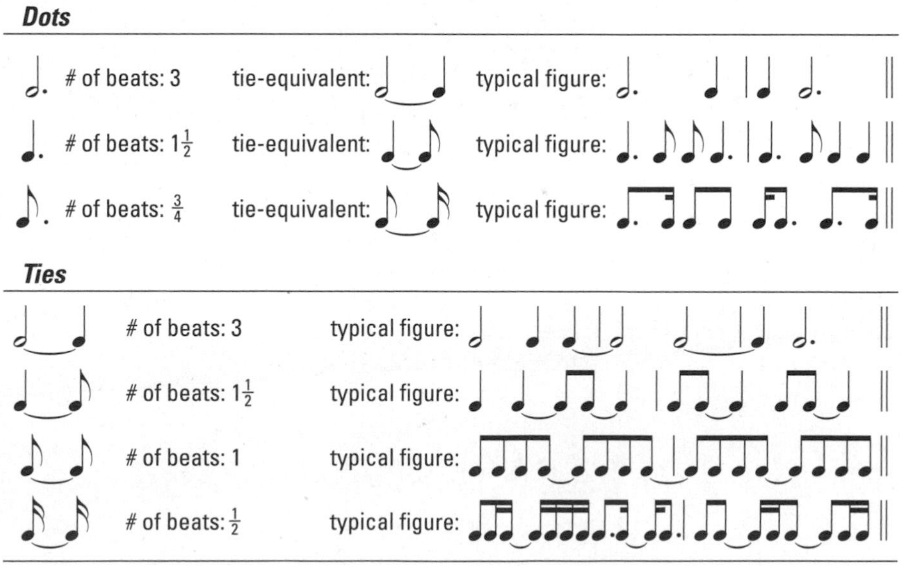

Book II

Sounds and Techniques

Figure 4-9:
Common syncopation features.

Playing syncopated figures

So much for the music theory behind syncopation. Now how do you actually play syncopated figures? Try jumping in and playing two progressions, one using eighth notes and one using 16th notes, that employ common syncopation patterns found in rock.

Figure 4-10 shows a useful syncopation scheme for an easy 4/4 rhythm at a moderate tempo. Pay close attention to the downstroke (⊓) and upstroke (∨) indications. Because the normal flow of down- and upstrokes is interrupted in syncopation, it's important to remember which stroke direction to play a note to avoid getting your strums out of synch.

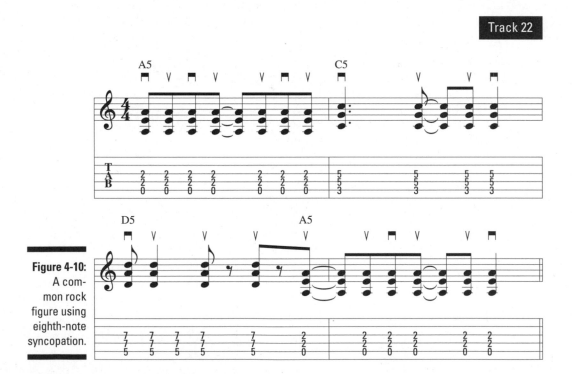

Track 22

Figure 4-10: A common rock figure using eighth-note syncopation.

Giving Your Left Hand a Break

If you listen closely to rhythm guitar in rock songs, you hear that strummed figures aren't one wall of sound — that minuscule breaks occur in between the strums. These breaks prevent the chord strums from running into each other and creating sonic mush. The little gaps in sound keep a strumming figure sounding crisp and controlled.

To form these breaks, or slight sonic pauses, you need to stop the strings from ringing momentarily. And we're talking very *small* moments here. Controlling the right hand's gas pedal with the left hand's brake pedal is a useful technique for cutting off the ring-out of the strings so they don't all run together.

Left-hand muting

To get the left-hand to mute the in-between sound between any two chords, just relax the fretting fingers enough to release pressure on the fretted strings. These strings will instantly deaden, or muffle, cutting off sound. What's more, if you keep your right-hand going along in the same strumming pattern, you produce a satisfying *thunk* sound as the right hand hits all these deadened strings. This percussive element, intermixed among the ringing notes, creates an ideal rock rhythm sound: part percussive, part syncopated, and all the while driving. If you relax the left hand even further so it goes limp across all six strings, then no strings will sound, not just the ones the left-hand fingers cover.

Also, allowing your left hand to do the muting means you can keep your right hand going, uninterrupted, in alternating down- and upstrokes. The notation indicates a left-hand mute with an *X* note head.

Book II

Sounds and Techniques

Implying syncopation

Figure 4-11 is technically a straight-ahead down-and-up eighth-note strum in the right hand. But because you employ left-hand muting, the sound seems to cut off in just the right places, creating an almost syncopated sound. Your right hand isn't performing true syncopation, because it's playing straight through. It's just that some of the notes don't come through audibly. More than creating a syncopated sound, however, left-hand muting provides the guitarist with another means for controlling the strings' sound.

Figure 4-11:
Left-hand
muting
simulates
syncopation.

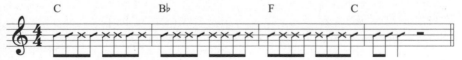

Left-hand muting is one of those rhythm techniques that guitarists just seem to develop naturally, almost as if it weren't a technique you *had* to learn because you'd invent it anyway, so obvious and useful is its benefit. And like riding a bicycle, left-hand muting is more difficult to execute slowly. So don't analyze it too much as you're learning; just strum and mute in the context of a medium-tempo groove. Your hands will magically synch up and you won't even have to think about it.

Although left-hand muting belongs to the hand not named in this chapter, its impetus is drawn from the right-hand motion. Plus, performing a left-hand mute is impossible without another hand to turn it into sound.

Suppressing the Right Hand

You can also mute with your *right* hand (using the heel of the palm), but this produces a different effect than left-hand muting. In right-hand muting you still hear the sound of the fretted string, but in a muted and subdued way. You don't use right-hand muting to stop the sound completely, as you do in a left-hand mute; you just want to suppress the string from ringing freely. Like left-hand muting, right-hand muting keeps your tone from experiencing runaway ring-out, but additionally it provides an almost murky, smoldering sound to the notes, which can be quite useful for dramatic effect. You sometimes hear this technique referred to as *chugging.*

You perform a right-hand mute by anchoring the heel of your right hand on the strings just above the bridge. Don't place your hand too far forward or you'll completely deaden the strings. Do it just enough so the strings are dampened (*damping* is a musical term which means to externally stop a string from ringing) slightly, but still ring through. Keep it there through the duration of the strum.

If a *palm mute* (as right-hand muting is known, abbreviated *P.M.*) de-emphasizes a string strike, then its evil twin, the *accent,* draws attention to a string strike. An accent is easy to execute: Just strike the string or strings harder than usual, and lift your right-hand palm from the strings as you do, to allow the strings to ring free. The result is that the accented strum stands out above the rest. An accent is indicated with a > just above or below the note head.

Palm mutes are much easier to perform if only one or two of the strings are struck, due to the restricted movement of the right hand caused by anchoring it to the strings' surface above the bridge. Figure 4-12 is a rhythm figure where you strike only the lowest note of the chord on the palm mutes, and the upper strings on the accents. Play this progression using all downstrokes to add intensity.

Figure 4-12:
A rhythm
figure
with palm
mutes and
accents.

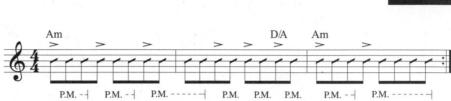

The interplay between the palm-muted notes and the accented chords creates a sound that makes it seem like two instruments playing.

Left-Hand Movement within a Right-Hand Strum

In this chapter you deal mostly with right-hand movement using static left-hand chord forms. When you begin to move the left hand in conjunction with the right, you uncover an exciting new dimension in rhythm guitar: left-hand movement simultaneous with right-hand rhythm. (It's what you flirted with in Figure 4-6, but you're now going to explore it fully.) This "liberating of the left hand" is also the first step in playing single-note riffs and leads on the guitar, which we get to in Chapter 3 in Book III.

Figure 4-13 features a classic left-hand figure that fits either a straight-eighth-note groove or a shuffle feel (although it's placed here in a straight-eighth setting). The changing notes in this example are the 5th degrees of each chord, which move momentarily to the 6th degree. So in an A chord, the E moves to F♯; in a D chord the A moves to B; and in an E chord the B moves to C♯.

This pattern is known by various names, but we call it the "5-6 move." (Clever, eh?) You can find it in songs by Chuck Berry, the Beatles, ZZ Top, and plenty of blues-rock tunes. The 5-6 move fits over any I-IV-V progression, but you see it here in the key of A.

Note that to more easily accommodate the 5-6 move, the figure supplies alternate chords and fingering to satisfy the A, D, and E chords. In each case the chords use only three strings, all adjacent to each other.

And even though it's in steady eighth notes, this progression should be played using all right-hand downstrokes. If you can throw in some palm muting (as is done on the CD), so much the better!

Track 24

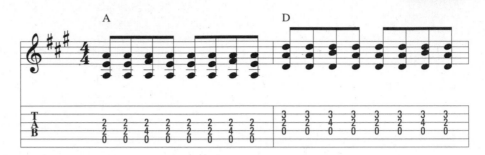

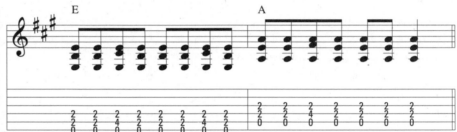

Figure 4-13: An eighth-note 5-6 move using all down-strokes and a moving left hand.

Giving Your Fingers Some Style

Fingerstyle, as the name implies, means you pluck the strings with the right-hand fingertips. For these times you can put the pick down, stick it between your teeth, or tuck it in your palm — whichever allows you to grab it the fastest after the fingerstyle passage is over.

Fingerstyle is especially suited to playing *arpeggios,* or chords played one note at a time in a given pattern. Fingerstyle is a much more simplistic way to play different strings in rapid succession, as you must do for arpeggiated passages. Generally speaking, the thumb plays the bass strings and the fingers play the upper three strings. Think of the opening figure to Kansas's "Dust in the Wind," Fleetwood Mac's "Landslide," or Simon and Garfunkel's "The Boxer," and imagine trying to play those patterns with your pick hopping frantically around the strings.

Position your right hand just above the strings, so your fingers can dangle freely but in reach of the individual strings. In Figure 4-14, the thumb plays the downstem notes and the right-hand fingers play the upper notes. (For you classical guitar aficionados out there: The standard way to notate the right-hand fingers is with the letters *p, i, m,* and *a,* for the Spanish words for the thumb, index, middle, and ring fingers.) In the example here, you don't need to be that careful about which fingers play which strings, so the figure doesn't indicate any left-hand fingerings. But a good way to approach Figure 4-14 is to use the index finger to play the 3rd string, the middle finger to play the 2nd string, and the ring finger to play the 1st string. Work for an even attack in the fingers and a smooth flow between the thumb and the fingers.

Book II

Sounds and Techniques

Track 25

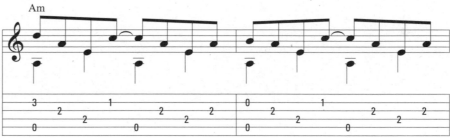

Figure 4-14: Fingerstyle arpeggios played with the right-hand thumb, index, middle, and ring fingers.

Of course, you don't *have* to play an arpeggiated passage fingerstyle if it's slow and there's relatively little string skipping involved. But for longer passages, or if the tempo is fairly rapid and the string skipping is relentless, work out the passage as a fingerstyle exercise.

Many players use a combination of pick and fingers when fingerpicking, called *hybrid picking.* Substitute the pick for the thumb, the middle finger for the index, and the ring for the middle finger.

Chapter 5

Playing Melodies in Position and in Double-Stops

*O*ne of the giveaways of beginning players is that they can play only down the neck, in open position, and that they play only single-string melodies. As you get to know the guitar better, you find you can use the whole neck to express your musical ideas, and that you're not limited to plunking out just single notes.

In this chapter, you venture out of open-position base camp into the higher altitudes of position playing. You also pick up the technique of playing in double-stops along the way.

Playing in Position

As you listen to complicated-sounding guitar music played by virtuoso guitarists, you may imagine their left hands leaping around the fretboard with abandon. But usually, if you watch those guitarists on stage or TV, you discover that their left hands hardly move at all. Those guitarists are playing in movable position, or for short, *playing in position*.

Playing in position means your left hand remains in a fixed location on the neck, with each finger more or less on permanent assignment to a specific fret, and that you fret every note — except for open position, of course. If you're playing in *5th position*, for example, your first finger plays the 5th fret, your second finger plays the 6th fret, your third finger plays the 7th fret, and your fourth finger plays the 8th fret. A *position,* therefore, gets its name from the fret that your first finger plays.

In addition to enabling you to play notes where they feel and sound best on the fingerboard — not just where you can most easily grab available notes (such as the open-string notes in open position), playing in position makes you look cool — like a nonbeginner! Think of it this way: A layup and a slam-dunk are both worth two points in basketball, but only in the latter case does the announcer scream, "And the crowd goes wild!"

Playing in position versus playing with open strings

Why play in position? Why not use open position and open strings all the time? Here are two key reasons:

- ✔ **It's easier to play high-note melodies.** Playing in open position allows you to play only up to the 4th or 5th fret. If you want to play higher than that, position playing enables you to play the notes smoothly and economically.

- ✔ **You can instantly transpose any pattern or phrase that you know in position to another key simply by moving your hand to another position.** Because position playing involves no open strings, everything you play in position is *movable.*

People have the idea that playing guitar in lower positions is easier than playing in higher ones. The higher notes actually aren't harder to play; they're just harder to read in standard notation if you don't get too far in a conventional method book (where reading high notes is usually saved till last). But here, you're not focusing on music reading but on guitar playing — so go for the high notes whenever you want.

Playing exercises in position

The major scale (you know, the familiar *do-re-me-fa-sol-la-ti-do* sound you get by playing the white keys on the piano starting from C) is a good place to start practicing the skills you need to play in position. Figure 5-1 shows a C major scale in 2nd position. Although you can play this scale in open position, play it as the tab staff in the figure indicates, because you want to start practicing your position playing.

The most important thing about playing in position is the location of your left hand — in particular, the position and placement of the fingers. The following list contains tips for positioning your left hand and fingers:

✔ **Keep your fingers over the appropriate frets the entire time you're playing.** Because you're in 2nd position for this scale, keep your first finger over the 2nd fret, your second finger over the 3rd fret, your third finger over the 4th fret, and your fourth finger over the 5th fret at all times — *even if they're not fretting any notes* at the moment.

✔ **Keep all of your fingers close to the fretboard, ready to play.** At first, your fingers may exhibit a tendency to straighten out and rise away from the fretboard. This tendency is natural, so work to keep them curled and to hold them down over the frets where they belong for the position.

✔ **Relax!** Although you may think that you need to intensely focus all of your energy on performing this maneuver correctly or positioning that finger just so, you don't. What you're actually working toward is simply adopting the most natural and relaxed approach to playing the guitar. (You may not think it all that natural right now, but eventually, you'll catch the drift.) So take things easy, but remain aware of your movements. Is your left shoulder, for example, riding up like Quasimodo's? Check it periodically to make sure it stays tension free. Remember to take frequent deep breaths, especially if you feel yourself tightening up. And practice in front of a mirror from time to time.

Figure 5-1:
A one-octave C major scale in 2nd position.

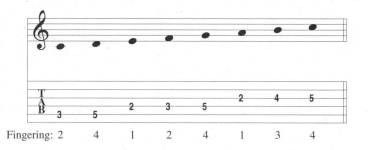

Fingering: 2   4   1   2   4   1   3   4

Look at Figure 5-1 and notice that the score indicates left-hand fingerings under the tab numbers. These indicators aren't essential because the position itself dictates these fingerings. But if you want, you can read the finger numbers (instead of the tab numbers) and play the C scale that way (keeping an eye on the tab staff to check which string you're on). Then, if you memorize the fingerings, you have a *movable pattern* that enables you to play a major scale in any key.

Play the *one-octave scale* (one having a range of only eight notes) shown in Figure 5-1 by using both down- and upstrokes — that is, by using alternate (down and up) picking. Try it descending as well (you should practice all scales ascending and descending). This scale isn't on the CD; you already know how it sounds — it's the familiar *do re mi fa sol la ti do.*

Figure 5-2 shows a two-octave C major scale (one with a range of 15 notes) in the 7th position. Notice that this scale requires you to play on all six strings.

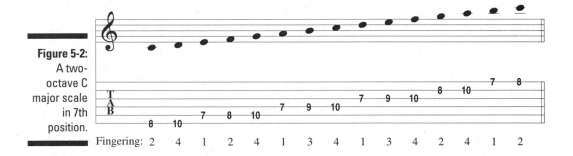

Figure 5-2:
A two-octave C major scale in 7th position.

To help you remember to hold your fingers over the appropriate frets all the time, even if they're not playing at the moment, and keep your fingers close to the fretboard, remember this twist on an old expression: Keep your friends close, your enemies closer, and your frets even closer than that.

Practice playing the scale shown in Figure 5-2 up and down the neck, using alternate picking. If you memorize the fingering pattern (shown under the tab numbers), you can play any major scale simply by moving your hand up or down to a different position. Try it. And then challenge the nearest piano player to a *transposing* (key-changing) contest using the major scale.

Play scales slowly at first to ensure clean and smooth notes; then gradually increase your speed. Start with a metronome at 60 beats per minute.

Shifting positions

Music isn't so simple that you can play it all in one position, and life would be pretty static if you could. In real-world situations, you must often play an uninterrupted passage that takes you through different positions. To do so successfully, you need to master the *position shift* like an old politician.

Andrés Segovia, legend of the classical guitar, devised fingerings for all 12 major and minor scales. Figure 5-3 shows how Segovia played the two-octave C major scale. It differs from the two scales in the preceding section in that it requires a position shift in the middle of the scale.

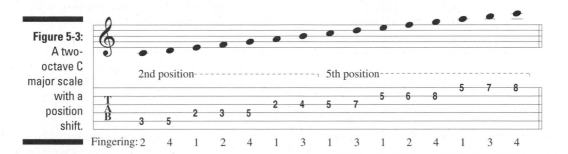

Figure 5-3: A two-octave C major scale with a position shift.

Play the first seven notes in 2nd position and then shift up to 5th position by smoothly gliding your first finger up to the 5th fret (3rd string). As you play the scale downward, play the first eight notes in 5th position, and then shift to 2nd position by smoothly gliding your third finger down to the 4th fret (3rd string). The important thing is that the position shift sound seamless.

Someone listening shouldn't be able to tell that you shift positions. The trick is in the smooth gliding of the first (while ascending) or third (while descending) finger. Practice this smooth glide to make it sound uninterrupted and seamless. Isolate just the two notes involved (3rd string, 4th fret, and 3rd string, 5th fret) and play them over and over as shown in the scale until you can make them sound as if you're making no position shift at all.

Building strength and dexterity by playing in position

Some people do all sorts of exercises to develop their position playing. They buy books that contain nothing but position-playing exercises. Some of these books aim to develop sight-reading skills, and others aim for left-hand finger strength and dexterity. But you don't really need such books. You can make up your own exercises to build finger strength and dexterity. (And sight-reading doesn't concern you now anyway because you're reading tab numbers.)

To create your own exercises, just take the two-octave major scale shown back in Figure 5-2 and number the 15 notes of the scale as 1 through 15. Then make up a few simple mathematical combinations that you can practice playing. Following are some examples:

- 1-2-3-1, 2-3-4-2, 3-4-5-3, 4-5-6-4, and so on. (See Figure 5-4a.)
- 1-3-2-4, 3-5-4-6, 5-7-6-8, 7-9-8-10, and so on. (See Figure 5-4b.)
- 15-14-13, 14-13-12, 13-12-11, 12-11-10, and so on. (See Figure 5-4c.)

Figure 5-4 shows how these numbers look in music and tab. Remember, these notes are just suggested patterns to memorize and help build dexterity.

You get the idea. You can make up literally hundreds of permutations and practice them endlessly — or until you get bored. Piano students have a book called *Hanon* that contains lots of scale permutations to help develop strength and independence of the fingers. You can check out that book for permutation ideas, but making up your own is probably just as easy.

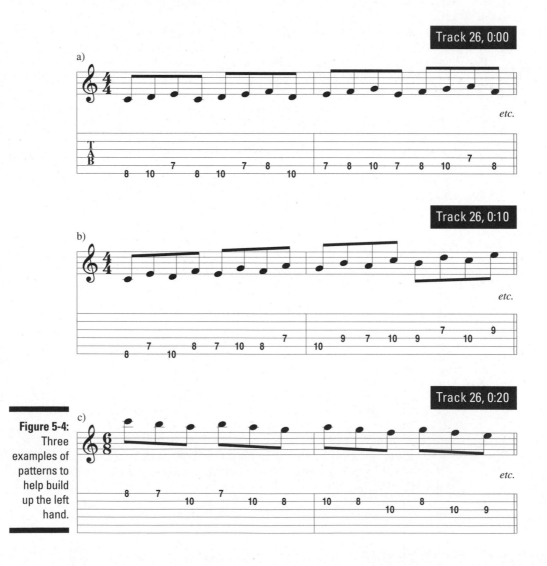

Figure 5-4: Three examples of patterns to help build up the left hand.

Double-Stops

Double-stop is guitar lingo for playing two notes at once — something the guitar can do with relative ease but that's impossible on woodwinds and only marginally successful on bowed string instruments. (Actually guitarists lifted the term from violin playing but quickly made double-stops truly their own.) By the way, you do nothing special in fretting the notes of a double-stop. Fret them the same way you do chords or single notes.

You experience the guitar's capability to play more than one note simultaneously as you strum a chord, but you can also play more than one note in a melodic context. Playing double-stops is a great way to play in harmony with yourself. So adept is the guitar at playing double-stops, in fact, that some musical forms — such as '50s rock 'n' roll, country, and Mariachi music (you know, the music that Mexican street bands play) — use double-stops as a hallmark of their styles.

Book II

Sounds and Techniques

Understanding double-stops

A double-stop is nothing more than two notes that you play at the same time. It falls somewhere between a single note (one note) and a chord (three or more notes). You can play a double-stop on adjacent strings or on nonadjacent strings (by skipping strings). The examples and songs that you find in this chapter, however, involve only adjacent-string double-stops because they're the easiest to play.

If you play a melody in double-stops, it sounds sweeter and richer, fuller and prettier than if you play it by using only single notes. And if you play a *riff* in double-stops, it sounds gutsier and fuller — the double-stops just create a bigger sound. Check out some Chuck Berry riffs — "Johnny B. Goode," for example — and you can hear that he uses double-stops all the time.

Playing exercises in double-stops

There are two general ways to play double-stops: You can play passages using only *one* pair of strings (the first two, for example) — moving the double-stops up and down the neck — or using *different* string pairs and moving the double-stops across the neck (first playing the 5th and 4th strings, for example, and then the 4th and 3rd, and so on).

Playing double-stops up and down the neck

Start with a C major scale that you play in double-stop *thirds* (notes that are two letter names apart, such as C-E, D-F, and so on), exclusively on the first two strings, moving up the neck. This type of double-stop pattern appears in Figure 5-5. The left-hand fingering doesn't appear below the tab numbers in this score, but that's not difficult to figure out. Start with your first finger for the first double-stop. (You need only one finger to fret this first double-stop because the 1st string remains open.) Then, for all the other double-stops in the scale, use fingers 1 and 3 if the notes are two frets apart (the second and third double-stops, for example) and use fingers 1 and 2 if the notes are one fret apart (the fourth and fifth double-stops, for example). With your right hand, strike only the 1st and 2nd strings.

Track 27, 0:00

Figure 5-5:
A C major scale in double-stops, moving up the neck.

Playing double-stops across the neck

Playing double-stops across the neck is probably more common than playing up and down the neck on a string pair. Figure 5-6 shows a C major scale that you play in thirds in open position, moving across the neck.

Track 27, 0:11

Figure 5-6:
A C major scale in double-stops, moving across the neck.

What's especially common in rock and blues songs is playing double-stops across the neck where the two notes that make up the double-stop are on the same fret (which you play as a two-string barre). Check out Books III and IV for more information on rock and blues.

Again, the example in Figure 5-6 doesn't show the fingerings for each double-stop. But you can use fingers 1 and 2 if the notes are one fret apart and fingers 1 and 3 if the notes are two frets apart.

Double-stops occur in the opening of Jimmy Buffett's "Margaritaville," Leo Kottke's version of the Allman Brothers' "Little Martha," Van Morrison's "Brown-Eyed Girl," Chuck Berry's "Johnny B. Goode," and the intros to Simon and Garfunkel's "Homeward Bound" and "Bookends."

Book II

Sounds and Techniques

Playing Songs in Position and in Double-Stops

Certain keys fall comfortably into certain positions on the guitar. Songs are based in keys, so if you play a song in a particular key, the song will also fall comfortably into a certain position. Rock, jazz, blues, and country lead playing all demand certain positions to render an authentic sound.

Telling you that the melody of a song sounds best if you play it in one position rather than another may seem a bit arbitrary to you. But trust us on this one — playing a Chuck Berry lick in A is almost impossible in anything *but* 5th position. Country licks that you play in A, on the other hand, fall most comfortably in 2nd position, and trying to play them anywhere else is just making things hard on yourself.

The best position for a certain style not only sounds best to your ears, but also feels best to your hands. And that's what makes playing the guitar so much fun.

Play the two songs in this section by reading the tab numbers and listening to the CD; notice how cool playing up the neck feels instead of playing way down in open position, where those beginners play.

When you're playing in position, remember to keep your left hand in a fixed position, perpendicular to the neck, with your first finger at a given fret and the other fingers following in order, one per fret. Hold the fingers over the appropriate frets, close to the fretboard, even when they're not fretting notes.

Here is some useful information to help you play the songs:

- **Turkey in the Straw:** To play this song, you need to know how to play in 7th position (see the section "Playing in Position," earlier in this chapter) and what saying "day-day to the wagon tongue" means.

- **Aura Lee:** To play this song, you need to know how to play double-stops up and down the neck on the 1st and 2nd strings (see the aptly entitled section "Playing double-stops up and down the neck," earlier in this chapter) and how to gyrate your pelvis while raising one side of your upper lip.

  You play this arrangement of "Aura Lee" — a song made famous by Elvis Presley as "Love Me Tender" — exclusively on the first two strings, moving up and down the neck. In the double-stop scales that you practice in Figures 5-5 and 5-6, the two notes of the double-stop move up or down together. In "Aura Lee" the two notes of the double-stop sometimes move in the same direction and sometimes in opposite directions. Other times, one of the notes moves up or down while the other remains stationary. Mixing directions makes an arrangement more interesting. Play and listen to "Aura Lee" to hear this for yourself.

  Notice that the left-hand fingerings appear under the tab numbers. If the same finger plays successive notes, but at different frets, a slanted line indicates the position shift (as in measures 5, 7, and 9). For your right-hand picking, use all downstrokes. Remember to repeat the first four bars (as the repeat signs around them indicate) before continuing to bar 5. And make the song tender, just as Elvis did. Uh-thank yew verrah much.

Track 28

Turkey in the Straw

Fingering: 1 4 2 2 4 2 1 3 4 1 1 1 2 4

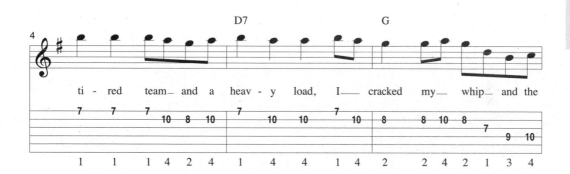

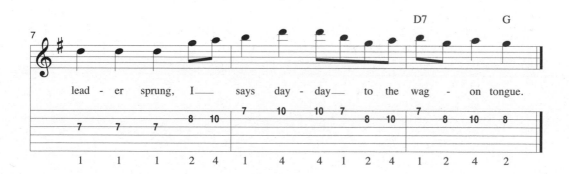

Book II

Sounds and Techniques

Track 29

Aura Lee

Book III
Rock Guitar

"Now this little plant is called Emma. Emma blooms best to the scathing guitar riffs of Ted Nugent and Eddie Van Halen."

In this book . . .

So you wanna be a rock 'n' roll star . . . coming right up! This book covers the whole history of rock, from its beginnings in the mid-20th century right through to today. The best of the best guitar greats are covered here, and each one is analyzed with the purpose of discovering why they were so great and how they perfected their particular sound. You also get the goods on the workings of electric guitars and amps, playing lead, practicing riffs, and moving up the neck of your guitar. By the end, all you'll need are those distressed leather pants . . .

Here are the contents of Book III at a glance.

Chapter 1

It's Only Rock Guitar, but I Like It

Rock guitar does not have a dignified history in music. It doesn't come from a long lineage of historical development where composers such as Bach, Beethoven, and Brahms wrote lovingly for it, composing concertos and sonatas highlighting its piquant and gentle qualities. It wasn't played in the great European concert halls or in the parlors of fine households.

Not only was rock guitar unknown to the great composers of the ages, but they couldn't have even conceived of such a thing in their worst nightmares. Imagine what they would have thought of an Ozzy Osbourne concert — a nightmare no matter which century you hail from! Indeed, even if they could have heard, through some sort of time travel, an electric guitar banging out the riff to "Satisfaction," they would have hardly recognized it as music.

Rock guitar is a mid-late-20th-century invention. It has no memory of a bygone era when youths were respectful of elders, music was a polite pursuit, and musicians cared about social acceptance. Rock guitar is for people who like their music loud, in your face, electric, and rebellious, and who owe no debt to history. Rock guitar is probably not the wisest choice of instruments to tackle if you want to garner acceptance from the music community.

So if you want respect, take up the flute. If you want to set the world on fire, attract adoring fans, and get back at your parents to boot — pick up an electric guitar and wail, baby, wail, because rock guitar will change your life.

First, though, you gotta learn how to play the thing.

Differentiating Between Rock and Acoustic Guitar: It Ain't Just Volume

When you see someone wailing away on rock guitar — on TV, in a film, or at a live concert — be aware that what you're seeing is only part of the story. Sure, someone playing rock guitar is holding an instrument with six strings, a neck, and a body — qualities that describe the instrument that classical guitarist Andrés Segovia played — but the sound couldn't be more different. That difference in sound is the key to understanding rock guitar. What's important is not the leather, the hair, the onstage theatrics, the posturing, the smoke bombs, or the bloody tongues — but the *sound* of that guitar.

It was the sound of the electric guitar — so different from that of its predecessor, the acoustic guitar — placed in the hands of some early, forward-looking visionaries that forced a cultural change, a musical modification, and a historical adjustment to the way we experience popular music. Songwriters had to write differently, recording engineers had to record differently, and listeners had to do a major attitude adjustment to get their ears around it. Heck, people even had to learn new dances.

But what makes the sound of an electric guitar so different from an acoustic one? If you didn't think about it, you might say, well, *volume.* Rock guitar is just a whole lot louder than its acoustic counterpart. Although that may be true most of the time, volume alone is not what makes rock guitar unique. True, you listen to rock at high volumes — its message tastes better served up loud — but volume is a byproduct, an after-effect, not what makes rock different or what drives it.

To really understand rock guitar, you need to explore some of its qualities *other* than volume. Don't worry, though; this chapter gets back to volume eventually.

Sound quality, or timbre

When guitarists "electrified" their acoustic guitars, they originally intended to give the guitar a fighting chance in the volume department. Unsatisfied with the results of placing a microphone in front of the guitar, they sent the guitar's sound to a speaker by placing a magnetic element called a *pickup* under the guitar's strings. (See "Signal" and "Distortion and sustain" later in this chapter for more on pickups.) Players quickly found, though, that, unlike a microphone, a pickup didn't just make the sound louder, it *changed* the tone too. How? It wasn't that obvious, but it was tangible.

The basic differences between a guitar coming out of a pickup and a guitar playing into a *mike* or *mic* (slang for *microphone*) are that the sound coming out of a pickup

- ✔ Is smoother and less woody.
- ✔ Is more electronic, with purer-sounding tones, like that of an organ.
- ✔ Has a less defined lifecycle, or *envelope* — a beginning, middle, and end. These stages, so clear in the sound of a plucked acoustic guitar string, are blurred together in an electric guitar.

Signal

When progressive-minded guitarists of the '30s and '40s first put electro-magnetic elements under their strings to "pick up" their vibrations and send them along a wire to an amplifier, they did a lot more than increase the volume — though they didn't know it at the time. They were on their way to creating one of those "happy accidents" so common in art and science (and this was a little of both, really).

Originally, jazz guitarists playing in the big bands of the day were merely seeking a way to cut through all the din of those blaring horns and thundering drums. The mellow guitar, regarded by most other musicians as a mere parlor instrument with dubious stage presence, was no match for the louder brass and percussion instruments. The banjo had a sharp, cutting quality, and was better at projecting on the bandstand, but its tone was falling out of fashion in favor of the more full-bodied, versatile tone of the guitar. Problem was, the guitar just wasn't that loud, so something had to be done.

Slapping on heavier-gauge (thicker) steel strings helped, but it still wasn't enough. Placing a mike in front of the guitar, as was done for vocalists, worked somewhat, but was cumbersome, and the mike picked up the sur-rounding sound as well as the guitar. Plus, who wanted to bother miking the lowly guitarist way over in the rhythm section when you had some hotshot crooner in the spotlight at center stage?

To avoid these problems, *luthiers* (guitar makers) got the idea to put a mag-netic element just underneath the strings to carry the signal electronically to an amplifier. Because the strings were metal — specifically, electrically conductive magnetic metal — the sound of the strings traveled electronically through the *pickup* (so called because it picked up the sound of the vibrating string), down the attached wire, into a portable amplifier, and then out of a speaker.

Book III

Rock Guitar

The electric guitar was born, but getting from electrification to rock 'n' roll nirvana was still a bit of a journey. It would be some time before guitarists recognized the monster they had spawned from the unholy union of electricity and acoustic guitar. (Get used to imagery involving evil, wickedness, and other bad stuff; it's all part of rock 'n' roll lore.)

Distortion and sustain

When the six-string Dr. Frankensteins of the '30s and '40s were electrifying their guitars, they weren't envisioning what Jimi Hendrix would do decades later at Woodstock and Monterey. Just like the well-meaning doctor in Mary Shelley's novel, early electronic guitar designers were wholesome and good. These pioneer inventors wanted to reproduce the sound of the acoustic guitar as faithfully as possible. Fortunately for us, they failed miserably. But electronics' loss was music's gain, because even though the electric guitar sound was nothing like the acoustic sound — or the acoustic guitar sound as heard through a microphone — it nonetheless had a very pleasing and musically useful quality.

The effort to produce an exact, amplified match of the original acoustic guitar failed primarily because it introduced *distortion* (an untrue representation of the sound) into the sound. The louder the sound, or the more the guitar "worked" the electronic circuitry, the more distorted the sound got. As the electronic signal "heated up," the sound became *fuzzier* (where the high frequencies became more muted), and the tone generally *warmed up* (sounding more rounded and less brittle). All of this distortion increased the *sustain* (the tendency for the tone to ring indefinitely at the same level), which was noticeable in even the lowest of volumes.

Distortion, normally a bad thing in just about any other electronic endeavor, had a nice effect for guitar tone. As the guitar became thought of more and more as a lead instrument, guitarists found they could work the distortion factor to their advantage. An electric guitar had a different, *better* tonal quality, called timbre.

This *timbre* (a musical term for tone, or sound quality), distortion, and increased sustain took the plunkiness out of the guitar's tone and made it more smoothly melodic — more like the buzzy, reedy qualities of, say, a saxophone or a blues vocalist, which is why so many early rock guitarists cut their musical teeth on the blues. Whereas the guitar had formerly been a rhythm instrument, owing to its clipped sound, rapid *decay* (the quality of a sound to die away), and strident tone, the "electronic" guitar now had properties more suited to melody-making. The guitar was poised to step out of the background and up to the spotlight itself. All it needed was some brave souls to tame this new sonic monster.

Plenty of acoustic guitarists at that time were playing melody, notably Django Reinhardt. Reinhardt even bent strings — something that would become the province of electric guitarists everywhere, but is generally shunned by classical guitarists who deem the technique "unacousticlike."

Oh yes, and volume

Of course, electrifying a guitar did accomplish what it set out to do — make the guitar louder. Although it needed an electronic crutch, in the form of amplification through an external apparatus, this system of pickups, wires, and a portable amplifier (where the guitarist didn't need to rely on the auditorium's sound engineer) gave guitarists the freedom to play in all sorts of styles — melodic, rhythmic, and chordal — and freed them from the "rhythm section ghetto."

An excellent example of an early electric guitarist who realized and exploited the newfound qualities of the electric guitar was jazz guitarist Charlie Christian. It's important to note that even though Christian was not a rock player (rock just didn't exist in the '30s), he is worshipped by electric guitarists everywhere — from blues to jazz to rock — as an incredible visionary who realized the power of the electric guitar's tone.

Some people may claim that Christian was, in part, responsible for inventing the electric guitar pickup, but this is just a myth. However, he certainly did his part to popularize the "pickup-configured" electronic guitar, and he is one of its best early practitioners, because he recognized — and exploited through his musical genius — its sustain qualities.

After the guitar could play as loud as the other, more charismatic instruments (such as the trumpet and saxophone), it wasn't long before the guitar would become a featured instrument, both from a personality perspective as well as an instrument for solo exhibitionism.

Book III

Rock
Guitar

Listening examples

You can talk all you want about the tone of the electric guitar, but the best way to understand its tonal qualities is to listen to some classic examples.

✔ Led Zeppelin's "Stairway to Heaven" is not only a classic song, it's one of the best illustrations of the differences between electric and acoustic guitar. The song begins with a plaintive vocal by Robert Plant, accompanied by a Renaissance-sounding acoustic guitar. The accompaniment gradually builds, and then at 6:42 guitarist Jimmy Page launches into the solo section with an opening *phrase* (a musically complete passage or thought of any given length) that sums up the essence of the electric guitar in just two measures. Listen to the first note, which seems to hang in midair and *sing*. The rest of the solo is a tour de force of technique, phrasing, and tone, but it's that opening *riff* (a self-contained musical phrase) that grabs you.

✔ Another well-known example is the guitar solo section of the Eagles' "Hotel California," played by Joe Walsh and Don Felder. This solo is given plenty of room to breathe by the accompaniment. The gliding quality at the end of Walsh's first short phrase (the fifth note in the opening sequence) is a *string bend,* where you stretch the string by pushing it out of its normal alignment causing the pitch to rise. Listen to how the note, again, *sings.* This quality, broken down to its component attributes, has a smooth sound (timbre); a reedy, fuzzy quality (distortion) that doesn't resemble the plucked sound of the acoustic guitar; and an elongated, non-decaying volume and intensity (sustain).

These examples are both in the melodic vein. Things really get weird when guitarists started abandoning melody altogether and choose to exploit timbre, distortion, and sustain for their own purposes. Jimi Hendrix, for example, took distortion and sustain to the nth degree.

Guitar, Amp, and Effects: The Power Trio

All right, the previous section helps you to understand the tonal differences of an electric guitar versus an acoustic one, and that an electric guitar has pickups (or magnetic elements) that carry the sound via an attached wire to a loudspeaker. What else do you need?

A burning question for most aspiring rock guitarists is, "Since I have an electric guitar here, does that mean I also have to have an amp?"

Yes, you do need an amplifier. Just as you can't hear a scream without ears, so, too, can you not hear a guitar without its amplifier and speaker (in guitar terms, an "amplifier" can refer to the amplifier circuitry *and* the speaker, which are often housed in the same box). Electric guitars can have the biggest, most-powerful, nuclear-charged pickups on board, but without an amp, the guitar will make no noise.

Sounds unbelievable, but it's true. No amp, no electric guitar sound. Anytime you see somebody walking around with an electric guitar, you can bet he or she is looking for an amp. Therefore, you must have at least two elements to even be audible on the electric guitar: the guitar itself and the amp. (Technically speaking, you also need a cord, or wire, to attach the electric guitar to the amp.)

Realistically, however, guitarists these days routinely introduce a third element into the *signal chain* (as the path from the originating guitar pickups to the terminating amp speaker is known): intermediary electronic gizmos known as *effects*. These typically sit between a guitar and an amp, and connect to each other with short cords, via in and out *jacks* (the electronic term for sockets, or something you can insert plugs into).

The electric guitar

The electric guitar is the principal player in the three-part system that comprises the rock guitar sound. And whether it has a natural mahogany finish or is painted Day-Glo green with purple lightning bolts across the body, all electric guitars have common properties. Like an acoustic guitar, an electric has a neck and a body, six strings, and tuning keys on the top of the neck that allow you to tighten or loosen the strings to the desired pitch — the process known as tuning. (See Chapter 1 in Book I for details.) Unlike the acoustic guitar, however, an electric guitar sports *pickups* (electromagnetic devices that "sense" the strings' vibrations and create a small current), knobs, and switches for controlling the pickups, and possibly other hardware (such as a *bar,* described in the following bulleted list) that acoustic guitars don't have. Figure 1-1 shows the various parts of the electric guitar.

Here's a quick overview of the functions of the various parts of the electric guitar (refer to Chapter 1 in Book I for a fuller run-down).

- **Bar:** A metal rod or arm attached to the bridge that varies the string tension by tilting the bridge back and forth. It's also called the tremolo bar, whammy bar, vibrato bar, and wang bar.

- **Body:** The large, shapely wooden mass that provides an anchor for the neck and bridge. The body can either be solid, hollow, or partially hollow, and houses the bridge assembly and electronics (pickups as well as tone and volume controls).

- **Bridge:** The metal assembly that anchors the strings to the body.

- **End pin:** A metal post screwed into the body, where the rear end of the strap connects. The other end of the strap connects to the strap pin.

- **Fretboard:** A flat, plank-like piece of wood that sits atop the neck and has frets embedded in it. This is where you place your left-hand fingers to produce notes and chords. It is also known as the fingerboard.

- **Frets:** Thin metal bars embedded perpendicular to the strings that shorten the effective vibrating length of a string, enabling it to produce different pitches.

- **Headstock:** The section that holds the tuning machines and provides a place for the manufacturer to display its logo.

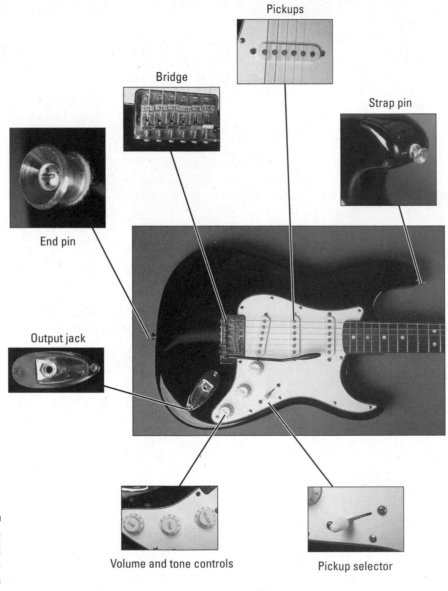

Pickups

Bridge

Strap pin

End pin

Output jack

Figure 1-1:
A typical
electric gui-
tar with its
major parts
labeled.

Volume and tone controls

Pickup selector

Tuning machines/ Post

Tuning machines/
Tuning key

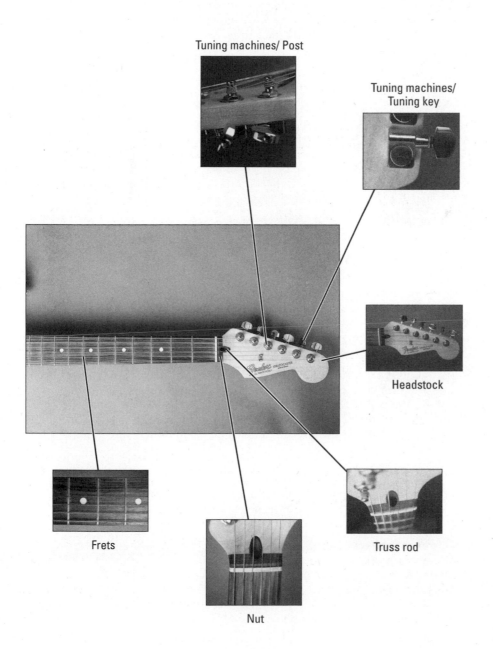

Headstock

Frets

Nut

Truss rod

- ✔ **Neck:** The long, club-like wooden piece that connects the headstock to the body. Some guitarists like to wield their guitars like clubs, and usually do so by holding them by the neck.

- ✔ **Nut:** A slotted sliver of stiff nylon or other synthetic substance that stops the strings from vibrating beyond the neck. The strings pass through the slots on their way to the tuners in the headstock. The nut is one of the two points at which the vibrating area of the string ends. (The bridge is the other.)

- ✔ **Output jack:** The insertion point, or jack, for the cord that connects the guitar to the amplifier or other electronic device. You will sometimes hear this jack called an *input* because guitarists think of putting a cord "into" the jack. Electronically speaking, however, this is an *output* jack because it carries signal out of the guitar.

- ✔ **Pickup selector:** A switch that determines which pickup or pickups are currently active.

- ✔ **Pickups:** Bar-like magnets that create the electrical current that the amplifier converts into musical sound.

- ✔ **Strap pin:** The metal post where the front, or top, end of the strap connects. The strap pin is screwed into either the guitar's back (as on a Gibson Les Paul) or into the end of one of the "horns" (as on a Fender Stratocaster). The other end of the strap connects to a corresponding pin, the end pin.

- ✔ **Strings:** The six metal wires that, drawn taut, produce the notes of the guitar. Although not strictly part of the actual guitar (you attach and remove them at will), strings are an integral part of the whole system, and a guitar's entire design and structure revolves around making the strings ring out with passion and musicality (and don't forget volume!).

- ✔ **Top:** The face of the guitar's body. The top is often a cosmetic or decorative cap that overlays the rest of the body material.

- ✔ **Trussrod:** An adjustable steel rod that can be rotated using a special wrench and which helps keep the neck straight. You gain access to the rod through a hole in the headstock or at the base of the neck.

- ✔ **Tuning machines:** Geared mechanisms that raise and lower the tension of the strings, drawing them to different pitches. The string wraps tightly around a post that sticks out through the top, or face, of the headstock. The post passes through to the back of the headstock, where gears connect it to a tuning key. Tuning machines are also known as tuners, tuning pegs, tuning keys, tuning knobs, and tuning gears.

- ✔ **Volume and tone controls:** Knobs that adjust the loudness of the guitar's sound and its bass and treble frequencies.

The amplifier

The *amplifier* is an all-electronic device with no moving parts (except for its knobs and switches, which control the volume and tone of the incoming signal). You may think that those rather pedestrian-looking, geometrically plain boxes that do nothing but a lot of internal electrical processing are functional and necessary, but not particularly sexy (well, not by electric guitar standards, anyway). Amp lore, however, is every bit as epic and mythological as guitar lore. Entire subcultures (that all, curiously, seem to have an Internet newsgroup devoted to their cause) are devoted to assessing, proselytizing, and otherwise pondering the mysteries and myths of the perfect guitar amplifier. (See Chapter 2 in Book III for more on setting up your amp.)

In any quest for the perfect tone, you must have an amp in the equation, and the history and contributions of such legendary amp manufacturers as Fender, Marshall, and Vox are an inextricable part of the rock 'n' roll gear legacy. Plus, you have to have someplace to set your drink when you go onstage. Figure 1-2 shows the various parts of an electric guitar amplifier.

The following list tells you the functions of the various parts of an amplifier.

- **Cabinet:** The box that houses the speaker and electronic components. It's typically made of plywood or pressure-treated wood and encased in a durable protective covering.

- **Effects:** Many modern amps also include onboard digital signal processing, such as reverb, delay, chorus, and flange.

- **Front panel** or **face plate:** The metal plate through which knobs and switches protrude to protect the controls that sit just below the surface.

- **Grille cloth:** The mesh-like fabric, usually made of a synthetic weave, that allows sound to pass through, but keeps foreign, and potentially harmful, objects (such as a boot) away from sensitive speaker surfaces.

- **Input jack:** The socket where you put the cord from your electric guitar or the cord from the output of the last effect in your signal chain.

- **Power switch:** A switch that turns the amp on and off.

- **Tone switch:** Two-position, or toggle, switches (not rotary or continuous) that provide additional tonal control.

- **Volume and tone controls:** Rotary knobs that provide continuous control over the outgoing signal.

Book III

Rock Guitar

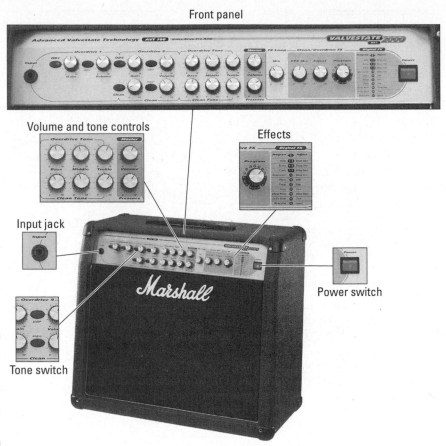

Figure 1-2:
A typical guitar amp with its major parts labeled.

Effects

The newest member of the triumvirate of principal players is the group whose members are electronic effects. These self-contained units range in size anywhere from a cigarette pack to a VCR deck. Figure 1-3 shows four of the most common electronic effects used by rock guitarists.

Here's what the four most common effects do:

✓ **Digital delay:** Creates an echo by digitally recording the signal and playing it back at adjustable times after the principal signal has sounded.

✓ **Chorus:** Creates a thick, swirly effect of two or more guitars playing in tandem, but not quite with the exact tuning or timing.

String length and tension: Les Paul versus Stratocaster

One of the biggest differences between two icons of electric guitar models, the Gibson Les Paul and the Fender Stratocaster, is that their string lengths are different.

The Les Paul has a vibrating string length of 24.75 inches; the Strat (as it's known to its friends) has a vibrating length of 25.5 inches. Not much difference, maybe, but enough to make a perceptible difference to the hands.

Physics tells us that two different string lengths drawn to produce the same pitch (as they must to be in tune) will have different tensions. The Strat has the longer string length, and therefore has slightly higher string tension than does the Les Paul. This creates two key differences in playability for the electric guitarist: tighter, or springier, string response and larger frets in the Strat; and looser, or spongier, string response and smaller frets in the Les Paul.

Figure 1-3: Four common effects (left to right): digital delay, chorus, distortion, wah-wah.

Book III

Rock Guitar

✔ **Distortion:** Simulates the sound of an amp that's played too loud to handle a signal cleanly. Distortion devices are convenient: The guitarist doesn't have to keep adjusting the amp controls to get a distorted sound.

✔ **Wah-wah:** A foot-pedal, rocked by the guitarist's foot, that creates a tonal variation that resembles a horn with a mute, or a human voice saying the phrase "wah wah" (thus the name).

Accessorizing Your Guitar

The accessories don't stop at effects. You may also want to acquire some other useful, but not essential, components, including various accessories that all serve to make rock guitar playing a little easier. Figure 1-4 shows an assortment of guitar accessories that any rock guitarist should have.

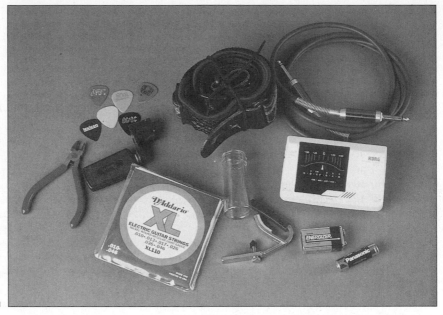

Figure 1-4:
Clockwise, from top left: picks, strap, cord, electronic tuner, batteries, capo, slide, extra strings, peg winder, wire cutters.

Picks

An optional item for acoustic guitarists, a pick is a near-requirement for playing rock guitar (exceptions include Mark Knopfler and Jeff Beck, among others). Sometimes called a *plectrum,* a pick is a small triangular- or teardrop-shaped piece of thin plastic or nylon, about the size of a quarter, that's held between the thumb and index finger of the right, or strumming, hand. When you strum a chord or pluck a note, you use your pick to make contact.

You can buy guitar picks (there's no distinction between electric guitar and acoustic guitar picks) at any music store, in a variety of colors, shapes, and thickness (called *gauges*). Buy 'em by the bucketful, because you'll lose, break, give away, and squander plenty in your guitar-playing career.

Straps

A strap is also an absolute necessity, but under only one condition: if you plan to play while standing. Straps *can* be used while sitting, but that's a matter of personal preference. Most people who are interested in playing rock guitar live, however, will want to stand for at least some of that time. A strap is always a good thing to have rolled up and tucked away in your guitar case, even if you do most of your playing sitting down.

Straps come in all materials, from leather to fabric to space-age mesh, so you'll certainly be able find one that suits your sense of fashion. You can even have a custom-made strap with your initials or name emblazoned on the side that faces the audience. Looks great on TV.

Cords

A *cord,* sometimes referred to as a *cable,* is the technical term for the wire, or lead, that connects electric guitars to amps and other components, so you need at least one. If you use one electronic effects device you'll need two cords — one to connect the guitar to the effect's input, and one to connect the effect's output to the amp. If you have two effects, you'll need three cords, and so on. But whether you use effects or not, carrying an extra cable with you is always a good idea (like straps, cables can be coiled up and unobtrusively stashed in a guitar case). An extra cable is cheap insurance; a bad cable can silence you as quickly as a broken guitar neck or blown speaker.

Tuners

A tuner is a device that helps you to tune your instruments. It won't turn the pegs for you, but its meters tell you when a string is flat or sharp with much more accuracy than your ear can — even if you have perfect pitch. (Chapter 1 in Book I talks more about guitar tuners.) And what's the definition of perfect pitch, you ask? That's when you can toss a banjo into a Dumpster without hitting the sides.

Book III

Rock Guitar

Headphone and virtual amps

For $20 to $50 you can pick up a small device, such as the Vox Classic Rock headphone amp, and play as loud as you want without bothering your roommates or family. The battery-powered units plug right into your guitar and accept standard headphones, such as those for an iPod. Some of them come with effects, too, so choose according to your playing style.

You can also create classic amp and effects setups on your computer. Native Instruments' Guitar Rig 3, for example, is a hardware-software combo that connects your guitar with your computer via a foot pedal. The onboard soundcard sends the signal to the speakers. The software offers lots of classic amps, cabinets, microphones, and effects. The outfit currently sells for around $550.

Chapter 2

All about Amplifiers

*J*on Chappell here with a personal story: When I was a kid, I pined for an eternity (okay, it was one summer) for my first guitar, which hung, unattainable, in the music store window. After several agonizing months of paper routes, odd jobs, and bottle recycling, I finally bought my dream guitar. As the salesman pulled my hard-won treasure from the window, he commented casually, "Yeah, good guitar you're getting here. Whatcha got for an amp?"

An *amp?* I'd never even thought about it! Did I need an amp? Of course I did, but all my energies had gone into buying this guitar. As the meaning of his words flooded over me like a giant tidal wave, I realized I hadn't even considered that I needed something to plug into to be heard. My mom wasn't about to spend one red cent more than she had already contributed to my musical cause, so she called an electrician friend who ran an appliance repair store across town. To my utter humiliation, we found ourselves in a washing machine fix-it shop buying what looked like a converted toaster oven. It took me six more months to get a *real* amp, which helped me to get up the nerve to play in front of my friends (junior high school kids can be *so* cruel, you know). So take it from one who's been there, don't forget the amp! It does wonders for your guitar sound (not to mention your self-esteem).

You may not think that the amp is a very flashy player in the cast of rock guitar characters, especially when it has to share the limelight with its more glamorous counterpart, the electric guitar. But amps are essential to creating a great rock guitar sound and literally contribute one half of the effort. The more you understand your amp, the more passionate you become. In this chapter, you think "inside the box," separating the amp system into the smaller sections that all amps of various makes and models have in common. You then drill down one level to see how you can manipulate the controls that govern those parts. And don't worry, you don't need a driver's license — or even a learner's permit — to operate one of these babies.

Amps are all-electronic devices, and let's face it, that scares some people. Or at least it's intimidating enough that many beginner guitarists have a tougher time relating to an amp than, say, to something you can *play,* such as a guitar. Just as you can appreciate a sports car's power and performance without knowing the physics of the internal combustion engine, so, too, can you enjoy the "internal combustion" of an amp just by taking it for a ride. Like a well-made car, a great amp has a personality, responds to your every movement, and gives you the giddy sense that you're sitting atop something *really* powerful. Knowing just a little bit about what's going on under the hood of your amp increases not only your appreciation, but your pleasure as well.

Following the Signal Chain

An amp has a big job to do, when you think about it. It receives from the guitar a signal that is quite sensitive, having started life as a tiny current produced by skinny vibrating strings and a simple magnet. The amp must then respect the tiniest nuances of those vibrating strings, because you the player know exactly what you played, and if you don't hear that at the end of the process — coming out of the speakers — the amp has failed in its mission.

The amp, therefore, must shepherd the signal through an electronic journey, all the while preserving its integrity. The amp must then switch gears, applying huge amounts of power to this once-sensitive electrical impulse, to rock stadiums and pulverize screaming fans. That's not an easy task for a box with no moving parts.

A good amp can do all this, plus excite you as a listener and inspire you as a performer in the process. The electronic journey is called the *signal chain.* Technically speaking, the entire signal chain includes at its source the guitar, from whence the signal originates (by you striking the strings), and at its terminus the speaker (which, in a "combo" configuration, is housed in the same box), which converts the electrical signal back into acoustic energy — you know, earth-shattering, filling-rattling AC/DC riffs.

In this section, you find out what happens to the signal after it's inside the amplifier — this sets the stage (so to speak!) for you to better understand how to manipulate the controls and to shape the sound. A guitar signal's journey through the amp goes something like this: An anemic (by electrical standards) signal enters the guitar amp at the preamp stage where sensitive circuitry optimized for handling low levels boosts the signal and sends it through to the section where the amp shapes the tone and adds effects. The signal then goes into the power amp, which applies massive amounts of juice behind it to drive speakers and produce audible — often *extremely* audible — sound waves we can crowd surf to.

Preamp

Every amplifier, whether it's for a guitar or keyboard — or inside a home stereo receiver — has two stages to actually amplify, or boost, the signal: the preamp and the power amp (which is covered later in this chapter). In amp systems made for guitars, the *preamp* takes the puny signal from the guitar (which is, after all, produced by mere magnets), jacks it up so the power amp can deal with it, and turns it into the screaming tones of death that eventually burst forth from stressed-to-the-brink speakers. The result is the sound that blows back the hair of the audience in the first ten rows.

The preamp is the daycare center of signal processing, designed to foster and nurture small impulses and guide them in their first baby steps through amp land. Preamps respond very well to the sensitive but relatively weak messages from the pickups.

The power amp can't do much with an untreated guitar signal, which comes way under its radar, preferring instead to deal with levels that a preamp generates. The power amp takes whatever it sees coming at its input and attempts to churn out an exact copy, but thousands of times bigger (at a strength known as *line level* in electronic terms). A power amp may not be able to do justice to an untreated guitar signal, but it can take a preamp signal, puff it up, and use it to beat the stuffing out of a speaker.

Think of the preamp as a struggling talent agent and the power amp as a big Hollywood movie producer: The preamp polishes the talent of the small-time artist and prepares it for the big screen — er, speaker. The power amp doesn't muck about with the little people, but has the might to take the prepared talent and turn it into box-office dynamite.

The idea of two volume controls is unique to guitar amplification. Normally, household stereo amps don't give users separate access to the preamp and power amp controls. Stereo listeners just want the best *fidelity* (the most accurate signal) possible from their system. But in guitar amps, you can use the relationship of the preamp volume to the power amp volume to actually degrade the fidelity (in the form of distortion, or overdrive) to musical effect, as you find out later in this chapter.

Tone controls

After coming out of the preamp, the signal then passes through a series of electronic filters, which selectively increase or reduce the level of certain frequencies. Known collectively as the tone controls, these filters make up the *equalization,* or *EQ,* section. Applying EQ is sometimes referred to as *tone shaping.*

Book III

Rock Guitar

You sometimes hear the term EQ (pronounced "Ee-Cue") when discussing tonal issues. EQ is short for "equalization" (the bass and treble components of the tone) or "equalizer" (a box or circuit that affects tone). Following are three different uses of the term "EQ" that guitarists often hear:

✔ **As an intangible noun (an entity):** "The overall EQ of your guitar sound makes me feel like I'm chewing aluminum foil. Can't you make it less harsh?"

✔ **As a tangible noun (a device):** "Howdy! I'm your new bass player! Can we borrow your 10-band EQ? I forgot mine."

✔ **As a verb:** "Can you *please* EQ that amp so that it doesn't sound like a chainsaw on a blackboard? Thank you *so* much."

The tone controls on your guitar amp act just like the bass and treble knobs of your stereo: They make your sound *boomier* or *tinnier*. Because these filters don't affect all frequencies equally (which would result in an overall *volume* increase or reduction), but only in specific ranges, we hear the resultant sound as a *tonal* difference. Unlike a stereo receiver, however, a guitar amp has more than just a bass and treble control. Most amps feature at least one in-between knob called, logically enough, the *midrange* (usually abbreviated as *mid*) control. More sophisticated amps even have a *presence* control, which is between the midrange and treble control, and is especially suited to guitar frequencies. Still others have a contour control, and some have two knobs for the midrange that work in tandem — one to select the frequency and another to boost or cut the level of that frequency. But however a specific amp is configured, the controls in the tone-shaping section serve to change the bass, midrange, and treble content put out by the preamp.

Don't worry too much about understanding the technical differences between the variously named tone controls. Good tone production involves knowing very little science (at least from the *player's* perspective, anyway), because guitarists — even the best ones — just fiddle with the knobs until they find something they like. Fiddling with knobs is probably not the best way to deliver nuclear power to a city, but it works fine for guitarists searching for that special tone.

Effects

From the EQ, or tone-shaping section, the signal next proceeds to the effects section, which usually consists of at least a reverb control, and may have tremolo, vibrato, or chorus. You can use effects to subtly enhance a sound, giving it a certain ambience, warmth, fullness, or just a little more "life."

Or not. You can also use effects to make your playing sound completely off the wall, alien, space age, underwater, distorted, tortured, or to give it any other wholly unnatural quality. How you use effects (on your amp and/or elsewhere in the signal chain) is strictly a matter of taste and depends on the response you want to evoke from your listeners. Ugly, scary, brutal, and just plain rude are all worthy qualities completely at home in rock guitar (especially for punk and heavy metal!), and you often enlist effects (along with sheer overpowering volume) to help you achieve your aesthetic goal. But unless you're going for a *really* wacky sound, you find, as your playing develops, that using effects subtly is best for most musical situations.

Power amp

The final stop on the signal's electrical journey to the speaker is the *power amp* — a robust, no-nonsense electrical place where treated but underpowered signals get pumped up into sound-wave warriors. The power amp adds very little color to the sound — at least compared to the three previous stages — because its primary function is to reproduce, as faithfully as possible, the signal it receives from the preamp, tone, and effects sections. You may think, therefore, that the power amp section is comprised of fairly straightforward, unimaginative stuff, which actually isn't the case.

Although its function may be simple to describe, the power amp's processing is a fairly complex and demanding electronic project. In more powerful amps, the power amp section is bigger, heavier, and more expensive to build. And in tube amps, which are objects of lust among amp aficionados, the power amp also adds a bit of color to the sound — something it's ideally not supposed to do (that task being the exclusive domain of the preamp tubes). But at least where tubes are concerned, the result is so musical that guitarists find it pleasing and make an exception — sort of like the famous adage about sausage: If you love it, you don't want to know how it's made.

Book III

Rock Guitar

Taking a Guided Tour of the Amp

The following sections offer a walking tour through each of the amp's individual components. The sections here are grouped linearly, from start to finish. The exception is the preamp and power amp volume controls, which are tackled simultaneously because, although they are at the front and back of the amp's signal chain, respectively, you can best appreciate their functions and how they work together by dealing with them in tandem and in relation to each other — like bookends.

Boxing it in: The cabinet

The *cabinet* is a sturdy wooden box that houses the speaker, controls, and electrical guts so they don't fall all over the floor in a great big mess. The cabinet protects the speaker's surface with a grille cloth stretched taut across its front, serves as an anchor for the *chassis* (which houses the electronics) and the reverb tank (if present), and provides a frame for the *baffle* (the open-holed board that the speaker mounts to). The cabinet is also the acoustic place where the speaker lives and moves, however, and therefore contributes to the overall sound and performance of the amp. It also supports a sweating beverage bottle a *lot* better than the headstock of a guitar. Figure 2-1 shows the cabinet of a typical combo amp.

Figure 2-1:
The cabinet is the wooden box that houses the amp.

The cabinet can be open in the back (exposing the amp's interior and offering easy access to the speaker), closed, or sealed (leaving no opening), or "half back," which is like an open-back cab, but with a plank of wood across the opening. Sonically, an open back provides a rounder fuller tone, because sound escapes from both sides of the amp, back and front. A closed-back cab yields a punchier result because all sound is forced through the front of the amp (producing a boost in the bass frequencies in particular), and a half-back cab is a mix of the two sounds, but is closer to the open-back cab in quality.

Taking control: The control panel

The *control panel* is a metal plate that plays host to the amp's knobs, switches, and sockets. Under the knobs and sticking through holes in the control panel are *shanks,* or *spindles,* which rotate, sending messages to the electronic components within the *chassis* (the metal tray or compartment housing the amp's electronics). The control panel and its knobs are often recessed or angled in such a way to protect them from getting damaged. This helps keep them from getting sheared off as you load your amp into the trunk of a car and you don't quite clear the back of the trunk. (I *hate* when that happens.) The control panel is where the brains of the operation sit. It is to the signal chain what Houston is to a NASA space shuttle. Figure 2-2 shows a control panel of a typical combo amp.

Figure 2-2: The control panel groups an amp's jacks, switches, and knobs.

Book III

Rock Guitar

Channel inputs

Channel inputs are the sockets, or jacks, where you insert your guitar cord for access to a particular channel. A *channel* is an individual path through the amp's signal-processing sections. Many amps have two channels optimized for producing different sounds. Typically, one channel favors setting up a "clean" sound, the other a high-volume, distorted sound. One input often serves two channels, allowing you to switch between channels instantly via a footswitch, without having to re-plug (see the section on channel switching later in this chapter).

Some multichannel, multi-input amps even accept two instruments simultaneously — great for keeping handy two different types of guitars that you must switch between quickly, such as a 12-string and a six-string, or an acoustic-electric and a regular electric.

Preamp and power amp controls

The *preamp* takes a signal and boosts it so it can survive the journey through the tone-shaping and effects sections and wind up intact for the G-forces it's subjected to in the power amp section. The *power amp* determines the actual human-hearing volume coming out of the speaker. Guitarists control the output of each of these stages with separate level, or volume, knobs. Figure 2-3 shows the volume controls of the preamp and power amp.

Figure 2-3:
A tale of two volumes: preamp and power amp, channel, and master.

Here's a list of preamp and power amp controls:

✔ **Gain/drive:** *Gain* and *drive* are synonymous terms that simply describe the volume controls for the preamp. The higher you turn *any* preamp volume control, the more distortion you introduce into the signal. Preamp volume distorts in musically pleasing ways, however, and rock guitarists use that as part of their tone quality and sustain. (See Chapter 1 in Book III for more detailed descriptions of the electric guitar's sustain and tone quality.)

✔ **Volume/master volume:** The power amp volume control determines the overall or absolute loudness of the amp. In amps containing more than one channel, the term *master volume* distinguishes the power amp control from the channels' preamp controls. If you run the master volume high (on high numbers, such as 6, 7, 8, 9, and 10), the sound coming out of the amp is loud. If you run the master volume low (1, 2, and 3), the amp is soft. This is important to remember when balancing the preamp channel volume with the power amp master volume (see the section on setting the controls later in this chapter).

✔ **Boost switch:** Often an amp has a switch that activates a boost circuit, which just jacks up the power amp's volume by a fixed level. A boost switch can be very handy because it keeps your basic sound intact, retaining the specific tone and effects settings, and applies a volume increase. This way, a guitarist can have two versions of a carefully crafted sound: loud and really loud.

Tone controls

In the tone-shaping stage of an amp, various electronic filters add or subtract frequencies, giving the guitarist tonal control over the sound apart from what the volume and effects controls provide. Most of the tone controls are intuitively named and produce expected results. For example, when you turn up the treble you brighten the tone. Figure 2-4 shows the tone-shaping section of an amp's control panel.

Figure 2-4: The tone controls of an amp's EQ, or tone-shaping, section.

Book III

Rock Guitar

Check out the following tone controls:

- ✔ **Bass:** The bass control determines how low or boomy the sound is. Turning up the bass provides more "girth;" turning down the bass reduces "rumble."

- ✔ **Middle or midrange:** For a fuller or warmer sound, guitarists reach for the midrange control. Conversely, to sharpen a sound, or to accentuate high highs and low lows, guitarists will cut, or "dial out," midrange frequencies. Heavy metal bands such as Pantera and Metallica often cut, or "scoop," their midrange frequencies.

- ✔ **Treble:** The highest of the tone controls, the treble can restore luster to a signal that's become dull from passing through too many effects pedals. If a signal is too harsh sounding, cutting back the treble makes it mellower.

- ✔ **Presence:** Technically, this is a high-mid control that sonically resides somewhere between the mids and the treble. "Presence" is sort of a misnomer because applying it doesn't really bring the sound any closer to the listener; it just adds a gloss or sheen. Presence can really sweeten up a signal, but too much of it can fatigue the ears and create a saccharine sound.

✔ **Bright switch:** The bright switch is a two-position *toggle* (a switch that alternates between two states) that selects between the normal sound and a brighter sound. Most rock guitarists who have amps with bright switches keep them on all the time. For that occasional jazzy passage, however, you may want to flick it to the "normal" position.

Don't think that just because you adjust one control that you're affecting only one range of notes. For example, turning down the treble doesn't affect just the high notes; it affects the entire high frequency content of the signal. So even if you play only low notes, turning down the treble will affect the high end of those low notes, inhibiting their ability to "sparkle."

Amp effects

Although most tone-shaping sections on amps are fairly standardized, amp manufacturers differ widely with respect to what effects they include. Following are some fairly universal effects found on many guitar amps.

✔ **Reverb:** *Reverb* is short for "reverberation" and is a basic staple guitar effect, one that is heard on virtually every recorded example of rock guitar music. Older amplifiers use metal springs (secured in a box or *tank* bolted to the inside of the cabinet) that will jiggle and make a crashing sound if you shake the amp. Newer amps deliver reverb through the less-costly technology of microchips and digital circuitry, but the intent is the same: to simulate the sound of a guitar played in different acoustical settings, from a small room to a concert stage to a giant cavern or cathedral. A single knob controls the intensity of the effect. Figure 2-5 shows the reverb control knob on an amp.

Figure 2-5:
The control for amp reverb is usually limited to one knob.

✔ **Tremolo:** *Tremolo* is regular, rapid wavering of a signal's volume. Old Fender amps used two controls, *speed* (the rate of the fluctuations) and *intensity* (to determine the distance between the loud and soft portions of the sound). At lower settings, the sound has a slight quiver. With the intensity cranked, it sounds like you're playing through an electric fan. These days, newer amps include tremolo only if they're going for that vintage vibe.

You sometimes hear amp tremolo described as "vibrato," but this is a misnomer. *Vibrato* is the rapid fluctuation of *pitch;* tremolo the rapid fluctuation of *volume.* Fender has an entire series of amps with the prefix "Vibro" to describe amps sporting a feature that is actually tremolo. Rock guitar is full of misnomers, but that's just part of its rebellious charm.

✔ **Flanger:** A *flanger* gives a kind of swirling, spacey effect to a guitar's sound. It does this by mixing two identical signals, but time-delaying one by a varying amount to create a kind of sweeping, up-and-down-the-sound spectrum.

✔ **Chorus:** *Chorus* simulates the sound of many guitars playing at once, creating an overall fuller sound that's slightly swirly. Turning up the speed yields a warbling effect; increasing the intensity produces lush, whooshy sounds. Figure 2-6 shows the chorus controls of an amp made famous by its classic onboard chorus: the Roland JC-120.

Book III

Rock Guitar

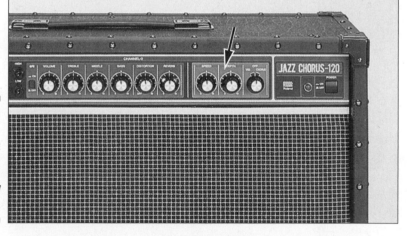

Figure 2-6: The two controls that modify the chorus here are *speed* and *depth.*

Making a graceful exit

Other than pumping the signal out through a speaker, an amp can output a signal through other points. Knowing these different output destinations helps in understanding how the amp contributes to the quality of the sound, rather than just acting as a "guitar megaphone." Alternate outputs allow for options like sending your guitar signal to a P.A. (sound system), headphones, and mixing boards for recording. An amp's output jacks are typically found on the back panel.

Speaker out

The main *speaker out* is an output jack that connects the amp's power amp to its internal speaker (if it's a combo) or to the main cab (if the amp is in a separate housing from the speaker). Some amps offer additional speaker outs for hooking up additional cabs. Ninety-nine times out of 100, you want your amp sound coming out through the speaker, because this is how electric guitars are heard — realized through a speaker. This is different than, say, a piano, flute, or even *acoustic* guitar where we can experience them live, without the benefit of a speaker. It's only on recordings where we must enlist the aid of a speaker. But an electric guitar knows no audio reality — live *or* recorded — without a speaker. Even if a direct out is used (as described later in this section), a speaker simulator is thrown in to simulate the sound of the signal coming through a speaker.

Headphone out

In the iPod era, everyone understands the importance of listening to music through headphones. Many amp makers realize this too, and so provide a headphone output for speaker-less listening. By listening to your guitar through headphones, you can wail away to your heart's content (and experience thundering levels of distortion via an overdriven preamp) and still not disturb the person next to you watching TV. Headphone outputs are great for practicing late at night or in close proximity to other humans.

Direct out

You sometimes want the signal to not go into the power amp and through the speaker but to some other destination, such as a mixing board (for recording directly onto tape or hard disk) or even to another amp. You can't successfully plug a guitar directly into a mixer channel, because you need the treatment that the amp's preamp, tone-shaping, and possibly effects sections provide. But an amp's power amp and speaker exist only to make the sound audible in the room, which is not necessarily what you want when sending a *direct-out signal.* You want to route the signal to a mixer or recording deck where you can then *monitor* (listen to the resultant sound) from the mixer or deck's headphone jack or speakers.

Effects loop

You can insert an outboard effect device between the preamp and the power amp sections of the amp, which is the optimal place for many effects, like delay, chorus, and flange, that just sound better placed between the preamp and the power amp, rather than before the preamp, which is the situation when using pedals. If you desire an effect not provided by your amp's built-in circuitry, but that you have in an external box, you use the effects loop to "patch" it in.

The *effects loop* consists of two jacks, an output and an input. With an extra guitar cord you plug the output (sometimes called *send*) of the amp into the input of the external effects box. You then take another cord and plug the output of the effects box back into the amp, at the input (sometimes called the *return*) jack. The amp has provided a "loop" for you to route the signal out and back in, allowing you to enhance it along the way. Figure 2-7 shows the diagram for plugging in an external device via the effects loop.

Figure 2-7: With an effects loop, you can route signals out for processing and then back in.

Power amp in

You may have occasion to use your amp just for its power amp capabilities only — to make an external sound source (such as a CD player) audible by means of the amp's speaker. In this case, the sound comes to the power amp from a source other than the amp's onboard preamp. For those situations, you take the output of the external device and insert it into the *power amp in* jack. Doing this skips all the circuitry before the power amp stage (preamp, tone-shaping, and effects sections), which the CD player doesn't need or want.

Use the power amp in jack to patch in a CD player (although you may have to tweak the tone controls to get a decent sound). This allows you to perform two common and useful tasks:

✔ Play recorded music in close proximity to your guitar-playing activities, instead of over the stereo speakers — wherever they are.

✔ Play recorded music through your amp on a gig during the break. (This is great if the venue has no "house system" of its own, or if you want to control what the audience hears — such as your newly minted demo!)

Various other "holes"

The preceding sections tackle the important jacks that appear on most amps, but you may discover amp models that have additional jacks.

- ✔ A *footswitch jack* allows you to plug in a pedal that you can operate with your foot for instantaneous and hands-free control. Typical footswitch jacks include channel switching, effects on/off, and, on digital amps, *preset advance* (where you can "step through" different setups you've created and stored in the amp's memory).

- ✔ High-quality amps often include several places where you can *tap* (gain access to) the signal: after the preamp, after the power amp but at non-speaker-level (for additional processing), and speaker level (which can only be connected to a speaker, lest you risk damaging the amplifier's circuitry).

- ✔ Some amps offer additional inputs, too, like an *aux in,* which allows you to plug in, say, a CD player so you can practice along with your favorite CD.

Sounding out: The speaker

The speaker's function is pretty obvious to anyone who's grown up around stereos, radios, and TVs: It magically converts that mystical stuff called electricity into acoustic sound waves that we can hear with our ears and feel in our bodies (if it's loud enough).

For all the advancements in electronics, speakers today look and operate pretty much the same as they did half a century ago. Electricity passes through a cylindrical metal coil at the speaker's center, surrounded by a doughnut-shaped magnet. This causes the coil to vibrate inside a magnetic field. The speaker's cone of paper-like material exaggerates and amplifies this movement, creating audible sound. If this process sounds familiar it should: It's essentially the way a pickup works — but in reverse (see Chapter 1 in Book III for more on the pickup's workings).

Speakers are delicate by design, because they must react to the minute electrical fluctuations in the coil. Guitar amp speakers are called *woofers* (as opposed to their higher-pitched brethren, *tweeters*) and are suited for cranking out the midrange-rich frequencies of electric guitars. The majority of guitar speakers measure 12 inches in diameter, though 10 inches is quite popular too. In general, the larger the speaker, the louder and stronger it sounds. Figure 2-8 shows a typical guitar speaker.

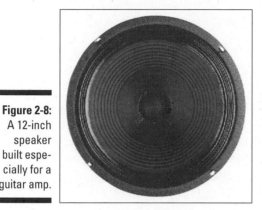 

Figure 2-8:
A 12-inch speaker built especially for a guitar amp.

Plugging In and Turning On

Because an amplifier plugs into the wall, and because it's capable of delivering signals both electrical and acoustic in high doses, you must follow some simple but vital rules for operating an amp. Do not skip the following sections!

Book III

Rock
Guitar

Safety first

First and foremost, a guitar amplifier is a high-voltage, electricity-driven device, such as any TV, stereo, radio, or appliance in your kitchen. Follow these directives to keep you and those near you safe and injury free.

- ✔ **Never stick your hands inside the amp to check connections, to find loose or rattling parts, or to otherwise poke around.** Even when you unplug the amp, its components store electricity for several minutes afterward.

- ✔ **Never operate an amp with water anywhere in the vicinity, either on your body or in an open container.** Mixing water with a plugged-in amp — even if it's not turned on — can be lethal. Treat the cord to the wall socket with respect and care. Always turn off the power switch when the amp is not in use for an extended period of time, and always turn off the power switch before unplugging the amp.

- ✔ **Never operate an amp in the rain or near a sprinkler or garden hose (which may happen if you play in a garage, backyard, or patio).** Have fun with your music, but always treat electricity with grave seriousness.

The six-step program

Following is a quick-start list of six steps for plugging your guitar in and turning it on in the right order. Doing this protects your speakers from sonic assaults and rude pops, and preserves your eardrums from unexpected, irritating — and potentially damaging — sonic blasts.

To turn on an amp:

1. **Turn all amp volume controls off or to their minimum position.**

2. **Plug one end of the guitar cord into the guitar, the other end into the amp.**

3. **Turn the amp's power switch on.**

4. **Turn the volume knob(s) of your guitar all the way up.**

5. **Turn up the amp's master volume to about 4 or 5, or up to about halfway.**

6. **Slowly turn the preamp or channel volume knob up and check for the presence of audible signal by strumming your guitar.**

Here's how you reverse the process to ensure a safe and pop-free shutdown routine. To shut off an amp:

1. **Turn off the guitar's volume knob(s).**

   Do this as a courtesy so unintended sound won't escape from the ringing open strings as you reach over to the amp's controls.

2. **Turn down the amp's master volume controls.**

3. **Optional: Turn down the channel or preamp volume control(s).**

   Do this as a courtesy to the next player — even if that's you — so she can make her own preamp adjustments. Conversely, you can *keep the preamp volume level where it is* to recall easily your sound upon restart.

4. **Turn off the power switch.**

5. **Optional: If you're leaving the amp unattended for a long period of time, or you can't predict who will be in the room with the amp when you're not there, unplug the amp from the wall socket.**

6. **Unplug the cord from the amp, and unplug the cord from the guitar.**

Additional hints:

- ✔ Never unplug a guitar cord — from either the guitar or the amp — without first turning down the master volume knob all the way.

Sudden loud noises in the form of "pops" from inopportunely connected or disconnected cords can damage the speaker (and at the very least are amateurish and annoying).

✔ Never move an amp any significant distance without turning down the volume and shutting off the power. This is important to consider when you're attached to a long extension cord.

✔ When plugging different guitars into one amp in rapid succession (such as when you're auditioning a bunch of guitarists), turn down only the master volume control. This shuts off the signal from reaching the speaker. Note the volume knob's position before you bring it down so you can restore it to the same place after you have safely unplugged and plugged in the guitar cord.

Getting a Sound

When you have an understanding of the amp's different sections and the controls that govern them, use them to set up your own sound. You can't make any mistakes when creating a sound, so experiment until you find something you like — something that's not too loud or too soft, too muddy or too shrill. Then go from there.

First decide what kind of sound you want. Something clean and crisp, say, for chords? Or something raunchy and snarly for low-note Led Zeppelin-type *riffs* (self-contained single-note phrases). Always have a vision in your mind's eye — make that ear — of what you're seeking, rather than blindly spinning controls hoping to stumble onto something you like.

Book III

Rock Guitar

Setting the controls

Start with your tone controls in the 12:00 position, or at "5," so they're *flat* (adding no boost or cut). That will help you hear your basic guitar sound in the amp's most neutral setting. Turn off all effects too, so you hear the pure guitar signal through the circuitry. Then decide whether you want a sound that's *clean* or *distorted.* Figure 2-9 shows an amp with its controls in the neutral position.

✔ **Clean:** The term *clean* in guitar parlance simply means distortion free and is not necessarily better or worse than an *overdriven,* or heavily distorted, sound. You can obtain a clean sound by running the power amp volume (or master volume) high and the channel, or preamp, volume relatively low. If you want the sound louder, turn up the master volume, not the channel volume.

✔ **Distorted:** If you're trying to get a distorted sound from an older amp that has no separate volume controls for the channel and the master (sometimes referred to as *non-master-volume models*), you have but one choice: crank that sucker until the sound starts to break up. In the process, hope that the neighbors don't call the police. If your amp has two volume controls, though, your options are a little more versatile. Set up the master volume to about halfway, and bring up the channel volume to a comfortable listening level (whatever that is, depending on your environment).

To create a distorted sound using the two volume controls in conjunction with each other, turn up the channel volume and compensate for the increased volume by turning down the master volume. By turning down the master as you turn up the channel, your overall loudness should remain fairly constant. But as the preamp works harder and harder, it will begin to distort — even though the volume doesn't change. The twin-volume approach to distortion is a beautiful thing for guitarists, because it means you can achieve overdriven preamp distortion at low volumes.

Don't get too caught up in all the semantics and synonyms for distortion. Technically, *distortion* is the result of any signal that gets overdriven.

Figure 2-9:
Place the controls in a neutral position with the volume reduced, effects off, and tone controls "flat."

Figure 2-10 shows two setups, one clean, and the other overdriven. In both settings the overall volume — or absolute loudness — is about the same. Only the distortion content changes.

Figure 2-10:
The left settings produce a clean, undistorted sound; the right gives distortion.

Channel switching

Most modern amps that allow you to create sounds on separate channels also allow you to switch between them by means of a front-panel switch. This enables you to set up two channels independently and switch between them instantly and at will. Typically, you assign two contrasting sounds for these channels, such as clean and distorted, or variations on those qualities (perhaps "ultra-sheen" and "super-stun").

Careful crafting of two independent clean and distorted sounds may produce righteous tones on their own, but they aren't much use to a guitarist who in the same song wants a clean sound on the verses (to, say, accompany a singer), and mondo-distortion for the Big Guitar Solo (and rock guitarists should *insist* every song include at least one of these). In a single-channel amp, reconfiguring the controls for real-time use between song sections is a practical impossibility, and in multiple channels, even throwing a front-panel switch requires the guitarist to take one hand off the instrument and reach for the amp. And hey, who has that kind of time?

The *footswitch* is an inexpensive (about $20, if not already included with the amp), "stompable" device that sits on the floor and plugs in the back of your amp. Its sole purpose in life is to alternate between two states — 1 and 2, A and B, on and off, and so on. A footswitch allows the guitarist to play with both hands on the guitar the entire time, and when the moment comes to switch seamlessly from dutiful backup drudge to distortion-diva superstar, she can step surreptitiously on a pedal and have her sound magically and instantly launch into hyperspace.

A footswitch has other uses besides hands-free channel switching. You can use a footswitch to turn your effects on and off. Or you can try to step on two footswitches at once, to turn on the effects *and* to change channels. This sometimes poses a problem because you have to twist your foot sideways so your toe and heel can simultaneously press two switches at once. Miscalculation of this move may leave audience members wondering, "Why did that knock-kneed guitarist suddenly fall over just before the guitar solo?"

Book III

Rock Guitar

Making Do If You Don't Have an Amp

Certainly a guitar amp is an important thing to have. But sometimes you simply have to choose between getting a really good guitar now and waiting for an amp, or spending the same money for two pieces — and comprising on the quality of both.

For those who have faced this cosmic struggle, know that you have alternate means of amplification available to you that won't cost nearly as much as a quality amplifier. You may even have the technology right now and not even realize it. (Cue mysterious organ music.)

Plugging into a home stereo or boombox

You can get away without buying an amp at all, if you plug your electric guitar into the auxiliary input of your home stereo. All you need is a special, inexpensive adapter. You can readily purchase these devices at electronic or music stores for less than $5. (Just tell the salesperson what you want to do, and he can supply the correct unit.) The adapter is just a metal or plastic-coated plug that has a female $\frac{1}{4}$-inch jack on one end and a male RCA (sometimes called *phono*) plug on the other. Many boomboxes have inputs as well, but use a $\frac{1}{8}$-inch connection, so for one of these you need a female $\frac{1}{4}$-inch jack on one end and a male $\frac{1}{8}$-inch stereo plug on the other. Make sure, if you buy your adapter at a place other than a music store, that the adapter's female end is mono; that's the end you plug your guitar cord into.

Before you go plugging anything in to a stereo or boombox, make sure the volume control on the receiver is all the way down. This precaution prevents any sudden pop or surge in the system, which can potentially damage the speakers.

Because you plug into, say, the left input of your receiver, you hear music only out of the left speaker. This is normal. Some higher-end receivers enable you to set the *output mode* (the stereo configuration) of the source signal. If you see a bunch of settings such as L, R, L+R, and so on, set that knob to L (which routes the left channel to both speakers). The resultant sound is not stereo, but it sounds fuller and more widely dispersed than if your guitar comes out of only one speaker. And hey, it's better than a converted toaster oven any day!

Figure 2-11 shows how to plug into the back of your receiver. Plug one end of the guitar cord into your guitar and the other end into the adapter. Check to see that the receiver's volume is down. Plug the adapter into the left auxiliary input in the back of your receiver. On the receiver's front panel, select "Aux 1" or whatever is the corresponding name of the input into which you plugged your guitar. (It may be called "Tape 1" or some other name — check the input itself or your owner's manual if in doubt.) Turn your guitar's volume up full. Then slowly turn up the receiver's volume knob until you hear sound at a comfortable listening level. You can adjust the receiver's tone controls to better shape your sound as well.

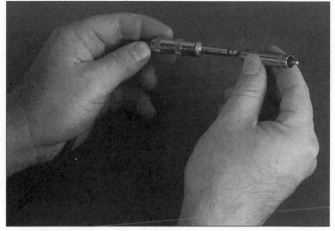

Figure 2-11:
An adapter allows you to use your stereo or boombox as an amp.

Book III

Rock Guitar

Headphone amps

Because of the miniaturization of all things electronic, you can now get full-sounding, authentic guitar sounds from a unit the size of a disposable camera — as long as you listen to it through headphones (meaning that it has no speaker or power amp of its own). These strap-on wonders are battery powered for untethered practicing (great for walking into the bathroom and standing in front of the mirror to check your stage moves). And virtually all headphone amps offer distortion, EQ, reverb, and other digital effects, many of them simultaneously. So a headphone amp can usually double as a multi-effects processor, which is quite cool.

Headphone amps also provide numerous *presets* — sounds preprogrammed, or set up, by the manufacturer, plus full stereo sound (especially effective over headphones). Headphone amps are great for playing in a moving vehicle, at the beach, in a hotel room, or in the airport lounge, and they can even output the signal to tape or disk, suitable for recording. The cost starts from about $200 (the Korg Pandora, Scholz Rockman, Ibanez Rock 'n' Play, and Zoom 9000 series are just some makes and models) and are well worth the price if portability, privacy, and authentic tone are important for your practice routine. Figure 2-12 shows a headphone amp for guitar.

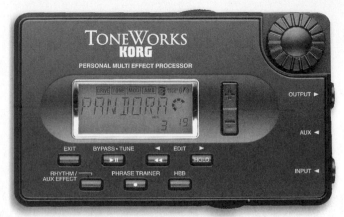

Figure 2-12:
The Korg
Pandora
PX-3
features
several
types of dis-
tortion, EQ,
and effects.

Demystifying the Gizmology

Amp functions and their controls may seem daunting at first, but if you just remember to break them down to their basic sections, you'll have a much better time dealing with them. When you shop for an amp and are faced with myriad choices, remember that the rows of dials, knobs, and switches all have common purposes among models. Occasionally, you see something unique to that manufacturer or model, but if you come prepared in the basics, you should have an easier time recognizing what that feature is and to what section it belongs.

Above all, don't let the number of knobs intimidate or impress you. The important thing about an amp is how it sounds — and more specifically, how it sounds to you when you play your guitar through it. Some of the best amps in the world have very few knobs and look rather low tech.

So make sure you check out an amp the way you would a guitar — by listening to it as well as playing through it, and developing a rapport and feel for the vibe it produces.

Chapter 3

Playing Lead

. . . .

In This Chapter

▶ Mastering scales, arpeggios, and lead patterns

▶ Reading notation

▶ Practicing riffs

▶ Improvising good solos

. . . .

Lead guitar is without a doubt the most spectacular and dazzling feature of rock guitar playing. Lead guitar can embody emotions that run the gamut from mournful and soulful to screaming, frenzied abandon — sometimes in the same solo. Whereas *riffs* are grounded, composed, and can manifest their power through their unflinching solidity, lead is beckoned by the music to launch into divinely inspired flights of fancy — to be forever soaring.

The greatest lead rock guitarists, from Eric Clapton and Jimi Hendrix to Eddie Van Halen and Steve Vai, have all been able to soar, but they have also all been disciplined masters of their instruments. They have resolved the ultimate artistic paradox: total freedom through total control.

Left-hand movement and precise single-string picking are the focus in this chapter. As you begin developing the basic technique for playing lead, never forget that your playing possesses the potential for evoking enormous emotional power. And kick over a few amplifiers while you're at it too!

Taking the Lead

You must play many before you can play one, Grasshopper.

This saying of unknown but vaguely Eastern origin certainly applies to rock guitar playing, because you need to learn to play *chords* (note groupings of at least three notes) before you can learn single notes — the stuff of leads.

Actually, you don't *have* to learn chords before lead, but in rock guitar it's a good idea, at least from a technical standpoint, because when playing rhythm you don't have to be as precise with your right-hand motions. Most beginning guitarists find striking multiple strings easier than plucking individual ones. (You can find the basics of rhythm techniques in Chapter 4 in Book II.)

Now, however, the time has come to venture into the world of single-note playing, where you pick only one string at a time, and which string you play is critical. Single-note playing also involves a lot more movement from the left hand.

Single-note takes on a number of different musical forms. Four of the most important ones for playing rock include the following:

- **Melody:** A major component of single-note playing on the guitar is melody. *Melody* can be the composed tune of the song played instrumentally, or it can be an improvised break or solo, using the melody as the point of departure.

- **Arpeggio:** An *arpeggio* is playing a chord one note at a time, so, by definition, it's a single-note technique. You can use arpeggios as an accompaniment figure (as you do in the fingerstyle example in Chapter 4 in Book II) or as lead material, as many hard rock and heavy metal guitarists, such as Eddie Van Halen and Randy Rhoads, have done. Lead guitarists burn up many a measure just by playing arpeggios in their lead breaks, and the results can be thrilling.

- **Riff:** A *riff* is a self-contained musical phrase, usually composed of single notes and used as a structural component of a song or song section. A riff straddles the line between melody and rhythm guitar because it contains elements of both. A riff is typically repeated and serves as a backing figure for a song section.

  Think of the signature riffs to the Beatles' "Day Tripper" and "Birthday," the Rolling Stones' "Satisfaction," Aerosmith's "Walk This Way," Cream's "Sunshine of Your Love," Led Zeppelin's "Whole Lotta Love" and "Black Dog," Ozzy Osbourne's "Crazy Train," and Bon Jovi's "You Give Love a Bad Name." These are all songs based on highly identifiable and memorable riffs.

  Riffs aren't always composed of just single notes. Deep Purple's "Smoke on the Water" and Black Sabbath's "Iron Man" are actually composed of multiple-sounding notes moving in unison. And two or more guitars can play riffs in harmony too. The Allman Brothers and the Eagles are famous for this.

- **Free improvisation:** This isn't a recognized technical term, but you can think of *free improvisation* as lead material not necessarily derived from the melody. It doesn't even have to be melodic in nature. Wide interval skips, percussive playing, effects used as music, and melodic note sequences (such as patterns of fast repeated notes, or even one note) can all contribute to an exciting lead guitar solo or passage.

The yin and yang of rhythm and lead

If a band has two guitarists, a logical division of duties is to have one guitarist play rhythm and the other play lead. Often, the better guitarist is the lead guitarist. Sometimes, though, you divide the duties not necessarily for reasons of musical talent, but because the rhythm guitarist is the principal songwriter (as in the case of Tom Petty and Metallica). In many bands with two guitarists, the divisions of lead and rhythm are not clearly defined, as with Lynyrd Skynyrd, the Allman Brothers, and Judas Priest. In the following list, however, the duties between lead and rhythm are (or were) clearly separated.

Group	Rhythm	Lead
The Beatles	John Lennon	George Harrison
The Rolling Stones	Keith Richards	Brian Jones/Mick Taylor/ Ron Wood
The Kinks	Ray Davies	Dave Davies
The Grateful Dead	Bob Weir	Jerry Garcia
AC/DC	Malcolm Young	Angus Young
Creedence Clearwater Revival	Tom Fogerty	John Fogerty
Aerosmith	Brad Whitford	Joe Perry
Kiss	Paul Stanley	Ace Frehley
Tom Petty and the Heartbreakers	Tom Petty	Mike Campbell
The Cars	Ric Ocasek	Elliot Easton
The Clash	Joe Strummer	Mick Jones
Def Leppard	Steve Clark	Phil Collen
Bruce Springsteen and the E Street Band	Bruce Springsteen	Nils Lofgren
Metallica	James Hetfield	Kirk Hammett
Guns N' Roses	Izzy Stradlin	Slash

Book III

Rock Guitar

The terms *lead, melody, single line, riff, solo,* and *improv* are all types of single-note playing and are often used interchangeably. The phrase *single-note playing* is a little cumbersome, so you can refer to any playing that is not rhythm playing as lead playing, even if it's to indicate playing a riff.

Strictly speaking, lead playing is the *featured* guitar, which is usually playing a single-note-based line. But it doesn't always have to be playing only single notes; it could be playing *double-stops,* which are two notes played together (they're introduced in Chapter 5 in Book II). Also, the designation *lead guitar* helps to distinguish that guitar from the other guitar(s) in the band that are playing rhythm guitar.

Sometimes the featured guitar can consist of a strummed chordal figure. The guitar break in Buddy Holly's "Peggy Sue" and the opening riff to the Who's "Pinball Wizard" are two standout examples of the rhythm guitar taking a featured role.

Holding the pick

You don't need to hold the pick any differently for lead playing than you do for rhythm playing. Have the tip of the pick extending perpendicularly from the side of your thumb and bring your hand close to the individual string you want to play. You may find yourself sometimes gripping the pick a little more firmly, especially when you dig in to play loudly or aggressively. This is fine. In time, the pick becomes almost like a natural extension of one of your fingers.

Attacking the problem

The sounding or striking of a note, in musical terms, is called an *attack*. It doesn't necessarily mean you have to do it aggressively; it's just a term that differentiates the beginning of the note from the *sustain* part (the part that rings, after the percussive sound).

To attack an individual string, position the pick so it touches or is slightly above the string's upper side (the side toward the ceiling) and bring it through with a quick, smooth motion. Use just enough force to clear the string, but not enough to sound the next string down. This motion is known as a downstroke, which is just like the downstroke discussed in Chapter 4 in Book II, except that here you strike only one string. To play an upstroke, simply reverse the motion.

The ups and downs of lead playing

Striking a string with a downward motion is called a *downstroke* and is indicated by the symbol ⊓. Striking the string by bringing the hand up is called an *upstroke* and is indicated by the symbol ∨. In rock guitar, rhythm guitarists tend to favor downstrokes. Downstrokes are more forceful and are generally used to accentuate notes to play even, deliberate rhythms. Alternating downstrokes and upstrokes is called *alternate picking* (covered later in this chapter) and is essential for playing lead guitar.

Playing Single Notes

Playing chords involves a lot of arm and wrist movement. Single-note playing requires much less arm movement, because most of the energy comes from the wrist. You may be tempted to anchor the heel of your right hand on the bridge, which is okay as long as you don't unintentionally dampen the strings in the process.

As you move from playing notes on the lower strings to notes on the higher strings, your right-hand heel will naturally want to adjust itself and slide along the bridge. Of course, you don't *have* to anchor your hand on the strings at all, either; you can just let your hand float in the area above the bridge.

Even when you play loud and aggressively, your right-hand movements should remain fairly controlled and contained. When you see your favorite rock stars on stage flailing away, arms wildly windmilling in circular motions of large diameters, that's rhythm playing, not single-note playing.

In the following sections, you start out with some easy exercises for learning to play single notes on the guitar and then move to things that actually sound cool and are fun to play.

Book III

Rock Guitar

Single-note technique

Using all downstrokes, play the music in Figure 3-1. These are six passages, each on separate strings that require you to play three different notes. All the melodies are in quarter notes, which means the notes come one per beat (or one per foot tap if you're tapping along in tempo).

The trick here is to play single notes on individual strings accurately, without accidentally hitting the wrong string. You don't have to play any fancy rhythms or down- and upstroke combinations; you just have to hit the desired string cleanly. Obviously, it's harder to do that on the interior strings (2nd, 3rd, 4th, 5th) than on exterior ones (1st, 6th).

Each exercise is written in a different feel (as evidenced by the CD recording), but don't let that throw you. As long as you count out the quarter notes with the count-off on the CD (heard as the percussive click of the struck hi-hat cymbals, as a drummer would do when counting off a song) and focus on playing smooth, one-note-per-foot-tap notes, you should do fine.

Track 30, 0:00

Figure 3-1: Quarter-note melodies on each of the guitar's six strings in open position.

The next exercise is a bit harder, because it requires you to switch strings as you play. When you play the example in Figure 3-2, try to go between the strings smoothly, without breaking the rhythm, and without varying your *dynamics* (the intensity of your pick attack) as you switch strings.

Track 30, 1:12

Figure 3-2:
A quarter-note melody played across different strings.

As a guitarist, you not only have to focus on keeping the rhythm steady between bars, but also when switching strings.

Alternate picking in down- and upstrokes

You double the pace by introducing eighth notes into your playing. Keep in mind that in rhythm playing, you can often play eighth notes by just speeding up your downstroke picking. But in lead playing, you must always play eighth notes using the technique called *alternate picking*.

Alternate picking requires you to follow a simple rule: Downbeat notes are played with downstrokes; upbeat notes are played with upstrokes. Sounds mundanely simple, but in practice, maintaining this strict alternating pattern while crossing — and even skipping — strings can be difficult. Still, alternate picking works, even when it seems illogical, or at least inefficient, and virtually every guitarist on the planet who plays with any facility uses alternate picking.

The alternate-picking technique doesn't care whether you have to cross strings or not. In an eighth-note melody, the alternate-picking technique requires that the downbeat notes take downstrokes and the upbeat notes (the ones that fall in between the beats) take upstrokes — which should be easy to remember.

Book III

Rock Guitar

Scales

By definition, a *scale* proceeds in stepwise motion. Scales are the dreaded means of musical torture wielded by Dickensian disciplinarians (like your fourth-grade piano teacher), but they do serve a purpose. They're a great way to warm up your fingers within a recognizable structure, and they reveal available notes on the fingerboard within a key.

Plus, playing scales provides a familiar-sounding melody *(do re mi fa sol la ti do)* that yields a certain satisfaction upon correct execution — at least until you've done them two or three billion times and you can't stand it anymore. But for now, you're going to try an ascending, contiguously sequenced set of natural notes in the key of C beginning on the root (the 1st degree of the scale or chord) — a C major scale.

Playing in the majors

Figure 3-3 is a one-octave C major scale in eighth notes. Note that the pick-stroke indications are given for the first two beats, and then the term *sim.* (which is short for *simile,* or "in the same fashion") tells you to continue on in the same way.

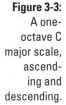

Figure 3-3: A one-octave C major scale, ascending and descending.

Left-hand fingerings are also provided in the standard music notation staff. The idea is not that you sight read all this stuff — the notes, the right- and left-hand indications, and so forth — but that you learn this C scale and play it whenever you feel like warming up. Or you can just play the scale when inspiration waits in the wing space of your mind, mute and mocking, and you can't think of anything else musically cohesive to play.

Now for another scale that's musically about the same, but in a different key, and somewhat harder to play. Figure 3-4 shows a two-octave G major scale, ascending and descending. What makes it harder is the left-hand fingering: You use all of your left-hand fingers for this scale, in a four-fret span.

Figure 3-4: A two-octave G major scale, ascending and descending.

Keep your left hand fairly stationary above the strings, and let your fingers stretch and reach for their correspondingly numbered fret (the first, or index, finger plays the 1st fret; the second, or middle, finger, plays the 2nd fret; and so forth). As your hand becomes more agile, your finger span will widen and you'll be able to reach the frets comfortably while keeping your left hand almost perfectly stationary.

A minor adjustment

Because you backed into scales by way of stepwise motion, you should get equal time with the major scale's gloomier cousin, the minor scale.

Actually the "family" analogy isn't that far off because minor scales are related to major scales. Every major scale has a corresponding minor scale, the *relative minor,* which you can play in its entirety using the same key signature. In any major key, the *natural minor scale* (so called because you can play it naturally, with no altering of the major-scale notes) begins at the 6th degree. (For more on all of this, see Chapter 3 in Book VII.)

So in the key of C, the 6th degree would be A (remember the musical alphabet only goes up to G), so Am is the relative minor of C major. Figure 3-5 is a minor scale, in eighth notes, starting on the open 5th string, A.

Figure 3-5:
A one-octave A minor scale.

Skips

Skips are melodic movements of noncontiguous letter names, such as A, C, E, G, B. Skips can be of any interval and don't have to follow the notes of a chord. So all arpeggios are skips (but not all skips are arpeggios). Figure 3-6 shows an Am7 arpeggio. The notes of the chord are played one after the other: A-C-E-G.

Figure 3-6:
An Am7 arpeggio.

Combining steps and skips

Most melodies are composed of a mix of stepwise motion and skips, and sometimes melodies can include an arpeggio (such as in the Army bugle calls "Taps" and "Reveille"). Scales, again, are a series of notes organized by key, where you play the notes in order, ascending and/or descending. Arpeggios can be skips in any order, but are limited to the notes of the chord.

Starting at the Bottom:
Low-Note Melodies

For some reason, all traditional guitar method books start with the guitar's top strings and work their way down to the low strings. But in the true rebellious spirit of both rock 'n' roll and the *For Dummies* series, this book starts at the bottom.

The reason for starting at the bottom is not just pure rebelliousness, either (although it certainly is fun to be contrary for its own sake!): It's because the impetus for so many of the world's greatest melodies, riffs, and rock rhythm figures have low-born origins (from a guitar perspective, anyway). Think of all the classic riffs already mentioned in this chapter — "Smoke on the Water," "Iron Man," "Day Tripper" — and how many of them are low-note riffs.

So in that spirit, try Figure 3-7, which is a low-note melody in the style of a classic-rock riff. Note how it almost revels in its own subterranean girth. Spinal Tap would be proud.

Track 31, 0:00

Figure 3-7:
A rocking low-note melody, exploiting the low strings of the guitar.

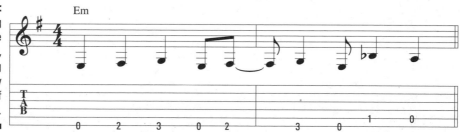

Figure 3-8 is another melody, nimbler than the one in Figure 3-7. This figure moves in steady eighth notes and features some unexpected changes in direction. It also contains a series of melodic skips, which in this case is an arpeggio because it outlines the notes of an A minor chord.

Track 31, 0:11

Figure 3-8:
A low-note melody in moving eighth notes.

Book III

Rock Guitar

Going to the Top: High-Note Melodies

Lead playing typically exploits the upper registers of the guitar, where melodic material is most naturally situated. Before you get really high up on the neck, play the melodic example in Figure 3-9 to hear the ability of the guitar's upper registers to cut through the rhythm section's din.

Track 31, 0:26

Figure 3-9:
A high-note
melody
in open
position.

If your guitar sounds twangy instead of smooth and creamy, try increasing the distortion factor of your sound. See Chapter 2 in Book III for information on how to dial up a more distorted sound if necessary.

Playing in Position

So far you've played all of your melodies and exercises in the lower regions of the neck, between the 1st and 4th frets. This is where it's easiest to place the notes that you see written on paper onto frets of the guitar neck.

But the guitar has many more frets on the neck than just the first four. Playing in the lowest regions of the neck is where you play most of your low-note riffs, a lot of chords, and some lead work, but the bulk of your lead playing takes place in the upper regions of the neck for two reasons:

✔ The higher on the neck you are, the higher the notes you can hit. The guitar is sort of a low instrument — in fact, the notes you read on the treble clef are actually an octave higher than the notes of the guitar. For this reason, it's a good idea to get as far up the neck as possible if you want to distinguish yourself melodically above the low-end rumble of basses, drums — and, of course, other guitars playing rhythm in the lower range.

✔ Up the neck the strings are more flexible and easily manipulated by the left hand, which means you have better expressive opportunities for bends, vibrato, hammer-ons, pull-offs, slides, and other expressive devices.

Open position

Playing in open position is where you've spent your time thus far, but by *design*. When you have complete command of the entire neck and you can play anywhere you can find the note, playing in open position will be a *choice*. In other words, ultimately you should play in open position only because you want to, because it suits your musical purpose.

Rock guitar uses both open position and the upper positions (the positions' names are defined by where the left-hand index finger falls) for the different musical colorings they offer. By contrast, jazz guitar tends to avoid open position completely, and folk guitar uses open position exclusively. But rock uses both, and so you need to understand the strengths offered by both open position and the upper positions.

Remember the G scale of Figure 3-4? That's an open position G scale because it uses the open strings of the guitar. Now it's time to explore playing the same exact notes in the same exact rhythm another way.

Book III

Rock Guitar

Movable, or closed, position

Playing in a *movable position* allows you to take a passage of music and play it anywhere on the neck. If you play a melody on all fretted strings (incorporating no open strings), it doesn't matter if you play it at the 1st fret or the 15th. The notes will preserve the same melodic relationship. It's sort of like swimming: After you learn the technique of keeping yourself afloat and moving, it doesn't matter if the water is 5 feet or 5 miles deep — except if you're in 5-mile deep water, it's probably a lot colder.

A movable position is sometimes called *closed position,* because it involves no open strings. After you play anything on all-fretted strings, you have created a great opportunity to slide it anywhere on the neck and have it play exactly the same — except of course that you're apt to find yourself in another key. This has equally profound implications for chords, as you find out in Chapter 3 in Book II in the sections on movable chords and barre chords.

The best part is the ability to move closed-position melodies around — instantly transposing their key — which is something that no piano player, trumpet player, or flute player can do easily, and they'll be eternally jealous of you.

To demonstrate a movable position, first take your two-octave G major scale and play exactly the same pitches, but place them on all fretted strings. Figure 3-10 is, then, a two-octave G major scale in 2nd position. It's 2nd position because the lowest fret played defines the position's name, and here it's the 2nd fret.

Figure 3-10: A two-octave G major scale in 2nd position.

After you master Figure 3-10, try sliding your hand up and down the neck, playing the scale in different positions. By doing this you'll *transpose* your G major scale into other keys.

Getting in Tune with Lower Register Riffs

The example on low-note melodies earlier in this chapter tackles the topic of riffs, but now you should take a look at them in earnest — not because they help illustrate alternate picking or string-crossing strings, but for their own sake. Finally, you're making music to make music!

The best thing about the lower register of the guitar is its powerful bass notes. You simply have no better arsenal for grinding out earth-shattering, filling-rattling, brain-splattering tones than the lower register of the guitar, so this is where 99 percent of all the greatest riffs are written.

Start off with a classic riff in quarter notes, called, variously, *boogie-woogie,* *boogie,* or *walking bass.* Figure 3-11 is a classic boogie figure using only the notes of the chord, plus one, the 6th degree, in a fixed pattern for each chord. But notice that its repetition is its strength. Your ears want to hear the same pattern for each of the chords, so infectious is the sound!

Track 32

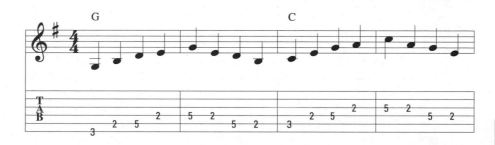

Figure 3-11: A classic walking bass/ boogie-woogie riff in G.

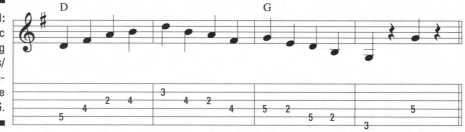

Making It Easy: The Pentatonic Scale

The major and minor scales may be music-education stalwarts, but as melodic material they sound, well, academic when used over chord progressions. Rock guitarists have a much better scale to supply them with melodic fodder: the pentatonic scale. The *pentatonic scale* isn't the only scale available for playing rock lead, but it's the most widely used and easiest to learn. The beauty of this scale is that it sounds great over every chord change in a key, and you can begin to make music with it almost immediately.

As its name implies, the pentatonic scale contains five notes, which is two notes shy of the normal seven-note major and minor scales. This creates a more open and less linear sound than either the major or minor scale. The pentatonic scale is also more ambiguous, but this is a good thing, because it means that it's harder to play *bad* notes — notes that, although they're within the key, may not fit well against any given chord in the progression. The pentatonic scale uses just the most universal note choices.

The importance of the pentatonic scale can't be emphasized enough. It ranks with anesthesia, the printing press, and the cordless screwdriver as indispensable to modern civilization.

The first scale you should learn is the A minor pentatonic. A minor pentatonic can be used as a lead scale over chord progressions in A minor, C major, and A blues ("blues" can imply a specific, six-note scale, as well as a chord progression). It also works pretty well over A major and C blues. Not bad for a scale that's two notes shy of a major scale.

Figure 3-12 is a neck diagram outlining a pentatonic scale form in 5th position. The neck is positioned as if you're facing a guitar that is laid on its side, with the neck to your left. So it looks like tablature in the sense that the first string is on top, but it's a schematic of the actual neck instead of the tab staff. On Track 33 on the CD, it's played from top (1st string, 8th fret) to bottom (6th string, 5th fret) in quarter notes. Try playing it, and don't worry about playing along in rhythm with the CD; the track is just there so you can make sure you're in the right position hitting the right notes.

Track 33

Figure 3-12: The pentatonic scale in 5th position.

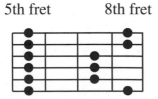

5th fret   8th fret

In the neck diagram, just like in a tab staff, the 1st string is the top line. This isn't a chord, but all the available notes for the pentatonic scale. The left-hand index finger plays all the notes on the 5th fret; the ring finger plays all the 7th-fret notes; and the little finger plays all the 8th-fret notes. In this particular scale pattern, the middle finger doesn't play at all.

Playing the Pentatonic Scale: Three Ways to Solo

In the following sections you learn to play one pentatonic scale pattern in three different musical contexts:

- ✔ A progression in a major key
- ✔ A progression in a minor key
- ✔ A blues progression

You can use just one pattern to satisfy all three musical settings. This is an unbelievable stroke of luck for beginning guitarists, and you can apply a shortcut, a quick mental calculation, that allows you to instantly wail away in a major-key song, a minor-key song, or a blues song — simply by performing what is essentially a musical parlor trick. This is a great quick-fix solution to get you playing decent-sounding music virtually instantly. As you get more into the music, however, you'll want to know why these notes are working the way they do. But until then, let's jam!

Place your index finger on the 5th fret, 1st string. Relax your hand so your other fingers naturally drape over the neck, hovering above the 6th, 7th, and 8th frets. You are now in 5th position, ready to play. Work to play each note singly, from top to bottom, so you get your fingers used to playing the frets and switching strings. Don't worry about playing downstrokes and upstrokes until you're comfortable moving your left-hand fingers up and down the strings, like a spider walking across its web.

Now try Figure 3-13, a descending scale in C pentatonic major in eighth notes, beginning with your left-hand little finger on the 1st string, 8th fret.

Book III

Rock Guitar

Track 34, 0:00

Figure 3-13:
A descending eighth-note C pentatonic major scale.

This particular pentatonic pattern allows you to keep your left hand stationary; all the fingers can reach their respective fret easily without stretching or requiring left-hand movement.

Now that you've played the scale, try it in a musical context. This is where you witness the magic that transpires when you play the same notes over different feels in different keys. Let the games begin!

Pentatonics over a major key

Figure 3-14 is a C major progression in a medium-tempo 4/4 groove. The written solo is a mix of quarter notes and eighth notes comprised of notes from the C major pentatonic scale, moving up and down the neck. The left channel of your CD has the rhythm instruments, and the right features the lead guitar. As soon as you get the idea about how the lead sounds, dial it out and try to play the melody against the recorded rhythm sound by yourself. Then check your work by dialing back in the right channel and see how close you got.

Pentatonics over a minor key

And now, as Monty Python once said, for something completely different. Or is it? In Figure 3-15, the feel changes (to a heavy back-beat 4/4), the key changes (to A minor), but you still play the same notes. Notice the strikingly different results.

Figure 3-14: Solo in C major over a medium-tempo 4/4.

Figure 3-15: An A minor solo over a heavy back-beat 4/4.

Book III

Rock Guitar

Pentatonics over a blues progression

And here is yet another groove that works with the same scale. Figure 3-16 is an up-tempo blues shuffle in A. Note that the eighth notes in this example *swing* — they're to be played in a long-short scheme. Make it cry.

Figure 3-16:
An A blues
solo over an
up-tempo
shuffle.

Improvising Leads

In rock, jazz, and blues, improvisation plays a great role. In fact, being a good improviser is much more important than being a good technician. It's much more important to create honest, credible, and inspired music through improvisation than it is to play with technical accuracy and perfection.

The best musicians in the world are the best improvisers, but they're not necessarily the best practitioners of the instrument. About the only thing that competes with the ability to improvise a good solo is the ability to write a song.

And so the last exercise in this chapter is devoted to improvising — where you take a collection of notes and turn it into music. To do this, use the 5th-position pentatonic scale you learned earlier in this chapter. Figure 3-17 is a slow, gutbucket blues shuffle in A. Don't forget to swing those eighth notes and remember the blues credo: You don't have to feel bad to play the blues . . . but it helps.

Track 35

Book III

Rock
Guitar

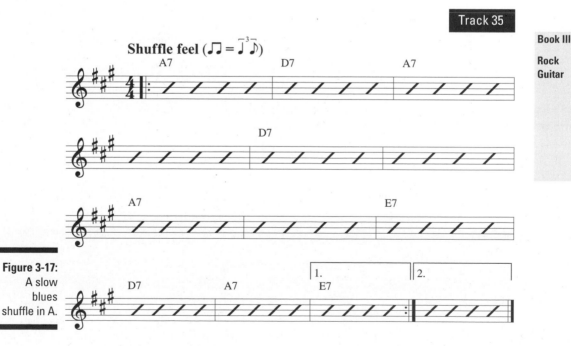

Figure 3-17:
A slow
blues
shuffle in A.

Improvising is, at the same time, one of the easiest things to do (just find your notes and go) and one of the hardest (try to make up a meaningful melody on the spot). The more note choices you have, the more vocabulary you'll be able to pull from to express your message.

Practice to get your fingers working smoothly through the notes up and down the neck. Try to surprise yourself by changing direction, skipping strings, and even repeating notes for dramatic effect. Some of the highest musical moments of your improvising career will be the results of something completely unintentional — a happy accident. But to have such "musical mishaps," you must put yourself in harm's way. Be bold, be daring, take chances, improvise.

The pentatonic scale is a great way to start making music immediately, but plenty of other scales exist to help you in your music making. And you still have to listen to other guitarists for ideas. Go outside any scale you use to get unusual notes, and learn passages of classic solos on recordings to see what makes them tick. Above all, you must develop your own sense of phrasing and your own voice.

Chapter 4

Groovin' on Riffs

- -

In This Chapter

▶ Working out with basic riffs

▶ Doing double-time with double-stops

▶ Combining riffs and chords

▶ Playing rhythm figures

- -

*R*iffs are often the most memorable component of a rock 'n' roll song and can form the perfect bridge between a chord progression and a melodic lead phrase. Although technically a short, self-contained musical phrase, a *riff* is much, much more than that. A riff sticks in your head long after you forget the lyrics — and even the melody — and at a noisy party, it is the riff that makes a song instantly recognizable when you can't quite make out the rest of the music. In many cases, the riff is the backbone of the song, its *raison d'être* (a fancy French term for mojo), and the rhythm, melody, and chords are all derived from the riff.

In this chapter, you venture deep into riff territory to see where rock 'n' roll *lives* and discover why riffs themselves are such a vital and inextricable component of rock 'n' roll. (Hey, where do you think the phrase "a riff-roarin' good time" came from?) This chapter also briefly looks at two other rock staples, the *power chord* and the *double-stop*. Power chords are actually easier to play than the open-position chords covered in Chapter 3 in Book II, and a *whole* lot easier than the dreaded barre chords also discussed in that chapter. (Oh, barre chords aren't *that* bad, really — at least for us electric guitarists.)

Then, just when you think having any more fun in this chapter couldn't possibly be legal, you find out how to combine riffs, power chords, and double-stops into full-blown, fully realized rhythm figures. *Rhythm figures* embody the total approach to rhythm guitar, and virtually any strumming or single-note technique you can come up with can be pressed into rhythm-guitar service and incorporated into a rhythm figure. And although lead guitar may be the brain surgery of the rock world — the glamorous specialty skill — rhythm guitar is the daily exercise and good living that keeps you healthy and prospering.

Getting Your Groove On: Basic Riffs

This chapter starts off with riffs that exploit the lower register of the guitar. Make sure you strike only one string at a time, but that your pick strokes carry the same confidence and power that they have when playing chords. Even if the riffs sound familiar, make sure you execute the rhythms and articulations precisely as written; don't let your ears allow you to gloss over the tricky parts.

Half- and whole-note riffs

A riff doesn't have to be flashy to be memorable. Figure 4-1, in the style of the band Black Sabbath, uses only half notes and whole notes to create an eerie, menacing effect.

Track 36, 0:00

Figure 4-1:
A powerful-
sounding riff
using only
half notes
and whole
notes.

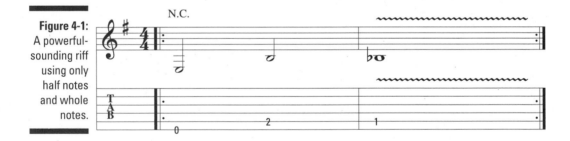

You can give fretted notes with long values (half notes and whole notes) more life by applying left-hand *vibrato* to them. Gently pull and release the string (causing it to bend slightly) very rapidly, causing the note to waver. Vibrato helps give slower notes more intensity. A wavy line placed above the note (〰) tells you to apply vibrato.

Eighth- and quarter-note riffs

Other than slow riffs created from half notes and whole notes, the simplest riffs to play are formed from the straightforward, nonsyncopated rhythmic units of quarter notes and eighth notes. Figures 4-2 and 4-3 are riffs that mix quarter notes and eighth notes. Be sure to observe the pick-stroke indications for downstrokes and upstrokes (⊓ and V, respectively).

Track 36, 0:11

Figure 4-2: A riff comprised of mostly quarter notes, with one eighth-note pair.

Track 36, 0:19

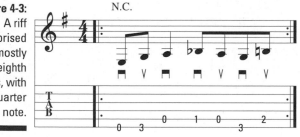

Figure 4-3: A riff comprised of mostly eighth notes, with one quarter note.

Book III

Rock
Guitar

Note the presence of F♯ in the key signature of Figures 4-2 and 4-3. This means that all Fs are sharped, and that the key is either G major or E minor. So even though these two riffs don't contain any Fs, we can see that the examples are in E minor, because the riffs gravitate to and around the root note, E.

Now try the boogie riff in Figure 4-4 (an expansion of the boogie riffs presented in Chapter 3 in Book III), which is comprised of mostly quarter notes, but with a couple of shuffle eighth notes thrown in to give the groove an extra kick. The tempo is fairly bright here, so watch that you execute the long-short rhythm of the shuffle eighth notes correctly.

Track 36, 0:27

Figure 4-4: A boogie shuffle in quarter notes, with eighth notes thrown in.

Riffs that consist of all eighth notes create a sense of continuous motion and can really help propel a song along. Figure 4-5 is in all eighth notes, and notice how easily the end of the measure leads into the beginning of the second measure, creating a seamless sound. Note too the presence of the B♭ and D♯ — two *chromatic,* or out of key, notes in E minor.

Track 36, 0:37

Figure 4-5: A steady-eighth-note riff in E minor.

While Figure 4-5 is a simple one-bar riff that repeats over and over, Figure 4-6 is a longer, steady eighth-note phrase that goes for two measures before repeating.

Because riffs are short and self-contained, they can be easily *looped,* or repeated back to back with no break. All the riffs in this chapter can be played seamlessly, and you're encouraged to play multiple repetitions until you execute the notes flawlessly — both from a technical standpoint (no missed or *fluffed* notes, no buzzing) as well as a rhythmic one. Pay particular attention when *rounding the corner* (going from the end of the riff back to the beginning). The barrier preventing a smooth transition can be more psychological than technical.

Track 36, 0:45

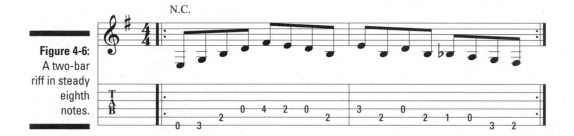

Figure 4-6:
A two-bar riff in steady eighth notes.

It's one thing to maintain a steady, consistent delivery for two bars. It's quite another to stay solid over bars upon bars or minutes upon minutes of playing the same riff within a groove. So repeat the riffs in this chapter in a loop fashion; that is, play them numerous times until you're sure you've got the long-term as well as the short-term consistency considerations under control. Or at least repeat the riffs until you can't stand it anymore. Either way, it's good training for playing with any band claiming the Allman Brothers, the Grateful Dead, or Phish as an influence.

16th-note riffs

A 16th-note riff doesn't have to be fast or syncopated (for more on syncopation, see Chapter 4 in Book II) just because it contains 16th notes. Figure 4-7 is a riff that builds up speed by going first through quarter notes, then eighth notes, then 16ths. Does this riff sound familiar?

Track 36, 0:57

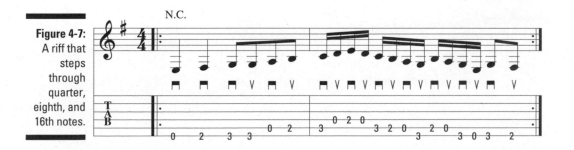

Figure 4-7:
A riff that steps through quarter, eighth, and 16th notes.

Book III

Rock Guitar

Many hard rock and heavy metal riffs are based in 16th notes, including the infamous "gallop" pattern. Figure 4-8 is a gallop riff that takes you on a wild ride. Buckle up — or should that be saddle up?

Track 36, 1:12

Figure 4-8: A heavy metal gallop in eighth and 16th notes.

Then again, sometimes a riff written in 16th notes really is just plain dog-gone fast, such as the hard-rock groove in Figure 4-9. Be sure to observe the alternate-picking indications in this example.

Track 36, 1:23

Figure 4-9: A fast 16th-note-based riff in a hard rock style.

Eighth-note syncopation

Technically, playing a syncopated riff is no harder than playing a nonsyncopated riff; it's just trickier to read in printed music. The more experience you have with syncopation, the more you can learn to recognize typical syncopation patterns. So you don't have to count your brains out with every dot and tie that appears, you can use your memory to help you. Syncopation is not intentionally designed to trip you up (although it may seem like that at first); it's there to put a kick into the music. Learn a few patterns and combinations, and you'll start to recognize them when they reappear. Memorizing a vocabulary of pre-existing syncopation patterns helps so you don't have to reinvent the wheel every time you encounter a syncopated rhythm.

A great example of eighth-note syncopation occurs in the first line of the Beatles song "Eleanor Rigby." If you tap your hand or foot in time and sing, or say in rhythm, the words "Eleanor Rigby picks up the rice in the church where a wedding has been," you notice that the words "Rigby," "rice," "church," "wedding," and "been" all fall on the offbeat.

Figure 4-10 is a steady eighth-note figure where only the last eighth note in the bar is syncopated — here, through the use of a tie that binds it to the first note of the next measure. This particular syncopation device is called an *anticipation,* because it anticipates the downbeat, or first — and strongest — beat, of the measure. In fact, an anticipation is such a common and cool-sounding syncopation device that often players will introduce it, even when it's not written into the music. It's one of those rock 'n' roll situations where something can be justified simply because "it's a feel thing."

Track 36, 1:33

Figure 4-10: Beat 1 is tied over from beat four-and-a-half.

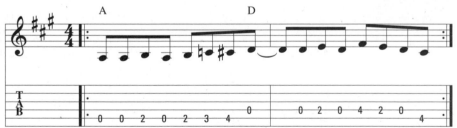

Now, double your syncopation efforts and put anticipations before beat 3 (the beginning of the second half of the bar) as well as beat 1, in Figure 4-11.

The melody to the Beatles' "Eleanor Rigby" is highly syncopated. In the same scheme as used in Figure 4-11, beats 1 and 3 are anticipated throughout the verse section.

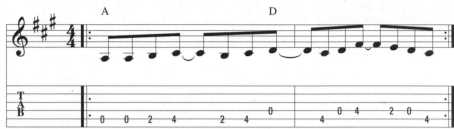

Figure 4-11: An eighth-note riff with anticipations on beats 1 and 3.

Track 36, 1:46

Finally, Figure 4-12 is an ultra-syncopated figure where none of the notes in bar 2 fall on the beat; they all fall in between. The band Deep Purple wrote the riff to their classic hit, "Smoke on the Water," using a similar syncopation scheme.

Track 36, 1:58

Figure 4-12: A highly syncopated eighth-note riff.

Playing Two Notes Can Be Better than One: Double-Stops

Stuck in a categorical netherworld between single notes and power chords is the two-note phenomenon known as the double-stop. A *double-stop* is simply two notes played simultaneously — on adjacent strings or separated by one to four (the maximum) strings in between.

Because it's obviously not a single note, and because a chord requires at least three notes, the double-stop wanders between the two camps like some musical double agent — sometimes masquerading as a chord, sometimes exhibiting single-note properties. As such, it's a tremendously useful tool in rhythm guitar playing. Because of its facile properties, you can use it for lead playing, too (which is covered in Chapter 3 in Book III).

Right now, though, you're going to employ double-stops in a rhythm context. A two-note power chord is technically a double-stop, because it's two strings played together. But conceptually, guitarists don't really think of power chords as double-stops. Figure 4-13 is more of a true double-stop, especially in its usage here. Note how its movement — between the fretted and open strings — is much easier to execute and less clunky than, say, switching between two chords (such as A and G) in the same tempo. Yet the double-stop movement still retains a chord-like sound and feel.

Track 37, 0:00

Figure 4-13:
A moving double-stop figure, used as a chordal device.

Book III

Rock Guitar

Note that you've crept up, register-wise on the guitar. You're now not playing just low notes, but have moved to the midrange of open position.

Figure 4-14 is a chord progression based on A, D, and E minor, but the ascending double-stop movement lends a nice melodic, quasi-single-line feel to the passage. In this case, the double-stops aren't on adjacent strings, as in Figure 4-13. Here, they have a string separating them (the open 3rd string, G), so you have to "pinch" the 2nd and 4th strings with your right-hand middle finger, or, if you want to employ a little fingerstyle action, the middle or index finger and thumb.

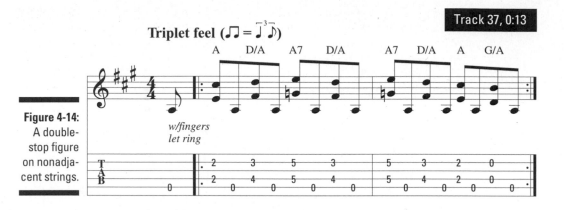

Track 37, 0:13

Figure 4-14:
A double-
stop figure
on nonadja-
cent strings.

If you accidentally let the middle string (the open G) ring while playing Figure 4-14, you notice it doesn't sound half bad. So try playing the open G string intentionally, either by plucking all three strings, or by strumming the three interior strings (4th, 3rd, and 2nd) with your pick. The unchanging bass note (the open A string) sounded against changing ones (in this case the ascending double-stops) is called a *pedal tone,* or just a *pedal,* in music. Usually a pedal is the bass note, less often it's the highest note, but sometimes it's in the middle.

Combining Single-Note Riffs and Chords

Whereas lead guitar is a studied craft with an established orthodoxy (that is, you can buy books on the subject), rhythm guitar is a universe without many rules. No one can say for sure what makes up a good rhythm guitar part, but you sure know one when you hear it. The best rhythm players in rock — such as Pete Townshend, U2's The Edge, Andy Summers, Peter Buck, Neil Young, and Keith Richards, just to name a few — all play in styles that are hard to label or analyze. But part of that indefinable magic comes from the fact that these guitarists don't limit themselves to just chords when playing rhythm guitar. They mix a healthy dose of single notes into their playing.

Although he was known for his fiery leads and stage antics (such as playing with his teeth and lighting his guitar on fire), Jimi Hendrix was a superb rhythm player. In his ballads, notably "Little Wing" and "The Wind Cries Mary," Hendrix plays lovely Curtis Mayfield–inspired R&B chords that sound like a cross between gospel, country, and piano figures. Hendrix also played his share of double-stops, too.

Figure 4-15 is a hard rock progression that mixes power chords, open position chords, and single notes into one cohesive part. Note how it builds up dramatic power by starting slow and becoming increasingly active.

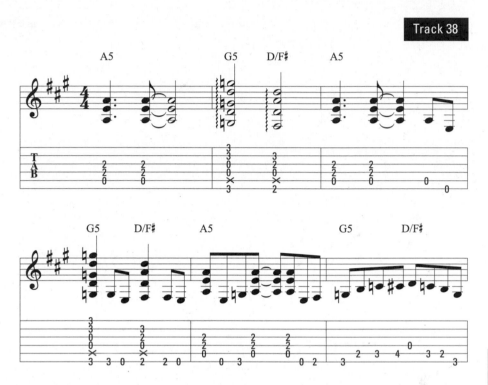

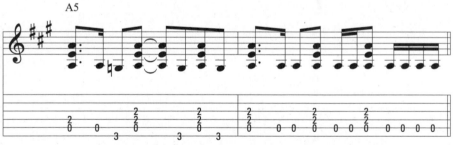

Figure 4-15: A hard rock progression mixing chords and single notes.

The squiggly vertical lines in bar 2 of Figure 4-15 tell you to draw the pick across the string in a quick arpeggio, creating a *kerrang* sound. Experiment to see just how long you can drag out the strums without losing the sense of the rhythm.

Discovering Your Own Style

Don't be discouraged if you can't make the riffs you see written in the notation sound exactly like what you hear on the CD. As long as you can play the correct pitches in the specified rhythm, you're doing fine. You have to find your own style. That's why even though Mozart wrote a piano sonata one way, there are as many interpretations for that written piece as there are musicians playing it. The same is true for rhythm guitar. Each guitarist will play a 12-bar blues, or a power-chord sequence, or a double-stop figure in a slightly different way. But as long as that individual guitarist believes in what he is doing, each rendition will be unique, honest, and heartfelt.

Don't forget to use a metronome if you get confused by any rhythm you're playing on guitar. But the most important thing when tackling these — or any — rhythm figures is to develop a natural feel for them. A natural, comfortable, and confident delivery in rhythm guitar playing is vitally important — more important even than in lead playing. So repeat these exercises till you know them cold, till you own them, and then relax and play them like it ain't no thang.

Chapter 5

Playing Up the Neck

· ·

· ·

*T*o sound like a true rock 'n' roller and to share the stratospheric heights frequented by the legions of wailing guitar heroes, you must learn to play up the neck — that is, the frets closest to the body of the guitar. We take you up the neck in Chapter 3 in Book III, which introduces the pentatonic scale, but in this chapter, you go beyond that and find out how to *think* up the neck.

Playing up the neck requires both a theoretical approach and a technical adjustment. In fact, it's probably a little harder on the brain (at least at first) to figure out what to play than it is for the fingers to fall in line. Those smart-alecky digits, which acclimate very quickly, just prove the old saying, "the flesh is willing but the spirit is weak." Or something like that.

Rock players play up the neck a lot — a whole lot. Many rock players play way, way up the neck, higher than any folk-based music would dare venture, and beyond the range of many jazz players. In many folk-based and singer-songwriter-type songs, you often don't have to play beyond open position at all. Or if you do, it's just to grab the occasional oddball, up-the-neck chord.

In rock, however, playing up the neck is essential, especially for lead playing. Playing up the neck not only gives you access to the higher-pitched and more brilliant-sounding notes, but also allows you to play the same notes many different ways. Barre chords (see Chapter 3 in Book II) also allow you to use chords of the same name but which appear in different parts of the neck (all of them "up" from open position). When you add barre chords you then have a complete picture of what it's like to play using the entire neck of the guitar. And to suddenly glimpse what it's like to have a command of the entire fret-board is a very exciting and empowering feeling.

Beyond Open Position: Going Up the Neck

You are now leaving the relatively safe haven of open position for the great unknown — that vast uncharted sea of wire and wood they call (cue dramatic music) . . . the upper frets! It's time to unbolt those training wheels, cut the apron strings, loose the surly bonds of earthbound music, and fly high. You're going up into the wild blue yonder.

Playing up the neck opens up a whole new world of possibilities for playing rock guitar music. If you know only one way to play an A chord — or to play a riff one way when you hear an A chord — then all of your music will have a certain sameness about it.

But if you have the entire neck at your disposal, are able to play A chords in several different places, can form lead lines in four or five places, and have opinions and associations on what effect you'll produce when you choose one over the other, then you're tapping the true potential of the possibilities the guitar neck has to offer.

When playing up the neck, you really need to keep an eye on what your left hand is doing, unlike playing chords and riffs in open position where you really don't need to (or shouldn't have to) keep an eye on your left hand. So get used to keeping your head cocked to the left (if you're right-handed) and really looking at — and learning the locations of — those fret markers (the dots or other decorative inlays on the side of the neck and sunk into the fingerboard). They'll be your signposts in your up-the-neck journeys.

Choking up on the neck

The best way to get moving up the neck is to start out with an exercise that doesn't introduce any new or intimidating techniques, either chordal or melodic. You're just going to get your left hand moving around the neck a little. So you start with some known chord forms that you can move up and down to good musical effect over an open-D-string pedal (see the explanation of *pedal tone* in Chapter 4 in Book III).

Figure 5-1 is a rhythm figure that pits an open D string against some chord forms that move up and down the neck. Notice that forms themselves are the familiar D, Dm, Dm7, and D7 shapes. But they move around the frets, rather than staying in one place, as they do when they're just doing "D" duty in open position. Be sure you observe carefully the fret-number indications in the diagrams.

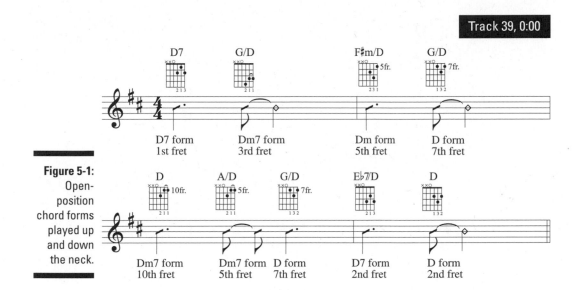

Track 39, 0:00

Figure 5-1:
Open-
position
chord forms
played up
and down
the neck.

Conveniently, you can refer to these forms by their open-position shapes: D, Dm, Dm7, and D7. But these forms don't necessarily *sound* like those chords, because they've been moved or transposed. When they're moved out of their original, open position, they now produce a different-sounding chord. When discussing chord forms, be aware of the difference between a D *shape* versus a D *chord*. A D shape played at the 7th position actually sounds like a G chord — for the very good reason that it *is* a G chord. You can play many different forms to create a given chord, so chords are named by their absolute sound — their *musical* result — not the shape used to create them.

Book III

Rock
Guitar

Playing double-stops on the move

Now move to the interior of the guitar's strings and play a rhythm figure comprised of moving double-stops on adjacent strings. Figure 5-2 is a hard-rock figure that creates drama by moving a series of melodic-oriented double-stops up and down two strings, the 3rd and the 4th, over an open-A pedal. This is a great exercise to get your eyes and left hand used to playing the up-the-neck frets accurately.

Because Figure 5-2 creates an interplay between the open A string and the moving double-stops, try increasing that sense of delineation by applying palm mutes (see Chapter 4 in Book II for an explanation of palm mutes) to the open A string and accents to the fretted double-stop notes. You can hear this effect on the CD performance.

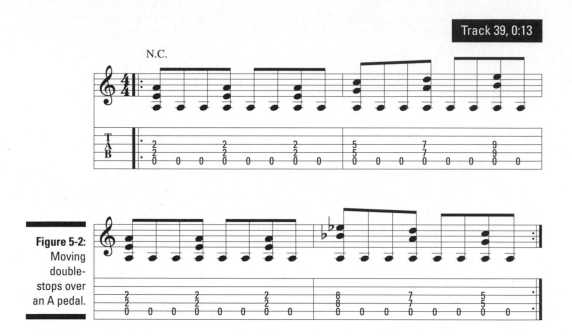

Figure 5-2: Moving double-stops over an A pedal.

Track 39, 0:13

After you've gotten a feel for what it's like to move around the neck, you can see that not only won't you get hurt, but also it's kind of cool to do. The next section shows some movable lead patterns that will get you sounding and thinking like a pro in no time.

Playing Closed-Position Lead Patterns

Playing in closed position means that you employ no open strings to play your chords, melodies, or riffs. That may seem like a restriction, but it actually frees you from the tyranny of open position, allowing you to transpose instantly and easily. But getting comfortable playing all fretted strings takes a bit of an adjustment.

The first lesson about playing up the neck is that you can no longer rely on your dear friends, the open strings. When you first learn the guitar, the open strings are like spin doctors to your politically incorrect blunders: They can shield your most embarrassing gaffes by running sonic interference. The open strings will ring through clearly while your fingers struggle with a tough chord change, muffling and buzzing their way to coherence.

But in up-the-neck playing, if you relax your left hand — even for the briefest moment — the sound disappears. So you have to be really sensitive to what's happening on both sides of the notes, the attack as well as the *cut-off* — the point your finger leaves the current fret to go do something else. And without the benefit of open strings, you have to actively work to get the notes to connect to each other smoothly. You do that by employing legato.

Letting notes ring for their full term is called playing *legato,* and after guitarists no longer have ringing strings to provide the sonic glue, achieving legato turns from a passive let-it-just-happen affair into a concerted effort.

So as you begin playing up the neck, in closed position, keep an ear out for making the notes ring for their full value. Don't let a note stop ringing until it's time for the new note to take over. Often that's as simple as leaving full pressure on your finger before releasing it at the last possible moment to play a new note on the same string (if the next note is lower), or placing an additional finger down on the same string (if the next note is higher). We call this the "lazy-finger approach" — where a finger doesn't move — or release pressure — until it absolutely has to. So you are hereby granted permission to be "digitally lethargic" and practice the lazy-finger approach to develop a legato technique on closed, or fretted, strings.

Learning to play patterns that employ no open strings has big-time benefits. Playing all-fretted patterns presents a clear advantage in one respect: The pattern can be transposed easily.

Playing in Position

So you don't just go tearing up the neck willy-nilly, you need to know some zones, or positions, to give your up-the-neck forays some purpose. Guitarists don't just go up the neck because it's higher up there (although that's sometimes a desired result — to produce higher-pitched notes); they do so because a certain position gives them better access to the notes or figures they want to play. Going to a certain zone on the neck to better facilitate playing in a given key is called *playing in position*.

Positions defined

A *position* is defined as the lowest-numbered fret the left-hand index finger plays in a given passage. So to play in 5th position, place your left hand so the index finger can comfortably fret the 5th fret on any string. If your hand is relaxed and the ball-side of the ridge of knuckles on your left-hand palm is resting near the neck, parallel to it, your remaining fingers — the middle, ring, and little — should be able to fret comfortably the 6th, 7th, and 8th frets, respectively. Figure 5-3 shows a neck diagram outlining the available notes of the pentatonic scale in 5th position.

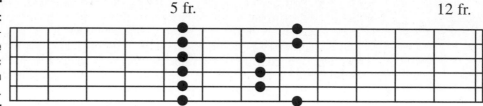

Figure 5-3:
The available pentatonic frets in 5th position.

5 fr.   12 fr.

A firm position

Now that you have the answer to what playing in position means, the next question is what specific benefits playing in position brings — other than allowing you access to higher-pitched notes not available in open position? The answer is that certain positions favor certain keys, scales, figures, or styles, better than other positions do. Here are the three most common criteria for determining the best position in which to play a given passage of music:

✔ **Key:** The chief way to determine at what position to play a certain piece of music is by its key. To use the example in Figures 5-3 and 5-4, 5th position favors very much the major keys of C and F. If you have melodic material in the key of C or F, you'd be well advised to first try playing it in 5th position. Chances are, you'd find the notes fall easily and naturally under your fingers. The relative minors of C and F, A minor and D minor, also fall very comfortably in 5th position. This is no accident, because these minor keys share the same key signature, which means they use exactly the same *pitch class* (a term you learn in music school for collection of notes, not necessarily in any given order) as their major-key counterparts.

The pitch class of the C major and A minor pentatonic scale is A C D E G. The order of the notes changes depending on the context. For example, in the key of C, where the root is C, the notes read C D E G A. In A minor, A is the root, so the notes are ordered as A C D E G. After you start to play, however, the order becomes less important than the collection of notes (which is exactly the same for both keys), because life would be pretty boring if music was played in order of the notes in the scale or key from which they were derived.

✔ **From a scale:** A scale can be derived from a key, but often the scale you want isn't extracted from a traditional major or minor key. For example, the blues scale is one of the most useful scales in rock, but it's not pulled from an existing major or minor key. So C *blues* is better played out of 8th position, not 5th.

✔ **From a chord:** Sometimes you may not care anything about scales or keys because you find a chord whose sound you can manipulate by pressing down additional fingers or lifting up existing fingers to create a cool chord move. The technical term for this is *a cool chord move,* and often the movement doesn't involve melodic or scalar movement, just a neat way to move your fingers that results in a nice sound. Rock guitar moves are often discovered and adopted simply because they feel comfortable to perform or involve satisfying a natural impulse.

Using the Movable Pentatonic Scale

Probably the greatest invention ever created for lead rock guitarists is the pentatonic scale, to which we pay homage in Chapter 3 in Book III. Its construction and theory have spawned countless theoretical discussions, but for rock guitar purposes, it just sounds good, and you're going to focus your efforts on figuring out as many ways to use it as possible. The following sections focus on moving it around the neck at will, changing the fingering to fit all sorts of different positions. And you can do this while maintaining the same notes in the same key.

Staying at home position

The main position for the pentatonic scale is placed in 5th position. This is the home position of the pentatonic scale in C major or A minor. For simplicity's sake, one scale, A minor, is used in the pentatonic studies for the remainder of this chapter. But be aware that most of the same qualities discussed can be applied to C major as well. Figure 5-4 is the A minor pentatonic scale in 5th position.

Book III

Rock Guitar

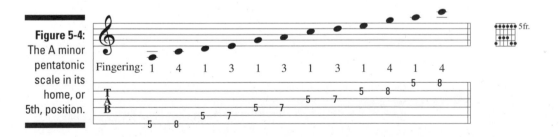

Figure 5-4: The A minor pentatonic scale in its home, or 5th, position.

Although this scale looks to be positioned fairly high up the neck, only two of its notes — the 8th-fret C and 5th-fret A, both on the 1st string — are out of range in open position. The rest of the pitches can be found in other places in open position. For example, the 8th fret on the 2nd string is a G, which is the same G as the 1st string, 3rd fret — a note that's easily played in open position. So as you step through these notes in 5th position, be aware that you can play almost all of those same pitches in an open-position location as well.

The next step is to learn the various ways to play the same scale but in a different position, starting on a different note. This is known in music as an *inversion.* An inversion of something (a scale, a chord) is a different ordering of the same elements.

Going above home position

After the home position, you may feel restless and yearn to break out of the box. To extend your reach, learn the pentatonic scale in the position immediately above the home position. Figure 5-5 is a map of the A minor pentatonic scale in 7th position.

Figure 5-5:
Notes of the A minor pentatonic scale in 7th position.

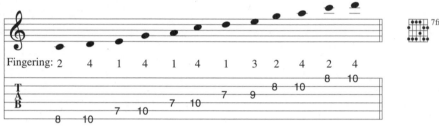

These are exactly the same notes (except the highest note, the 1st string, 9th fret, which is out of the home position's range) as those found in 5th position.

Dropping below home position

To apply some symmetry in your life, learn the pentatonic scale form immediately below the home position. Figure 5-6 shows the scale form immediately below the home position. It's played out of 2nd position and has one note on the bottom that the 5th position doesn't have, the low G on the 6th string, 3rd fret.

Take a moment and see what you've accomplished so far. You can now play one scale, the A minor pentatonic, in three different positions: 2nd, 5th (the home position), and 7th. If you look at the neck diagram with all three patterns superimposed on the frets, it looks like Figure 5-7. It's presented in two ways: as three separate but interlocking patterns (triangles, dots, and squares), and the union of those patterns, the actual notes available (as just dots).

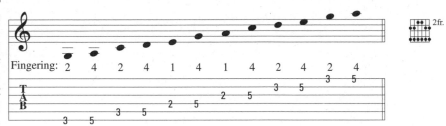

Figure 5-6: The 2nd-position A minor pentatonic scale, just below home position.

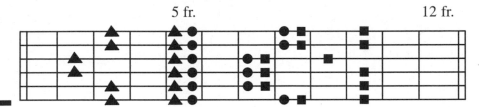

Figure 5-7: Three pentatonic scale forms shown as interlocking patterns and notes.

Note how the patterns *dovetail,* or overlap: The bottom of the 5th position acts as the top of the 2nd position, and the top of the 5th position acts as the bottom of the 7th position. It's like Paul Simon once said: "One man's ceiling is another man's floor."

Moving between positions

Okay, you've seen the way to play a given pentatonic scale in three positions. Now it's time to put these patterns into motion by actually moving between them. This way you not only get to travel laterally, across the neck, but longitudinally, up and down the neck. Can you stand it?

Book III

Rock Guitar

The shift

Figure 5-8 shows two simple melodic segments that go from 2nd position to 5th position and 5th position to 7th position via a *shift*. To perform a shift, slide your left-hand finger from one fret to another above or below it, maintaining contact with the string. In the first segment, Figure 5-8a shifts up from the 5th fret to the 7th fret on the third finger of the left hand, hitching a ride on the 5th string. Shifting this way takes you from 2nd position to 5th position. In Figure 5-8b, slide up on the little finger.

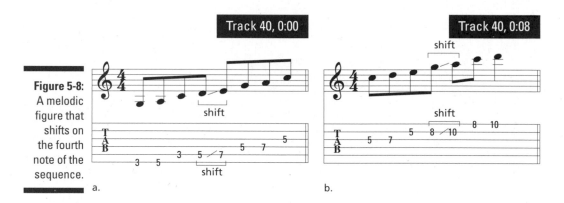

Figure 5-8: A melodic figure that shifts on the fourth note of the sequence.

Sometimes the finger you slide up with isn't the proper finger for that fret and string in the new position. But you can usually correct it easily enough on a subsequent move.

The slide, reach, and jump

A *slide* is one of two ways to shift positions while playing. A *reach* is the other. When you reach, either upward or downward, you stretch your hand out so a left-hand finger can play a note out of position. You can always *jump* or *leap*, too, which just means that you don't leave any fingers down, or maintain any contact with the old position. Mostly, you just do whatever works.

Lateral versus longitudinal

Figure 5-9 is an example of an ascending melodic line that illustrates the difference between playing laterally versus longitudinally. The first ascending and descending sequence takes you across the fingerboard in a stationary position. Then on the second ascent, the line shifts to reach the upper notes, rather than playing to the upper strings on the same position. You have to play this one up to tempo to hear how the same pitches sound when played in two different places.

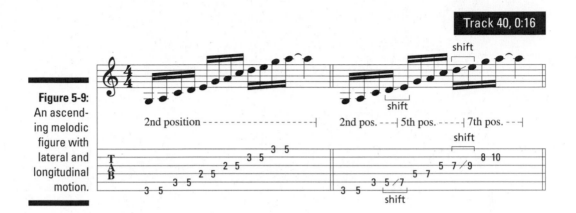

Figure 5-9:
An ascending melodic figure with lateral and longitudinal motion.

Seeking Out the Five Positions of the Pentatonic Scale

Figure 5-10, for your amazement, lays out on one long neck diagram the five positions of the pentatonic scale. Although Figure 5-10 maps out the notes to only one key and its relative minor, you can fit this pattern to all 12 keys — and their relative majors or minors — simply by moving it up or down to the appropriate fret (for example, up three frets for E♭, down four frets to A♭, and so forth).

Book III

Rock Guitar

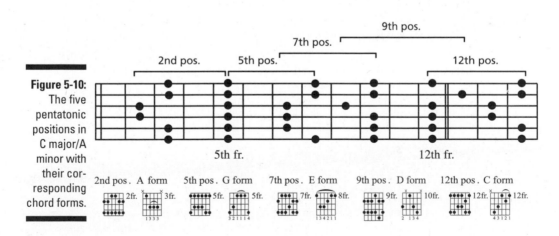

Figure 5-10:
The five pentatonic positions in C major/A minor with their corresponding chord forms.

Almost as important, each of these patterns has an associated chord form. For example, the home position corresponds to an open position G chord. The scale just below the home position looks like an A chord. The position immediately above the home position is based on an E chord. The appropriate chords are also shown in Figure 5-10 relative to their corresponding scale forms.

You can begin to see how the many frets of the guitar neck begin to become demystified. This one scale occupies so many different positions on the neck. And this is only one scale, in one key, with only five notes. The shapes used to plot the notes help you to differentiate visually among the patterns.

With five positions of the same scale at your disposal, try Figure 5-11, which is a melody based on the pentatonic scale and can be played in all five positions. The rests separating the phrases should give you ample time to switch to the new position.

Track 41

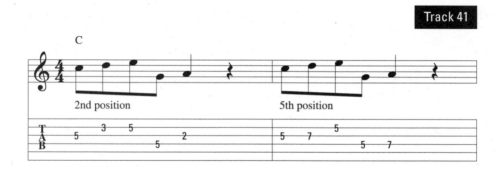

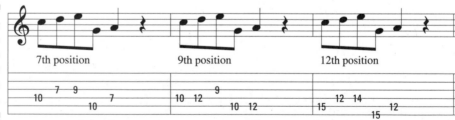

Figure 5-11: A pentatonic melody in all five positions.

In the Beatles' "Let It Be," lead guitarist George Harrison plays a terrific guitar solo in the middle of the song, based entirely in the C pentatonic scale. He shifts artfully between several different positions, proving he obviously had an advance copy (*way* advance) of *Rock Guitar For Dummies*.

Chord licks, lead licks

In rock, a *lick* is a short, self-contained melodic phrase. This may sound suspiciously close to the definition of a riff, but there is a slight difference. While "riff" and "lick" are often used interchangeably, most guitarists agree that a riff is a repeated figure that can be used to form the basis of a song, while a lick is more of a melodic snippet, fleeting in nature, and is not generally used to form the basis of a rhythm figure.

Like riffs, licks are usually single-note affairs. But sometimes a lick can be chord based. If the distinction between a riff and a lick is a little fuzzy on the single-note front, it's even more obscure when dealing with chords. In other words, there's not much difference from a chord-based riff and a chord-based lick. It's sort of like distinguishing between good tequila and bad tequila: It's hard to do because the best tequila you've ever had in your life doesn't taste a whole lot different than the worst tequila you've ever had in your life.

Nevertheless, in an effort to pigeonhole, classify, and label all things musical, some famous chord-based licks throughout the history of rock 'n' roll include the Doobie Brothers' "Listen to the Music" and "Long Train Running," Jimi Hendrix's "Hey Joe," "The Wind Cries Mary," and "Little Wing," and Led Zeppelin's "Stairway to Heaven" (the section right before the line "Ooh, and it makes me wonder").

Changing Your Position

Book III

Rock
Guitar

What's cool about playing up the neck is how often you get to shift positions while doing it. And make no mistake, shifting is cool. You get to move your whole hand instead of just your fingers. That looks really good on TV.

Now that you've gone from one pentatonic scale position to another via a shift, you're ready to try some real licks. These licks aren't limited to notes drawn from the pentatonic scale, as previous figures in the chapter were. Going forward, you're allowed the luxury of some *chromatic* (out of key) additions. You're playing real music now! Anything goes.

Licks that transport

Just like life, a lick can start you out in one location and take you to another unexpected place — often with delightful results. Figure 5-12 begins in 5th position, but quickly shoots up to 7th and finishes in 8th position with a bluesy flourish. The added chromatic note here is the flat five in A minor, E♭, which is called a *blue note* (so named because it's the note that creates a sad or blue sound). The left-hand fingering indications will help you to play this smoothly.

Track 42, 0:00

Figure 5-12:
A short blues lick starting in 5th position and ending up in 7th position.

Adding E♭ to the A minor pentatonic scale creates a six-note scale called the *blues scale*. The blues scale in that case is spelled A C D E♭ E G. The numeric formula (the "interval recipe," if you will) for the blues scale is 1 ♭3 4 ♭5 5 ♭7. The ♭5 can also be written as a ♯4, the ♭5's *enharmonic* equivalent. So, applying this formula to a C major scale (C D E F G A B) produces C E♭ F G♭ G B♭, the C blues scale. (See Book IV for a whole lot more on the blues.)

Of course, you can start high and end low — which might be bad in the world of finance or investments but is perfectly fine in music. Figure 5-13 is a lick that begins in 5th position and takes an unexpected dip into 2nd position for some low-end gravity.

Track 42, 0:09

Figure 5-13:
A lick that dips down to 2nd position to get some "big bottom."

From the depths to the heights

For the ultimate exercise in shifting, try Figure 5-14, which starts in 2nd position, goes through 5th position, then 7th, and finally winds up in 9th — ending on a high, 12th-fret E on the 1st string. This allows you to "end on a high note" (albeit through low humor).

Figure 5-14: An ascending line that progresses through three position shifts.

Track 42, 0:18

Although you've practiced different positions, various ways to shift, and five versions of the pentatonic scale, you've never left the key of C major/A minor.

Knowing Where to Play

After you get your hand moving comfortably around the neck, and you have a solid foundation in the A minor pentatonic scale and its different positions, try playing the pentatonic scale in its various forms in different keys. To do that, you must know how to place the scale patterns on the different regions of the neck.

Book III

Rock Guitar

Associating keys with positions

Some keys just fall more comfortably in certain positions than in others, so this section starts with the obvious, default positions for three common keys. Remember, any pentatonic scale satisfies two (related) keys: a major and its relative minor, or a minor and its relative major, depending on your orientation.

G positions

The home position for G major falls in open position or 12th position (which is exactly an octave higher). Because these are two extremes of the neck (and the open-position version defeats the purpose of this exercise), you might try to play G-based stuff out of 7th position. Figure 5-15 is a riff in 7th-position G major pentatonic (with one out-of-key note, the A♭ in bar 1), and its corresponding neck diagram.

Track 43, 0:00

Triplet feel ($\sqcap$ = $\overset{3}{\sqcap}$ $\flat$)

Figure 5-15:
A riff in
7th-position
G major
pentatonic.

F positions

F is a common key for blues, especially if you jam with horn players. Figure 5-16 is a bluesy riff in F major, with an added flat 3, A♭. This riff sits well in 7th-position F major pentatonic. Note that because F is one whole step down from G, its five pentatonic scale positions are the same as the key of G, but shifted down two frets.

Track 43, 0:08

Triplet feel ($\sqcap$ = $\overset{3}{\sqcap}$ $\flat$)

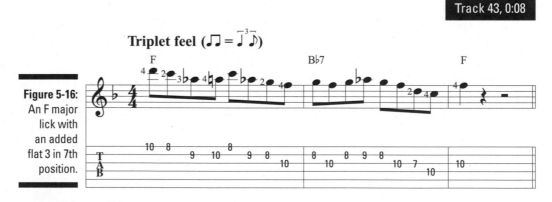

Figure 5-16:
An F major
lick with
an added
flat 3 in 7th
position.

Note that even though this lick is in 7th position, it's in F, not G, and so uses a different pentatonic scale form than the 7th-position form designated for G or E minor.

F minor positions

The key of F minor (and its relative major, A♭) is the interval of a major 3rd (four frets) lower than our dearly beloved A minor, so all of its pentatonic scale positions are shifted down four frets, relative to A minor. Its home position falls in 1st position, which means all subsequent positions are up from that. So even though the A minor example had a position lower than the home position, in the F minor example, that lower position gets "rotated" up the neck to the 10th position. Figure 5-17 is an earthy minor riff that takes advantage of its low position on the neck — the lowest possible closed-position pentatonic scale.

Track 43, 0:18

Figure 5-17: A low riff in 1st-position F minor pentatonic.

Placing positions

One great advantage to the guitar is that after you learn one pattern, in any key, you can instantly adapt it to any other key without much thought at all. Unlike piano players, flute players, and trombonists — who have to transpose, remember key signatures, and create different fingerings to play the same phrase in another key — guitarists just have to shift their left hand up or down the neck a few frets. But the pattern — what you actually play — remains the same.

It's as if you wanted to learn a foreign language, but instead of learning new words for all the nouns and verbs you know in English, you simply had to raise or lower your voice. Speak in a high, squeaky voice, and you're talking French. Say the same words in a deep, booming voice and you're conversing in Chinese. That's what transposing is like for the guitarist.

To help you know which positions are good for which keys, look at the table in Figure 5-18. This table is by no means exhaustive and by no means the final word on where to place your pentatonic positions. It merely gives you a jumping off point to know in what general vicinity to put your hands to improvise in, say, the key of A♭.

Major/minor key	Pentatonic pattern/fret #	Chord forms
A major/F♯ minor	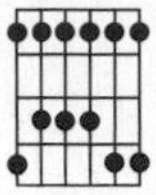 2nd fret	G/Em
B♭ major/G minor	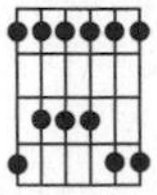 3rd fret	G/Em
B major/G♯ minor	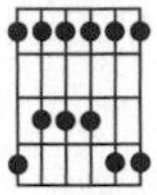 4th fret	G/Em
C major/A minor	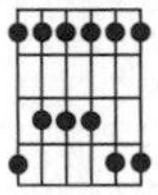 5th fret	G/Em
D♭ major/B♭ minor	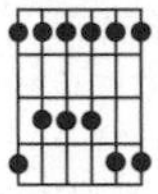 6th fret	G/Em
D major/B minor	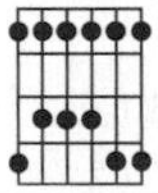 7th fret	G/Em
E♭ major/C minor	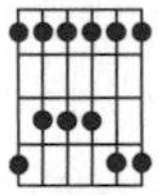 8th fret	G/Em
E major/C♯ minor	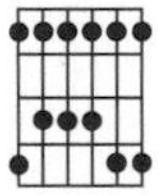 9th fret	G/Em
F major/D minor	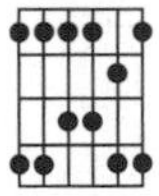 5th fret	C/Am
G♭ major/E♭ minor	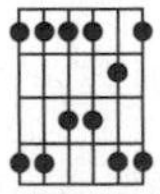 6th fret	C/Am
G major/E minor	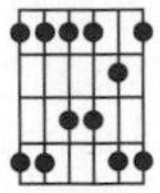 7th fret	C/Am
A♭ major/F minor	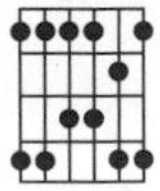 1st fret	G/Em

Figure 5-18:
A table showing the 12 keys and their relative minors, the fret number, appropriate pentatonic pattern, and chord form.

Putting the five positions into play

After you learn the pentatonic scale in five positions, you are more than 90 percent there, technically. The next hurdle is more mental than anything else. You simply have to be able to calculate where to play any given key, and which pentatonic pattern best suits your mood. Here are some exercises you can do to limber up your brain, learn the fretboard, and become acquainted with the differing characteristics offered by each of the five pentatonic positions:

- ✔ **Work out in different keys, spot transpose:** Don't just always play in A minor and C. Jam along to the radio, which often has strange (at least for guitarists) keys.

- ✔ **Arpeggiate the chords you're playing over:** Remember from Figure 5-10 that all these scale positions have associated chord forms. Try arpeggiating (playing one at a time) the notes of the chord whenever that chord comes up in the progression. This is a great way to break up linear playing, and it forces you to think of the notes of the chord, rather than playing memorized patterns.

- ✔ **Work out in different positions:** It's one thing to work out in different keys. It's another to work out in different positions. Make sure that you mix it up with respect to positions as well as keys.

We're all human and we tend to favor routines and tread familiar ground. With pentatonic scale patterns, the comfort zone lies in the home position and the ones immediately above and below. Make an effort to treat all the positions equally, however, so you can breeze through an ascending or descending line without hesitating as to where the correct notes are.

If you work to become fluid in all keys, all positions, and all patterns, the neck becomes your musical magic carpet and can transport you effortlessly to magical lands.

The fret markers on the neck are not just there to look pretty. They make it easier to find positions up the neck. Use them!

Book III

Rock Guitar

Chapter 6

Rock Guitar Legends, Styles, and Genres

Rock 'n' roll was created from a hybrid of styles that included traditional blues, country and western, rhythm and blues (R&B), and mainstream popular music. Many rock pioneers, such as the Beatles, claim to have been influenced by the older blues players, yet their music was sunny, pop-ish, and of the stuff that made teenage girls giggle, scream, and faint. No prison chain-gang song, field holler, or other traditional blues form could do that. So clearly something else was going on.

Early rock songs clearly showed their roots, because a "universal rock style" hadn't yet developed. Like immigrants meeting in a new land, everyone was there to pursue a common purpose, build a common community, and speak a common language, but they all still carried with them habits and dialects of the Old Country from which they came. Buddy Holly and Elvis had clear southern roots (Texas and Memphis, respectively), and Chuck Berry and Bo Diddley were definitely a product of more northern climes (Chicago's Chess Records). Yet all were learning from each other, while converting listeners who heard them and influencing every guitarist who followed them. This early era in rock 'n' roll was a musical melting pot of styles.

Those styles led to an explosion of rock "genres" over the next half century, led by a procession of rock guitar gods. To try to cover just the best legends would easily take up several books. In this chapter, you get merely a taste of those musicians whose playing added significantly to rock guitar history.

Bo Diddley

One of the biggest influences in rock was rhythm and blues (or R&B), which would continue to develop on its own (see Book IV), but also had a profound effect on rock 'n' roll. Some performers, such as pianist/vocalist Fats Domino, weren't really rock musicians, but enjoyed mainstream success because radio playlists and record-sales charts hadn't distinguished between the two genres yet.

However, one of the biggest influences in bringing the R&B sound mainstream was the late Bo Diddley. Born Ellas McDaniel in McComb, Mississippi, Diddley grew up in Chicago, where he moved to at age 5. He was a self-invented phenomenon who played a homemade, rectangular-shaped guitar with his teeth and behind his back, brandishing it in a sexually suggestive manner — all techniques that would be brought to high art by Jimi Hendrix. One of Diddley's best-known songs was an anthem he composed for himself, named after himself, and which used a syncopated rhythm that became synonymous with his name. That must be some kind of record: a person, song, and a rhythm, all having the same name.

Figure 6-1 is a rhythm passage that employs the "Bo Diddley Beat." Note how "scratchy" it is, and how the left-hand mutes are actually written as X-shaped noteheads in the notation. Above the music are *rhythm slashes,* which show what the rhythm section does to accompany the guitar figure below it.

Track 44

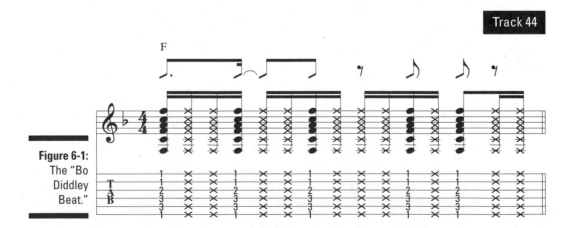

Figure 6-1:
The "Bo Diddley Beat."

Buddy Holly

The southern U.S. still has a regional flavor when it comes to its native-born musicians producing music, but it was even more pervasive in the 1950s.

Although the Deep South produced blues (the Delta blues being the most famous), "Texas twang" also had its place in rock development.

Everyone knows Lubbock-born Buddy Holly because of his unique status in rock 'n' roll history: He was part of the trio of rock performers (along with Ritchie Valens and the Big Bopper) that went down in the tragic plane crash in 1959 (immortalized in Don McLean's song "American Pie" as "the day the music died"). He also composed and sang some memorable songs, including "That'll Be the Day," "Not Fade Away," "Every Day," and "Peggy Sue." Holly made a lasting contribution to rock guitar, however, in addition to achieving mythic status as a rock martyr: He was one of the first to popularize the Fender Stratocaster; he played, wrote, and recorded his own music with his own band (being one of the first to use multi-tracking in the studio to enhance his performances); and he played the featured guitar himself. All while wearing thick-framed glasses.

Figure 6-2 shows a blues turnaround with a distinctly Holly-like treatment, followed by a boldly strummed chordal statement.

Figure 6-2: A bluesy double-stop riff and a featured chordal figure.

Book III

Rock Guitar

Chuck Berry

More than any other guitarist, Chuck Berry defines the single point at which rock 'n' roll guitar became a bona fide style. And he is considered a real innovator, a true hero, rubbing shoulders with the ranks of Eric Clapton, Jimi Hendrix, and Eddie Van Halen. Berry had down cold the entire ethos of rock 'n' roll: the rhythm, the lead, the attitude, the lyrical double-entendre, and the moves (his famous "duck walk"). And he did it many years before any of these guitar heroes were on the scene, between 1957 and 1960.

Figure 6-3 is the familiar-sounding rhythm figure, which owes its signature sound to the movement of the chord's 5th degree momentarily up to the 6th degree, and then resolving back to the 5th. You can play the 5-to-6 movement on the I, IV, and V chords (for example A, D, and E), and in either a straight-eighth or shuffle feel. (See Chapter 4 in Book VII for more on the I, IV, and V chords in relation to music theory.) It's a stationary, one-note adaptation of the boogie-woogie line played by R&B pianists and bass players. Chuck Berry didn't invent it, but he sure made it popular, and it's often referred to in various appellations using his name.

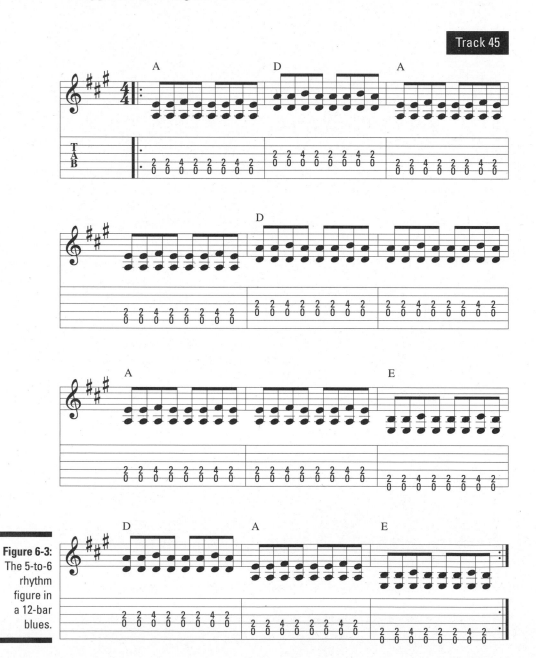

Figure 6-3:
The 5-to-6 rhythm figure in a 12-bar blues.

Hold your left-hand first and third fingers stationary while reaching up with your fourth finger to momentarily fret the 6th degree of the chord. Be careful not to shift the already-fretted fingers as you fret and release the fourth finger.

John Lennon and George Harrison

The so-called *British Invasion* was a clever catch phrase and headline dreamed up by some savvy media type to describe the flood of British rock bands that gained popularity in the early to mid-'60s, the most famous being the Beatles from Liverpool. The band's guitarists, John Lennon on rhythm and George Harrison on lead, really built the bridge between early rock and classic rock. They did straight covers and knockoffs of Chuck Berry tunes, but later transcended early rock and came to master just about any sub-genre they touched until they broke up in 1970.

The rhythm riff to the early Beatles song "I Saw Her Standing There" is highly twangy and percussive-sounding. You just can't get this sound out of a barre chord, proving that open-position chords do indeed have their place in rock. Figure 6-4 requires a tightly controlled rhythm guitar approach, using open-position chords, while "keeping a lid on them" through heavy left-hand muting. The harder you hit the strings, the more dynamic and choppy-sounding (in a good way) your sound is, but the more potential it has to get out of control.

Book III

Rock Guitar

Track 46

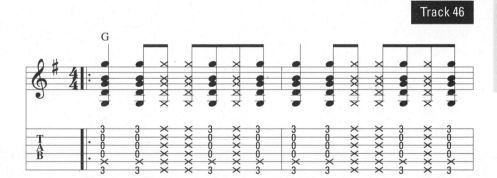

Figure 6-4: A progression using all open-position chords for their twang factor.

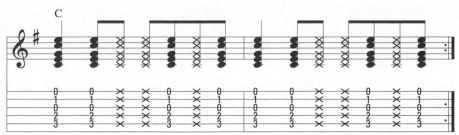

Instead of just strumming, you can use a slow pick drag — either as an up- or a downstroke — to draw out the notes in a quick arpeggio. You can hear this technique on the CD, although it's not written into the music.

Pete Townshend

You don't have to "carve" wailing leads to be a rock player. The Who's Pete Townshend didn't play stellar lead, for example, but he had the best rhythm sound in rock. He elevated rhythm guitar to a high art. And it was great theater in the best rock tradition. To add emphasis or a sense of excitement, Townshend often threw in a quick 16th-note-strummed flourish with a quick down-up-down–stroked sequence in his right hand. Guitarists often describe this sound to each other as *chick-a-CHOW* (you won't find *that* in any college music-theory book). Even quarter notes would be treated to the "windmill," where Townshend would fully extend his long arm and make large sweeping circular motions, striking the strings as his hand passed his midsection.

Figure 6-5 shows a rhythm guitar part in the Pete Townshend style with plenty of dynamics and syncopations.

Track 47

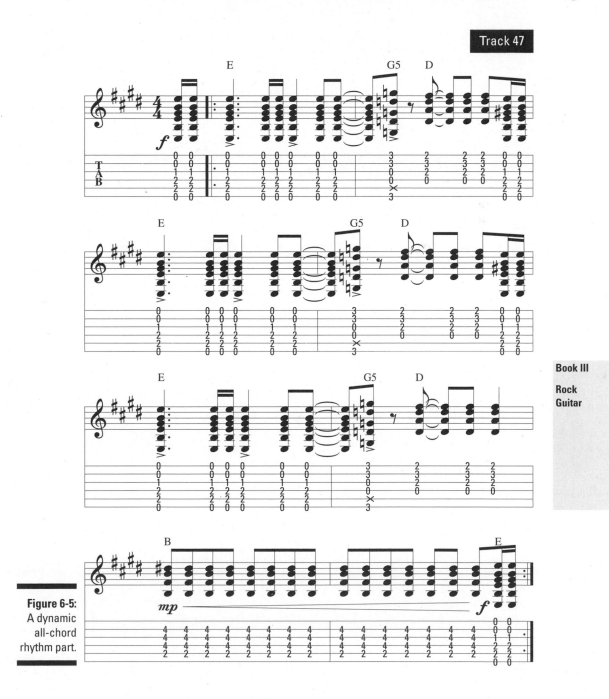

Figure 6-5:
A dynamic all-chord rhythm part.

Keith Richards

Keith Richards is a founder and musical anchor of one of the most enduring and successful rock bands of all time, the Rolling Stones. He is a highly original musician who plays chiefly rhythm guitar. The riff to "Satisfaction" (1965), which Richards composed, is arguably one of the most recognizable and classic of all time. It proved that rock didn't have to use clever and inventive melodies to be effective. This riff is only three different notes having a range of $1\frac{1}{2}$ steps. On paper (to coin a phrase), it didn't seem all that distinctive, and yet it launched a huge number-one hit and was a harbinger of the petulant and rebellious future of rock. The Rolling Stones presented rock 'n' roll as it was meant to be: simple, grammatically incorrect, and immortal.

Keith Richards is a human riff machine, creating memorable hooks to such immortal songs as "Start Me Up," "Honky-tonk Women," "Jumping Jack Flash," "Last Time," and "Brown Sugar." The aforementioned songs all benefited from Richards's patented "chordal riff" approach, where the musical motion, interest, and impetus comes from not moving chords — nor single lines based on chords — but available movement within a left-hand chord form. Figure 6-6 is a blend of chordal riffs, played within a fairly stationary left-hand chord-form setting.

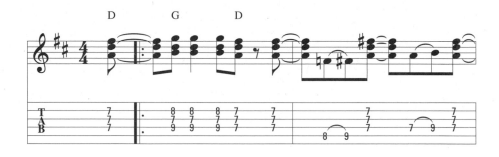

Figure 6-6: Chordal riffing inside assorted left-hand chord forms.

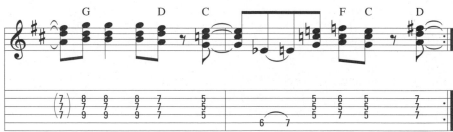

Eric Clapton

One of the primary forces that defined the post–British Invasion classic-rock era was the maturing of the electric blues style, as typified by Eric Clapton, Jimmy Page, and Jimi Hendrix. Many bands had readily acknowledged R&B and early rock greats Chuck Berry and Bo Diddley as influences, but either covered their material directly or ignored it completely in favor of a pop sound. But with the coming of age of Clapton, Page, and Hendrix, a new synthesis was taking place where the electric blues was about to enjoy not only a renaissance, but a transformation.

Clapton got his start in the Yardbirds (as did Jeff Beck and Jimmy Page), but left to join John Mayall's Bluesbreakers where he honed soulful and lyrical lead skills. He became a bona fide superstar of the guitar (and was the first "guitar god" — all over London graffiti artists scrawled "Clapton Is God") and helped revive popular interest in many of the blues legends he drew inspiration from, including Robert Johnson, Blind Lemmon Jefferson, Son House, Skip James, Elmore James, Freddie King, Buddy Guy, B.B. King, Otis Rush, Albert King, and many others.

Clapton earned the nickname "Slowhand" because of his supreme ease in playing and the effortless way he moved over the fretboard. Following his stint with the Bluesbreakers, he founded Cream, often credited as the first true supergroup comprised of recognized virtuosos. The heaviness of their hit songs, including "White Room," "Sunshine of Your Love," and "Badge," helped to define the era of the "power trio" and to establish the blues as viable rock material, both creatively and commercially. "Crossroads," a song by Robert Johnson, captured in a live version on the album *Wheels of Fire* (1968), contains one of the greatest guitar solos of all time. Eddie Van Halen learned it note for note and, in concert, would drop it into a song's improvisational section as a tribute.

Figure 6-7 is a bluesy solo, employing many of the techniques Clapton used to infuse his solos with expression: bends, hammers, pulls, slides, and left-hand vibrato. Notice that much of this solo takes place comfortably in the home position of the pentatonic scale. This is the way Clapton plays: not with gratuitous flash, but with restraint, precision, and taste.

Book III

Rock Guitar

Figure 6-7: A blues-based lead solo in the style of Eric Clapton.

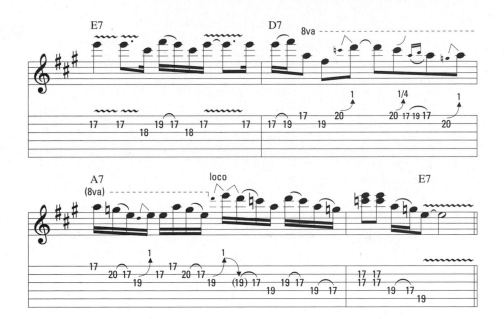

Jimi Hendrix

Jimi Hendrix is hailed as perhaps the greatest rock guitarist of all time. He combined the best elements of electric blues, psychedelic abandon, sonic sculpting, and pure inspiration. Although he died at only 27 in 1970, his legacy is the most enduring and studied of any guitarist. He started off in the R&B circuit as a sideman, playing with the Isley Brothers and Little Richard, to name two, but quickly developed his own style and became a local legend revered for his other-worldly technique and far-out stage performances.

Hendrix was a superior showman as well as guitarist, and could play the guitar behind his back and with his teeth. Like Jimmy Page and Jeff Beck, Hendrix saw the guitar as a total sonic instrument and was a master of marshaling such effects as distortion, *feedback* (the high-pitched howl that occurs when you face the guitar's pickups directly at a cranked-up amp), and the wah-wah pedal. Hendrix recorded three albums, *Are You Experienced* (1967), *Axis: Bold As Love* (1967), and *Electric Ladyland* (1968), containing such classics as "Purple Haze," "Hey Joe," "All Along the Watchtower," "Little Wing," and "Voodoo Child (Slight Return)." He played left-handed, using a "flipped" right-handed guitar (usually a Strat), restrung.

Figure 6-8 is a lead figure using several techniques of which Hendrix was an acknowledged master: blues playing, string bending, whammy bar manipulation, and effects use (wah-wah pedal and distortion).

Figure 6-8:
A Hendrix-style lead featuring bent notes and whammy bar moves.

Try getting the pitches and rhythms under your fingers first, before incorporating the bar moves. Then work to make the combination of blues soloing, whammy bar manipulation, and effects use as cohesive as possible.

Jimmy Page

Jimmy Page was a seasoned sideman and session player, and, perhaps because of this, was able to drive his band Led Zeppelin into producing the ultimate in finely crafted songs and perfectly orchestrated instrumental parts. Although a virtuoso, Page never overplayed, preferring to showcase his genius through his composed riffs, arranging skill, and songwriting savvy. Led Zeppelin could seemingly take on any music form and make it work: traditional blues-based material ("Since I've Been Loving You"), Eastern-influenced music ("Kashmir"), folk influences ("Bron-Y-Aur Stomp"), flat-out rockers ("Whole Lotta Love," "Heartbreaker"), trippy psychedelia ("Dazed and Confused"), and epic anthems ("Stairway to Heaven"). Many people consider Zeppelin to be the prototype for heavy metal.

If you had to pick one band from the entire classic rock era that encompassed everything — great blues-based guitar playing, immortal riffs, successfully eclectic material (from blues to folk to exotic to metal), and superior songwriting, it would have to be Led Zeppelin. No other band comes close in defining the classic rock era.

Figure 6-9 is a riff based on the Led Zeppelin sound — massively heavy, tinged with blues, and with a dash of the exotic thrown in.

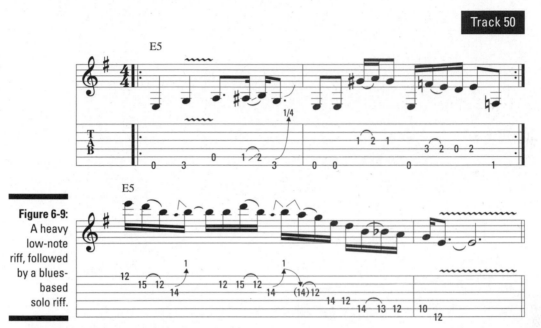

Track 50

Figure 6-9:
A heavy
low-note
riff, followed
by a blues-
based
solo riff.

Book III

Rock Guitar

Carlos Santana

Mexican-born Carlos Santana rose to prominence in the early 1970s, leading a big band that played Latin rock, but with a guitar sound so lyrical, so big, so mature, he became an unavoidable and irresistible influence for any other guitarist who heard him. Santana was equally at home playing in a flashy, virtuosic style as he was in a slower, more soulful one, but it was his thick, creamy, blues-based sound that most people associate him with. His minor-key lines were especially achingly expressive. Through his hits "Evil Ways" (1970), "Black Magic Woman" (1970), and "Oye Como Va" (1971, written by Latin percussion great Tito Puente), Santana established himself as a true guitar hero along the lines of Clapton and Page.

Figure 6-10 is a lyrical, melodic line played over a Latin-rock-flavored beat. The progression here outlines the Dorian mode, which is like the minor scale but with a raised 6th degree. The quarter-note triplets (which are twice as long as eighth-note triplets, or three for every two beats) help lend an expressive, lyrical quality to the line.

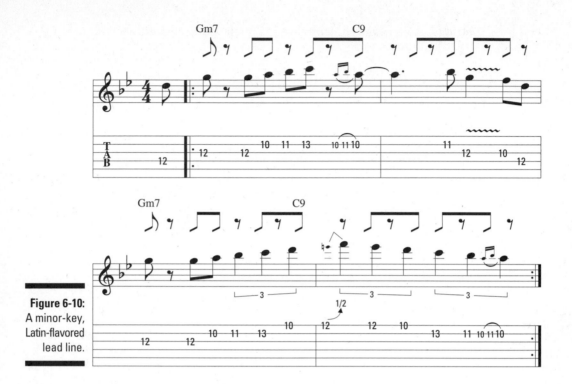

Figure 6-10:
A minor-key,
Latin-flavored
lead line.

Stevie Ray Vaughan

Although primarily considered a blues guitarist and coming later than classic rock's acknowledged heyday, the brilliant Stevie Ray Vaughan simply demands inclusion in any discussion about rock, because he played with as much exuberance and abandon as any rock player since Hendrix. He revived the dying blues movement in the early 1980s, after, improbably, getting his professional start as a sideman with the godfather of glam, David Bowie. He was profoundly influenced by Jimi Hendrix and often performed Hendrix's famed ballad "Little Wing." Vaughan was an inspiration to fellow-Texan and guitar great Eric Johnson, as well as any rock player who's ever heard him and tried to fuse together the already-close sensibilities of electric blues and rock. He fronted his own band, playing inspired rhythm as well as lead, and was at the height of his career before his death in a helicopter crash in 1990.

Figure 6-11 is a rhythm riff in the style of Stevie Ray Vaughan that features a hard-swinging rhythm part punctuated with short single-note phrases, followed by an aggressive lead phrase. The key here is to dig in on the notes, with both the right and left hands, especially on the lead parts. Part of what gave Vaughan his sound was that he strung his guitar with heavy-gauge strings. This produced a big, fat tone, to be sure, but required him to really attack the guitar aggressively to subordinate the string tension that fought him, especially when bending strings. But you could see in his performances that he enjoyed working hard at it, that he loved the struggle.

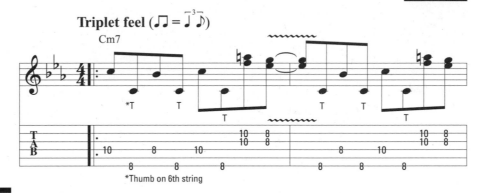

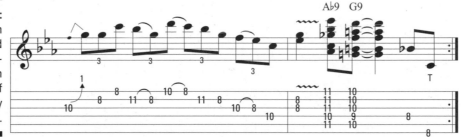

Figure 6-11: A rhythm figure and lead passage in the style of Stevie Ray Vaughan.

Book III

Rock Guitar

U2's The Edge

Hailing from Dublin, Ireland, U2 is one of the world's biggest bands, packing stadiums and creating multi-platinum-selling albums such as *War, Unforgettable Fire, The Joshua Tree, Rattle and Hum, Achtung Baby,* and *Zooropa.* The band won two Grammy Awards in 1987, including Album of the Year *(The Joshua Tree).* The band's success continues with their most recent Grammy Awards for *How to Dismantle an Atomic Bomb,* released in 2004.

U2's guitarist David Evans, known as The Edge, is a strikingly original player whose style is difficult to categorize. He is the master of treating the guitar as an ensemble instrument and a leader in the group of expert effects users and minimalists that includes Brian May of Queen, Andy Summers of the Police, and Robert Fripp of King Crimson. He uses signal processors and effects to high art, and it's often hard to tell that what you're listening to is even a guitar. He regards the guitar as a tool for creating texture rather than just as a weapon to pound out chords or a device for taking the obligatory single-line solo. The Edge was a lightning bolt of creative inspiration to rock, making the guitar important again in ways no one imagined.

Figure 6-12 is a rhythm figure in the style of The Edge, using some of his hallmarks: an arpeggiated treatment of an exotic chord progression, a deftly placed harmonic, and a reliance of outboard effects to achieve a rich, textured approach to rhythm-track layering.

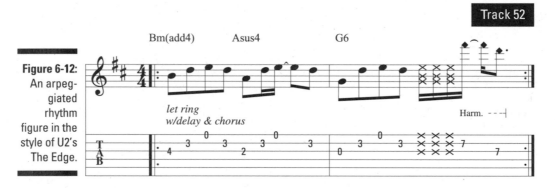

Figure 6-12: An arpeggiated rhythm figure in the style of U2's The Edge.

Let the arpeggios ring out as long as possible and play exactly in rhythm so the delay repeats stay in sync with the played notes. Work to make the final harmonic speak out among the normally picked notes.

Tony Iommi

Led Zeppelin may have been the driving force behind 1970s heavy metal, but none would dispute Black Sabbath's place in the grand metal pantheon. The members of Sabbath distilled a grim view of reality and turned it into something darker and more sinister sounding than anything Jimmy Page ever came up with. Fronting Black Sabbath was the twin force of vocalist Ozzy Osbourne and guitarist Tony Iommi. Although Ozzy was barely a singer in technical terms, he proved a devastatingly effective and charismatic frontman. Iommi, who could turn the basic power chord into a towering wall of doom and gloom, was a surprisingly nimble soloist — especially for a guy missing parts of some fingers. (Remember that when you're whining about fingering!)

Iommi's combination of distorted, two-note power chords and fast pentatonic-based solos (on a Gibson SG) helped carve out the sound of early metal. Iommi uses this signature approach on such classic Sabbath tracks as "Paranoid," "War Pigs," "N.I.B.," and the FM radio staple "Iron Man."

In all, Black Sabbath was a group that played a brand of rock 'n' roll that was grimy, violent, and full of darkness. As such, you can see why contemporary thrash acts such as Metallica and Megadeth preferred the killer riffs of Sabbath over the polished guitar licks of Led Zeppelin. Figure 6-13 shows a power-chord riff that is very much in the style of Iommi — simple, heavy, and menacing. Amazingly, Tony himself is a very sweet-natured, charming man in person. Just goes to show that you can't judge a metalhead by his riffs.

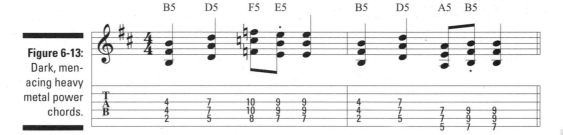

Figure 6-13: Dark, menacing heavy metal power chords.

Ritchie Blackmore

Book III

Rock Guitar

Deep Purple was another top metal band of the 1970s, inspiring everyone from Judas Priest to Yngwie Malmsteen. Purple guitarist Ritchie Blackmore is very influential, being the first major player to meld a heavy guitar tone with classical technique and harmony. He also follows Jimi Hendrix's example and uses a Stratocaster through Marshalls (most early metal players preferred a solid body with humbuckers, such as a Gibson Les Paul). Deep Purple's most celebrated song is "Smoke on the Water," a 1972 hit with dead-simple riffs and slippery Blackmore solos. Other tracks — such as "Strange Kind of Woman," "Mistreated," "Woman from Tokyo," and "Burn" — also display Blackmore's fast hammer-on runs, violent vibrato bar, and melodic phrasing.

One of the best examples of his classical side is on "Highway Star" (from *Machine Head*). Here, Blackmore weaves quickly picked intervals based on Bach into his lead. The lick in Figure 6-14 offers a simplified Baroque-era-influenced phrase in the Blackmore tradition. Try it slowly at first and then bring it up to speed.

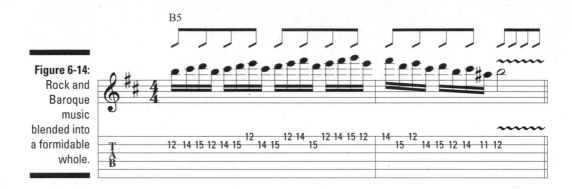

Figure 6-14:
Rock and
Baroque
music
blended into
a formidable
whole.

Eddie Van Halen

Rock guitar was getting pretty stale and boring in the late 1970s, with most rock guitarists relying on the same pentatonic-blues scales for their solos that Clapton, Beck, Page, and Hendrix had introduced a decade earlier. Then came Eddie Van Halen. Fronting his band of the same name, Eddie Van Halen strapped on a homemade Strat-style electric and blasted out solos of fluid hammer-ons, crazed whammy bar dives, and a wacky two-handed striking technique.

Perhaps the most obvious Van Halen trademark is the two-handed tap (where notes are sounded using the right-hand fingertips to slam the string onto the fretboard, rather than brushing the strings). A right-hand tap is always followed by a right-hand pull-off, either to a fretted or an open string. Then a left-hand finger hammers and pulls off as well. This produces a strikingly fluid sound and enables the guitarist to play wider intervals than possible with conventional left-hand technique.

Figure 6-15 is an example of right-hand tapping technique over an eight-bar, classically constructed chord progression. The taps arpeggiate the chords in a smooth and fluid manner that conventional techniques can't emulate.

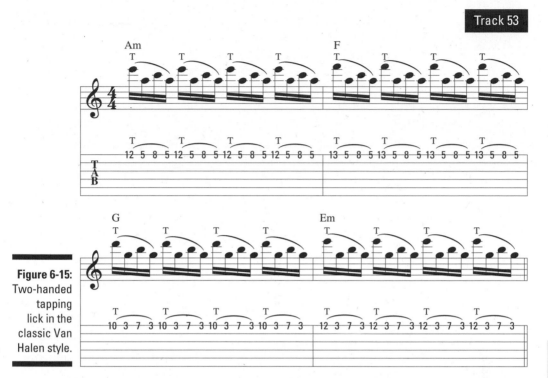

Figure 6-15: Two-handed tapping lick in the classic Van Halen style.

Angus Young

During the 1980s, when speed and virtuoso technique dominated most rock guitarists' styles, the Australian band AC/DC rocked the globe with clean power chords, economical rhythm arrangements, and aggressive, blues-based solos. With his brother Malcolm playing kick-ass power chords, Angus Young relies on slow solos and Chuck Berry-style double-stops in solos to hard-rocking anthems such as "You Shook Me All Night Long," "Highway to Hell," and "Shoot to Thrill." The key to emulating Angus's solos is not to listen to other metal players, but instead blues guitarists such as B.B. King, Eric Clapton, or Stevie Ray Vaughan and bend the strings with soul.

Figure 6-16 shows a simple, bluesy lick in the style of Angus Young. Here again, the emphasis is on feel over speed.

Figure 6-16:
Straight-
ahead
blues-rock.

David Gilmour

If Pink Floyd is the ultimate "space rock" band, then David Gilmour is its pilot. While other progressive rock players exude strange and exotic influences in their solos, Gilmour is on the traditional side, more of a bluesy guitarist in the mold of Eric Clapton than a sonic revolutionary. Nevertheless, his haunting solos help define the Floyd sound as much as the obscure lyrics and ethereal synthesizers.

Listen to "Time" (from the mega-platinum *Dark Side of the Moon*), where Gilmour cuts an echoey lead laced with string bends. "Shine On You Crazy Diamond" (from 1975's *Wish You Were Here*) includes a series of soulful solos over a basic minor-blues backbeat. His best-known break, however, is in the power ballad from *The Wall,* "Comfortably Numb." Technically, it's a basic blues-rock solo, but one that's elevated to operatic proportions due to a highly dramatic chord progression. In Figure 6-17, the secret to success is that it's in a "space rock" context, however — not a conventional blues one. Imagine B.B. King jamming with Yanni and you'll get the picture.

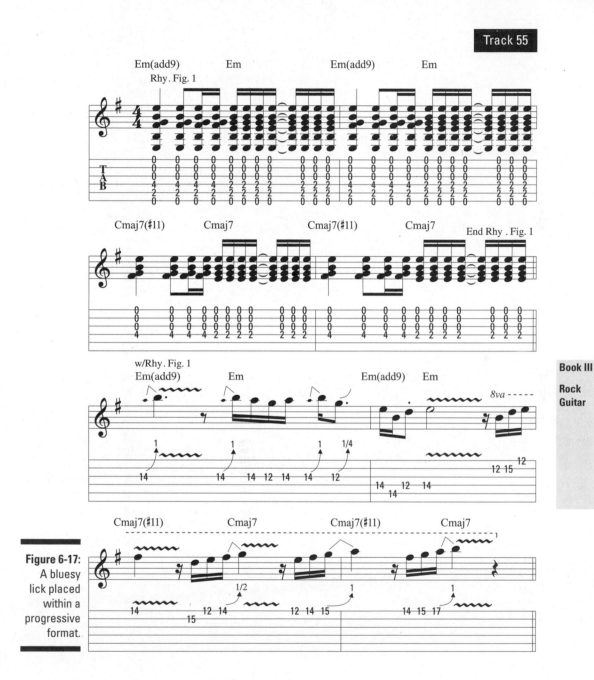

Figure 6-17: A bluesy lick placed within a progressive format.

Book III

Rock Guitar

Alex Lifeson

A powerhouse player, Alex Lifeson remains among the most innovative rock guitarists of the last three decades. His work with the Canadian power trio Rush is marked by blazing melodic solos, shimmering rhythm parts, and a frequent use of chorus and echo. Some of his best electric solos are in tracks such as "La Villa Strangiato," a complex instrumental, and "Limelight," which includes tasteful tremolo bar effects and a strong sense of melody.

In addition to his fiery lead work, Lifeson is also a skilled rhythm guitarist and makes extensive use of chorus effects in his arpeggiated chord progressions. He is equally at home with electric, acoustic, or classical guitars. A veritable jack-of-all-guitar-trades, Lifeson often pushes the envelope of rock guitar — and licks and stamps it, too.

Figure 6-18 concentrates on Lifeson's unique chord parts. Instead of block barre chords, Lifeson often lets the upper E and B strings ring open, making his 6-string guitars sound like 12-strings. Add a chorus pedal to heighten the effect.

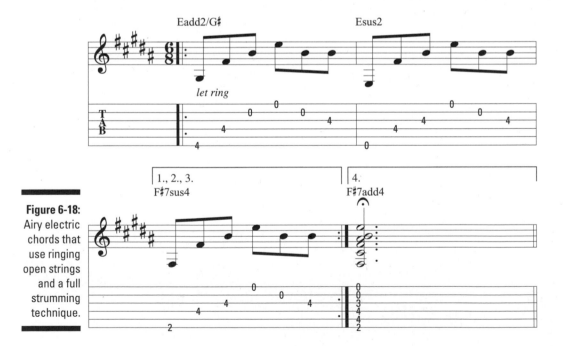

Figure 6-18:
Airy electric chords that use ringing open strings and a full strumming technique.

Book IV
Blues Guitar

In this book . . .

From its humble beginnings on Southern front porches to the dazzling nightlife of the Chicago blues scene, the blues genre is 100 percent American. The blues went on to influence everything from rock to country. From the early genius of Robert Johnson to B.B. King and the legend of Lucille, we take you on a wide-ranging tour of what the blues is, why it's so great, and how to play it on the guitar.

Here are the contents of Book IV at a glance.

Chapter 1

Blues Meets Guitar: A Match Made in Heaven

In This Chapter

▶ What defines blues guitar music

▶ How acoustic and electric guitars each make the blues in their own way

▶ The essential gear you need to play the blues

The guitar and blues go together like apple and pie. The guitar allows you to sing along with yourself (try that with a flute), and singing is the way the blues started. And a guitar is much easier to bring out on the front porch than a piano. It's also cheaper to own (or make yourself) than many other instruments, and that helped bring blues music to many poor folks — the people who really had the blues.

Because the blues was concentrated in the rural South, in the time before musical instruments adopted electricity, the earliest blues guitar music was played on acoustics. The "Delta blues" style was the first recognized style of the blues and consisted of strummed and plucked acoustic guitars with chords formed as in other forms of folk music.

As the blues developed, guitar makers adopted features that helped bring out the qualities of the blues to even better effect. An electric guitar is played with two hands and leaves your mouth free to sing (as an acoustic does), but electrics, with their skinnier strings, are easier to bend — stretching the string while it's ringing produces a gradual, continuous rise in pitch — and electronic amplification helps project the guitar's sound out into the audience of (often raucous and noisy) blues-loving listeners. In this chapter, you discover in detail why the blues and the guitar make great music together.

Beyond the Delta: Defining the Blues Guitar Sound

Blues guitar can take many forms and has grown dramatically since its humble beginnings in the southern United States. Blues players were traditionally self-taught, and many were illiterate. One of the easiest ways to create different chords was to tune the guitar to an open chord, such as G major or E major, and then use a *slide* — such as a pocket knife or bottle neck — to change chords. In both slide and fretted guitar styles, guitarists would emphasize the driving rhythm of the blues by thumping out steady bass notes on the low strings with their thumb while fingerpicking upper strings for chords, melodic riffs, and fills.

Playing simple chords to back up a blues singer is still a form of blues guitar — as is playing chords with a slide. You can't help but sound bluesy when you move a slide from one position to another to play the different chords in a song, especially if you do it expressively. But beyond this, you can ascribe certain musical hallmarks to the blues that don't make you play any more soulfully but provide you with a deeper understanding when you hear the blues.

The following sections break down the elements of the blues into four musical concepts. Keep in mind that these concepts are the main ones and there are certainly more, but thinking of and listening to the blues while considering these criteria helps in your understanding of this sometimes elusive music form. You may not be able to define the blues, but you know it when you hear it. Or as Sonny Terry says:

> Sometimes I want to holler,
> Sometimes I want to shout,
> Sometimes I want to cry,
> But I wonder what about.
> I think I got the blues.

The method to the music: Chord progressions

What defines a blues song is the way chords are put together, or the *chord progression.* Although there's such a thing as a jazz chord, there's not really a blues chord (there's no such thing as a classical chord, either). But if you put certain chords together in a certain way, you can definitely have a blues chord progression. The most common blues progression is the 12-bar blues, which is covered, along with the others, in Chapter 3 in Book IV.

Chords used in blues include major and minor triads (simple, three-note chords), dominant 7 chords — triads with the flatted (lowered by a half step) 7th added — and sometimes even jazz chords (with complex-sounding names like G13♭9/♭5).

The guitarist's language of melody

The blues definitely has a harmonic and melodic language. It even has a scale named after it: the six-note blues scale. If music is described as "bluesy," it usually means that the melody borrows or enlists notes from the blues scale (nicknamed "blue notes") rather than the standard major and minor scales that make up other, non-blues styles. Blue notes are the minor 3rd, minor 7th, and flatted 5th (in shorthand, flat 3 or ♭3, ♭5, and ♭7). Figure 1-1 shows the C major scale (the familiar *do, re, mi,* and so forth) with the blue notes shown beneath their unaltered counterparts.

Figure 1-1:
The C major
scale with
blues notes.

C major:	C	D	E	F	G	A	B	(C)
Blue notes:			E♭		G♭		B♭	

When discussing scales, you don't include the octave note, in this case, the second, higher C. That's why it's in parentheses. So a major scale is really a seven-note scale, though in practice musicians usually include the octave eighth note.

When playing the blues, guitarists incorporate aspects of both the major scale and the blue notes to come up with two new scales of their own: the six-note blues scale and the five-note minor pentatonic scale (covered in Chapter 3 in Book III). Figure 1-2 shows both scales in the key of C in letter names and in music notation.

If all this talk of scales, intervals, and flat this and that are making your eyes roll, don't worry. You don't need to know any of this to play the blues or to even hear it. It's a peek under the hood, is all.

Book IV

**Blues
Guitar**

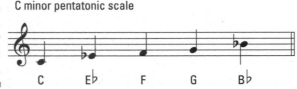

Figure 1-2:
The six-note
blues scale
and the five-
note minor
pentatonic
scale.

The expression that invokes your senses

One of the best things about the blues — and a huge relief to beginning
guitarists — is that the blues isn't all that hard to play, technically speaking.
Playing lead or rhythm in most blues songs requires only intermediate technique. What is harder to do — in fact, you never stop figuring out how to do
it better — is to play expressively. *Expression* in the blues is what turns craft
into art. Check out these ways to make your music more bluesy:

- **Use bent notes:** Bent notes are notes where the pitch is raised slowly
  upward in a continuous fashion, and this element is closely identified
  with the blues.

- **Make your music shake:** Vibrato is a technique that makes the notes of
  the music quiver by using left-hand finger wiggling, which gives blues a
  signature sound. B.B. King is well-known for his expressive and soulful
  vibrato. Because much of the blues is set to medium tempos, players
  hold notes for long periods of time. Vibrato is a great way to bring notes
  to life, so they don't just sit there.

- **Give it some slide:** If you don't hit notes straight on but rather slide into
  notes from above and below, you give music a bluesy feel and breathe
  some life into your notes. Guitarists often draw their inspiration from
  vocalists and horn players (saxophone, trumpet, trombone, and so on),
  who exercise the slide technique on a regular basis.

- **Slur your notes:** Connecting notes through slurs — where you don't
  restrike the second note with the right hand — is a good way to loosen
  up your playing in the typical way a blues player does.

- **Allow the rhythm to flow:** Blues also allows a certain rhythmic liberty
  to be taken with melodies — especially letting the melody notes deliberately fall after, or behind, the beat. It's been described as lazy, devil may
  care, or cavalier. Whatever you call it, it sure makes the notes sound
  more bluesy.

The groove that sets the pace

Groove is often used informally to mean "on the mark" or "in sync with," but here the term refers to the meter, rhythmic feel, and tempo, and the instruments' role in providing the accompaniment, or backing figures. Several different grooves exist within the blues:

- A *shuffle* is a type of groove that uses triplet eighth notes with the emphasis on sounding just the first and third notes played at a medium tempo. "Sweet Home Chicago" is an example of a song in a shuffle groove.

- A slow 12/8 *blues* (the "12/8" refers to the time signature) is another type of groove that's also based on three-note groups, but the tempo is slower and all three notes of the beat are pronounced. "Stormy Monday" is a song in a slow 12/8 feel.

- A straight-four *groove* is where the eighth notes are evenly spaced apart, rather than in the long-short scheme of a shuffle. "Johnny B. Goode" is in a straight-four.

Given the infinite forms of expression the blues takes, it's nice to know that at least from a technical standpoint, you need to master only a few grooves to play most of the blues music out there.

Dissecting Acoustic and Electric Blues Guitars

Anatomically speaking, guitars come in two sexes: acoustic and electric. Because solid-body electric guitars don't make sound acoustically but through electronics, like females they have more chromosomal material — er, components — than do acoustics. Some of the functions of these gizmos aren't even obvious until you plug in and start messing around with them.

About the only thing that can go wrong with an acoustic is that a string breaks. On an electric, more moving and electronic parts are subject to failure, so you have a little more to keep track of on an electric. And all guitars, being made of wood and moving parts, can go out of whack and need periodic adjustment to keep them humming and happy. (Flip to Chapter 1 in Book I for details on all the parts of a guitar — both the acoustic version and the electric kind.)

The practical differences between the two types of guitars is, in sum, that an electric guitar needs to plug in to an amp and have electricity to be heard, but it's easier to play than an acoustic. An acoustic works with nothing but the fingers nature gave you, and its loudness is limited to a range of a few dozen feet, and in a quiet environment — unless it is miked, of course. Acoustics can't sustain like electrics can, either, so their lead qualities are more restricted, too. In this section, you get details on both guitars, but take note that the fundamental principles for acoustic guitars, and the way their strings produce notes, apply to electrics as well — the acoustic is that baby's daddy, after all.

The foundation for all guitar playing: Acoustic guitars

In the old days, gut- and steel-string acoustics were used as a means to accompany a singing voice or another melodic instrument, like the fiddle. Gradually the rhythms evolved into single-note figures (riffs), and then finally into a solo instrument, where the guitar would carry the melody. Blues played on the acoustic guitar remains a viable style today, as evidenced by the work of Rory Block, Roy Book Binder, John Hammond, Keb' Mo', and Chris Thomas King, among others. So the first step in playing the blues is to understand how acoustic guitars work and why they're so perfect for playing the blues.

In guitar, the hands perform different functions — unlike, say, the piano or saxophone where the hands work the same way. In guitar playing, the left-hand fingers press down the strings at different frets, which creates different sounding pitches. The right hand actually produces the sound by strumming or plucking the strings. So the two hands need each other, and they must coordinate their efforts so they move together to create chords and single notes in rhythm. In blues guitar playing, unlike large governmental bureaucracies, the right hand must know what the left hand is doing, and vice versa.

 Good guitar players, who know the fingerboard, can identify any string/fret location by its pitch (note name), no matter where it falls. The better guitar player you become, the more you're able to look at the neck and quickly see notes and patterns.

Shifting acoustic to overdrive: Electric guitars

As soon as electric guitars were available, blues players of the day made the transition quickly and easily from their acoustic versions. An electric guitar uses the same approach to neck and frets and the way the left and right hands share separate but equally important roles — but it provides some advantages that the acoustic guitar doesn't, in addition to the most obvious one: increased volume through electronic amplification. The amplified electric guitar certainly changed the music world, but in many more ways than just being able to be heard over the rest of the band. The entire tonal character of the instrument changed, in addition to the way you had to play it.

Technologically speaking, an electric guitar is no more complicated than an eighth-grade science project: A wire (the string) hovers over a magnet (the pickup), which forms a magnetic field. When you set the wire in motion (by plucking it), the vibrating, or oscillating, string creates a disturbance in the magnetic field, which produces an electrical current. This current travels down a cord (the one sticking out the side of your guitar) and into an amplifier, where it's cranked up to levels that people can hear — to say the least.

Naturally, there's a lot more to the way electric guitars make music than this description, but what's significant is that an electric guitar doesn't make its sound acoustically. Even though you can hear the string when the guitar's not plugged in, that's not what the guitar "hears." The guitar converts a disturbance in the pickup's magnetic field to a current. This all-electronic process is different than "pre-electric guitar amplification," which consisted of placing a microphone in front of a guitar.

In an electric guitar, you must use metal strings, because nylon ones don't have magnetic properties. The fact that you need only a metal wire and a pickup to make sound — rather than a resonating chamber — meant electric guitars could be built differently from their acoustic counterparts. And they were played differently, though that took some time to evolve.

Bending strings

As a guitar player, what you notice as soon as you pick up an electric guitar is how easy it is to play. For the blues, as far as physical effort is concerned, electric guitars are much easier than acoustic guitars because

- The neck is shallower.
- The fingerboard width is thinner.
- The strings are lighter than those found on an acoustic.
- The action, or distance from the strings to the frets, is lower, so it frets almost effortlessly.

But the lighter strings have another advantage crucial to blues playing, other than being easier to play: They're easier to bend. Bending strings just sounds bluesy. It allows electric guitarists to be more expressive in their lead playing, and allows the guitar to better emulate the vocal stylings of blues singers, who use their flexible approach to pitch to sing soulful blues notes. Figure 1-3 shows what it looks like to bend a string on an electric. The string is physically pushed sideways on the fretboard by the left hand, stretching it.

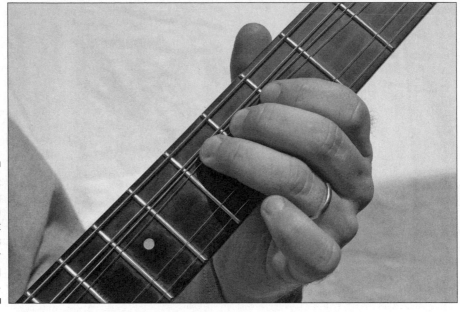

Figure 1-3:
Bending
strings with
your left
hand makes
your guitar
playing
bluesier.

Noticing increased sustain

In the process of electrifying a guitar, blues players noticed something besides the loudness advantage: Electric guitars *sustained* longer. The notes just seemed to hang on longer instead of dying away quickly, as they did on acoustic guitars and banjos before that. As a result of this increased sustain, electric guitars were able to produce more substantial vibrated notes, bent notes, and long notes that held their sound. Along with jazz players, blues players found they could now more closely emulate vocal and horn stylings. A saxophone note, for example, will sound as long as your breath holds out, instead of decaying as an acoustic guitar note does. This change encouraged a more versatile approach to single-note, or lead, playing. Before the electric guitar, the guitar was largely a rhythm instrument, with some notable exceptions, such as the jazz playing of Eddie Lang, Lonnie Johnson, and gypsy guitarist Django Reinhardt.

What Your Guitar Needs to Get Your Blues Groove On

To be a well-appointed blues guitar player, you need to have not only your acoustic or electric guitar, but also some other stuff that allows you to play to your fullest. Check out this list:

✔ **Picks:** Being able to play with a pick is an important skill in blues play-ing, and you should learn to play with one before deciding to be a rebel and go without. True, some traditional players of both acoustic and elec-tric blues don't use a pick. They use the unadorned fingers of the right hand to produce all of their blues sounds, from full strummed chords to riffs to leads.

✔ **Spare strings:** As far as "string breakage," it's not a question of if, but when. Strings break all on their own, even if you don't play hard or bend them, but blues bending certainly shortens their lifespans. Carry spares so a sudden "string mishap" doesn't shut down your jam for the night. (See Chapter 3 in Book I to find out how to change strings.)

✔ **Tuner:** Most guitar teachers will tell you that it should be illegal to allow beginning guitarists to roam the earth without a tuner. These days, the word "tuner" usually means "electronic tuner" — the battery-operated kind that you can plug into (or use the onboard mic, if you're playing an acoustic). An electronic tuner is designed for quick and easy guitar tuning, and you can tune silently to boot. You can use other tuning methods — such as employing a pitch pipe, tuning fork, or the relative method (see Chapter 1 in Book I) — but the recommended way is to use a tuner. Given the distinctive quality of the blues notes, a tuner is an essential tool — and courtesy — for all who appreciate in-tune music.

✔ **Effects pedals:** Many blues players get along with just an amp, but most blues guitarists augment their sound with outboard effects — each about the size of a packet of index cards — to get even more sonic pos-sibilities. Effects can make it sound like your guitar was recorded in a recording studio, or produce otherworldly sounds that may have more of a theatrical application than a musical one. But perhaps the biggest use of effects in the blues is to get a distorted sound. An effects pedal gives you this quality at low amp volumes. There are more distortion effects available than any other kind, and they'll keep coming.

✔ **Slide:** To play slide, you need a slide apparatus, in the form of a metal or glass tube, bottle neck (you may as well use the beer you cried into), or medicine bottle. Or lots of other things. You can also buy a professional slide. They're not expensive.

Book IV

Blues Guitar

Chapter 2

Playing Blues Rhythm

• •

In This Chapter

▶ Mixing up your blues playing: Downstrokes and upstrokes

▶ Applying syncopation to your sound

▶ Discovering different muting techniques

▶ Checking out some classic fingerstyle blues

▶ Playing different grooves and feels

• •

Chords don't by themselves convey anything meaningful. They're just raw building materials of music until you arrange and play them in a certain way. For guitarists, the playing part comes when you add in the right hand. By playing chords with the right hand in a certain tempo, rhythm, and strumming pattern, you enter into the world of rhythm guitar — an indispensable part of the blues.

Strumming Along

One of the most basic ways you can play chords is with a strum. *Strumming* involves taking your right hand and, with a pick, thumb, or the back of your fingernails, brushing it across several or all the strings, sounding them all together at once. A strum can be slow, fast, hard, or gentle, or any of the infinite shadings in between. When you strum, bring your hand from the top of the guitar (closest to the ceiling) to the bottom (toward the floor) in one motion, striking the strings along the way.

 If you've never played with a pick before, you may find it takes a little time and practice to figure out how tightly to hold the pick when strumming (see Chapter 2 in Book I for more on picks). If you grip it too tightly, the pick gets tripped up in the strings and your right hand doesn't flow smoothly. On the other hand, if you hold the pick too loosely, it may spring out of your fingers when you strike the strings. The important thing is to keep the right hand and arm flowing smoothly while you find just the right grip.

Stroking down . . .

You may not have thought of basic strumming as "executing a downstroke," but that's what you're doing when you naturally strike the strings on a guitar. When you get to more complex strumming patterns — especially ones involving syncopation — you distinguish between downstrokes and upstrokes (see the next section). But for now, focus on the more popular and prevalent downstroke strum.

A *downstroke* (indicated in written music with the symbol ⊓) is played with a downward motion of the pick, toward the floor — the way you naturally strike a guitar. You can strum multiple strings or pick an individual string with a downstroke.

. . . And stroking up

An *upstroke* (indicated by the symbol ∨) is played upward, toward the ceiling, in the opposite direction of a downstroke. So instead of dragging your pick down toward the floor, as you do in a downstroke, you start from a position below the first string and drag your pick upward across the strings, from 1st to 6th. This motion may seem a little less natural and comfortable than a downstroke, but with practice, you can perform upstrokes as easily and with as much control as downstrokes.

In an upstroke, you don't need to worry about hitting all the strings. The top three or four strings are usually sufficient. For example, when playing an E chord with an upstroke, you don't have to strum the strings all the way from the 1st to the 6th, just up to about the 3rd or 4th string. There are exceptions to this rule, but generally, in the blues, you don't hit as many strings on an upstroke strum as you do in a downstroke.

Upstrokes don't get equal playing time with downstrokes. You typically use upstrokes only in conjunction with downstrokes, but you use downstrokes by themselves fairly often in blues playing.

Combining down and up

In certain fast lead passages, upstrokes alternate with downstrokes equally. For fast eighth notes, the strict observance of upstrokes following downstrokes is called *alternate picking*. Alternate picking is the key to playing fast leads smoothly. The best thing is to practice upstrokes as they occur in their natural state — in an eighth-note rhythm in between downstrokes.

Striking to a beat

Regardless of whether your hand moves up or down when it strikes the strings, the important thing to remember is that you're striking in a rhythm — or in sync with the beat. If you strike the strings once per beat, you're playing quarter notes. If you play two strokes per beat, you're playing in eighth notes, which come twice as fast as quarter notes.

If you need help hearing just what the beat is, get a *metronome* — an electronic device that taps out the beat for you. You can buy a metronome at any music store, and many models are small enough to fit right in your guitar case.

Quarter-note striking, beat by beat

Figure 2-1 shows two bars of an E chord with quarter-note slashes. You play four strums for each bar for a total of eight strums. The quarter notes tell you that the strums occur once per beat.

Figure 2-1:
Strumming an E chord in quarter notes for two bars.

Eighth-note striking, twice per beat

Eighth notes occur twice as frequently as quarter notes in the same tempo, or two for every beat instead of one. In written guitar notation, instead of the slashes shown in Figure 2-1, you now face slashes with *beams* — horizontal lines that connect the stems. Quarter notes have just a stem attached to them; eighth notes have stems with beams connecting them to each other. An eighth note by itself has a flag instead of a beam: ♪.

For the eighth notes that appear in Figure 2-2, you strum twice as fast — twice per beat — as you do for the quarter notes. You can do this easily using only downstrokes at most blues tempos, which are slow to moderate (between 60 and 160 beats per minute). To make things interesting, you change chords and introduce A and B7 into the mix. Note that in the figure, the last note of each bar is a quarter note, which gives you a little more time than two eighth notes would for changing chords. Aren't we nice?

Book IV

Blues Guitar

Figure 2-2:
Eighth- and
quarter-note
down-
strokes.

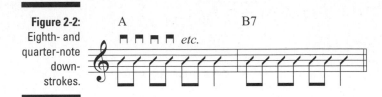

Figure 2-3 combines downstrokes and upstrokes in an eighth-note rhythm. As you practice this passage, keep a relaxed, free-swinging, up-and-down arm motion going. Also work to get equal emphasis on the downstrokes and upstrokes. You may notice that your downstrokes naturally include more and lower strings, while the upstrokes play just the top strings and fewer of them. This is perfectly natural.

Figure 2-3:
Eighth- and
quarter-note
upstrokes
and down-
strokes.

At a moderate tempo, you can easily play Figure 2-3 with all downstrokes, but that variation gives the figure a different feel — more driving and intense. It may be a subtle difference, but playing an eighth-note figure in all down-strokes — versus playing it with alternating downstrokes and upstrokes — is a musical choice, not a technical consideration.

Mixing Single Notes and Strumming

Downstrokes and upstrokes are used for playing single notes, as well as for strumming. Combining single notes with strums is an important part of blues rhythm guitar playing and gives you more options than just strumming. For example, a piano player doesn't plunk down all of her fingers at once every time she plays, and guitarists shouldn't have to strike all the strings every time they bring their picks down (or up).

Because of their instrument's layout, keyboardists play bass notes with the left hand and chords with the right hand. When guitarists separate the bass notes from the chord, they do it with just the right hand, but the principle is the same.

Separating bass and treble: The pick-strum

Separating the bass and treble so they play independently is a great way to provide rhythmic variety and introduce different textures into your playing. In the pick-strum pattern, the _pick_ refers to picking the single bass note, and the _strum_ refers to the upper-string chord that follows. Both the pick and the strum are played with the pick in downstrokes.

Figure 2-4 is a simple pick-strum pattern that's used in many folk blues and country blues songs. This notation mixes single notes (which appear with normal, rounded noteheads) and rhythm slashes (with the narrower, elongated noteheads).

Track 56

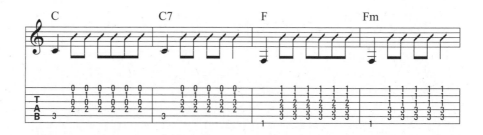

Figure 2-4: Pick-strum pattern for country blues.

Book IV

Blues Guitar

Playing common pick-strum patterns

Most strumming patterns in blues are either all strums or a pick-strum combination, and which approach you use depends on the instruments in your ensemble at the time. A pick-strum approach is good for solo playing or if you're the only rhythm instrument, because the bass notes fall on different parts of the measure than the chord parts.

If you're playing solo guitar, you play a lot more pick-strum patterns. In a band setting, you usually have a bass player who handles the bass duties, and it's more appropriate to play all strumming patterns so as not to get in his way. The following sections describe two pick-strum patterns for the most common blues feels.

Two-beat or cut shuffle

This is sometimes referred to as a *boom-chick* pattern because the bass note and chords alternate, as shown in Figure 2-5. A two-beat feel is common in other forms of music (Dixieland and big-band jazz, polka, samba, and country), but it has its place in the blues, too.

Track 57

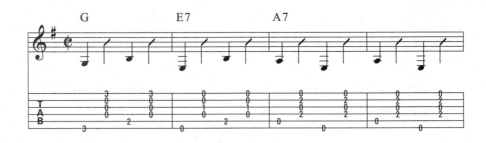

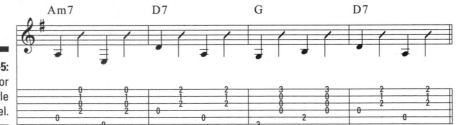

Figure 2-5: Two-beat or cut shuffle feel.

12/8 groove

This is the slowest pattern of the blues, so it helps to have the bass note play twice on beats 1 and 3, while the chords play on beats 2 and 4, as shown in Figure 2-6.

Track 58

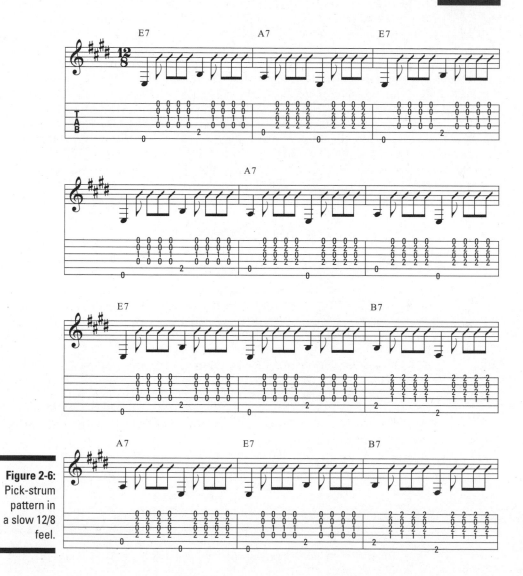

Figure 2-6:
Pick-strum
pattern in
a slow 12/8
feel.

Shuffling the Beats with Syncopated Strumming

After you develop a feel for strumming in different combinations of quarters, eighths, and 16ths — which come *four* per beat, or twice as fast as eighth notes — you can increase the rhythmic variation to these various groupings by applying syncopation. *Syncopation* is the disruption or alteration of the expected sounds of notes. In blues rhythm playing, you can apply syncopation by staggering your strum and mixing up your up- and downstrokes to strike during different parts of the beats. By doing so, you let the agents of syncopation — dots, ties, and rests — steer your rhythmic strumming to a more dramatic and interesting course.

A bit of notation: Dots that extend and ties that bind

In written music, a *dot* attached to a note increases its rhythmic value by half the original length. So a dot attached to a half note (two beats) makes it three beats long. A dotted quarter note is one and a half beats long — or the total of a quarter note plus an eighth note.

A *tie* is a curved line that connects two notes of the same pitch. The value of the tied note adds to the original, so that only the first note is sounded, but the note is held for the duration of the two notes added together.

Figure 2-7 shows a chart of how dots and ties alter the standard note values of eighth, quarter, and half notes.

Figure 2-7:
Dots, ties, rests, and other common syncopation marks.

- whole rest, 4 beats
- half rest, 2 beats
- quarter rest, 1 beat
- eighth rest, 1/2 beat
- 16th rest, 1/4 beat

Syncopation: Playing with dots and ties

So how do dots and ties actually make syncopation work in a musical context? There are two progressions — one in a straight-eighth feel and another in a shuffle — that you can practice playing in this section. They both have common syncopation figures used in the blues.

The normal flow of down- and upstrokes is interrupted in syncopation, so it's important to recall which stroke direction to play a note to avoid getting your strums out of sync.

In both Figures 2-8 and 2-9, pay close attention to the downstroke (⊓) and upstroke (∨) indications.

Book IV

Blues Guitar

✔ Figure 2-8 is a straight-eighth-note feel, in the key of A. The use of dots and ties signals a syncopated rhythm. If the tied figures present a problem, practice the figure by first ignoring the ties (in other words, play the tied note).

Track 59, 0:00

Figure 2-8:
Straight-eighth progression in A with syncopation.

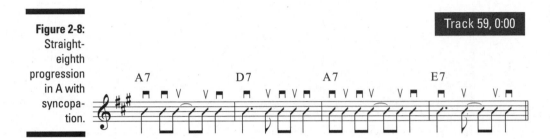

✔ Figure 2-9 is in a shuffle feel in the key of A. A shuffle rhythm divides the quarter note into two eighth notes — but the first eighth note is held longer than the second, producing a swinging, lilting feel. The same syncopation scheme appears here as it did in Figure 2-8, but the shuffle feel makes it fall in a slightly different place in the beat.

Track 59, 0:16

Figure 2-9:
Shuffle in A with syncopation.

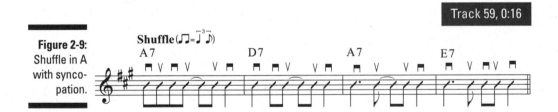

Stopping the Strings from Ringing (Just for a Sec)

Listen to blues rhythm guitar and you hear that it's not one repetitive wall of sound, but an open, varied sound with breathing room and subtle breaks. It's these breaks that prevent the chord strums from running into each other and creating sonic mush. The little gaps in sound keep a strumming figure sounding crisp and controlled.

Muting the sound between two chords (left hand)

To create a rhythm guitar part with some breathing space between the notes, you need to stop the strings from ringing momentarily. And we're talking very small moments here — much smaller than can be indicated by a rest symbol in the music. You can stop the strings instantly with the left hand. Letting the left hand go limp is the best and quickest way to stop a string from ringing — far faster and more controlled than anything you can do with the right hand. This is actually a coordinated effort between the two hands, because it can only occur when the right hand plays.

To get the left hand to mute (indicated in written notation by an X notehead) the in-between sound between any two chords, just relax the fretting fingers enough to release pressure on the fretted strings. The strings instantly deaden, completely cutting off the sound. If your right hand keeps going in the established strumming pattern, you produce a satisfying thunk sound as the right hand hits the deadened strings.

The muted strings intermixed with the sounding strings create a percussive and syncopated rhythm. Allowing your left hand to mute means you don't have to stop and start your right hand to produce syncopation. You can keep it going uninterrupted, in alternating down- and upstrokes.

Simulating syncopation with left-hand muting

Left-hand muting gives you the means to control the strings' sound. Figure 2-10 is technically a straight-ahead down-up eighth-note strum in the right hand. But because you employ left-hand muting, the sound seems to cut off in just the right places, creating a syncopated sound. Your right hand isn't performing true syncopation, because it's playing straight through. It's just that some of the notes don't come through audibly.

Book IV

Blues Guitar

Track 59, 0:32

Figure 2-10: Left-hand muting can simulate syncopation.

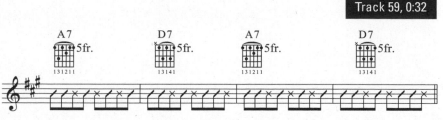

Guitarists seem to develop left-hand muting naturally, almost as if it isn't a technique you have to learn but a way of playing that is self-evident. So don't try to analyze it too much or slow your playing down as you're learning; just strum and relax and tighten your left hand in the context of a medium-tempo groove. Eventually, your two hands sync up without even thinking about it.

Muting the sound of a note (right hand)

Right-hand muting is entirely separate from left-hand muting and produces a totally different effect. When you mute with your right hand, you still hear the pitch and tone of the vibrating string but in a subdued way — more like a true *mute,* in the musical sense. Right-hand muting keeps the string from ringing freely and reduces the volume and ringing of your strings while still maintaining drive and intensity. This technique is a great way to add dramatic variation to your playing.

Palm mute is another name for right-hand muting. It's executed by resting the heel of your right hand on the strings just above the bridge. If you place your hand too far forward, you completely deaden the strings, so place it just forward enough of the bridge that the strings still sound but are dampened. Keep your hand in position through the duration of the strum.

The *accent* is the opposite of a palm mute: It highlights a strike and lets the resulting sound ring out. To accent a chord, just strike it harder than usual and allow the strings to ring free. An accent is indicated with a > mark, just above or below the notehead.

Palm mutes are usually applied to only one or two strings, because the right hand is restricted when you rest it directly on the strings above the bridge. Figure 2-11 is a rhythm figure where you strike only the lowest two strings of the chord during the palm mutes and the upper strings on the accents. Play this progression by using all downstrokes to add intensity.

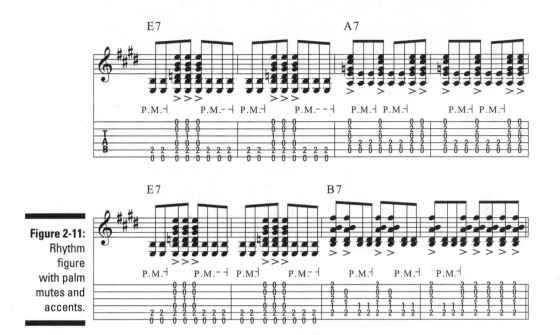

Figure 2-11: Rhythm figure with palm mutes and accents.

Copying the Classics: Plucking Fingerstyle Blues

If you want to make money playing the blues, you should probably get yourself an electric guitar and play it with a pick. But if you want insight into the roots of the blues, grab an acoustic and play it fingerstyle. Acoustic fingerstyle blues is a wonderful tradition, populated with such immortal figures as Robert Johnson, Skip James, Lightnin' Hopkins, Mance Lipscomb, Leadbelly, Mississippi John Hurt, Reverend Gary Davis, John Hammond, Rory Block, Roy Book Binder, Bob Brozman, Jerry Reed, and Chet Atkins.

Early solo blues guitar players quickly realized that separating the thumb and fingers was a great way to get the bass line going independent of the chords and riffs above it. Acoustic fingerstyle blues is best played with an independent thumb. You use the thumb to hit the bass notes while the fingers brush the treble strings, but *independent thumb* means that the thumb and fingers can play separate musical roles — almost like a mini rhythm section. The thumb can be the bass player, and the fingers can provide chords like the guitar's traditional role.

Book IV

Blues Guitar

Figure 2-12 shows a basic fingerstyle pattern where the thumb drives out a steady quarter note rhythm on the low strings, and the thumb plays chords on the offbeats. Listen closely to the CD to capture the shuffle feel in this figure.

Track 60

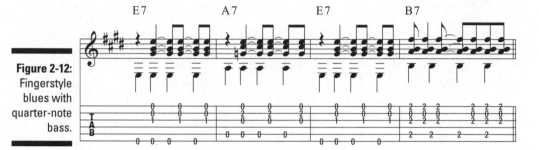

Figure 2-12: Fingerstyle blues with quarter-note bass.

Feels and Grooves: Different Rhythm Styles to Play

Blues consists of a few different *feels* or *grooves* — rhythm styles — and if some songs sound like others, as many say, it's partly because of the relatively few feels. Table 2-1 is a list of the common blues feels and well-known songs written in that feel (and if you don't know these songs, find them and listen to them).

Table 2-1	Blues Songs by Groove	
Feel	*Song*	*Artist*
Shuffle	Sweet Home Chicago	Robert Johnson, The Blues Brothers
	Blue Suede Shoes	Carl Perkins, Elvis Presley
	Midnight Special	Leadbelly
	Hide Away	Freddie King, Eric Clapton, Stevie Ray Vaughan

Feel	Song	Artist
Straight-four	The Thrill Is Gone	B.B. King
	Killing Floor	Howlin' Wolf, Mike Bloomfield, Jimi Hendrix
	Crossroads	Robert Johnson, Cream
	Born Under a Bad Sign	Albert King, Cream
12/8	Stormy Monday	Allman Brothers, T-Bone Walker
	Red House	Jimi Hendrix
	At Last	Etta James
	The Sky Is Crying	Elmore James, Stevie Ray Vaughan
16 feel	Hard to Handle	Otis Redding, Black Crowes
	Little Wing	Jimi Hendrix, Stevie Ray Vaughan
	Mary Had a Little Lamb	Buddy Guy, Stevie Ray Vaughan

The shuffle groove

The shuffle groove is certainly the most common feel in blues — even more common than the straight-four and slow 12/8 feel. There's one small hurdle to get over: A shuffle feel uses a triplet-based rhythmic division, where each quarter note is divided into three eighth notes, called *triplets*. The typical melodic division is two eighth notes, where the first note is held for the duration of the first two notes of the triplet, and the second eighth note is the third note of the triplet. This yields a lopsided, lilting feel in the eighth-note flow that's the heart of the shuffle sound.

Figure 2-13 is a progression in a shuffle feel. Practice while listening to the CD on this one to make sure that you get the sound of the shuffle.

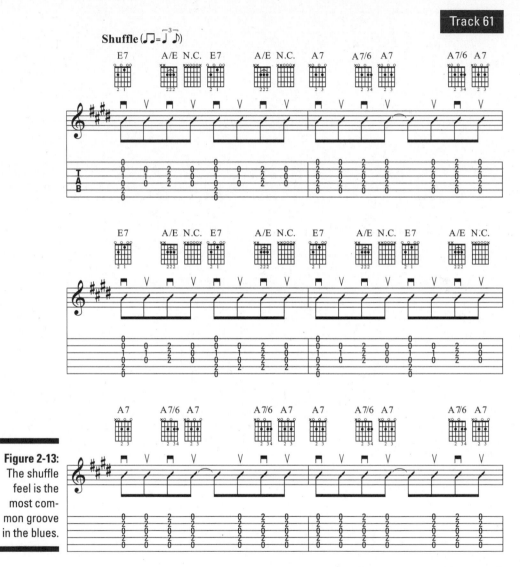

Figure 2-13: The shuffle feel is the most common groove in the blues.

(continued)

(continued)

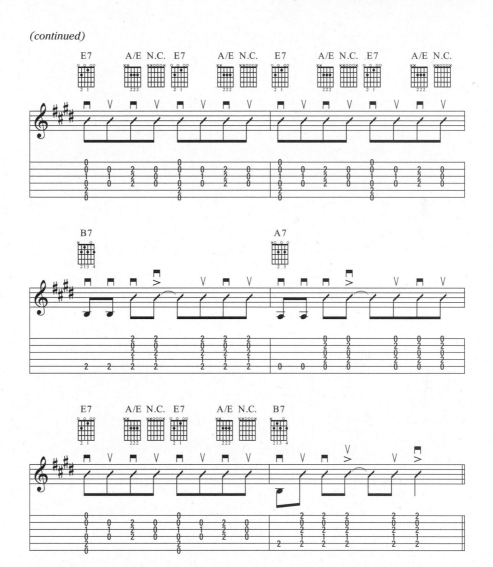

The driving straight-four

The *straight* in *straight-four* refers to the eighth notes being evenly spaced, just as they are in most normal music forms you encounter. The *four* is 4/4 time, which is the most common time signature for blues. This explanation may sound mundane, except when you consider that most blues is in a shuffle feel, so the word *straight* indicates that you're doing something a little uncommon for the blues. Figure 2-14 shows a driving straight-four groove.

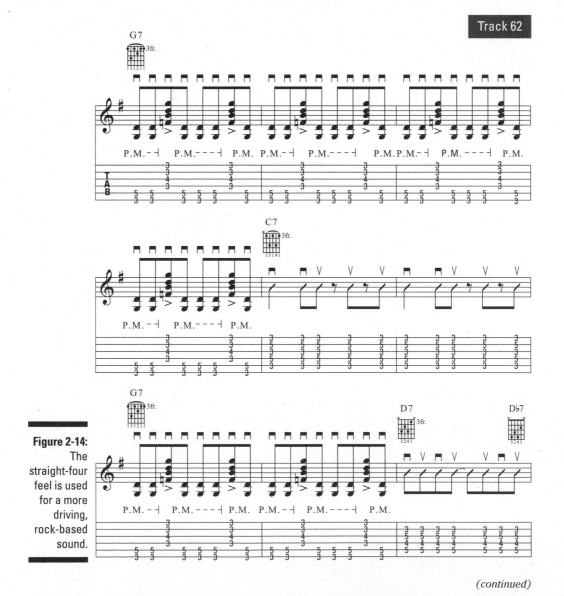

Figure 2-14: The straight-four feel is used for a more driving, rock-based sound.

(continued)

(continued)

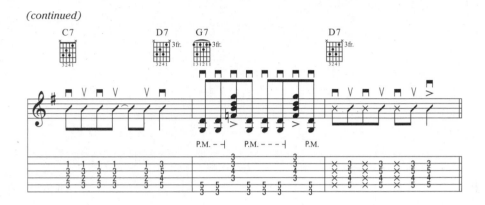

The slow 12/8, with groups of three

The *slow* part of the slow 12/8 feel is easy to grasp. The 12/8 is related to the shuffle, because a shuffle is a 4/4 feel based on triplet divisions of eighth notes. But in 12/8, the feel is slower, and the individual eighth notes (they're not called triplets, because their grouping of three is built into the time signature) are given more prominence.

Don't be intimidated by the 12/8 part of this feel. There are 12 eighth notes to the bar, and each eighth note gets one beat. In practice though, the eighth notes are grouped in four units of three each. So it's a lot like 4/4 time with eighth-note triplets on every beat. If it's a slow blues and you can hear note-groupings of three, it's probably a 12/8 feel.

Famous blues songs in 12/8 include T-Bone Walker's "Stormy Monday," covered by the Allman Brothers on their Live at Fillmore album. Figure 2-15 is a passage in the style of "Stormy Monday."

Book IV

Blues Guitar

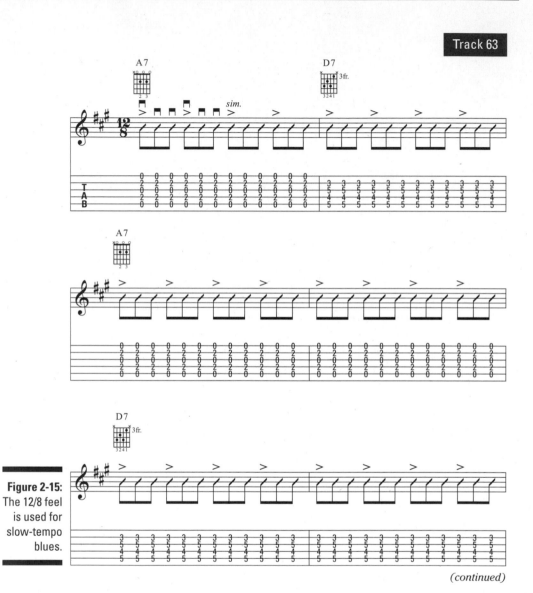

Figure 2-15:
The 12/8 feel
is used for
slow-tempo
blues.

(continued)

(continued)

The slow and funky 16 feel

More modern blues grooves include the *16 feel,* which has a slower tempo but funkier sound due to the 16th-note subdivisions. (James Brown's "I Feel Good" and "Papa's Got a Brand New Bag" are classic examples of 16th-note–based funk.) "Hard to Handle," written by Otis Redding and covered by the Black Crowes, is a famous example of 16-feel blues. Figure 2-16 is medium tempo, funky groove in a 16 feel.

Track 64

Figure 2-16: The 16 feel is used for funky-sounding blues grooves.

(continued)

(continued)

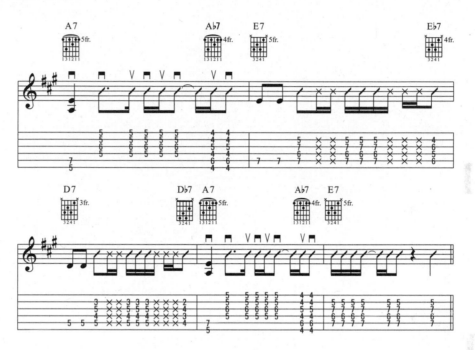

Chapter 3

Blues Progressions, Song Forms, and Moves

In This Chapter

▶ Distinguishing the primary key families and their chords

▶ Recognizing the structure of a blues song

▶ Connecting structures and keys

▶ Playing intros, turnarounds, endings, and high moves

*T*he blues is a welcoming, beckoning music for both listener and performer that says, "Join in and start contributing!" The blues' repetition and call-and-response qualities — derived from its forebears, the work song and field holler — make it easy for people to join in a song on the fly. Musicians grasp the form quickly, and listeners have an expectation that's set up by each phrase, which is then satisfied by the lyrics or the chord progression. Best of all, these simple, infectious, and ingenious devices that make the blues relatable are easy to understand and master, and are covered in this chapter.

Blues by the Numbers

You can learn music a lot quicker if you associate chords and keys by their numerical equivalents. In any key, the *root* or *tonic* (the tone that names the key or chord) is called I, and subsequent pitches become II, III, IV, and so on, numbers expressed in Roman numerals. So in the key of C, the numbers are broken down like this:

✔ C is I

✔ D is II

✔ E is III

✔ F is IV

And so on.

As keys change, so do the notes, expressed as letter names — but the numbers, or relationships, remain the same, allowing you to treat all keys equally. The number system works well for building chords by intervals, too, but in the blues, you're more concerned with chords formed on the notes of the scale of a key.

If you memorize the basic blues chord formula in numbers (I, IV, V), then you can figure out the progression in any key because the numbers — and therefore the relationships — don't change, no matter what key it's in. Many have realized that because there are only seven letters in music (A through G), you can just memorize the keys without converting numbers to letters. And the more experienced you become, the more your ears take you to the right chord without having to memorize anything. In short: The numbers reveal the underlying structure and are important in understanding the function of the chords.

Musicians often refer to chords by their numerical designation instead of their actual letter name. For example, when a musician says, "In that song, listen to what B.B. does when he goes to the IV chord," you know exactly where in the song that is (bar 5). If the musician had said, "When he goes to the D chord," you'd have to know what key he was in first, and you or the storyteller may not have that information.

Viewing music through these numbers makes the key irrelevant to a blues player. Or more precisely, the key can change all it wants, but the structure doesn't, and that's the important point of the exercise.

Recognizing the Big Dogs: Primary Key Families and Their Chords

Whether you play folk, rock, or blues, sooner or later you notice that certain chords seem to cluster together. If you think of these chords by their numerical assignments, or function, you see this phenomena is common to all keys. In every key, the main chords are the one, four, and five, represented by the Roman numerals I, IV, and V. These groupings of I, IV, V are known as *families*. It's a virtual certainty that whatever other chords you may find in a song, you always have a I, IV, and V. And many songs have *only* these three chords.

Here's an example of how to figure out the I, IV, and V of different keys:

- ✔ In the key of A, A is the I chord. Count on your fingers up to your fourth finger, saying the letters of the alphabet as you go, and you find that the IV chord in A is D. The V chord, then, is E.

- ✔ In the key of C, C is the I chord. The IV chord is F. And the V chord is G.

Try it yourself with other keys, starting on I with the letter that names the key (in the key of G, G is I). Table 3-1 shows common blues keys and their I, IV, and V chords. There are other keys (for example, B and A♭), but these are the most commonly used keys for blues guitar.

Table 3-1	The I, IV, and V Chords in Common Blues Keys		
Key	*I*	*IV*	*V*
A	A	D	E
B♭	B♭	E♭	F
C	C	F	G
D	D	G	A
E	E	A	B
F	F	B♭	C
G	G	C	D

For guitarists, some keys and chords lend themselves to certain movements that sound especially good for the blues; other keys are less successful. The following section mixes up the keys so you get familiar with the different families. But the blues is most accommodating to the keys of E and A, especially when using open-position chords.

The Structure of a Blues Song, Baby

It's time to give your hands some direction — to organize sounds into chord progressions and song forms. These larger organizing principles make the blues come alive and build a meaningful experience for the player and the listener. Through them, you watch techniques turn into expressions and patterns into musical messages. In this section, you take the shorter phrases of the right-hand patterns (covered in Chapter 2 in Book IV) and make them into actual songs.

A song is made up of a *chord progression*. The song's form and chord progression are concepts that can be used almost interchangeably, with chord progression describing more often the harmonic architecture of the song. Many people can recognize a song form — such as the 12-bar blues — but as a guitarist, you need to know the corresponding chord progression that makes up that 12-bar form. And you need to be able to identify the actual chords going by, as well as any variations to that form. In the blues, the progression is part of what makes the blues the blues. So, the progression is synonymous with the form. In other words, saying "the blues" implies a 12-bar structure with the chords falling at specific bars within that structure.

Book IV

Blues Guitar

A chord progression isn't the only aspect of a song, but it's a pretty important one because it forms the framework or structure that supports the other elements: melody, lyrics, riffs, and the solo sections.

Playing the 12-bar blues

The 12-bar blues is by far the most popular form for the blues. It consists of 12 measures and observes a particular scheme as shown in Figure 3-1.

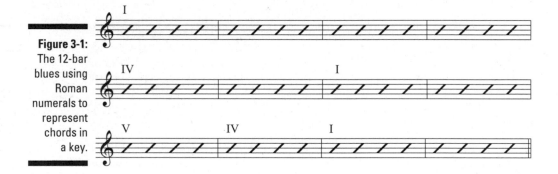

Figure 3-1:
The 12-bar blues using Roman numerals to represent chords in a key.

Figure 3-1 uses Roman numerals instead of letter names, because the progression is the same in every key. For example, if you play blues in E, then E is the I chord, A is the IV chord, and B or B7 is the V chord. With the corresponding letters substituted for the Roman numerals, the progression looks like Figure 3-2.

Track 65, 0:00

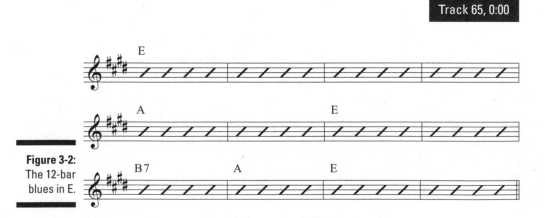

Figure 3-2:
The 12-bar blues in E.

B7 replaces B in Figure 3-2, mainly because B7 is easier to play. Technically, you could play B as a barre chord on the 2nd fret. But the main point is to convey the letter names dictated by the I, IV, and V, so playing either B7 or B is acceptable.

Because the slashes (those /// marks) leave some interpretation in what you're playing, try this exercise with shuffle eighth notes — eighth notes that have a long-short rhythm scheme, explained in detail in Chapter 2 in Book IV — in alternating downstrokes and upstrokes. You hear this version on the CD, so see if you can match the rhythm of the performance on the audio.

If you're a little shaky on the eighth-note strum for Figure 3-2, try first playing this blues with quarter-note downstrokes (also covered in Chapter 2 in Book IV). Don't worry, you're still in sync with the CD, but the guitar on the CD strums twice to your once. After you can play that comfortably, try playing with eighth-note downstrokes in a shuffle feel. And after that, try the alternate-picking approach, which is, not surprisingly, also discussed in Chapter 2 in Book IV.

The quick four

The *quick four* is a variation on the 12-bar blues that occurs in the second bar, where you go to a IV chord — for example, when you go to A in the key of E — for one bar, and go back to the I chord for two bars. The quick four, as shown in Figure 3-3, provides an opportunity for variation and interest in an otherwise unbroken stretch of four bars of the same chord.

Track 65, 0:37

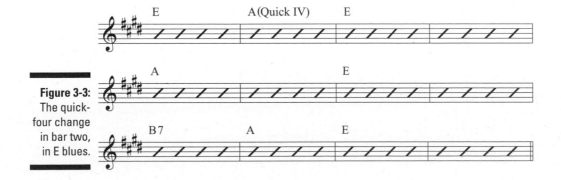

Figure 3-3:
The quick-four change in bar two, in E blues.

Book IV

Blues Guitar

The quick four happens almost as often as not in blues songs. Some songs that use the quick-four method include "Sweet Home Chicago" and "Hide

Away." Songs such as "Hound Dog" and "Johnny B. Goode" don't use this variation. Most blues guitarists don't think too much about whether a song has a quick four. They just look at someone else in the band who knows more than they do to see if they're going to make that move in bar two or not.

The quick four happens very soon after you start the song, so if you're at a jam session, or are playing along with a song for the first time, you must be on your toes to anticipate its use.

The turnaround

The *turnaround* is the last two bars of the progression that point the music back to the beginning. At the end of the 12-bar blues, you can repeat the progression or end it. Most of the time you repeat the progression to play additional verses and solos. To help get the progression ready for a repeat, you employ a turnaround, which sets up the repeat. At the most basic level, you can create a turnaround by just substituting a V chord for the I chord in the last bar — bar 12.

Practically all songs (blues or otherwise) end on the I chord, called the *tonic* chord of the key, so the substitution of the V chord creates a strong pull that brings the song back to the I chord at bar 1 of the progression. In any music, the V chord sounds like it wants to go back to the I chord. When the V chord occurs at the end of the progression, it tells musicians and listeners unmistakably that "we're going back around again." While the most basic application of a turnaround is just playing a V chord in the last bar, to most guitarists, a turnaround presents an opportunity to play a *riff* or *lick* (covered in Chapter 4 in Book IV). Figure 3-4 shows the last four bars of a 12-bar blues with a turnaround bar added.

Figure 3-4:
The turn-
around
usually has
a V chord in
the last bar.

Bar 9 of 12-bar blues

The 12-bar blues in song

If you're wondering how musical charts and symbols relate to the actual songs (melody and lyrics), here's the quick version:

✔ The 12-bar blues breaks down neatly into three lines of four bars each. These three lines correspond to the vocal phrases.

✔ The vocal scheme of the blues is A-A-B. Each letter represents a sentence, complete thought, or phrase of the lyric.

Think of any 12-bar blues, such as "Hound Dog," "Stormy Monday," "Kansas City," "St. Louis Blues," "Easy Rider," or "Corrina, Corrina." Each song has three lines per verse, with the first line repeated. Even though the first vocal line is repeated, it never sounds repetitious, because the chords underneath the lyric and melody change, which provides interest. You can actually sing any of these songs to any 12-bar progression.

You may see the V chord in the turnaround bar with parentheses around it. This method is shorthand for saying that you use the turnaround optionally or whenever you decide to repeat the progression. When you want the progression to end, you ignore the parentheses and continue playing the I chord from the previous bar.

Slow blues

Slow blues is usually a 12-bar blues, but played in 12/8 time, using three strums to the beat. Because of the slower tempo, there's often more opportunity to put in additional chords — especially 9th chords, a common slow-blues hallmark.

Figure 3-5 is a slow 12-bar blues in 12/8 time with its own moves added — moves that consist of adding chords a whole step higher before the main ones. But it's still a 12-bar blues. You can hear a lot of this quality in the playing of T-Bone Walker.

One irony of slow blues is that although the tempo is slower than a shuffle, and the changes come more slowly and are therefore more manageable, the lead playing is often very intricate, especially with regard to rhythm. If you ever get a chance to see transcribed guitar solos in print, look at the ones in a slow 12/8. The notation can get quite hairy!

Track 66

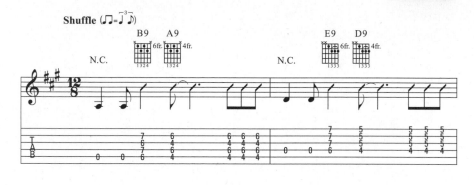

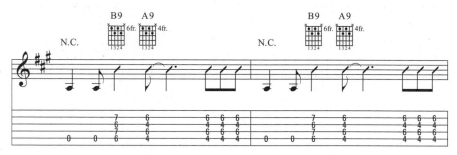

Figure 3-5:
A slow
blues in 12/8
with added
chords.

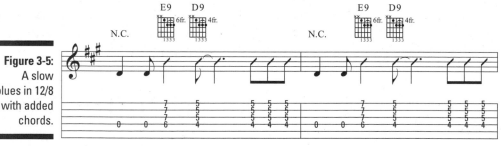

(continued)

(continued)

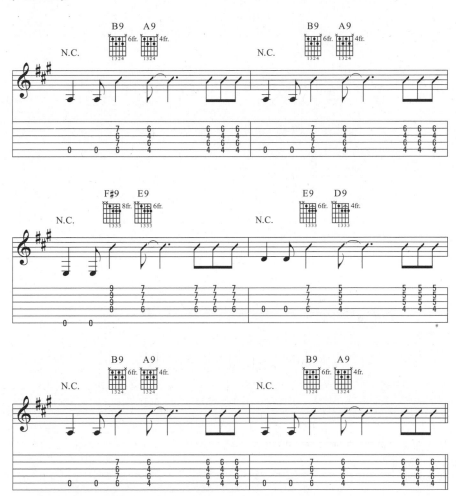

8-bar blues

The *8-bar blues* is four bars shorter than the 12-bar blues, but the 8-bar blues doesn't really follow a strict form the way the 12-bar blues does. The 8-bar blues encompasses several feels, tempos, and qualities — often an 8-bar blues has more chords in it than just the basic I, IV, and V, making it more "songlike" than a 12-bar blues. Figure 3-6 is an 8-bar blues played with a bass-strum pattern by using a variety of chords.

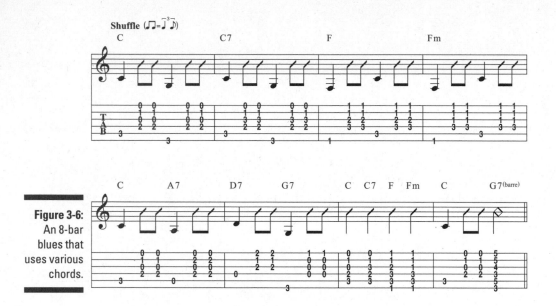

Figure 3-6: An 8-bar blues that uses various chords.

Straight-four (or rock blues)

Straight-four is sometimes called *rock blues* or *rock feel* and means that you play even eighth notes supported by a heavy backbeat (emphasis on beats 2 and 4, usually courtesy of a cracking snare drum). Most blues is in a non-straight feel, meaning it's either in a shuffle (a long-short scheme that derives from triplets) or a slow 12/8 feel (with three notes to the beat). So a straight-four, which is common in rock, is actually rare in traditional blues.

Some examples of well-known songs in a straight-four include "Roll Over Beethoven," "Johnny B. Goode," and Albert King's "Crosscut Saw." Figure 3-7 shows a straight-four progression in A with a variation on the 5-to-6 move (also called the Jimmy Reed, covered in the next section). This variation has the moving voice occasionally going up to the flat seven. (G in the A chord, C in the D chord, and D in the E chord.)

Track 67

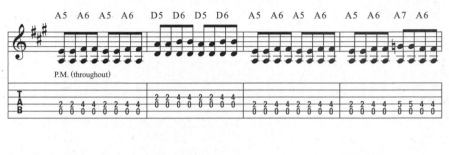

Figure 3-7:
A straight-four progression with a variation.

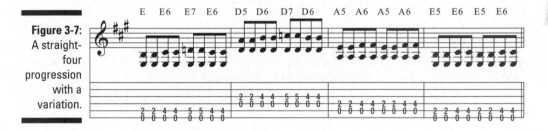

Applying Structures to Keys

Although every key is treated equally when discussing function and music theory (see "Blues by the Numbers" earlier in this chapter), the reality is that different keys and chords on the guitar present different moves. What you can do easily in E, you may not be able to do in G, and G has other options that E may not have. These variations are a delight (and frustration!) of playing the guitar. Each key has something idiomatic that can't be performed comfortably or convincingly in another key. Composers and musicians write and play songs in different keys to exploit these little differences that each key provides.

Book IV

Blues Guitar

A move with many chords: The Jimmy Reed move

If you have the basic 12-bar blues under your belt, including the quick four and turnaround bar, it's time to shake things up a bit. (See the corresponding sections earlier in this chapter if you look under your belt and nothing's there.) You can start off with a move that's been a blues and rock staple forever. It's known by many different names, but because this book is a blues book, you can attribute it to one of its most famous practitioners: Jimmy Reed.

The Jimmy Reed move — named after the Chicago harmonica player, singer, and guitarist — involves going from the 5th to the 6th degrees in each chord (the note E in a G chord, A in a C chord). Chuck Berry made this technique famous in a straight-eighth, rock 'n' roll setting in the late '50s and '60s. For now, don't worry about converting numbers to notes for the I, IV, and V chords; just figure out the left-hand part.

To play a "move," you put your left hand in motion. Figure 3-8 shows the Jimmy Reed move in the key of E, using E, A, and B power chords (for more on power chords, see Chapter 3 in Book II). The chord diagrams are given above the tab, allowing you to think of this move in two ways: as an extra chord inserted in between the ones you already know or as a simple one-finger move in the left hand. Whichever way works for you is the right one!

One of the best things about the Jimmy Reed move is that it works so well in different chords and keys. When played in different keys, the figure preserves the original relationship of the notes in the new key, but because it's in a different key, it just sounds, well, different. Not better or worse, perhaps, just different — and still very cool. It's like singing "Happy Birthday" in the key of G or E♭: You can recognize the melody in any key setting — but the Jimmy Reed move is so much hipper than "Happy Birthday."

Jimmy's move in G

If you had to play in the key of G, and you wanted to throw in the Jimmy Reed move, it would look like Figure 3-9. This move has a different character and is a little easier to play than the same move in E (discussed previously). The chord diagrams in the figure are presented above the staffs, so you can view the move as either a new chord inserted between the ones you already know or as just simply moving a finger over to play a previously open string on beats 2 and 4.

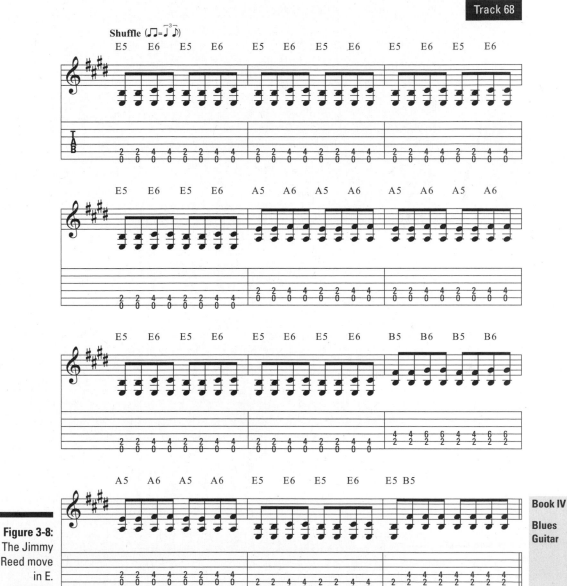

Figure 3-8:
The Jimmy
Reed move
in E.

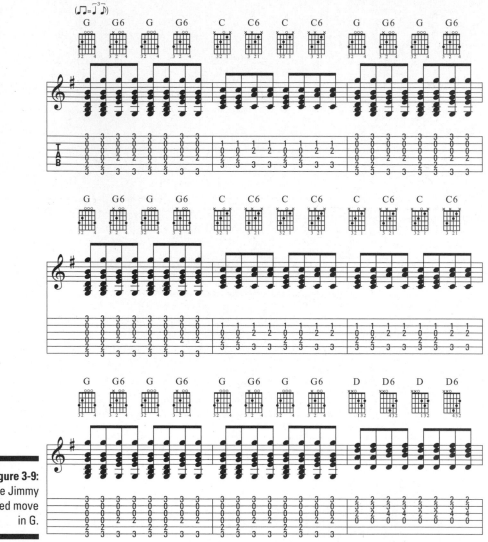

(continued)

(continued)

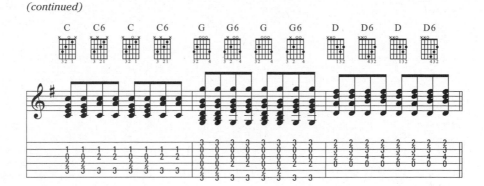

In the Jimmy Reed move in G, you have to mute the open string that your finger just left to play the new chord (indicated by an X in the chord diagram).

Jimmy's move in A

The move travels up the neck of the guitar to grab the IV and V chords. This sound is very rock 'n' roll (in a good way), and has a less folksy character than the G progression. The blues move in A has an entirely different feel than the same move in G, yet they're only one letter away — the basis for Chuck Berry's sound and for much of the "boogie" rock 'n' roll played by rockabilly artists of the '50s, '60s, and today.

The sound of sadness: Minor blues

For a different flavor of blues, consider the blues in a minor key setting. Minor keys in music sound sad or menacing or mysterious, and what better way to give the blues a double dose of trouble than to put it in a minor key? Putting the blues in minor also provides some variety. A minor blues doesn't say much about the form, only that it uses minor chords instead of the usual major or dominant-7 chords. A minor blues can be a 12-bar blues with minor chords or a straight-eighth (or non-shuffle feel), 16-bar format (instead of the more common 12-bar format).

"St. James Infirmary" and "The Thrill Is Gone" are two minor blues songs. "The Thrill Is Gone" is a popular format for more contemporary blues, and Figure 3-10 shows a progression more along the lines of this song. Notice the addition of minor 7th chords, which help give a jazzier feel.

Book IV

Blues Guitar

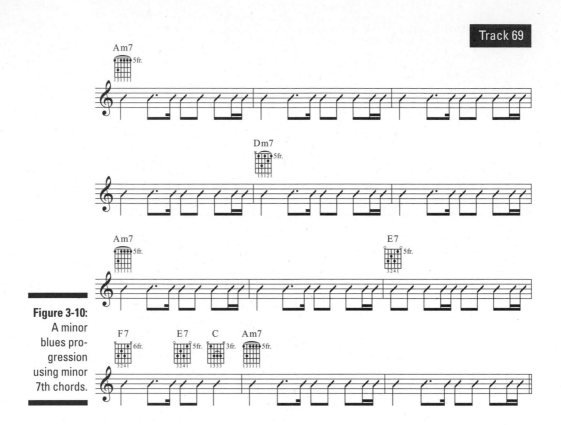

Track 69

Figure 3-10:
A minor blues progression using minor 7th chords.

Accessorizing the 12-Bar Blues: Intros, Turnarounds, and Endings

Intros (short, of course, for introductions), *turnarounds*, and *endings* are all enhancements to the 12-bar blues. They're used to steer the song toward repeats or resolutions and are all related. There are countless variations for these three devices, and they're often reworked versions of each other, where the only difference is how they end.

Intros

An intro often features a solo lick by the guitar, piano, or other instrument (think of "That'll Be the Day" by Buddy Holly). But sometimes the whole band plays the intro, and the guitar is expected to play rhythm guitar (licks and riffs are covered in Chapter 4 in Book IV).

Intros often borrow from their turnaround cousins, because the whole idea is to set up the I chord and the beginning of the progression — the same duties that the turnaround has.

Figure 3-11 shows a basic two-bar intro. The rhythm features a syncopation and then a held note, which creates a musical space (or hole) before the downbeat of the 12-bar progression. This space allows room for a vocal or instrumental melodic pickup — a phrase that starts before bar 1.

Figure 3-11:
A simple
2-bar intro.

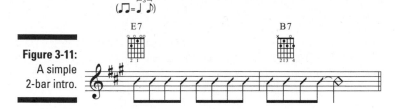

Figure 3-12 is a four-bar intro that is just the last four bars of the 12-bar blues. This intro is popular and is often announced by a musician saying, "Let's bring it in from the V," or "Let's walk it down from the V."

Figure 3-12:
A four-bar
intro.

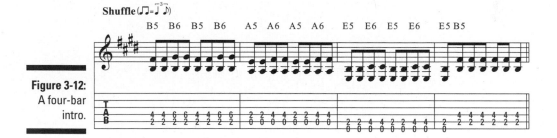

Turnarounds

A turnaround bar is a bar, as mentioned earlier, that substitutes a V chord for a I chord in the last bar of the progression — bar 12 in a 12-bar blues (see "Playing the 12-bar blues" earlier in this chapter). A true, full turnaround is, at minimum, a two-bar phrase that goes from the I chord to the V chord. *Note:* Entire books could be written on just turnarounds, but this section covers only a few rhythm approaches.

Figure 3-13 shows a simple two-bar turnaround using the Jimmy Reed move and syncopation.

Book IV

Blues Guitar

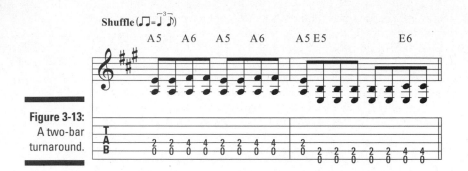

Figure 3-13:
A two-bar turnaround.

Figure 3-14 shows a more elaborate turnaround using one chord for every two beats or five different chords in all: C, C7, F, Fm, and G7 — all in the space of two bars.

Figure 3-14:
A two-bar turnaround with chord changes every two beats.

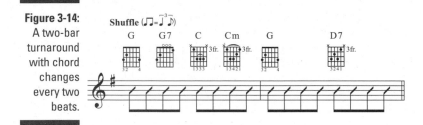

Figure 3-15 is a variation of Figure 3-14, with a chromatic move in the last part. It's also in an unusual key — B♭.

Figure 3-15:
A two-bar turnaround with chromatic movement.

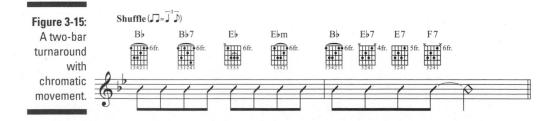

Endings

Endings are closely related to turnarounds, except for the last part of the last measure. The last measure terminates on a I chord of some type. Figure 3-16 shows an ending that a slow blues often uses — a 9th chord for the final chord of the piece.

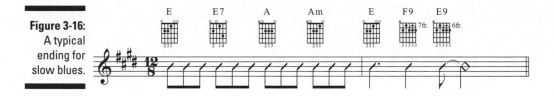

Figure 3-16: A typical ending for slow blues.

Figure 3-17 is an ending that's typical for medium-tempo shuffle tunes.

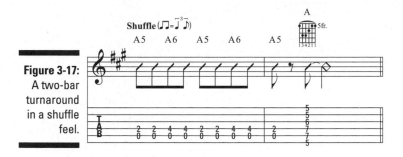

Figure 3-17: A two-bar turnaround in a shuffle feel.

High Moves

All the moves covered earlier in this chapter take place on the lower strings. But you can play them on the higher strings, too. These strings often involve the same notes that are played in the lower strings (the 5th and 6th of the chord featured in the Jimmy Reed move — covered in "Applying Structures to Keys" earlier in this chapter), but when played up high, it sounds more like a riff than a chord figure. This creates a bridge between chord figures and riffs and licks.

Think of these new, higher moves as chord forms added to your basic eighth-note strumming. As you play these added chords, notice that the sound produces a melodic motif. Figure 3-18 shows the first high-note move in the key of E. The two added chords are E7 chords with your fourth finger of the left hand playing notes on the second string.

Book IV

Blues Guitar

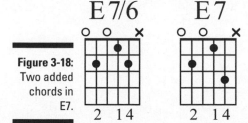

Figure 3-18: Two added chords in E7.

Now add two chords to the A7 chord sequence. The notes are the same relative ones you added to the E7 chord — the 6th and the 7th. Figure 3-19 shows the fingering with the added notes played by the fourth finger of the left hand.

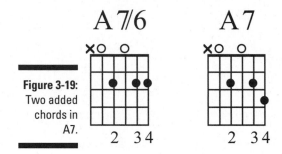

Figure 3-19:
Two added
chords in
A7.

For the B7 chord, in Figure 3-20, the fourth finger again plays the added note, but because the finger is already in place — on the 2nd fret, 1st string — you must move it up to the 3rd fret briefly. This may seem a bit awkward at first, and the stretch between your fourth and third fingers may take a while to get smoothly, but it will come in time.

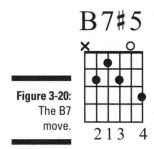

Figure 3-20:
The B7
move.

Figure 3-21 shows all three moves in a 12-bar blues. If some of the moves seem difficult, or come too fast, try leaving them out at first. As long as you don't break the rhythm in your right hand and you change left-hand chords where you're supposed to, the blues still sound fine. That's the beauty of the blues: You can play any variation on the basic structure — from simple to complex — and it always sounds good.

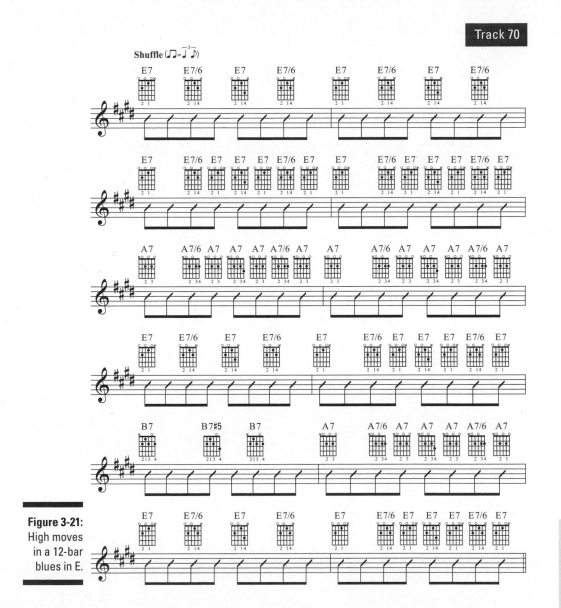

Figure 3-21:
High moves
in a 12-bar
blues in E.

Chapter 4

Blues Riffs: The Bedrock of the Blues

. . . .

In This Chapter

▶ Mastering the basics: Single-note riffs

▶ Exploring double-stop riffs

▶ Shooting for high-note riffs

▶ Taking your skills to the next level: Mastering rhythm figures

. . . .

*I*t can be tough to find your own blues voice because you can't randomly improvise the blues any more than you can make up baroque or bebop; you have to learn the vocabulary in order to improvise. And the vocabulary for blues includes licks and riffs.

Although related to chords, riffs aren't tethered to chords the way the rhythm-based approach is (Chapter 2 in Book IV discusses blues rhythm). It's always good to know where your riffs spring from — especially if they're derived out of a chord form. But you don't need to grab a chord first to play a riff. In this chapter, you play riffs with a liberated left hand.

When you learn chords, strumming, double-stops, and single-note riffs, you have most of the ingredients necessary to start really developing as a player. In the blues, cloning the greats and doing your own thing is always a delicate balance.

Basic Single-Note Riffs

A *riff* is a self-contained musical phrase, and it can be used to form the basis for a song. Riffs are the bridge between chords and lead guitar. They're usually based on single notes, but they can involve *double-stops* (two notes played simultaneously) and bits of full-chord playing.

You may hear the terms riff and lick used interchangeably in your blues guitar career. But try to think of a riff as more of a structural, repeatable phrase, and a lick as a cliché — that is, a self-contained lead figure that doesn't necessarily have structural importance (like those short, snappy melodic phrases played by blues and country guitarists between vocal lines).

The signature guitar parts in the Rolling Stones' "Satisfaction" and the Beatles' "Day Tripper" are classic examples of riffs. In blues, the crisp, ascending, horn-like melodic bursts in Freddie King's "Hide Away" are riffs, as is the repeating pattern in Bo Diddley's "I'm a Man."

In the next few sections, you look at riffs in order of increasing rhythmic activity, starting with quarter notes, advancing through eighth notes (the straight, shuffle, and triplet varieties), and moving to the more complex 16th-note–based and syncopated riffs (which involve eighths and 16ths). Just as you do when playing chords, you must play riffs with a solid and consistent approach to articulation (attack), rhythm, and dynamics (overall loud and soft) to help keep the drive in the guitar part.

Use a metronome to help keep yourself playing along with the beat, and use a combination of your ears and muscle memory to make sure you strike the strings with the same force for achieving consistent dynamics.

For the low-down bass notes: Quarter-note riffs

You may think you can't do much to groove hard with the boring ol' quarter note, but the quarter note drives a lot of boogie-woogie bass lines. Boogie-woogie and blues are close cousins, and you can always throw in a boogie bass as a variation to almost any medium- to uptempo shuffle. Figure 4-1 shows a common quarter-note boogie pattern that you can play easily with just downstrokes.

Figure 4-1:
A boogie
bass line
in quarter
notes.

The big daddy of riffs: Eighth-note riffs

Most riffs in blues are eighth-note based, so there's a wide range of music you can play in an eighth-note groove. But to start off, jump into eighth-note riffs by taking quarter-note riffs (from Figure 4-1) and doubling them up — that is, play two notes per beat instead of one. Figure 4-2 is a boogie-bass pattern in shuffle eighth-notes.

Figure 4-2: A boogie bass line with double-struck eighth notes.

Another popular riff is the stop-time feel. It features the low notes of the guitar. The entire band plays a figure in unison and stops at the downbeat of each measure in the phrase, like in "Blue Suede Shoes." This approach is used famously in the Muddy Waters tunes "Mannish Boy" and "Hoochie Coochie Man." A tribute to the stop-time riff is featured in Figure 4-3.

Figure 4-3: A stop-time riff in eighth notes.

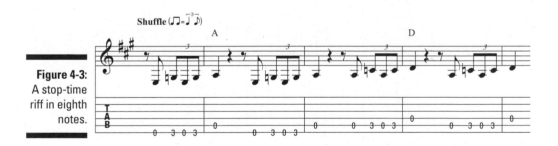

Book IV

Blues Guitar

Figure 4-4 shows a riff in the style of Freddie King's "Hide Away" — one of the most recognizable eighth-note riff-based songs in the blues repertoire.

Figure 4-4:
An eighth-note riff in the style of Freddie King's "Hide Away."

Adding a little funk: 16th-note riffs

Funky blues usually sound that way because 16th notes are in the mix. In a 16th-note groove, the tempos tend to be moderate. But because the beats use 16th-note subdivisions, the groove sounds quite active. Often the bass line and drums (particularly the hi-hat) employ 16th notes to lend support to the scratchings laid down by the guitar. Figure 4-5 is a 16th-note riff on the low strings that you play with strict alternate (down-up-down-up) picking.

Figure 4-5:
A 16th-note riff using alternate picking.

Throwing rhythm for a loop: Syncopated eighth-note riffs

Although syncopation isn't a huge influence in the blues (compared to, say, jazz, R&B, and funk), it's used sometimes and is always a welcome treat. (For more on syncopation and its mechanisms, flip to Chapter 2 in Book IV.) Figure 4-6 shows a syncopated blues line consisting of a dotted eighth, a tie, and 16th notes.

If you're practicing the syncopation in Figure 4-6 and it gives you trouble at first, try practicing the line without the tie (so you're playing both notes in the tie). Then, when you're confident with the figure, practice the tie by letting the note ring through.

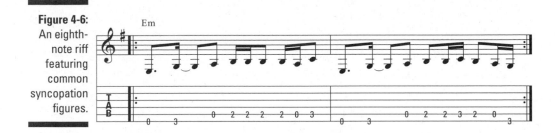

Figure 4-6: An eighth-note riff featuring common syncopation figures.

Double the Strings, Double the Fun: Double-Stops (Two-Note Riffs)

Riffs aren't restricted to single notes. In this section, you get to explore double-stops — a technique that doesn't strictly involve single notes. The term double-stop means two strings.

A double-stop applies to all string instruments when two notes are stopped or played together. Even when guitarists don't have to fret a string, they still refer to simultaneous two-string playing as double-stops. But more than just playing two strings (like in the Jimmy Reed figure covered in Chapter 3 in Book IV), double-stop playing implies moving in lock step — and even performing bends, slurs, and vibrato (sliding fretted notes back and forth to make them waver up and down in pitch) on two strings at once.

Part of the versatility of a two-note figure is that it can be played on any two strings — low, high, and in the middle — all for a slightly different effect. When you get tired of playing chords and single-note leads, a two-note riff can be just the ticket to give your playing (and your listeners) a much-needed dose of dual-string diversity.

The 5-6 riff is a blues-rhythm hallmark of going from the 5th to the 6th degree in a chord (such as E to F♯ in an A chord) and is technically a double-stop, although the string motion doesn't proceed in parallel motion. But the right-hand coordination is the same: You strike two strings as if they're one every time your right hand comes in contact with the strings. The 5-6 riff is also known as the Jimmy Reed move (see Chapter 3 in Book IV). The following sections cover two 5-6 riffs, each in a different feel.

Book IV

Blues Guitar

Straight feel

Straight-eighth notes are unusual in blues. But in blues-rock, classic rock 'n' roll, and rockabilly — all closely related to the blues — the straight-eighth feel rules. Straight eighths are spaced equally apart, whereas shuffle eighths follow a long-short scheme.

Figure 4-7 uses linear movement instead of the more static, back-and-forth 5-5-6-6-5-5-6-6. Also think of the riff to Roy Orbison's (and later Van Halen's) "Oh, Pretty Woman" for a classic straight-eighth approach to a low-note riff.

Figure 4-7:
An expanded version of the classic 5-6 move in straight eighths.

Many eighth-note riffs sound equally good in a shuffle or straight-eighth feel. And in many early rock and R&B recordings, such as Chuck Berry's "Johnny B. Goode" and "Carol," you can actually hear some instruments playing straight eighths and others playing shuffle eighths. Try the passage in Figure 4-7 in a shuffle feel to see if it translates. Some riffs will work, and some won't. You don't really know until you try, and there's no harm in that, even when it doesn't work out.

Shuffle, or swing, eighths

Most blues are in a shuffle feel, and shuffle-based eighth-note riffs (also called swing eighths) are the most popular and numerous types of blues riffs. Countless tunes employ eighth-note riffs, including such hits as "Dust My Broom," and "Sweet Home Chicago." Figure 4-8 shows you a classic shuffle rhythm that employs swing eighths and the occasional eighth-note triplet.

Figure 4-8:
A variation of the 5-6 move in swing eighths.

Figure 4-9 is an eighth-note riff with the melody weaving in and out of the low and high strings. This riff, once mastered, is tons of fun to play because it takes your left hand up and down and makes you look like you're really movin' on those strings.

Figure 4-9:
An expanded version of the classic 5-6 move.

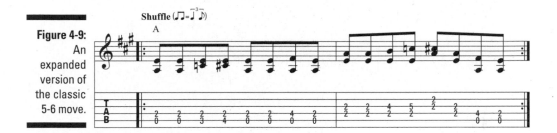

High-Note Riffs: The Bridge to Lead Blues Guitar

A high-note riff is very close — in words and in music — to a lick. But if you're mastering all that low-note stuff, you deserve to see what awaits you when you ascend the cellar stairs into the sunshine of high-note, melodic-based playing.

Keith Richards's borrowed trademark: Quick-four riffs

A quick four (in this section) refers to a double-stop riff that you play on the second and third strings within a measure of a I or IV chord. (Don't get this quick four confused with the kind of quick four that happens in bar 2 of a 12-bar blues, covered in Chapter 3 in Book IV.) When you play this riff during a chord, you create a temporary IV chord.

The Rolling Stones' Keith Richards carved out a very successful career exploiting this riff, and he learned from the great American blues masters. Figure 4-10 shows a four-bar phrase where the quick-four riff is applied at the end of each bar of an E and A chord.

Keith Richards's signature riffs in Stones classics like "Brown Sugar," "Honky-Tonk Women," and "Start Me Up" are actually in open-G tuning, which makes the quick four easy to access. Open tunings in G, A, D, and E were used extensively by prewar acoustic guitarists — such as Charlie Patton, Son House, and Robert Johnson — especially for slide.

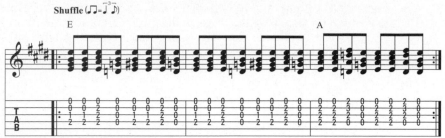

Figure 4-10:
The quick-four move over open-position E and A chords.

Intro, turnaround, and ending riffs

Intros, turnarounds, and ending riffs fill out the chord structure with melodic figures. As you play the figures in this section, try to hear the underlying structure — the rhythm guitar in your mind — playing along with you. You can play the chords according to the chord symbols above the music, but in this case the symbols identify the overall harmony and don't tell you what to actually play at that moment.

Intro, turnaround, and ending riffs have very similar DNA, so they can be mutated ever so slightly to change into one of the other two functions. You can easily adapt and add your own flavor to the examples (in the figures) in this section, so take a stab at converting the intro in Figure 4-11 into an ending that borrows from Figure 4-16. These practices get you used to taking other people's ideas and fashioning them into your own. That's how pre-existing riffs and licks get turned into an individual and original voice.

Intro riffs

Figure 4-11 is a snappy, triplet-based intro riff. The lower voice descends while the top voice stays fixed. Try playing this riff fingerstyle or with a pick and fingers.

Track 71, 0:00

Figure 4-11:
A triplet-based intro riff in E.

Figure 4-12 is related to Figure 4-11 in that the lower voice descends against a fixed upper-note. But here, the notes are played together as double-stops for a more obvious and dramatic harmonic clash of the two notes. This blues lick and the one in Figure 4-13 are borrowed from a famous pop song — Johnny Rivers's version of Chuck Berry's "Memphis." Play this lick fingerstyle or with pick and fingers.

Track 71, 0:11

Figure 4-12:
A double-stop intro riff in E.

The varying motion of the riff in Figure 4-13 makes it unpredictable and dramatic. The figure shows an all-single-note riff in triplets, ending in a B7 chord that comes on beat 2. The melody here changes direction often and can be a little tricky at first. But we're confident you'll get the hang of it with some practice.

Track 71, 0:21

Figure 4-13:
A melodic intro riff based in all triplet eighth notes.

Book IV

Blues Guitar

TIP

The last note of the melody, low B, is actually the root of the B7 chord that you play one moment later. So play that B with your left-hand second finger.

Turnaround riffs

Figure 4-14 can be used as an intro or a turnaround, but here it's cast as a turnaround. This is a double-stop riff in A with a descending lower voice, reminiscent of the playing of Robert Johnson.

Track 71, 0:30

Figure 4-14: A descending double-stop turnaround riff in A, in the style of Robert Johnson.

Figure 4-15 is a wide-voiced double-stop riff where the voices move in contrary motion (the bass ascends while the treble descends). This riff is great for any fingerstyle blues in E because it highlights the separation of the bass and treble voices — a signature feature of the fingerstyle approach.

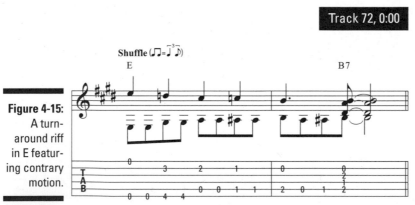

Track 72, 0:00

Figure 4-15: A turnaround riff in E featuring contrary motion.

If the double strikes in the bass give you trouble at first, try playing them as quarter notes, in lock step with the treble voice.

Combining single notes and chords

One way to get the best of both worlds — the lead and rhythm worlds, that is — is to combine single notes and chords. Many blues players don't make clear distinctions between chord playing, riff playing, or lead playing. Their technique just melds aspects of all these approaches into one cohesive style. And many of them do this while singing! Here are two examples:

✔ Stevie Ray Vaughan was a master of this style. He created full-sounding, active, and infinitely varied parts under his vocals as well as when he was just vamping along with the band.

✔ Eddie Van Halen, when in rare blues-mode (as opposed to his tapping, metal rock-god mode), was also an excellent practitioner of the integrated single-note-and-chord approach.

Today's students of the guitar tend to look at rhythm versus lead guitar as a black-and-white issue. But the history of blues shows that, until the advent of modern rock (from about the late 1960s on), players didn't really think of guitar-playing in those terms.

Be sure to also listen to the traditional players who sang and accompanied themselves on guitar:

✔ Robert Johnson

✔ John Lee Hooker

✔ Mississippi John Hurt

You hear the best examples of how to combine single notes and chords in those players' styles, and the musical playing is some of the best you may ever hear.

Figure 4-16 is an open-chord turnaround riff in C — the key for fingerpicking country blues like Mississippi John Hurt. The last chord is a treat: a jazzy G7 augmented (where the 5th of the chord, D, is raised a half step to D♯), which gives the progression a gospel feel with a little extra flavor.

Track 72, 0:12

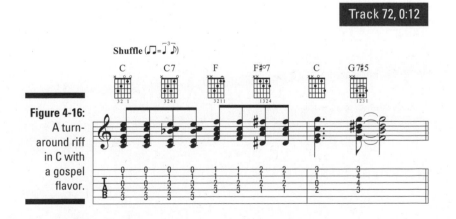

Figure 4-16: A turn-around riff in C with a gospel flavor.

Ending riffs

Ending riffs are similar to both intros and turnarounds, except ending riffs terminate on the I chord, not the V. Figure 4-17 is a triplet-based riff in 6ths, where the second string isn't played.

Figure 4-17: A triplet-based ending riff.

You can play this riff with just the pick, but it's easier with fingers or a pick and fingers. The open B string on the last triplet of beat 1 gives you a bit of a head start to get your hand up the neck to play the F9–E9 ending chords.

Figure 4-18 is a low note ending in E, using triplet eighths and a double-stop descending form. This riff is meaty and doesn't sound too melodic because it has more of a low, walking bass feel.

Figure 4-18: A low-note ending riff in E.

Mastering the Rhythm Figure

After you have a handle on the components of rhythm guitar — left-hand chords, right-hand strums, riffs, and combinations thereof — it's time to put them all together in various ways.

Here you can master the rhythm figure, which combines the components of rhythm guitar. In some musical circles, a rhythm figure — usually longer than a riff — describes any repeatable passage of music that forms the basis for a song or section of a song.

Rhythm figures can be as simple as a quarter-note chord strum, an eighth-note boogie pattern, or a wild hybrid containing everything but the kitchen sink, as evidenced by the complex, integrated rhythm work of Magic Sam, Freddie King, Jimi Hendrix, and Stevie Ray Vaughan.

Figure 4-19 is a 12-bar blues that uses chords, single-note bass runs (to bring you in and out of those chords), and single-note riffs that go into flights of blues fancy.

Figure 4-19: A rhythm groove over 12-bar blues in E.

Chapter 5

Blues Genres: Acoustic, Electric, and Blues-Rock

• •

In This Chapter

▶ Hammering out Delta, Piedmont, folk and country, and slide guitar blues

▶ Getting heavy with electric blues

▶ Checking out blues-rock, Southern blues, and the future of the blues

• •

*A*coustic-guitar blues is one of the earliest forms of blues. Before acoustic blues developed into its own instrumental style, the guitar was just a convenient instrument to play and accompany yourself while you sang. A performer naturally played rhythmically when singing and more melodically in between the vocal phrases. So the guitar style was woven into the singer's approach to accompanying himself on the guitar. Gradually, the guitar went from being just a background instrument into a solo, unaccompanied instrument and then evolved into the different branches of ragtime, country blues, and even rockabilly.

In this chapter, you take a grand tour of where the blues has gone in its long, illustrious journey, beginning with Delta blues, Piedmont blues, country and folk blues, and slide guitar, through electric and blues-rock, and ending with a few of the great up-and-coming blues players of today.

Delta Blues: Where It All Began

The famous *Delta* is an area of northern Mississippi and Arkansas that was agriculturally and musically fertile. When people refer to the "Delta blues," they describe the music specific to a geographic region and the hard-edged, acoustic blues played by Charlie Patton, Son House, and especially Robert Johnson — its most famous and influential practitioner, who contributed some of the best recorded examples.

Understanding the Delta technique

The Delta blues style is an acoustic, self-contained approach (rhythm and lead combined) used almost exclusively as accompaniment for a singer. The thumb and fingers often play different parts. The thumb plays either steady quarter notes or a shuffle-eighth-note rhythm, especially when the high notes are laying out. The Delta blues liberally uses the minor pentatonic scale. (For more on the minor pentatonic scale, see Chapter 3 in Book III.)

Figure 5-1 is a 12-bar blues in the Delta blues style. The thumb hammers out either quarter notes or shuffle eighths. In the spaces where the vocal rests, high notes are introduced as melodic fills.

Many Delta players use thumbpicks for extra power. For more rhythmic playing, thumbpicks are especially appropriate, even if you don't normally use them. The more experienced players try to incorporate licks and subtle chordal flourishes while keeping an insistent bass going.

The king of the Delta blues: Robert Johnson

Robert Johnson (1911–1938) is universally recognized as the "King of the Delta Blues," and for good reason. His influence is felt not only through those who followed but also in every student who picks up the guitar with a mind to play the blues. Johnson influenced many aspects of the blues — through his playing, his songwriting, and his aura. No performer has led — or was alleged to have led — a more mythic or legendary blues life. Some people believe that Johnson gained his talent in a deal with the devil; he died young and under mysterious circumstances, and his songs are haunting with chilling themes about the devil and death.

If you've grown up with blues as interpreted by B.B. King, Eric Clapton, Stevie Ray Vaughan, and other modern electric-blues masters, hearing the scratchy, raw recordings of Johnson can be quite startling. Johnson's thin, keening voice, his twangy guitar, and his sometimes irregular meter and quirky phrasing are definitely an acquired taste. But when you make the adjustment, the genius of him in these stark settings is awe-inspiring.

Robert Johnson's music embodied the Delta blues in its finished state. And there was no end to Johnson's innovation. He played with a slide and without, in altered tunings as well as standard, and he shifted from accompaniment to a featured guitar style effortlessly. Only one solo break of Johnson's talent exists on recording. To hear Robert Johnson play his only known recorded solo break, check out "Kind Hearted Woman Blues."

Figure 5-1:
12-bar blues in the Delta blues style.

Did Johnson sell his soul to the devil?

Almost certainly not. Robert Johnson wasn't always referenced with the devil. The myth only began in 1965 after blues scholar Pete Welding interviewed Son House. House talked about the amazing progress Johnson made on the guitar in such a short time and said, "He must have sold his soul to the devil to play like that."

Eric Clapton and his band Cream perpetuated the myth, perhaps inadvertently, when they changed Johnson's opening lines of "Crossroads Blues" from "I went to the cross road — fell down on my knee. I asked the Lord above, 'Have mercy — Save poor Bob, if you please'" to "'I went down to the cross road, fell down on my knees, saw the devil. I went up and I said, 'Take me if you please.'"

Johnson played his brand of blues in many keys and in many different tunings, but he's known for his work in the key of open A. Figure 5-2 shows a passage in standard tuning that Johnson frequently used for intros, turnarounds, and endings. The lick in Figure 5-2 is similar to others that are covered in Chapter 3 in Book IV in the key of E. (Don't worry if you haven't looked at that chapter yet.) This figure uses a device called *oblique motion* — a fancy term for when one voice stays the same (the top) and another moves (the lower, descending).

Figure 5-2:
A lick in the key of A in the style of Robert Johnson.

Johnson's style was complex and hard to pin down. Some of his stylistic hallmarks include the following:

- An insistent bass in quarters and shuffle-eighths
- Up-the-neck chords
- Chromatic movement

> ✔ Melodic fills in between vocal phrases
>
> ✔ Classic turnaround figures

Johnson is one of the few Delta blues players known for his influential song-writing (Willie Dixon, the bass player and performer, is another) and for contributing to the blues repertoire with such standards as "Sweet Home Chicago" and "Crossroads." Besides composing two well-known hits with "Kind Hearted Woman Blues" and "Terraplane Blues," many of Johnson's songs are also historically significant.

The Piedmont Blues: Country Ragtime

The *Piedmont blues* feel is achieved by an alternating bass, where the bass plays on every quarter note, with accents and a root-fifth scheme on the first and third beats. This variation lends a two-beat, or boom-chick, sound. The sound of Piedmont blues is joyous and happy and is generally played more uptempo than Delta blues. The bouncy ragtime syncopations of ragtime piano — and especially the independence of the bass and treble voices — are often emulated in Piedmont blues, which further enhances its infectious, upbeat sound.

Practitioners of Piedmont picking include Blind Blake, Blind Boy Fuller, Barbecue Bob, Reverend Gary Davis, and Blind Willie McTell. Blind Willie McTell (1898–1959), one of the most famous early practitioners from the early Piedmont school, was a virtuoso 12-string guitarist. His "Statesboro Blues" from 1928, though neither his best nor most famous song, is a modern classic as the driving, electric shuffle version recorded by the Allman Brothers Band on *Live at the Fillmore East* in 1971 (the band had learned it from a Taj Mahal record).

Geographically, the "Piedmont" in Piedmont blues refers to the area quite a bit east of the Mississippi Delta, between the Appalachian Mountains and the Atlantic coastal plain, stretching from Richmond, Virginia, to Atlanta, Georgia. Piedmont is often called *country ragtime* because of its lively, driving flavor. This ragtime is different from the piano ragtime of Scott Joplin that you may be familiar with. Ragtime in Joplin's time was played straight without the shuffle feel of country ragtime.

Book IV

Blues Guitar

Figure 5-3 shows the driving, two-beat feel, accomplished through an alternating bass. This method is sometimes called *Travis picking,* after country performer Merle Travis, whose alternating thumb technique was widely popular (see the later sidebar "Country and folk blues had a baby: Rockabilly" for more on Travis). In this passage, in the key of C, the blue notes E♭ and B♭ figure prominently.

After you practice Figure 5-3 a few times, throw in some variety and mute the lower strings to add contrast between the bass and treble voices. This variation is performed on the accompanying CD.

Track 75

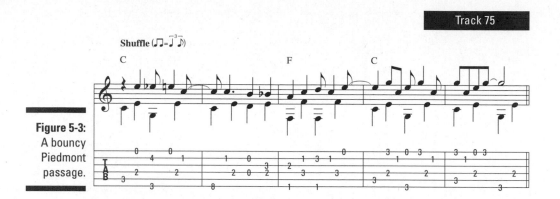

Figure 5-3:
A bouncy Piedmont passage.

Figure 5-4 shows a Piedmont style ragtime chord progression. This progression is typical, from the IV chord (F, in the key of C) that acts as the climax. ***Note:*** The walking bass runs seem to line up perfectly with the chord progression.

Figure 5-4:
A ragtime chord progression with bass runs.

Country and Folk Blues

For acoustic blues that isn't clearly Delta or Piedmont — or that may have elements of both — you can use the adjectives *country* and *folk*. In this case, country means old-time country, as in non-urban. It has nothing to do with Nashville, sequins, or Dolly Parton, but a lot to do with mountain hollers and shotgun shacks. Folk blues is more of a labeling convention, where certain performers, like Leadbelly, were considered folk musicians because they sang folk songs.

The repertoire that comprised country and folk blues was often just a loose mix of folk and popular songs that were given a bluesy treatment by blues-influenced performers. These performers often made no distinction between what was blues or not; they just played songs from any genre that suited

Country and folk blues had a baby: Rockabilly

An important offspring of country blues was the hard-driving, alternate-bass sound that came to be known as *rockabilly*. The style featured blues figures but at a supercharged pace and with a heavy backbeat (provided by a prominent drum sound) and often a heavy use of effects, such as reverb, slap-back echo, and tremolo.

Merle Travis was a rockabilly pioneer, along with Scotty Moore (Elvis Presley's first guitarist)

and James Burton (Elvis's second guitarist). Travis didn't invent the alternating bass sound of rockabilly, but he popularized his own hard-driving approach that featured a I-V-I-V bass motif in an uptempo two-beat feel, called *Travis picking*. Travis and his many followers, including Chet Atkins, Doc Watson, Leo Kottke, and Jerry Reed, made this a staple sound in acoustic playing, and it works well in upbeat blues.

their performance style. Audiences didn't notice, either. For example, no one could have led a more emblematic blues life than Leadbelly, yet his best known song was a waltz-time folk ditty called "Irene Goodnight."

Country and folk-style blues often includes an instrumental melody, usually syncopated on top of an alternating bass line. The guitar imitates the piano-based ragtime style of Scott Joplin's days. The key of C is the favorite for many country and ragtime blues songs. Ragtime chords in the key of C include E7, A7, D7, and G7, all of which fall nicely in open position and offer fingerpickers many options for bass runs, open strings, hammer-ons, and pull-offs.

For the audiences that found the Delta sound a little too dark or stark, country and folk music brought more tuneful melodies with a bluesy treatment that was more enjoyable. People who brought about this mix included Mance Lipscomb, Big Bill Broonzy, Reverend Gary Davis, and Mississippi John Hurt. Like Piedmont blues, these styles feature a lively, relentless, alternating bass line, and the songs themselves are drawn more from the folk repertoire than from the 12-bar blues arena.

The best way to understand country and folk blues is to listen to these styles. Songsters like Mississippi John Hurt wrote with a bouncy ragtime style and recorded famous songs such as "Candy Man Blues" (full of double meanings), "My Creole Belle," and "Make Me a Pallet on Your Floor." These lively songs featured Hurt's ingenious ragtime work and had a good blues backstory.

Figure 5-5 is a song that features a melody on top of an alternating bass pattern, similar to Mississippi John Hurt's style. Pay attention to the way his confident, driving bass notes (played with the thumb) contrast the high-note syncopated melodic figures (played with the fingers).

Book IV

Blues Guitar

Track 76

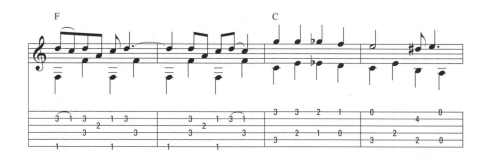

Figure 5-5: Country blues with a melody on top of an alternating bass.

*Barre at 3rd fret.

Quintessential Blues: Slide Guitar

Slide guitar may have become a stylistic choice over fretted guitar out of necessity by players who didn't have the skills or patience to fret the guitar and found it easy to slide a smooth, rounded object over the strings to achieve a similar effect. But for the greatest practitioners, such as Charlie Patton, Sylvester Weaver, Blind Willie Johnson, Son House, and Robert Johnson, slide guitar was an unparalleled mode of expression evocative of the human voice as well as the wail of train whistles — a sound near and dear to country blues guitarists. Slide guitar is a staple of the acoustic blues guitar sound, unlikely to ever be imitated by synthetic, digital means.

The tools that let you slide

Early, rural-dwelling slide players used anything they could find to produce the slide effect. The edge of a pocket knife, a length of pipe, a section of bone from a ham or beef shank, or a medicine bottle were among some of the top "tools" used. The most popular and effective was a broken bottle neck (filed or fired to eliminate the sharp edges). Slide blues guitar is sometimes called *bottleneck guitar.*

These days, you're likely to acquire your slippery weapon of choice by going to a music store and selecting from the prepackaged slides in the display case:

- ✔ Metal slides, especially those made from brass, are heavier (they have more mass), bolder sounding, and provide better sustain, but they're more difficult to master.
- ✔ Glass slides are light and have a rounder, mellower tone.

The sliding technique

Many Delta players combined slide technique with fretting, often having the slide play the melodic portions while their fretting fingers played chordal figures or kept the bass line going. This technique dictated the wearing of the slide on the fourth finger (the pinky). Follow the steps below to perfect your slide technique:

1. **Slide an object like a glass or metal tube over a left-hand finger (usually the third or fourth).**

2. **Rest the slide on the strings (not pressed down), directly over the fret wire.**

   Resting the slide on the strings and playing over the fret (instead of behind it as you do when fretting) takes a little finesse, but eventually, your *intonation* (the ability to play pitches in tune) and *tone* (the right pressure that produces rattle-free sustain) will improve.

3. **Change pitch by gliding the slide along the string.**

   This process produces a smooth, continuous change in pitch (sometimes called a glissando, or portamento, which is more correct).

Book IV

Blues
Guitar

At first, your slide playing may sound clangy and rattly as you move the slide around. You can improve your sound by using one of two techniques:

- ✔ Dampening (or muting), which involves placing your unused left-hand fingers lightly on the strings behind the slide (toward the nut)

- ✔ Employing right-hand palm mutes

Slide guitar is physically easy in one sense. You just drag a slide over the strings, and you can instantly hear the effect, right? Well, it can be difficult to get it under control to play in tune and keep the accompanying buzzing and rattling artifacts to a minimum. Slide guitar doesn't require left-hand strength the way normal acoustic guitar playing does, but it does require finesse. Focus on intonation first, rhythm second, and dampening third. Also, it can be instructive to check your intonation with an electronic tuner — an advantage you have over someone like Robert Johnson.

Tuning for slide guitar

Slide guitar can be played in standard or open tunings, but standard may be easier because your melodic instincts don't have to be translated to the altered tuning of the guitar. However, in standard tuning it's quite a challenge for a beginning slide guitarist to mute the unwanted strings that can create a sour, dissonant sound, as opposed to the chordal harmony of open tunings. So standard tuning presents more of a technical challenge, while open tuning presents a "thinking" challenge as you translate your instincts to fit a different tuning. The solution? Play both ways! The following sections explain what you need to do.

Open tunings favor the technical side of common blues licks. And the main tunings, open E and open A (which are the same, relatively speaking, as open D and open G), each have their specific idiomatic licks. Don't press too hard when applying the slide or the strings will buzz against the fret wire and fingerboard. Try to keep the rattle noise to a minimum when going from open strings to slide-stopped strings.

Standard tuning licks

Standard tuning and open E tuning both feature the root of the chord on the top string and an interval of a 4th between the 1st and 2nd strings. The lower note is the 5th of the chord and makes for powerful-sounding licks, as Figure 5-6 shows. The passage isn't difficult, and the slide doesn't do that much. But what it does is very effective, even in small doses.

The lick in Figure 5-6 is the characteristic sound of one of the most famous slide sounds of all time: "Dust My Broom" — a song originally by Robert Johnson with conventional fretting but covered in the most famous version by electric slide player Elmore James.

Figure 5-6:
A standard-
tuning slide
lick in the
style of
"Dust My
Broom."

Figure 5-6:
A standard-
tuning slide
lick in the
style of
"Dust My
Broom."

Open E and open D tuning

Open tunings have many technical advantages over standard tuning. The most prevalent is that an open tuning provides a major chord across all six strings, so holding the slide straight across at any fret yields a chord on any set of strings.

Open E (E, B, E, G♯, B, E, low to high) is close to standard tuning because the top two strings are tuned the same, and many blues slide licks lie well in this tuning, because they require only slight movement of a couple of frets above or below to play an entire passage.

Open D is the same as open E but tuned a whole step (two frets) lower (D, A, D, F♯, A, D). Elmore James and Duane Allman (one of the greatest blues-rock slide guitarists and founder of the Allman Brothers Band) played in open E. Figure 5-7 shows a typical lick in open E.

Track 77

*Open E tuning: E B E G♯ B E, low to high.

Figure 5-7:
A slide lick
in open E.

Book IV

**Blues
Guitar**

Open A tuning

In open A, the strings are tuned E, A, E, A, C♯, E, low to high. The root of the chord on the 5th string provides a major chord on the top three strings. Having a minor 3rd interval between the top two strings allows for some idiomatic blues moves, especially the chromatic descending lick in 3rds.

The Birth of Classic Electric Blues

Early electric guitars, even ones with pickups, weren't much different from acoustic guitars in construction, but gradually the manufacturing approaches diverged to produce two entirely different species. And along with the evolution of the electric guitar, so followed the electric blues guitar player's technique.

Today, of course, the electric guitar in blues (as it is in other genres) is far more popular than its older, acoustic counterpart. Think of the biggest blues guitar names playing today — Eric Clapton, B.B. King, Buddy Guy, Bonnie Raitt, Robert Cray. All are electric blues players. The acoustic-blues players of today — Rory Block, John Hammond Jr., Taj Mahal, Keb' Mo', Corey Harris, Roy Book Binder, and Bob Brozman — are no less talented, but don't enjoy household-name status.

The rise of the electric guitar in blues

At first, early electric guitarists simply played the way they always played when playing acoustic and appreciated the benefits of not having to play harder to play louder (instead they just turned up the amp). But as techniques developed, players began to understand that the electric was an entirely different instrument from the traditional acoustic, or "Spanish" guitar. Musicians started adjusting their techniques — and their whole approach to music — to suit the new medium. With a guitar that could hold its own with other principal instruments on the bandstand, guitarists now focused more on melodic and lead playing.

When pickups were developed, guitarists leapt at the opportunity to have at least a fighting chance to be louder. The new electrified sound allowed guitars to take the spotlight as the featured instrument. Searing slide solos, sustained string bends, and a more instrumentally virtuosic approach were the order of the day, fueled by restless musicians anxious to infuse this previously rural sound with urban postwar energy.

Increased sustain is probably the number-one advantage of electric guitars, allowing long, fluid, horn-like melodic lines. Overdriving an amp into distortion creates the illusion of even longer sustain because the signal is clipped and compressed, with a steady volume level until it decays.

The earliest electric pioneer: T-Bone Walker

Although electric guitarists became a dime a dozen after electrics became affordable, one name stands alone as the early voice of electric blues guitar: T-Bone Walker. He is one of the most influential blues guitarists of all time because he bridged the gap from acoustic country blues into the urbanized, electric sounds of Memphis, Kansas City, and Chicago. Walker's style and musical sensibilities were sophisticated and jazzy, and he was a versatile and skilled musician. He incorporated jazz-type harmony and phrasing in his playing, using 9th chords in his rhythm playing and crafting lead lines that were melodically and rhythmically complex.

Figure 5-8 shows a passage in the style of Walker's "Call It Stormy Monday" — his own tune and one where he really stretched out, taking the blues to places other melodic players of the day had never been. He achieved this end by throwing in unusual (for the time) string bends, jazzy phrases, and a harmonic sophistication his Delta counterparts would hardly recognize. But it was all grounded in the blues vocabulary.

Figure 5-8:
A slow blues in the style of T-Bone Walker.

Book IV

Blues Guitar

Walker influenced countless players, including Muddy Waters, Eric Clapton, Otis Rush, Magic Sam, Buddy Guy, Albert King, Albert Collins, Freddie King, and B.B. King. His showmanship, such as playing the guitar behind his head, was also imitated by many players.

Electric Blues' Sweet Home: Chicago

Many people think they know what Chicago blues is, but the more they discover the diverse influences, overlapping associations, time periods, and even the geography of the city, the more they realize what an open issue the notion of Chicago blues is. Still, if you just try to enjoy the music without engaging in too much analysis, you realize how important the Windy City is to the development of the blues.

Before World War II, important performers included Big Bill Broonzy, Tampa Red, and Memphis Minnie, who played electrically and acoustically. In the postwar period — and after T-Bone Walker's electric influence was felt by all who heard him — the Chicago scene, fueled by an influx of southern talent, took off. Table 5-1 shows some of the important blues guitarists who called Chicago home.

Table 5-1	Chicago Blues Players	
Artist	**Style**	**Association**
Big Bill Broonzy (1893–1968)	Acoustic folk blues	Friend to Muddy Waters
Tampa Red (1900–81)	Electric, slide, hokum	Influenced Muddy Waters, Elmore James, and Robert Nighthawk
Robert Nighthawk (1909–67)	Acoustic, electric	Delta influence; the slide link between Tampa Red and Earl Hooker
Howlin' Wolf (1910–76)	Electric	Delta influence in the direct lineage back to Charlie Patton ("Founder of Delta Blues"); Muddy Waters's contemporary and sometimes-rival
Muddy Waters (1915–83)	Electric, slide	Delta influence; leader of the first generation of postwar Chicago scene for decades

Artist	Style	Association
Elmore James (1918–63)	Electric, slide	Delta influence; the most influential electric slide guitarist of the time, and a contemporary of Robert Johnson
Earl Hooker (1930–70)	Electric lead, slide	Delta influence; followed Tampa Red and Robert Nighthawk; influenced B.B. King, Buddy Guy, Jimmy Page
Otis Rush (b. 1934)	Electric lead	Second generation Chicago; West Side sound; influenced Clapton, Stevie Ray Vaughan, and Peter Green; played "upside-down" guitar
Buddy Guy (b. 1936)	Electric lead	Second generation Chicago; West Side sound; backed Muddy Waters, among others; had a long association with harp man Junior Wells; influenced Jimi Hendrix and Eric Clapton
Magic Sam (1937–69)	Electric, fingerstyle	Second generation Chicago; West Side sound; influenced Robert Cray

The fertile postwar Chicago scene had several players, led primarily by the bigwigs in the following sections.

Muddy Waters, leader of the pack

Born in Jug's Corner, Mississippi, in 1915, Muddy Waters (birth name McKinley Morganfield) came north to Chicago in 1945 and became the leader of Chicago's South Side blues scene. A large and imposing man, Waters dominated the stage, the scene, and the entire city in all things blues. He had talented contemporaries, like Howlin' Wolf and Sonny Boy Williamson II, but no single person is more associated with the Chicago sound than Muddy. He had everything:

✔ A guitar style that included percussive, stinging single-note Delta riffs

✔ An aggressive, bone-chilling slide technique

✔ A big, raspy singing voice

✔ A commanding stage presence

✔ A long and prolific performing and recording career

Book IV

Blues Guitar

He played acoustic in Mississippi and electric in Chicago, single-handedly leading the charge to bridge the two styles. Figure 5-9 shows an electric guitar passage in the style of Muddy.

Figure 5-9:
A passage in the style of Muddy Waters.

Elmore James, slide guitarist extraordinaire

Elmore James was a Chicago-based blues player known for his electric slide work. James recast the signature lick from Robert Johnson's "I Believe I'll Dust My Broom" from conventional fretted playing to slide and recycled it many times in his other compositions. James's techniques with an electric guitar and his explosive assault on the strings turned "Dust My Broom" into a piece of blues immortality (his version is known by the shortened version of the title). James's slide lick is the first lick you need to learn; its importance is matched only by its accessibility, and it's what'll get you kicked out of the South Side if you don't play it correctly. James's "Dust My Broom," performed in open D tuning (D, A, D, F♯, A, D, low to high), is shown in Figure 5-10.

Magic Sam, a man who marched to the pluck of his own pick

Magic Sam (birth name Sam Maghett) was born on February 2, 1937, in Grenada, Mississippi, and was one of the architects of Chicago's West Side sound. Sam played in a unique style, a punctuated fingerpicking approach, dosed with amp tremolo and exhibited in such tunes as his debut single, "All Your Love." His nickname

"Magic" derived from his last name. For many, Sam's one-of-a-kind style, great voice, and singular performing persona made him the favorite of the West Side. Tragically Sam died at age 32 of a heart attack and didn't enjoy the fame and notoriety of some of the other figures of his time, such as Buddy Guy and Otis Rush.

Track 78

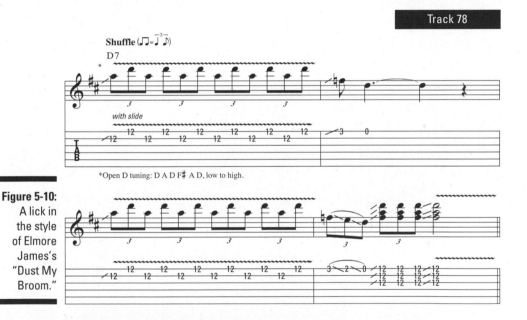

Figure 5-10: A lick in the style of Elmore James's "Dust My Broom."

Book IV

Blues Guitar

Otis Rush: A soulful player with a flair for vibrato

Born in Philadelphia, Mississippi, in 1934 as one of seven children, Otis Rush learned to play the guitar left-handed and upside down, like Albert King. Rush was exposed to Muddy Waters and Howlin' Wolf, but he also listened to B.B. and Albert King, who deeply influenced his lead approach. His first single, Willie Dixon's "I Can't Quit You Baby," made it to the top ten on Billboard's R&B chart.

"I Can't Quit You Baby," as well as the rhumba-flavored "All Your Love" and the minor-key songs "Double Trouble" and "My Love Will Never Die," show Rush's smooth, soulful single-string work and stinging vibrato.

Buddy Guy, the father of blues-rock

Buddy Guy, more than his contemporaries, seemed to foreshadow the blues-rock movement through his stage show. (Blues-rock is covered in more detail later in this chapter.) He played loudly and infused his playing with whammy-bar antics, distortion, and feedback. Guy influenced the early British blues-rock greats Jeff Beck, Eric Clapton, and the Rolling Stones, and toured the United Kingdom in 1965, sharing a bill with the Yardbirds. Stevie Ray Vaughan once said, "Without Buddy Guy, there would be no Stevie Ray Vaughan."

Guy is perhaps the single most important performer (trained by Waters and Howlin' Wolf) to bridge the Chicago sound with blues-rock. Through his exceptional talent and longevity, he has become a living legend whose albums have won Grammy Awards, and he's received the praises of later greats such as Eric Clapton, who calls Guy his "favorite blues axe man." Figure 5-11 is a passage that captures the essence of Buddy Guy's fiery and virtuosic style.

Figure 5-11:
A passage
in the style
of Buddy
Guy.

The Blues Sounds of Texas

As the blues grew up, it developed its own regional flavors beyond the already established locales of the Delta and Piedmont. So of course, Texas, being such a large and diverse state, has a sound and culture all its own when it comes to the blues. Of all the big blues regions, Texas, by virtue of its size and blues hotspots like Austin, Houston, and Dallas, still retains a meaningful connotation.

And speaking of the Lone Star State, when you say "Texas shuffle" to people attuned to the regional dialects of the blues, they instantly think of the many attributes of the shuffle:

✔ **Rhythm:** The rhythm section swings harder, influencing the lead guitarists' approach to their solos.

✔ **Swing:** The Texas shuffle has more swing than the slow grind of a Delta blues or the bouncy ragtime of the Piedmont.

✔ **Harmonic richness:** This genre also has a wider variety of notes (the major 3rd, major 6th, and chromatic neighbor tones) than the minor pentatonic or six-note blues of Delta players.

Any great blues musician knows a Texas shuffle. Figure 5-12 is a solo in a Texas shuffle setting. It incorporates a wide vocabulary of notes in the lead part. Note the liberal use of the sweet notes — the major 3rd and major 6th of the chords underneath.

Track 79

Figure 5-12: A classic Texas shuffle.

Famous early performers to come out of the Lone Star State include Blind Lemon Jefferson, Lightnin' Hopkins, T-Bone Walker, Clarence "Gatemouth" Brown, and Albert Collins. They performed vastly different music from one another, but all are connected through history and influence. A later generation of Texans includes several of the all-time greatest blues players of the post-Chicago heyday.

Johnny Winter, a Texas blues-rock titan

Blues-rock guitarist Johnny Winter exploded out of Texas in 1968 and proceeded to become one of the top concert draws of the early '70s. Winter was a virtuosic soloist who played with a thumbpick, and his speedy leads lit up a number of gold albums.

You can hear him trade red-hot blues leads with co-guitarist Rick Derringer on the 1971 cover of B.B. King's "It's My Own Fault." To play like Winter, develop the best blues vocabulary you can and work on making any phrase fit in any groove — straight, shuffle, or 16th-based, fast and slow.

Billy Gibbons and ZZ Top

The power trio ZZ Top is a powerful mix of Texan music and the blues. Guitarist Billy Gibbons isn't a high-speed player like Johnny Winter, but his slow, smoldering solos helped set the standard for "soulfulness" in the rock guitar world.

Gibbons is a masterful blues player with a well-rounded playing approach, but he's best known for his edge-of-the-pick (also known as *pinch*) harmonics. To play a pinch harmonic, follow these steps:

1. **Grasp your pick so only a small piece of the tip can be seen from between your thumb and index finger.**

2. **Just as you strike the string, give the pick a little forward twist, almost digging into the string and touching the flesh of your finger to the string, to stop or mute it slightly.**

   This technique takes some practice and getting use to, but the resulting note should have a harmonic (a high, bell-like sound resulting from the string being partially stopped) in it.

3. **Add plenty of distortion to help the effect "read" better.**

Gibbons's fat lead tone is legendary among rock players. He's particularly famous for using a flametop 1959 Gibson Les Paul Standard lovingly named "Pearly Gates," as well as a pink late-1950s Strat given to him by Jimi Hendrix, which greatly contribute to that tone. But did you know that he doesn't pick with a plastic piece, but with a real Mexican peso? Just a cool fact to know.

Stevie Ray Vaughan, the greatest modern bluesman of them all

Austin's legendary Stevie Ray Vaughan burst into the spotlight in 1983, first on David Bowie's *Let's Dance* album, and then on his solo debut, *Texas Flood*. Stevie Ray could channel Jimi Hendrix's Strat attack — he would often perform "Voodoo Child (Slight Return)" and "Little Wing" as a tribute — but he developed his own style that brought the Stratocaster back as the definitive blues-rock instrument.

Vaughan blew minds with both a blistering blues technique as well as the fattest guitar tone imaginable. He achieved his tone by using a combination of classic Fender, Marshall, and Dumble tube amps, pumped up with an Ibanez Tube Screamer TS-808 overdrive pedal, as well as a vintage Strat set up with heavy-gauge strings. He also tuned down a half-step, which contributed to his sound's girth.

Stevie Ray died in a helicopter crash in 1990, just after performing with Eric Clapton, but young guitarists are still mystified at how he achieved his one-and-only Strat sound, heard in such classics as "Pride and Joy," "Crossfire," and "The Sky Is Crying."

Vaughan's playing style was unique, evolved, and identifiable, with an integrated chord-and-single-note approach for rhythm as well as over-the-top lead playing that sounded on the verge of losing control (which he never did). To emulate the style of Vaughan, put heavy strings on your guitar, build up your arm strength, and combine melodic licks and riffs with open-position, jazz, and barre chords. (Listen to Figure 5-13 to hear how Stevie also threw tasty little chordal riffs into his solos — a hallmark of Texas blues guitar.) You must also play with complete authority, whipping off rhythm figures and lead lines with equal abandon.

Stevie Ray's brother, Jimmie Vaughan, is also an extraordinary blues guitarist, known for his work with the Fabulous Thunderbirds.

Book IV

Blues Guitar

Figure 5-13: Stevie Ray Vaughan often combined chord vamps with his leads.

Four Blues Giants: Three Kings and a Collins

Beyond the important regions, cultural developments, and trends in blues, individual performers often launch a trend in music. You'd be hard-pressed to find any single more influential individuals than the four giants of blues guitar covered in this section.

Albert King, the upside-down string bender

Mississippi-born, Arkansas-raised Albert King was a big man who squeezed the strings of his guitar into heartfelt submission. Because he played left-handed, upside-down guitar (where the low E string was closest to the floor), Albert's style was unorthodox, especially his approach to bending strings. He pulled the strings of his signature Gibson Flying V down toward the floor, which in part accounted for his unusual, expressive sound.

When Albert King was living in St. Louis in the late 1950s and then Memphis, he recorded for Stax Records and enjoyed real success, gaining visibility in both the blues and rock arenas. His soulful sound and R&B arrangements produced his best-known songs of the era, including "Laundromat Blues," "Cross Cut Saw," and "Born Under a Bad Sign," all of which placed on the pop charts. King influenced many guitarists, including Jimi Hendrix, Eric Clapton, Mike Bloomfield, Stevie Ray Vaughan, and Robert Cray.

B.B. King, the blues' king of kings

If you know only one name in the blues, it's probably B.B. King. B.B. is the rightly anointed, undisputed king of the blues. He has a deep, historical connection to the Delta performers and trod the early club circuit in the southern United States.

Born Riley B. King in 1925 in Indianola, Mississippi, B.B. King began to gain success in his early 20s in his adopted town of Memphis, playing clubs and appearing on radio. His on-air persona was "the Beale Street Blues Boy," eventually foreshortened to "B.B.", and he started recording in earnest in 1949 (only one year after Muddy Waters made his first recording in Chicago). B.B. soon had his first national R&B hit with "Three O'clock Blues" in 1951.

Book IV

Blues Guitar

Burning for Lucille

Lucille is the name B.B. King gives his main guitar (now a Gibson B.B. King signature edition, modeled after the ES-355). The story goes that King was playing in an Arkansas club when a fight broke out between two men over a woman. During the brawl a pail of kerosene that was being used to heat the club was knocked over, setting fire to the room. After escaping outside, King realized that he had left his guitar inside and rushed back into the burning club, risking his life to retrieve his axe. He later learned that the name of the woman the men had been fighting over was Lucille, and so King named his guitar Lucille and has since named many of his guitars in her honor.

B.B. King has it all: a soulful delivery, chops to burn, a vast vocabulary of blues licks in a variety of genres, and an inexhaustible reservoir of expressive techniques. He's perhaps most often cited for his vibrato, which is effortless and heart-rending. Figure 5-14 shows an example of how B.B. executes his brand of vibrato over a minor blues. To play like B.B., work to make every vibrato count, no matter how brief. That means applying a different intensity (rate of bend and depth of bend) to the note, based on the tempo and feel of the groove.

Freddie King, a two-pick man

Freddie King was a Texas-born guitarist who played with a plastic thumbpick and a metal fingerpick, in a two-finger fingerpicking style that he said he learned from Muddy Waters sideman Jimmy Rogers and Jimmy Reed sideman Eddie Taylor. His early influences included Lightnin' Hopkins and saxman/jump blues star Louis Jordan, but he's influenced others, too: Jeff Beck, Keith Richards, Jerry Garcia, Peter Green, Kenny Wayne Shepherd, and John Mayer.

Freddie's family moved from Texas to Chicago in 1950, when he was 16, and there he sneaked into clubs to hear the greats of that era: Muddy Waters, Howlin' Wolf (who took a liking to him), and Elmore James. He began recording as a sideman in the '50s while working in a steel mill.

Freddie King's best-known song is the instrumental "Hide Away," recorded in 1961, which was covered by John Mayall's Bluesbreakers with Eric Clapton, and Stevie Ray Vaughan — and every blues cover band in North America and Europe. Following the success of this tune, which placed on the pop charts as well as the R&B charts, Freddie followed up with more instrumentals, including "San-Ho-Zay," "The Stumble," and "Side Tracked."

Figure 5-15 shows a lick in the style of Freddie King's "Hide Away." Keep the approach light and crisp, as Freddie did, and play "on top of" (or slightly ahead of) the beat to capture his sound.

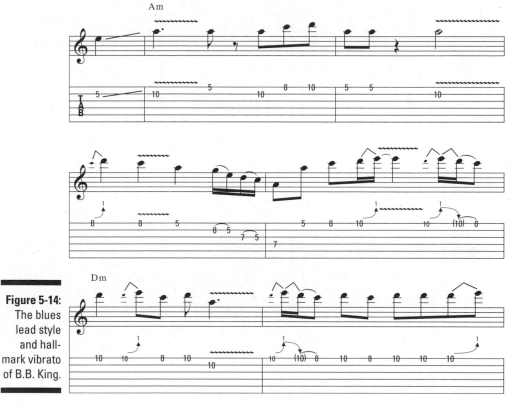

Figure 5-14:
The blues lead style and hallmark vibrato of B.B. King.

(continued)

Book IV

Blues Guitar

(continued)

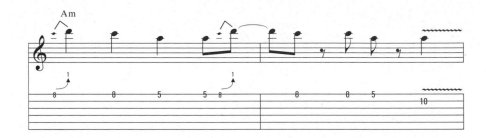

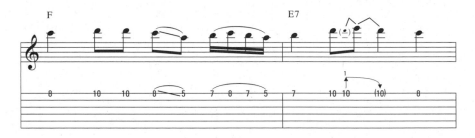

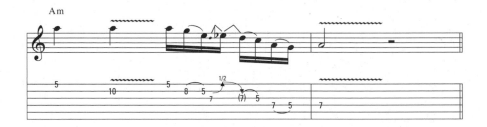

Albert Collins, master of the Telecaster

Albert Collins was an accomplished showman and a fierce guitarist. Born in 1932, in Leona, Texas, he received his initial musical training on the keyboards, but he soon picked up the guitar and started hanging out in Houston clubs and absorbing the influence of his Texas-based idols, Clarence "Gatemouth" Brown, Lightnin' Hopkins (a distant relative), T-Bone Walker, and John Lee Hooker.

Albert Collins concocted a unique recipe for playing guitar, consisting of a Fender Telecaster, a capo (which was often strapped on at the 5th, 7th, or even 9th frets), unorthodox tunings, and a stinging fingerstyle approach that

Figure 5-15: A lick in the infectious, melodic style of Freddie King.

fairly snapped notes out of the guitar. The essence of Albert Collins's style was his aggressive attack, piercing sound, and staccato phrasing. Plus he often tuned to an open minor chord.

Albert Collins had a string of instrumental hits in the late '50s and early '60s whose titles all had a "chilled" theme to them ("The Freeze," "Sno-Cone," "Icy Blue," and "Don't Lose Your Cool"). These songs earned him the nickname "The Iceman." In 1962, he released "Frosty," which became a big hit.

Blues-Rock and Southern Blues

The year 1965 was one of the most important years in popular music history. It was the year of Bob Dylan's "Like a Rolling Stone," and the Rolling Stones' "Satisfaction." For guitarists, it was also the beginning of a vast blues revival. Suddenly, mid-'60s electric guitarists on both sides of the Atlantic began re-exploring the blues and the roots of rock 'n' roll, along the way inventing an exciting, influential genre called *blues-rock*.

What traditional electric blues gave to the emerging style of blues-rock was widespread use of string bends and finger vibrato in composed melodic lines and improvised solos. Before the influence of blues, rockers in the '50s could

Book IV

Blues Guitar

buy only heavy-gauge guitar strings, but '60s blues-rockers learned how to bend new, lighter-gauge strings, develop a strong vibrato, and hold long, sustained notes. These blues techniques gave rock guitar leads a more human, vocal-like quality.

This new level of expression also gave birth to the "guitar hero." By the end of the 1960s, guitar gods like Eric Clapton, Michael Bloomfield, Jimi Hendrix, Jeff Beck, and Jimmy Page had become the gold standard of blues-rock currency. But these guitarists went beyond just bending strings — they also employed high-powered amplifiers, such as the fabled Marshall stack, to play blues guitar at previously unheard-of volumes, and infused their tone with tube overdrive, fuzzbox distortion, and the deep funk of wah-wah pedals.

When rock 'n' roll began in the mid-1950s, it was essentially a blend of R&B and jazz chord changes with country rhythms. Later, pop entered the genre via catchy tunes and more sophisticated lyrics. But the blues had only a negligible influence in a world of sweet and boppy melodies of the day — until one very stylish, duck-walking performer burst onto the scene: Chuck Berry. And following Berry was a whole movement of first British and later American artists who brought the blues to the world's screaming teens.

You can read about Chuck Berry, Bo Diddley, Eric Clapton, Jimi Hendrix, Jimmy Page, and other bluesy rock guitarists in Chapter 6 in Book III, which focuses more on rock than blues. Here, though, you can read about a decidedly more bluesy type of rock: southern rock.

Like the blues itself, there are few forms of popular music as quintessentially American as southern rock, which hails largely from the southeastern corner of the United States (notably Georgia and North Florida). Launched by the Allman Brothers Band, southern rock was the purest blues-rock sound ever created. The genre melded blues, country, gospel, and heavy rock. In all, the '70s southern rock sound had dozens of hot blues-rock players: The Outlaws ("Green Grass and High Tides"); The Marshall Tucker Band ("Can't You See"); and the fusion-fueled Dixie Dregs, featuring bluesy guitar virtuoso Steve Morse ("Take It Off The Top").

The Allman Brothers (especially Duane)

The original Allmans featured two excellent guitarists, Duane Allman and Dickey Betts. Both men could play the heck out of a 12-bar blues, but in Duane's brief career, he shined most on slide guitar (see Figure 5-16 for a slide solo, Allman-style). Allman's stylistic hallmarks were rapid up-and-down slides into and out of eighth notes, plus a penchant for throwing in large, unexpected melodic leaps to keep listeners on their toes. His exceptional slide work can be heard all over the famous *At Fillmore East* live album from 1971, especially on the blues masterpiece "Statesboro Blues." He died shortly thereafter, but his slide work was so ahead of its time that he set the bottleneck standard for the next 25 years.

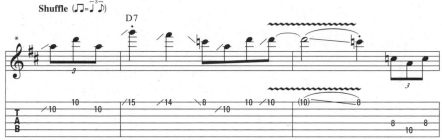

*Open E tuning: E B E G♯ B E, low to high.

Figure 5-16:
A slide riff in the style of the great Duane Allman.

Lynyrd Skynyrd

Lynyrd Skynyrd became the next southern supergroup, thanks to the 1974 smash, "Sweet Home Alabama." Skynyrd had three fine guitarists: Ed King, Gary Rossington, and Allen Collins. Rossington and Collins can be heard tearing up the concert favorite "Freebird." King is notable for a squealing, edgy tone (thanks to an electronic compressor) and for punching up the blues bends dramatically. King's solo in "Freebird" is inspired, yet controversial, because many claim that it's "in the wrong key." The song (whose first chord is D) is actually in the key of D. King himself admitted that he approached the solo as if it were in G, but most people agree the song is in D. Yet the solo seems to work anyway, and the song and King's solo both go down in history as one of the great events for guitar.

Blues in the 21st Century

Today's music scene may be dominated by computers and digital downloads, but happily, blues-rock, like traditional electric blues, has carved out a path and proceeds on its journey into the 21st century.

John Mayer and other new kids on the blues block

Among the brightest lights of the new millennium is singer-songwriter John Mayer, who fuses the best of Jimi Hendrix and Stevie Ray Vaughan into a stunning Strat style. Listen to "Route 66" from the *Cars* film soundtrack to hear this young picker play a joyous blues solo and throw down a wad of chunky chord work.

A few other young guns of modern blues worth checking out include the hot-pickin' Joe Bonamassa ("Travelin' South"), Kenny Wayne Shepherd ("Blue on Black"), and Henry Garza of Los Lonely Boys ("Heaven"). Coincidentally, or not, all of them play Fender Stratocasters, just like their blues-rock idols, Jimi Hendrix, Eric Clapton, and Stevie Ray Vaughan.

Allman Brothers redux: Warren Haynes and Derek Trucks, keepers of the flame

More than 35 years after their debut, the Allman Brothers are still a top concert draw, and the band's guitarists — Warren Haynes and Derek Trucks — have a huge part in the group's success.

✔ Haynes, who's been in the band longer than Duane Allman was, is a wizard at both straight soloing and the Duane Allman-style slide. To play slide like Haynes, keep your guitar in standard tuning and transcribe all Duane's moves (who played in open E) into standard tuning.

✔ Trucks, meanwhile, has taken bottleneck to a whole new dimension, infusing it with Indian music and bebop jazz influences from sax legend John Coltrane and trumpeter Miles Davis. You can hear both Derek and Warren just tearin' it up on "Firing Line" from the Allman Brothers album *Hittin' the Note.* To play like Trucks, you need to wear a slide and brush up on your bebop vocabulary. (If you want to check out Coltrane and Davis, get a copy of *Jazz For Dummies,* 2nd Edition, by Dirk Sutro [Wiley].)

Book V
Classical Guitar

The 5th Wave   By Rich Tennant

ON JULY 9th 1983, ANDRÉS SEGOVIA INEXPLICABLY BEGAN DUCK WALKING THROUGH THE ADAGIO SECTION OF BACH'S SUITE FOR GUITAR.

In this book . . .

From its very beginning, the guitar took to classical music. Vast swaths of the various periods of classical music turn out, in fact, to be quite playable on classical guitar. After it was invented, composers began scribbling pieces exclusively for the new instrument.

A classical guitar isn't the same as a regular acoustic, and it's not played the same way. This book gives you the scoop on the world of classical guitar music, which has developed separately from Western pop music but is certainly no less accomplished, to say the least.

Here are the contents of Book V at a glance.

Chapter 1

Introducing the Classical Guitar

*T*he first thing you have to sort out is just what's meant by the term *classical guitar*. It can describe both a type of instrument and a style of music played on it. When referring to the instrument itself, you're talking about a guitar that has a particular design and construction, is made of certain materials, and requires playing techniques that are unique to it, as compared to other guitars. To mine the depths of all the tonal and textural richness that await you in the world of classical guitar music, you must employ specific right- and left-hand techniques, which together comprise the classical guitar *style*.

A Brief History of Classical Guitar

The guitar is a relatively young instrument, having evolved to its present form in the 19th century. As such, it doesn't have the rich body of music available for it that, say, the violin does, which has been around for more than 500 years. But the classical guitar has been, how shall we say, *industrious* in the way it has "borrowed" music from other instruments to claim as its own. As a result, studying classical guitar means playing a lot of music that wasn't written for the guitar, by composers who wouldn't recognize the instrument. That's just part of the adventure of being a guitarist; you have to be somewhat of a pioneer with your instrument.

Nowadays composers write for the instrument all the time, ensuring its continued place in the field of serious musical instrument study. Many guitarists, associations, and organizations commission well-known composers to write compositions for the guitar in the same way that Beethoven and Mozart were commissioned to write symphonies and sonatas.

Some well-known composers from the 20th century who've written for the guitar include Heitor Villa-Lobos, Luciano Berio, Benjamin Britten, Elliott Carter, Peter Maxwell Davies, William Walton, Alberto Ginestera, Ástor Piazzolla, and Leo Brouwer. After taking a while to come into its own, the classical guitar is now a permanent member of the classical music community. Classical guitar is taught in universities and conservatories, it's a frequent program entry for concert and recital halls, and it's found readily in new recordings by major classical music record companies. As far as guitar music in general goes, however, it's definitely in the minority — with rock and pop being the major players.

How a Classical Guitar Is Different from Its Peers

They say a picture's worth a thousand words. Figure 1-1 shows a classical guitar with its main parts labeled (you see many of these parts on acoustic and electric guitars, too; flip to Chapter 1 in Book I for details).

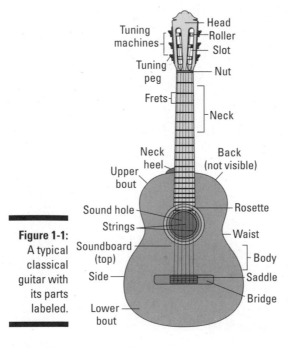

Figure 1-1:
A typical classical guitar with its parts labeled.

A classical guitar is like every other guitar in overall physique. And like other types of acoustic guitars, the classical guitar produces its sound *acoustically* — that is, without electric amplification — unlike the Stratocaster of Jimi Hendrix, which must be played through a guitar amplifier (though it's possible to amplify the classical guitar with a microphone).

Watch out when you hear the term *acoustic guitar.* A classical guitar produces its sound without amplification, so all classical guitars are in a sense acoustic guitars. But not all acoustics are classical.

Sometimes the best way to know what something is and what makes it special is to know what it isn't. Figure 1-2 shows a classical guitar and a popular traditional acoustic model.

Figure 1-2:
A classical guitar (left) with an acoustic steel-string model.

Classical guitar   Acoustic guitar

The following list sums up some of the major differences between classical guitars and acoustic guitars:

- **A classical guitar uses nylon strings.** All other acoustics used for unplugged purposes are built for steel stings. And you can't just swap out a set of nylons in your steel-string model and start playing Bach. The parts that connect the strings to the guitar are built differently, and you'd have a tough time securing a nylon string onto a steel-string guitar. Nylon strings have a gentler sound that suits classical guitar music better than the steel variety.

Some people use the adjective *folk* to mean any unamplified guitar, so it's always a good idea to clarify whether they mean the nylon-string (classical) or steel-string variety — assuming they're aware of the difference. The guitars played by James Taylor, Paul Simon, Bob Dylan, Joni Mitchell, Dave Matthews, and Sheryl Crow are all steel-string acoustics, though some folk, pop, and jazz musicians do play their brand of music on a classical guitar, including jazz guitarist Earl Klugh and, somewhat improbably, country music legend Willie Nelson.

Though the instrument is officially known as a *classical guitar,* other nicknames have sprung up for the "instrument played by classical guitarists." Some of these names include *nylon-string guitar, Spanish guitar, gut-string guitar,* and *flamenco guitar* (though that last appellation is sometimes used to distinguish a flamenco guitar from a classical guitar).

✔ **A classical guitar has only one body size.** Acoustic guitar bodies vary widely with regard to size and shape, with names like *jumbo, dreadnought, orchestra model,* and *grand auditorium* to help you keep track of them all. It's much easier with classical guitars — they're all the same size, and they all feel exactly alike when you hold them. So anything you learn on one classical guitar will transfer over to any other.

✔ **A classical guitar has no cutaway.** Many acoustic guitars have a scoop on the treble side of the upper bout that allows upper-fret access for the left hand. On a classical guitar, the body is symmetrical.

✔ **A classical guitar neck is wider than most steel-string guitar necks and joins the body at the 12th fret.** Steel-string necks are skinnier to facilitate strumming with a pick, and most modern-style steel-string necks join the body at the 14th fret. The wider frets of the classical guitar accommodate playing with the right-hand fingers, and tradition dictates the 12-fret union of neck and body (although some classical guitarists lament the more limited range of a 12-fret neck).

✔ **A classical guitar has no pick guard.** A pick guard helps protect the soundboard from the ravages of a pick. But because you don't play classical guitar with a pick, the pick guard is left off to expose more of the wooden surface. On flamenco guitars, though, a clear protective plate (called a *golpeador*) is added to protect the top from the percussive taps a performer is sometimes required to play as part of the style.

✔ **A classical guitar has no fret markers.** Acoustic guitars have inlay patterns both on the fingerboard and on the side of the neck. Sometimes these inlays can be quite elaborate, even gaudy. But classical guitars shun such showy displays and present the fingerboard in its natural, unadorned state. Occasionally, a classical guitar may have a single dot fret marker on the side of the neck.

✔ **A classical guitar never has the following images painted or stickered onto its surface:** skulls, lightning bolts, flames, your significant other's name, or inflammatory slogans of any kind.

Antonio Torres: Inventor of the modern classical guitar

Plucked string instruments have been around since ancient times, but the shape that all modern classical guitar makers follow was established by a *luthier* (guitar maker) named Antonio Torres (1817–1892), who lived in Spain and built guitars in the middle of the 19th century. Up until that time, a classical guitar could be found in a range of sizes, which affected the tuning and entire approach to playing the instrument. For the guitar to be accepted, it had to be standardized, and Torres did that. In fact, an 1863 Torres-made guitar is almost indistinguishable from ones built today.

One of the most important things Torres did was establish the string length at 650 millimeters, which hasn't changed. The string length has helped to determine other things: body proportions, neck length, and the guitar's overall dimensions. Many bold makers have tried alternate shapes and materials and added strings, but no one has successfully improved on the basic design of Torres's creation.

Modern improvements have been made, of course, especially in the manufacturing process and in some of the materials (such as synthetic substitutes for the bone or ivory nut and saddle, and better alloy chemistries for the metal tuning parts). But the woods and design have remained largely unchanged since Torres codified them back in the mid-1800s.

Beyond Physique: Other Unique Attributes of Classical Guitar

The most fundamental difference is that classical guitar is acoustic and played on a nylon-string guitar — but you could say that about other styles and other performers. (Willie Nelson is just one famous example of a nonclassical nylon-string guitar player.) So you have to dig deeper into the essence of classical guitar. In the following sections, you discover some of these key differences — in terms of the approach to the instrument — between classical guitar and other acoustic guitar styles.

Form and technique

Classical guitar requires that you hold the guitar and position your hands in a certain way (as you find out later in this chapter). Using these positions makes playing pieces easier, especially when you have to play up the neck or play notes with certain right-hand strokes to achieve the full tone of classical guitar music. The most important factors are how you hold the guitar, how you place your hands in playing position, and how your right-hand fingers pluck the strings.

Holding the instrument

You can hold an acoustic guitar a number of different ways: balanced on your right leg, balanced on your left leg (either between your legs or with your left leg crossed over your right), or dangling from a strap when you're standing up. But the classical guitar is played *only in a sitting position,* supported by the *left leg* — either with the left foot elevated or with a special support device (a cushion or frame) between the inner thigh and the guitar's body.

Placing your hands in position

In other styles, you can position the right hand in several ways, and no one will correct you as long as you sound good. But in classical guitar, you must hold your right-hand fingers perpendicular to the strings, without touching any other part of the guitar (such as the top and the bridge). You must also position your left hand so the knuckles farthest from the fingertips are parallel to the strings, not sloped away from the strings at the little finger, which some styles allow. And in classical guitar, the left-hand thumb stays braced at the center of the neck or can move toward the high strings, if necessary. But it should never be seen coming up from the bass-string side of the instrument, as you see in some fingerpicking styles.

Plucking the strings

To produce sounds on the guitar, you pluck the strings with the fingers of the right hand at a position over the sound hole (actually, the ideal position is not directly over the hole, but a little closer to the bridge than the fingerboard). With the left-hand fingers, you change the pitches of the notes by pressing the strings to the fretboard — a process known as *fretting* — which shortens the strings' vibrating length at a particular fret. (Violinists and other bowed string players don't have frets, so they refer to pressing fingers to the fingerboard as *stopping* the string, a term guitarists sometimes use, too.)

Unlike other forms of guitar playing, in classical guitar, you don't use a pick. All the sounds produced by the right hand are produced by the unadorned fingers, using the tips with a combination of the fleshy pad and a bit of fingernail (rarely strumming downward, or "brushing" them). The fingernail must extend slightly over the fingertip, and the guitarist must therefore maintain longer nails on the right hand than guitarists who play with a pick, or those who choose to fingerpick with just the flesh of the fingers.

Though classical guitar is played by picking with the fingers, the term *fingerpicking* isn't used, as it sometimes is with other styles. So don't ever call a serious classical guitarist a fingerpicker.

Musical knowledge and skills

Beyond perfecting the techniques necessary to execute classical music flaw-lessly (or getting ever nearer to that goal), classical guitarists develop their music-reading skills to cover more repertoire. And having more and more pieces under your belt means you can perform for longer periods of time and with more variety when entertaining listeners. The best classical guitarists also are technically superior to players of lesser abilities (a quality which isn't necessarily true in, say, pop music). The following sections outline why classical guitarists focus on improving their reading, mastering repertoire, and honing their technical skills.

Reading music

You can play many types of music without reading a single note. Certainly some of the best rock, blues, and folk players don't read music well or even at all, and it doesn't hamper their creative or technical abilities. But classical guitar relies on learning pieces, and the fastest, most efficient way to play through and memorize written music is to be able to read music well. That doesn't mean you have to sight read at a level where you can play the music perfectly and up to tempo the first time, but you should be able to read well enough to get a sense of the piece. (See Chapter 4 in Book I for a quick lesson in reading music.)

Mastering repertoire

If you play the classical guitar, you play *pieces* — classical compositions or arrangements written out from start to finish, with the exact notes you're to play indicated — and often the way to play them (with articulations, dynam-ics, and expression). You have to know written, composed music from start to finish, and most of the time you have to play it from memory.

Focusing on technical skill, virtuosity, and musicianship

Other styles of music may focus on the originality of the material or the inspired results of an improvisation. But in classical guitar, the primary focus is on technical mastery of the instrument. You work and work at improving your skill constantly your whole musical life, and your prowess is measured by how well you play standard pieces of repertoire. Simply put, classical guitarists are measured in the same way athletes are: The best classical guitarists are the most demonstrably technically proficient over their rivals.

One measure of technical proficiency is *virtuosity* — the ability to play extraordinarily difficult pieces with complete confidence, ease, and mas-tery. Along with technical prowess comes the not-so-showy quality called *musicianship,* which is understanding and executing the music with great accuracy, authority, and expression. In this way, the classical guitar has a lot in common with other classical instruments.

Now, if all this sounds like a lot of rules that may somehow restrict you, take heart. The *opposite* is true. The differences between classical technique and other techniques actually enable you to play notes more comfortably, easily, and with greater speed, accuracy, control, and range of expression. It may seem like a lot of do's and don'ts at first, but just as in ballet, architecture, and other art forms, you need to master the basic skills to open up a world of possibilities. To achieve total freedom of expression in playing classical guitar music, you first need to gain total control.

Situating Yourself to Play

Your first step in getting ready to play classical guitar is to make sure you're holding the instrument correctly and with your hands in the proper position. Unlike other styles of guitar playing, where common sense and comfort are often the only guidelines, classical guitar requires you to hold and position the instrument in certain ways that allow you to play more smoothly and to master the more difficult fingerings you may encounter. But though these requirements are specific, they're not difficult or restrictive in any way.

In proper position, a classical guitar makes contact with four points on your body. This allows you to keep a firm hold on the guitar while your hands enjoy the mobility they need to play freely. The four contact points support the guitar as follows (see Figure 1-3):

1. **Resting on the left leg.** This one's easy, because gravity does all the work. Set the guitar on your raised left leg (or use a support, explained later in this chapter) and proceed to the other points from here.

2. **Braced against the right leg.** The lower side of the guitar presses against the inner thigh of the right leg. You can move your leg around a bit if you feel the corner (the spot where the back and sides meet at a 90-degree angle) digging into your thigh in an uncomfortable way.

3. **Touching the chest.** The back of the guitar, just behind the bass side of the upper bout, should lightly touch the center of your chest.

4. **Lightly touching your right arm.** Your right arm rests, but doesn't press tightly, on the side. Avoid pushing the underside of the forearm into the guitar's top because that may impede its vibration and sound.

Figure 1-3:
Holding the guitar according to the four pressure points.

Taking your seat

Classical guitar is always played from a seated position. You never stand or kneel, or lie on your back, as some showoff rock guitarists do, and you never use a strap. In fact, a classical guitar doesn't even have strap pins.

Before you sit down just anywhere to hold the guitar, you should know that classical guitar prohibits certain types of seating arrangements. For one, you can't plop down on the living room couch or a beanbag chair. These two locations, as comfortable as they are for reading or messing around with *other* types of guitars, can't put you in the proper playing position for dealing with classical guitar technique. What you need is a sturdy, armless chair. Any kind of armless chair will do the job, including a dining room chair, a straight-back chair, a stool, or even a folding chair.

The chair you use should be relatively comfortable so you can spend long periods there without getting uncomfortable or risking strain or stiffness. If you use a normal metal folding chair, you may want to add a pad or cushion for comfort because you may be spending a good deal of time in that chair — especially if you want to get really good.

Supporting the guitar: Leg position

Another thing you have to attend to is a means to elevate your left foot off the floor about 4 to 6 inches. This is usually done with a footstool that's specially built for the classical guitarist. They're not very expensive (about $25), and you can buy them at any music store. If you don't have a footstool yet, just use a couple of hardcover books.

So to get started, find yourself a sturdy armless chair and sit toward the edge. Sit up straight with your legs slightly apart so you can set the waist of the guitar on your left leg. Place your foot on the footstool (or whatever improvised platform you have) and look straight ahead. Your position should look similar to that shown in Figure 1-4.

Figure 1-4:
Seated in the playing position with the left leg elevated.

An alternative to raising your leg is to use a specially made *support* or *cushion* on your left leg, which raises the guitar to the proper playing position while allowing you to keep both feet on the floor. Advocates of the support claim that it's better for your back because it doesn't require you to lift one leg in a sitting position, which causes strain. Figure 1-5 shows this alternate method, using an adjustable support that braces against the inner thigh and cradles the guitar by means of a curved piece that matches the contour of the side of the guitar's body.

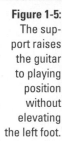

Figure 1-5: The support raises the guitar to playing position without elevating the left foot.

Some guitarists alternate the two, which mixes it up for the body, preventing them from having to maintain one position for too long. A guitarist may, for example, practice for two hours using the support, and then practice another hour with the footstool. Or he may choose to rehearse with the support and perform with the footstool. This is the approach we like, because although the support works, we like playing in the traditional way, too.

Embracing the guitar: Arm support

Classical guitarists don't invest in all the doodads and gadgetry available for other types of guitarists, but occasionally a device or accessory comes along that becomes part of the classical guitarist's bag of tricks. In addition to the support, another common external device you find is the *arm rest*. This fits on the guitar's side, on the bass side of the lower bout, directly under where the right arm sits, as shown in Figure 1-6. The arm rest lifts the forearm off the guitar's top, allowing the top to vibrate freely. Without the arm rest, the right arm inevitably touches the top. Because the arm rest prevents direct contact between the arm and the guitar, it also serves to prevent wear to the finish. Some arm rests lift the right arm off the instrument entirely, a benefit to big and tall players because it helps them maintain good posture and prevents them from having to hunch over the instrument.

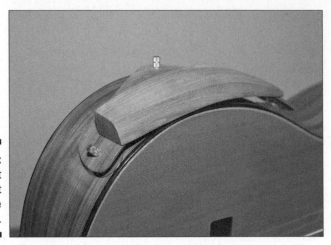

Figure 1-6:
An arm rest lifts the right arm off the guitar.

Placing your hands correctly

When you're in the proper sitting position and feeling comfortable, it's time to turn your attention to your hands. For now, all you're going to do here is *place* your hands in the proper position for playing. Don't worry just yet about actually making sounds. This is simply a check to make sure that your hands fall on the guitar in a natural, comfortable, and correct way.

The right hand

Assuming you're seated with the guitar balanced on your left leg, place your right hand so it hovers above the strings over the sound hole. Actually, don't center your hand directly over the sound hole, but slightly to the right of it, toward the bridge. Figure 1-7 shows how your right hand should look.

Figure 1-7:
Placing the right hand over the strings, a little toward the bridge.

Let your right forearm touch the edge of the guitar on the bass side of the lower bout. Your hand should be loose and relaxed with your wrist bent, or angled, in a way to cause the fingers, if you were to outstretch them, to lie perpendicular to the strings, as shown in Figure 1-8. In some situations, you may relax this "absolutely perpendicular" approach, allowing your hand to look like the position back in Figure 1-3.

Book V

Classical
Guitar

Figure 1-8:
Angling
your right
hand so
the fingers
fall perpen-
dicular to
the strings.

You should be able to pivot your right elbow so your right hand pulls away from the guitar without the guitar moving or going out of balance.

Try wiggling your fingers in the air above the strings. If you feel tension in your forearm muscle, you may be pressing your arm against the guitar's top too tightly. You don't need to hold the guitar in place with your right arm, so try lightening up a bit. The right arm and hand should almost float above the guitar and strings. And no part of your right hand should rest on the top of the guitar. All of your fingers should dangle freely above the strings. Make sure your shoulders are relaxed as well.

The left hand

When your right hand is in position, turn your focus — and your head — left. With the guitar balanced on your left leg, open your left hand slightly by separating the thumb from the fingers. Then slip your left hand around the neck and place your thumb on the center of the neck's back, allowing it to rest lightly there. Position your left-hand fingertips to press down on the strings on the top of the fingerboard. Figure 1-9 shows how your left hand should look from the back.

Turning your attention to the fingerboard side of the neck, check to see that the knuckles farthest from the fingertips are more or less parallel to the strings. Figure 1-10 shows the fingers arched and ready.

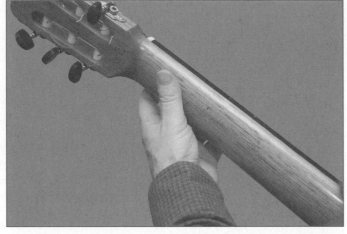

Figure 1-9:
The left
hand on the
neck with
the thumb
centered on
the neck's
back.

Figure 1-10:
The left-
hand fingers
ready to
press down
on the
strings.

A good check to see if the guitar is well-balanced is to take your left hand completely away from the guitar. The guitar shouldn't move at all because you don't use the left hand to support the neck.

Approaching the Strings with Your Hands

In classical guitar, left-hand techniques are intuitive and natural — not much different from left-hand techniques used in other types of guitar playing. In contrast, right-hand techniques are very specific and have to be learned, and they require you to not only position your hand so the fingers strike the strings at a perpendicular angle, but also to execute the notes using specific plucking methods, or strokes, called the *free stroke* and the *rest stroke*. The following sections walk you through these left-hand and right-hand techniques.

Fretting the strings: Left-hand form

Pressing the strings to the fretboard with the left-hand fingers is known as *fretting*. To fret a string, use a left-hand finger to press the string down to the fingerboard with just enough pressure to cause the string to ring clearly (without buzzing or muffling). To fret the strings as effectively and efficiently as possible, don't place your finger squarely in the middle of the two fret wires; play a little closer to the higher fret (the one closer to the bridge). This gives you better leverage when pressing down on the string, meaning it requires less strength to produce a strong, pure sound. Pressing closer to the higher fret helps eliminate buzzing, too.

When fretting a note, approach the string from above, rather than from the side, to get the maximum downward pressure against the fretboard, and keep your fingers rounded (not flat or hyper-extended) by curling your knuckles. This best applies your finger strength to the tip and provides the most effective fretting. Curving your fingers also helps you avoid accidentally touching adjacent strings. And you may be relieved to know that the left-hand fingernails can be kept short! In fact, if you're accustomed to having long left-hand fingernails, trim them to be flush with or below the fingertips.

Figures 1-11 and 1-12 show proper left-hand fretting technique.

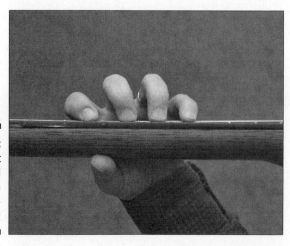

Figure 1-11:
The left hand placed correctly on the fingerboard.

Figure 1-12:
Keep fingers
curved and
approach
the string
from above.

Preparing to pluck: Right-hand form

Though you don't have to start out with long right-hand fingernails, sooner or later you have to grow and maintain them to be able to effect the tonal variations necessary for classical guitar playing. All classical guitarists agree that combining the nail with the fleshy part of the fingertip to pluck the string is essential in deriving the full spectrum of tonal colors and achieving the wide dynamic range required for classical guitar music.

Preparing your right-hand fingernails for action

To get "good guitar nails," let your right-hand fingernails grow so they extend about $\frac{1}{16}$ inch beyond the fingertip. This measurement is only an estimate, so just be sure you're able to get some of the nail in contact with the string when you pluck it. You may find it easier to keep your nails shorter as you're first learning to use them, allowing them to grow longer as you develop control. Many players like to have a slightly longer thumbnail for added bass note authority.

It's not enough just to have long fingernails. They also have to be properly shaped — that is, they should follow the shape of your fingertip — and you should keep them smooth and free of nicks and chips. To keep your fingernails at a consistent length and shape, care for them on a regular basis and invest in some "fingernail paraphernalia." A two-sided diamond nail file or a multisurface emery board are good options. For more on nail care, see the nearby sidebar, "A guitarist's guide to nail filing."

Making a beautiful sound: The nail-flesh tone

Anyone who studies the classical guitar spends long hours perfecting the development of the *nail-flesh tone* because it's such an inherent part of classical guitar technique and tone. Being able to combine the nail with the flesh (as shown in Figure 1-13) by angling the finger so more tip and less nail catches the string, in combinations that provide near-infinite degrees of tonal shading, is what makes the guitarist's palette of right-hand sounds so rich.

Figure 1-13: How to pluck to achieve the classical nail-flesh tone.

A guitarist's guide to nail filing

After your nails are long enough to give you some raw material to work with, follow these steps to shape and finish them so they can enhance your classical guitar tone (and they'll look nice too):

1. **Use the coarse surface of the file or emery board to get the nails into a basic rounded shape.** If you're using a multisurface emery board, start with the roughest-feeling grit. File down excess length and then shape the nail's edge to follow the contour of the fingertip in a symmetrical oval. Some classical guitarists recommend only filing in one direction to avoid tearing a nail. Check your progress frequently by holding your outstretched fingers in front of you, parallel to the wall, with your fingertips at eye level. Don't worry — no one's watching.

2. **Drag the file between the nail and the fingertip to round out any rough surface on the underside of the nail.**

3. **When the shape is curved and even, switch to a finer grit to smooth out any rough edges left by the coarser surface.** Eliminating snags or rough spots will make your sound smoother as well as prevent snagging on clothing and other fabrics, which can cause the nail to tear.

4. **When you've filed the nails smooth, try using fine grit sandpaper (600 or finer) or the emery board's finishing surface to make the nails even smoother, giving them an almost polished feel that protects them for longer periods between maintenance.**

Stroking the strings: Basic right-hand technique

In a *free stroke,* you pluck the string in an upward motion, leaving the finger "free," or dangling in the air, above the strings and poised to strike again.

The *rest stroke* is what classical guitar players use to produce strong, expressive, and powerful notes — more powerful than those that can be obtained by the free stroke. The "rest" part refers to the finger coming to a stop, or rest, on the next string in the direction of the stroke. Rest strokes are played with the fingers more often than the thumb and enable you to give notes more power and volume than a free stroke. But rest strokes are less nimble than free strokes, so you use them on notes that don't move quickly.

Many guitarists who first encounter free strokes and rest strokes often wonder when to use one or the other. See Table 1-1 for a handy list of which situation falls to the free stroke and which setting is a candidate for the rest stroke.

Table 1-1	Free Stroke versus Rest Stroke
Use the Free Stroke when You Play	*Use the Rest Stroke when You Play*
Arpeggios	Slower, more expressive melodies
Chords	Scales, scale sequences, and single-note passages
Light-sounding melodies, or filler notes between melody and bass parts	Loud notes, or notes requiring maximum performer volume or feeling of intensity
Passages where the rest stroke can't be applied because of tempo considerations, string conflicts, or awkwardness and impracticalities in the right-hand fingering	Passages that must be drawn out from their surroundings (either other notes from the guitar or in an ensemble setting), assuming no conflict with other strings

The free stroke

Playing the free stroke doesn't involve any specific trick or technique. It's a very natural way to play the guitar, and the way all styles of fingerpicking are performed. In fact, if you think about it too much, you may cause it to sound overly deliberate. Just pluck the string and do it several times to ensure an easy, natural approach.

To play a free stroke, place the index finger of your right hand on the 1st string. With a brisk motion, bending from the finger knuckle, pluck the string by drawing the finger toward the palm and slightly upward (being careful not to strike the 2nd string) so your finger ends up above the strings dangling freely, as shown in Figure 1-14.

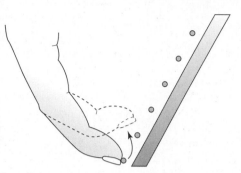

Figure 1-14:
Play a free stroke by plucking the 1st string and leaving your finger above the strings.

Repeat until you can play several plucks in a row smoothly. After you're comfortable playing free strokes with your index finger, play free strokes several times in a row using your middle finger. Then with your ring finger.

You almost never use the little finger of the right hand in classical guitar, so next try playing free strokes combining the three fingers. For example, play index, middle, index, middle; then index, middle, ring, index, middle, ring; then middle, ring, middle, ring; and finally, index, ring, index, ring.

Playing a free stroke with the thumb is just like playing a free stroke with the fingers, except you move in the opposite direction. Place it on the 6th string (nearest the ceiling). Then push through the string, plucking it, and bring your thumb slightly upward toward your palm so you don't strike the 5th string. Your thumb should end up above the strings, as shown in Figure 1-15.

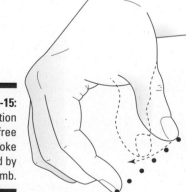

Figure 1-15:
The motion of the free stroke played by the thumb.

The rest stroke

A rest stroke always means coming to rest on the next adjacent string in the direction of the stroke. For the fingers, this means the next lower string in pitch (or next higher-numbered string). For example, if you play a rest stroke on the 2nd string, your finger rests on the 3rd string. Rest strokes must have a "place to park" after the string is played. Sometimes this creates a problem if the string underneath has to be played by the thumb or another finger, or if that string must be allowed to ring out from being previously plucked. In those cases, you must use a free stroke.

To play a rest stroke, plant your right-hand index finger on the 1st string. Then, in one motion, draw it back, plucking the string and following all the way through until your finger is stopped by the 2nd string. Be sure you don't play through the 2nd string; if you do, you're plucking too hard. It may help to think of drawing or pulling the finger downward into the guitar, rather than away from the guitar, as you do in a free stroke. Figure 1-16 shows the motion of the rest stroke.

Figure 1-16:
Playing a rest stroke on the 1st string and then stopping and resting on the 2nd string.

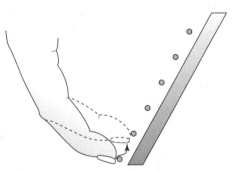

Because the rest stroke has a "landing string," it's a little more limited in its use than a free stroke is. For example, you can't use the rest stroke for arpeggios. But for bringing out a solo melody, nothing beats the expressive power of a rest stroke.

Playing rest strokes with the thumb is rare, though you sometimes play them this way to bring out a solo bass line or low-note melody. The principles for playing a rest stroke with the thumb are the same as with the fingers, except that your thumb moves in the opposite direction (toward the floor instead of the ceiling). To play a rest stroke with the thumb, plant your thumb on the 6th string. Then push your thumb so it plucks the 6th string and follows through to the 5th string, where it stops.

The birth of modern stroking technique

Because they imbue classical guitar music with its unique flavor, the rest stroke and nail sound may seem like they've always been around, preordained or something. But the rest stroke is only a recent practice and one largely promoted by the mentor of classical guitar great Andrés Segovia, Francisco Tárrega (1852–1909).

The rest stroke gave guitarists a much more powerful way to extract notes from the guitar than the free stroke could muster. And while Segovia adopted, embraced, and perfected Tárrega's rest stroke, he differed with him regarding the use of right-hand fingernails.

Tárrega and many others of the time were strongly opposed to using the nails. Emilio Pujol, a famous guitarist, composer, and Tárrega champion, thought the sound was "conical, pungent, and nasal," whereas the flesh-only sound "possesses an intrinsic beauty . . . as might be the notes of an ideally expressive and responsive harp."

But Segovia persevered and ultimately won out. It's a good thing, too, because without the use of the nail, the guitarist can't produce a sharp, percussive attack. And when playing the wide range of classical guitar music, guitarists need to be able to play bright, crisp sounds as well as soft, mellow ones.

Chapter 2

Playing Easy Pieces in Open Position

In This Chapter
▶ Exploring counterpoint
▶ Mastering melody and accompaniment
▶ Practicing pieces in different textures

*I*n this chapter the fun begins because you get to play honest-to-goodness classical guitar pieces. The pieces presented here are all rather easy to play. Where they differ is in texture.

What do we mean when we say the pieces are easy to play? First, they make use of lots of open strings — and as any guitarist knows, an open string is easier to play than a fretted one. Next, they contain no notes played above the 5th fret. Even though fretting a note at the 6th fret is technically no more difficult than playing a note at the 4th fret, people learning to read music on the guitar customarily begin with the lower frets and find playing music in low positions the easiest. Open strings and low positions naturally go together because scales and chords played in low positions often include open strings in their very makeup. (The higher you go on the neck, the less likely you are to encounter those easy-to-play open strings.)

And what do we mean when we say that the pieces differ in texture? Look at it this way: Lemon sorbet and rice pudding are both desserts, but one is light and smooth while the other is thick and chunky — that is, they have different textures. Musical compositions have texture, too. Some sound light and airy (a flute duet, for example), and others sound heavy and dense (a funeral march played by full orchestra, for instance). Texture can also refer to how the notes of a composition relate to each other. For example, are they played one at a time or all together? Do they work with each other or against each other? And how densely layered is the piece? Is it written for two instruments or 50? The classical guitar is such a versatile instrument that it can create myriad textures all by itself. In this chapter you discover two main classical guitar textures: first counterpoint, and then melody and accompaniment.

Coordinating Contrapuntal Music: Layered Melodies

Sometimes composers create music by combining individual melodies that are independent of each other yet sound good together. Music containing independent melodies is known as *counterpoint* — or, to use the adjective, *contrapuntal* music. Often (but not always), a contrapuntal piece includes nothing but those melodies; that is, no instrument plays any actual chords. If a chord does occur, it's because the various melodies happen to meet at a certain point and coincidentally (perhaps accidentally) produce one, not because the composer decided to put a chord there.

The simplest contrapuntal music is music that has two parts. That is, it contains just two melodies, usually a high one (often called the *treble,* or *treble part*) and a low one, which can sometimes be thought of as a bass line. J. S. Bach's two-part inventions (which he wrote for the keyboard) are well-known examples of two-part counterpoint. But how can you tell whether the low melody part is a true bass line or simply a low melody line? One answer is that it makes no difference what you prefer to call it. But perhaps a better answer is that it depends on how the low part sounds. For example, a low part made up of long, sustained notes, or of many repeated notes, can be considered a bass line, whereas a low part that moves a lot, as a melody does, can be thought of as part of the contrapuntal fabric (that is, as one of the independent melodies).

In classical guitar music, the low part (whether you choose to call it a bass line or a low melody) is always played by the thumb and the high part(s) by the fingers. By the way, in contrapuntal guitar compositions you rarely see more than two melodies combined, because playing more than two independent parts on the guitar is technically quite difficult. However, the upper melody can often be thickened with double-stops (two notes played simultaneously).

Another term for counterpoint is *polyphony,* which comes from the Greek and literally means "many voices." So, contrapuntal music (music containing a number of independent melodies) can also be referred to as *polyphonic* music.

Playing two melodies in sync rhythmically

The easiest way to start playing counterpoint is with music that contains only two lines (melodies) that happen to be in the same rhythm. Now, you can understandably argue that because they're in the same rhythm, the melodies aren't truly independent of each other — and you'd be right. But for now, concentrate on how your fingers and thumb work together to play two melodies without having to worry about executing independent rhythms. The exercise that follows gives your thumb and fingers a workout without taxing your rhythmic sense.

In Figure 2-1, a two-part arrangement of the famous Christmas carol "O Little Town of Bethlehem," play all the low notes with your thumb and use any comfortable combination of *i* and *m* for the top *voice* (also called part, or melody).

In classical guitar notation, *p* = thumb, *i* = index, *m* = middle, *a* = ring finger, and *c* = little finger. And because the thumb and one of the fingers sometimes must play on adjacent strings (making a rest stroke impossible), use all free strokes on this one (see Chapter 1 in Book V for more on free strokes).

Pay special attention to places where the thumb and finger play on adjacent strings. That's where the free stroke follow-through may cause your thumb and finger to bump into each other. But if you watch your right-hand position (that is, if you keep your right hand perpendicular to the strings), your thumb should extend well to the left of your fingers, and bumping shouldn't be a problem.

Book V

Classical Guitar

Track 80, 0:00

Figure 2-1: "O Little Town of Bethlehem" played with thumb and fingers together.

Opposing forces: Separating the thumb and fingers rhythmically

Music whose parts are all played in the same rhythm can become boring fast. In this section, your thumb and fingers play melodies that are truly independent; that is, they're independent in rhythm as well as in pitch.

The tricky part of playing two independent melodies is that you have to keep track of two rhythms at the same time, which, until you get used to it, is sort of like rubbing your stomach and patting your head. Just make sure to count the required number of beats in each measure properly. For example, in 3/4 time, even though you see what may look like six beats (three in the upper part and three in the lower), count the beats simultaneously for a total of three, not six.

Figure 2-2 comes from a *minuet* (a ballroom dance) by an unknown composer of the late 17th century. This arrangement (adaptation for guitar) is especially easy to play because of the numerous open strings in the bass part. Play this exercise using free strokes and with any comfortable combination of right-hand fingers.

Thickening the upper part by adding double-stops

The exercise in the previous section is pretty, but it doesn't sound especially full because it consists of only two single-note parts. In this section, you thicken the texture by adding some *double-stops* (two notes played together) to the upper part. Actually, if you play a double-stop in the upper part along with a bass note, you're playing three notes at once — a chord! And chords help classical guitar pieces sound full. Playing three notes at once isn't especially difficult. Just make sure to keep your right hand relaxed and your fingers nicely aligned. Depending on the strings involved, you can play the top notes of the chords with *i-m*, *m-a*, or *i-a*.

Figure 2-3 comes from a *gavotte* (a French dance popular in the 18th century) composed by German-born composer and organist George Frederick Handel (1685–1759), who, along with J. S. Bach, was the giant of music's Baroque era. This piece is good for practice because it offers a little of everything: single notes, double-stops (pinches), and three-note chords, with a variety of string combinations on those chords (that is, sometimes the strings that make up a chord are adjacent or close together; other times they're far apart).

Book V

Classical Guitar

Track 80, 0:23

Figure 2-2: "Minuet in A Minor" played with thumb and fingers separated rhythmically.

Track 80, 0:43

Figure 2-3: "Gavotte in A" played in contrapuntal style with texture thickened with chords.

Melody and Accompaniment: Using All of Your Fingers

The contrapuntal pieces discussed in this section have *two* melodies. But don't most musical compositions, you might point out, have just one melody? They do, and in this section you play pieces in which a single melody predominates. What makes this style — which we call *melody and accompaniment* — tricky is that while the melody is nothing but single notes, the accompaniment can take any form at all: full chords, double-stops, or anything that the composer (or an arranger) dreams up. Here you need to contend with, among other things, *four*-note chords and conflicting rhythms.

The technical term for music with one main melody (and accompaniment) — especially when the melody and accompaniment are in the same rhythm — is *homophony,* which comes from the Greek and literally means "same sound." So music in melody and accompaniment style can also be referred to as *homophonic* music.

Matching rhythm between accompaniment and melody

The simplest way to play melody and accompaniment style is to play the accompaniment in the same rhythm as the melody — an approach known as *block chord* style, or *block* style. It's simple because it allows you to concentrate on playing chords without concerning yourself with conflicting rhythms, which may exist between the melody and accompaniment.

When playing block style, even though you're playing nothing but chords, bring out the top note of each chord so the listener hears those top notes as the melody. You can't use rest strokes to bring out the top notes, however, because the lower adjacent string is also being played and needs to ring out. So accentuate the top notes simply by plucking them slightly louder than the other notes of the chord.

Figure 2-4, an arrangement of the famous Christmas carol "O Christmas Tree," combines the melody and accompaniment in a series of simple three-note chords. For the right hand, play all free strokes and use *p-i-m, p-m-a,* or *p-i-a,* depending on the strings involved and what feels comfortable to you.

Normally in printed classical guitar music, notes taken by the thumb are written with their stems pointing down from the note head (and this arrangement could have been notated that way). However, because the thumb and fingers play in the same rhythm, indicating separate voices (with up and down stems) is unnecessary. Nevertheless, make sure to play the bottom note of each three-note chord with your thumb.

Track 80, 0:59

Figure 2-4: "O Christmas Tree" played in three-note block chord style.

Getting creative with the flow: Two parts, two rhythms

Now we break away from block style to examine melody and accompaniment the way it most often appears — with the rhythm of the accompaniment *not* paralleling that of the melody. In other words, the accompaniment has its own rhythm. But whereas in counterpoint a melody is supported by another melody, in melody and accompaniment style the melody is supported by, well, an accompaniment — and by that we mean an accompaniment that's mainly chordal in nature. So in this section you play music that contains melody and chords, but because their rhythms are different, the music seems to flow along nicely.

In melody and accompaniment playing (whether block style or normal, "flowing" style), bring out the top notes so a listener will discern them as a melody.

Figure 2-5 comes from an *andante* (a piece played at a moderately slow tempo) by Spanish guitar composer and virtuoso Fernando Sor (1778–1839). Although the melody and accompaniment are in different rhythms, they're rather simple, so you shouldn't have difficulty combining them.

Track 80, 1:18

Figure 2-5: "Andante in E Minor" played in flowing melody and accompaniment style.

Playing Easy Pieces in Different Textural Styles

The four pieces in this section — in different styles and by a variety of composers — sound like what they are: real guitar performance pieces. These are pieces that you can play for your friends (or your parents or your date, as the case may be) and duly impress them with your talent and skill. Here's some useful information about the pieces to help you:

✔ **"Minuet in G":** This minuet by German composer and organist J. S. Bach (1685–1750) wasn't originally written for guitar but, because of its beauty and simplicity, is performed by guitarists with great frequency. The piece is quite famous, too. As explained by the character Mr. Holland in the 1995 film *Mr. Holland's Opus,* it was used as the basis for the 1965 pop hit "A Lover's Concerto" by the Toys.

Notice that when one voice is rhythmically active (playing eighth notes), the other is relatively inactive (playing longer notes), and that the active part sometimes switches from voice to voice. This type of interplay (with fast notes against slow ones and with the active rhythm moving from voice to voice) is typical of Bach's music and of contrapuntal music in general. And that's a good thing, not only because it makes the music interesting, but also because on the guitar it's easier to play one actively moving voice than two. If you focus on the rhythm of the active part, the rhythm of the other part seems to automatically take care of itself.

✓ **"Air in A Minor":** *Air* is another word for melody or song, and this one was written by the preeminent English Baroque composer Henry Purcell (1659–1695). The arrangement offers single notes, pinches, and chords — and a nice variety of string combinations on those chords.

Note that in measure 9, beat 3, the upper voice moves so low that it actually converges with the bass. Although that note has stems pointing both up and down, implying that it can be taken by either the thumb or a finger, you'll find it easier to take with the thumb. Also notice that in bars 3 and 4 the fingering is tricky because the first finger must suddenly jump from the 2nd string down to the 6th and then up to the 3rd. You may find it helpful to isolate those two measures for special practice.

✓ **"America (My Country 'Tis of Thee)":** This arrangement uses many four-note chords in block style. The melody is taken from the British national anthem "God Save the King," whose composer is unknown. When playing four-note chords, keep your hand in a steady but relaxed position and let all the motion come only from the thumb and fingers. But the arrangement also contains three-note chords and pinches — and a couple of single notes to boot. In other words, a little of everything, so it's a good piece for practice. As always, use the thumb for all notes with stems down. For notes with stems up, use whichever fingers feel most natural (but with four-note chords always finger *p-i-m-a*).

✓ **"Andante in G":** This andante was composed by Fernando Sor, and it offers some nice interplay between melody and accompaniment. Pay special attention to the rests; that is, don't let a note before a rest continue to ring into the beat the rest falls on. If that note happens to be fretted (measure 5, beat 3, for example), simply release the left-hand finger pressure to stop the note from sounding. But if the string is open (measure 13, beat 3, for instance), you need to lightly touch it with a finger (of whichever hand feels more natural) to stop it from sounding. As you become proficient, your hands will automatically stop strings from sounding when necessary without you having to think about it.

As usual, take advantage of all guide finger opportunities, as in measures 7, 9, 10, 15, and 16. Measures 15 and 16, in fact, are a guide finger extravaganza. You use two guide fingers at the same time (fingers 1 and 2), making it a "double guide finger," and those fingers guide your hand down the neck twice in a row (from 3rd position to 2nd, then from 2nd position to 1st), making it a "double double guide finger."

Minuet in G

TRACK 82

Air in A Minor

America (My Country 'Tis of Thee)

Book V

Classical
Guitar

Andante in G

Moderately slow

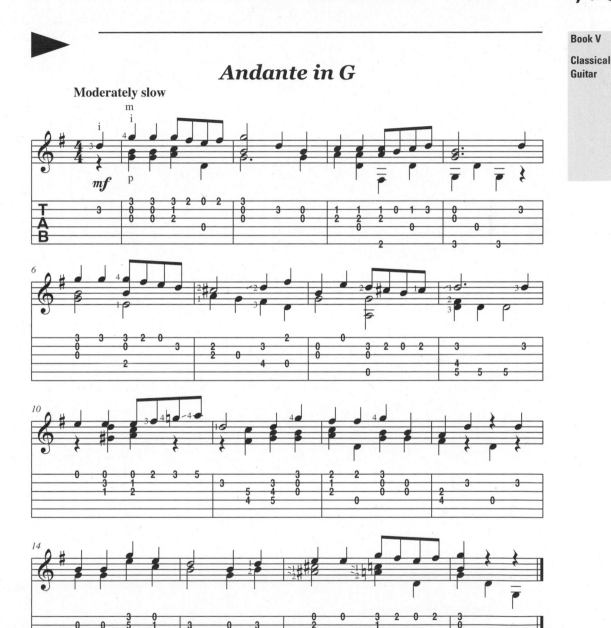

Chapter 3

Combining Arpeggios and Melody

*P*erhaps nothing is more satisfying to a classical guitarist than a composition that deftly combines *arpeggios* (notes of a chord played separately) and melodies. And the reason is simple: To a listener, the piece sounds intricate and advanced (sometimes even virtuosic), yet typically, it's not very difficult to play. So, with such pieces, you can amaze your friends without actually being a Segovia.

In this chapter, you discover how melody and arpeggios work together quite simply to create beautiful pieces, and you learn how to play them with ease.

In classical guitar notation, *p* = thumb, *i* = index, *m* = middle, *a* = ring finger, and *c* = little finger.

Grasping the Combination in Context

Combining a melody with an arpeggio is often a matter of simply playing the notes you're already fingering (rather than having to play additional notes) — the melody's notes are usually contained within the arpeggio itself. Also, when you play an arpeggio, all or many of the chord's notes are either open strings or are already held down (as a chord) by your left hand. Your right-hand fingers, too, are already in position — each resting in preparedness against its respective string. In other words, your hands hardly move for the duration of each arpeggio.

How, you may wonder, can you simultaneously play notes with various values (that is, quarter notes, whole notes, eighth notes, and so on) and keep them from sounding like a blur of overlapping pitches while also letting them all ring out as long as possible in each measure? The answer is that you actually play the notes at different levels of loudness — or, perhaps, different levels of emphasis. You do that by giving more *oomph* to some notes than to others.

The human touch (your touch, as determined by your understanding of the notes' roles and interactions) imparts the proper textural feel to the listener — and that's what makes playing such pieces so exciting. If you give the right amount of emphasis to the respective notes (even merely psychologically), the effect comes across to the listener, who hears the music not as just a blur of overlapping pitches but as a melody, an accompaniment, and a bass line. The technique for doing that varies, depending on whether you play the melody with your thumb or fingers.

When playing arpeggios, hold down your left-hand fingers as a chord whenever possible and for as long as possible. And keep the motion of your right hand to a minimum by resting your fingers ahead of time against the strings they need to play in each arpeggio. For example, before playing an A minor arpeggio (as in measure 1 in Figure 3-1), your thumb should be resting against the 5th string, your index finger against the 3rd string, and your middle finger against the 2nd string. While playing each arpeggio, your right hand itself doesn't move; only your fingers and thumb move as they strike their respective strings.

In the sections that follow, the exercises allow you to combine arpeggios with melodies in the bass (played by the thumb) and the treble (played by the fingers), and we explore ways to draw the melody out of the background and into the limelight, where it belongs.

Going Downtown: Melody in the Bass

The melody of a classical guitar piece, though usually played by the fingers on the high strings (in the treble), is sometimes played by the thumb on the low strings (in the bass). This concept applies to the piano, too, by the way. The right hand plays the melody of most pieces, though for a different effect, the melody can be placed in the left hand.

You may find it easier to combine arpeggios with a melody played by your thumb than by your fingers. For one thing, your thumb usually plays *on* the beat (rather than between the beats, as the fingers do). For another, you have no decisions to make about *which* finger plays the melody; that is, your thumb, acting alone, plays nothing but the melody notes while your fingers play nothing but the accompaniment (the higher notes of each arpeggio).

Don't worry about having to hunt down the melody in a piece. The melody usually reveals itself soon enough when you start to play, just in the way the composer or arranger wrote the notes. Sometimes the written music itself even offers clues, such as giving the melody its own stem direction. When you can hear where the melody falls, you can work to bring it out further, using slightly stronger strokes on the melody notes themselves. Or, if there's no melody at all (which sometimes happens in short passages between melodic phrases), you hear that, too, and give no emphasis to any particular notes.

Playing a melody within arpeggios in the bass

How do you bring out the notes when the melody is in the bass line? Just play them a little louder (striking them a little harder) than the other notes, and make sure the other notes are consistent with each other in loudness.

Figure 3-1 is an exercise that offers you an opportunity to practice the basic technique of combining arpeggios with a bass melody without having to worry about any of the complicated rhythms or unusual left-hand fingerings that real-life pieces may contain.

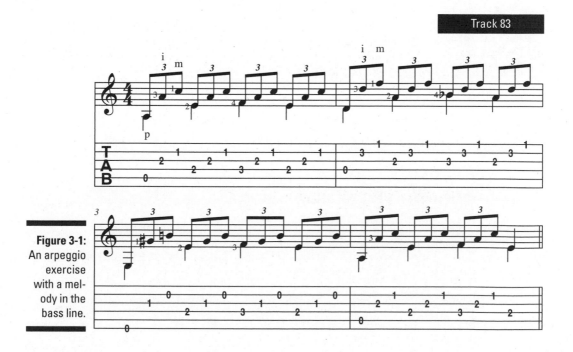

Track 83

Figure 3-1: An arpeggio exercise with a melody in the bass line.

Note that the first note of each triplet group has a downward stem (in addition to an upward stem). Those downward stems tell you not only to play those notes with your thumb but also to play them as quarter notes — in other words, to let them ring throughout the beat.

One of the rules of arpeggio playing is that all the notes of an arpeggio should ring out rather than be stopped short — so all of those bass notes sound as quarter notes anyway. So, in reality, those downward stems on the first note of each triplet group tell you not only to play them with the thumb and to let them ring out, but also to bring out those thumb notes so a listener will hear them as an independent melody.

Measure 2 presents an interesting right-hand fingering dilemma. Normal, or typical, right-hand position has the index finger assigned to the 3rd string, the middle finger to the 2nd, and the ring finger to the 1st. Also, you generally try not to move the right hand itself, if at all possible. For those reasons, you'd expect to use fingers *m* and *a* to play the top two notes of the D minor arpeggio.

But another rule of arpeggio playing says you should use the strongest fingers whenever possible — and the combination of *i* and *m* is stronger than that of *m* and *a*. So, according to that rule, you should use *i* and *m* for the top two strings even though you have to move your right hand across the neck a bit. Hence the dilemma.

When you have a situation in which those right-hand fingering rules conflict, the "strong fingers" rule takes precedence over the "minimize motion" rule, and thus we indicate in measure 2 that you play the top two notes of the D minor arpeggio with *i* and *m*.

Figure 3-1 presents no technical difficulties, but for best results, follow the left-hand fingering carefully and keep the rhythm as steady and even as possible.

Practicing making a bass melody stand out

Figure 3-2 is taken from a study by early 19th-century Spanish guitar virtuoso Dionisio Aguado. It features a single right-hand pattern throughout *(p-i-m-i)* and a uniform rhythm. That's what makes it easy to play. But at the same time, the study is somewhat challenging for a few reasons.

✔ First, the notes are 16th notes, which means they move along rather briskly. So start out by practicing slowly and then gradually increase the tempo.

✔ Second, the bass notes — because they're all chord tones that occur at the beginning of each four-note group — have a tendency to sound like nothing more than simply the first note of each arpeggio. So it's your job to make them especially melodic; that is, bring them out forcefully — but smoothly and sweetly — so a listener hears a "tune" in the bass.

✔ Finally, you play some of the notes on strings you may not expect. Check out measure 2, beat 4, for example, where, in order to preserve the right-hand pattern (and flow), you play the C on the 3rd string, and the repeated Es alternate between the 2nd and 1st strings.

Figure 3-2:
Study in A
Minor with
the melody
in the bass.

For ease of playing, pay special attention to the left-hand fingering (and especially to the guide finger indications). And for an effective performance, keep the rhythm as even as possible.

Moving Uptown: Melody in the Treble

We start with melodies in the bass because, as we explain earlier, they're a bit easier to combine with arpeggios than are melodies in the treble. Alas, arpeggio pieces with melodies in the treble are actually more common than those with melodies in the bass. In this section, we look at the technique you use to play such pieces.

Playing arpeggios with the melody in the treble rather than the bass can be a bit trickier for a few reasons:

- ✔ **Question of fingering:** Technically, any given melody note can be taken with any available finger — *i, m,* or *a* — and it's often up to you to decide which to use.

- ✔ **Use of the ring finger:** Because the *i* and *m* fingers usually play accompaniment notes on the inner strings, the *a* finger takes many melody notes. The problem is that the melody notes must be emphasized, but the ring finger is the weakest.

- ✔ **Question of right-hand technique:** As explained in the sections that follow, you have more than one way to bring out a treble melody from an arpeggio, and it's up to you to decide which technique to use.

- ✔ **Use of rest strokes:** Whereas you play arpeggios with a melody in the bass with free strokes only, you generally combine rest strokes and free strokes when you play arpeggios with a melody in the treble.

- ✔ **Complexity of notation:** Standard music notation for arpeggio pieces with a melody in the treble often requires the indication of three separate parts, or *voices* — one each for the melody, the accompaniment (usually filler notes on the inner strings), and the bass. Normally, stem directions tell you which notes belong to which part (for example, notes with stems up are melody and notes with stems down are bass). Depending on the musical context (or sometimes simply on the amount of available space), the accompaniment notes may be stemmed either down (sometimes making them hard to distinguish from bass notes) or up (sometimes hard to distinguish from melody notes). Sometimes, at the whim of a composer or arranger, the melody and accompaniment notes are combined into a single voice (as a continuous flow of upstemmed eighth notes, for example), and it's up to you, using your ear, to discover the real melody.

Although the aforementioned potential complications may cause you concern, most arpeggiated pieces — even those with the melody in the treble — aren't difficult to play. That's because, as stated, in such pieces, the left-hand generally holds down a chord, and the melody notes themselves are often contained within that chord.

To bring out the melody in the treble, you have to make it either louder than, or different in tone from, the other notes. You can do this simply by

- ✔ Making the melody notes sound stronger than the others by playing them with rest strokes (and the accompaniment notes with free strokes — see Chapter 1 in Book V for more on rest and free strokes). You can also try the techniques in the following bullets, but this technique — the use of rest strokes for melody notes — is generally used by classical guitarists, and it's the one you should strive to perfect.

✔ Striking the melody notes harder than the others, as you do when you bring out a bass melody with the thumb.

✔ Making the melody notes brighter sounding than the others by using more nail when you strike them — that is, if you play with a combination of flesh and nail, use more nail than flesh on the melody notes, and more flesh than nail on the accompaniment notes. (See Chapter 1 in Book V for details on the nail-flesh tone.)

Playing a treble melody within arpeggios

Figure 3-3 is an exercise that allows you to combine a treble melody with a series of arpeggios. Note that you play the melody in quarter notes (indicated by upward quarter-note stems), that the bass notes are whole notes (and thus must ring throughout each measure), and that the accompaniment notes are eighth-note triplets, which, though they are written as short notes, should also ring out (according to the general rules of arpeggio playing).

Track 84

Figure 3-3:
An arpeggio
exercise
with a
melody in
the treble.

Practice Figure 3-3 using rest strokes on all the melody notes. Start out playing slowly (but evenly), and then gradually increase your speed. Follow the left-hand fingerings to ensure that you can hold down each chord with your left hand for as long as possible. If necessary, listen to the CD to hear how the piece works rhythmically and how the separate voices interact.

Practicing making a treble melody stand out

Figure 3-4 comes from a study by late 19th-century Spanish guitar virtuoso Francisco Tárrega. It employs a consistent right-hand pattern throughout: *p-i-m, a-m-i, a-m-i, a-m-i.* Play all the melody notes as rest strokes with the ring finger.

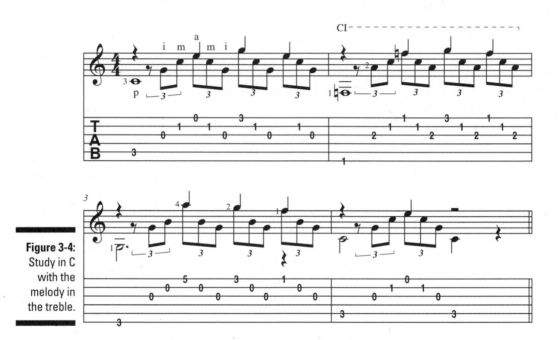

Figure 3-4: Study in C with the melody in the treble.

Note that the bass notes sustain throughout each arpeggio, but in measure 3, fingering requirements force you to stop the bass from ringing one beat early (because the finger that plays the bass note, the first finger, is suddenly needed on the 1st string to play the last melody note of the measure).

Mixing Up Your Melodic Moves: The Thumb and Fingers Take Turns

Not all arpeggiated passages are as straightforward as those you encounter earlier in this chapter — where the melody occurs consistently in either the treble or bass part. In some cases the melody moves back and forth between the treble and bass, and in others the treble and bass parts contain melodic motion simultaneously. Fortunately, the playing of such pieces requires no new techniques, but it does require a heightened awareness (on your part) of where the melody is and how to bring it out.

Playing a shifting treble-and-bass melody within arpeggios

In Figure 3-5, from measure to measure, the melody alternates between the treble and bass. In the odd-numbered measures, which have the melody in the treble, bring out the melody (the upstemmed notes) with rest strokes. For the even-numbered measures, which have the melody in the bass, bring out the melody (the downstemmed notes) by giving the first note of each triplet a little more *oomph* than the other notes.

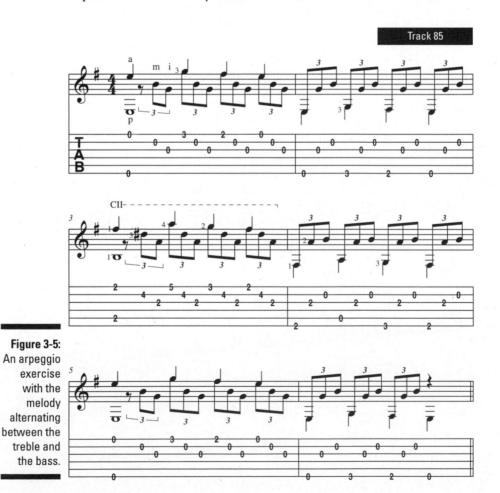

Figure 3-5: An arpeggio exercise with the melody alternating between the treble and the bass.

Note that the melody note that occurs on the third beat of each measure is a *dissonance* (that is, it's not a member of the chord being arpeggiated), but that it passes smoothly from one chord tone to another. For example, in measure 1, in which an E minor chord (made up of the notes E, G, and B) is arpeggiated, the F♯ on beat 3 functions as a *passing tone* (a dissonance that, in stepwise motion, passes between, and thus fills the gap between, two chord tones — in this case, G and E). Also note, as a point of interest, that each bass melody is a repetition, but two octaves lower, of the treble melody that precedes it. Repetition imparts structural unity and thus a sense of balance to a composition.

Practicing making a shifting melody stand out

Figure 3-6 is an excerpt from a waltz from the guitar method of early 19th-century Italian guitar composer and virtuoso Ferdinando Carulli. A glance at the music reveals that the melody begins in the bass (measures 1 and 2) and moves to the treble (measures 3 through 5).

Figure 3-6: "Waltz in E Minor" with the melody alternating between the bass and treble.

In measures 3 and 4, note that in the written notation, for the sake of simplicity, the composer combined the melody (the upstemmed notes on the beats: F♯-G-F♯, G-F♯-G) and the accompaniment notes (the open B's) into a single voice. What you need to realize is that although the melody notes are written as eighths, they are to be rendered in performance as quarters.

In Figure 3-5 you play a dissonance known as a *passing tone.* "Waltz in E Minor" presents another type of dissonance: the neighboring tone. A *neighboring tone* is a non-chord tone that, in stepwise motion, follows a chord tone and then returns to it (with the word "neighboring" obviously coming from the idea that, being just one step away from the chord tone, the dissonant note is like the chord tone's next-door neighbor). For example, in measure 3 you arpeggiate a B chord (B-D♯-F♯), and the G on beat 2 follows and then returns to the chord tone F♯. Because G is above F♯ in the scale, it's called, specifically, an *upper neighbor.* In the following measure you arpeggiate an E minor chord (E-G-B), and the F♯ on beat 2 (following and then returning to G) is a *lower neighbor.*

Playing Pieces that Combine Arpeggios and Melodies

Unlike simple arpeggio-and-melody practice exercises, which generally feature easy left-hand fingerings or consistent right-hand patterns, real-life pieces often contain complications in the form of some not-so-easy fingerings and not-so-consistent patterns. In this section we offer, for your practice and enjoyment, pieces by classical guitar masters that combine arpeggios with melodies — one with the melody in the bass, one with the melody in the treble, and one with a melody that moves between the treble and bass.

Here's some information to help you with the pieces:

✔ **"Ländler in D":** A *ländler* is an Austrian folk dance in 3/4 time (or a musical piece to accompany such a dance), and this one was composed by 19th-century Hungarian guitar virtuoso Johann Kaspar Mertz.

Play notes with stems both up and down (generally on beats 1 and 3 in the first section and on each beat in the second) with the thumb, and bring them out as a melody (and remember to hold down all the notes of each measure as a chord whenever possible).

In measures 13 through 20, you play only a single note after each bass note, so the patterns aren't true arpeggios. That is, an arpeggio is a "broken chord," and a chord, by definition, contains three or more notes. However, in that section, if you think of each beat as a two-note "chord," you can see that you're still playing in arpeggio style (meaning that the thumb and fingers alternate).

In two-note arpeggio figures (as in measures 13 through 20), your thumb, of course, plays all the bass notes. You play the treble notes, if they change pitch from beat to beat, by alternating between *i* and *m*. But if the pitch of the treble notes remains constant, as in this instance, you usually play the notes with just one finger — either *i* or *m* (depending on which strings your thumb plays and how close they are to the treble string in question). Try measures 13 through 20 first using *i* for all the open E's and then using *m*, and see which fingering you prefer.

✔ **"Romanza":** This is one of the all-time most famous classical guitar pieces; virtually every classical guitarist encounters it and plays it at some time or another. It's known by several titles, including "Romanza," "Romance," "Spanish Romance," and "Romance d'Amour." In most collections that include it, the composer is said to be anonymous, which may lead you to believe that the piece was written hundreds of years ago. Actually, the piece isn't nearly that old, and the identity of the composer isn't so much unknown as it is in doubt or in dispute; a number of composers have claimed authorship of this piece.

As indicated, play all the melody notes with the *a* (ring) finger, and bring them out by emphasizing, or accenting, them slightly. Even though *a* may be the weakest finger, it's charged with the important work of carrying the melody here.

What makes this piece relatively easy is the great number of open strings (as is typically the case with pieces in the key of E minor). What makes it difficult (besides the many barre chords) are the left-hand stretches in measures 10, 27, and 28. Isolate those measures and practice them separately, if necessary. And what makes the piece interesting (besides its inherent beauty) is the shift from the minor to the major key in the second section (at measure 17), and then the return to the minor key after measure 32. The major section is more difficult than the minor because it has fewer open strings, so you may need to practice that section a bit more.

✔ **"Andante in C":** Just as Carulli did with "Waltz in E Minor" in Figure 3-6, so too did early 19th-century Italian guitar virtuoso Matteo Carcassi combine the melody and accompaniment notes into a single part. But whereas in the Carulli piece it's obvious which notes are melody and which are accompaniment, this piece has a certain amount of ambiguity. Sometimes, as in the first two full measures, it's easy to discern the melody: it's made up of the notes that occur at beats 1, 2, and 4 (and

Book V

Classical Guitar

which should be rendered in performance as a quarter note, a half note, and a quarter). But in the next measure, is the A on beat 4 melody or accompaniment? And in the measure after, are the final three notes (G, F, and D) melody or accompaniment? Only Carcassi could answer definitively, but because you can't ask him, it's up to you, the performer, to answer such questions by bringing out (or not bringing out) those ambiguous notes accordingly.

If you look at the piece's second section (measures 10 through 17), you see that the upper voice contains a melody (albeit intermingled with accompaniment notes in the same voice) and that the bass part also moves melodically. This really gives you an opportunity to practice your melody/arpeggio chops (or to display them, as the case may be). All at once you have to decide which of the upstemmed notes you consider the real melody notes, to bring out those notes from the notes that function merely as accompaniment, and to also bring out the separate melody that occurs in the bass!

Because Carcassi's notation leaves some unanswered questions, you may wonder why he didn't employ three separate voices in his notation — one for the upper melody, one for the filler (accompaniment) notes, and one for the bass line. He could have, and some pieces are so notated. However, the risk is that the notation is so complicated that it's counterproductive. That's why Carcassi chose to notate the piece as he did. But that doesn't mean a different composer may have notated it as three separate voices.

Ländler in D

(continued)

(continued)

Book V

Classical Guitar

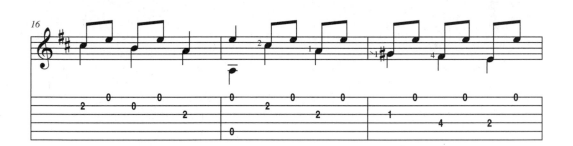

D.C. al Fine

Romanza

(continued)

(continued)

Book V

Classical Guitar

(continued)

(continued)

Book V

Classical Guitar

Andante in C

Moderately slow, in 2

Fine

(continued)

(continued)

D.S. al Fine

Chapter 4

Classical Guitar Genres: The Renaissance to the 20th Century

● ●

● ●

Music historians like to divide music into well-defined periods, or eras. Music from before around 1450 — the *Middle Ages,* or *medieval period* — was mainly sung in church, and today it sounds so primitive that it's hardly ever played on guitar. The next period, from about 1450 to around 1600, is known as the *Renaissance era,* and the following period, from around 1600 to 1750, is the *Baroque era* — and the music of those eras does still sound good on guitar.

The Baroque era was rather complex. Bach's counterpoint was sometimes intricate to the extreme, as were many of the instrumental ornaments (trills, turns, and so on) that were written into the music and improvised by the era's virtuoso performers. After the death of Bach (1750), as a reaction against the showy aspect of Baroque (which means "ornate") music, composers began to write pieces that were more formal, sedate, elegant, and graceful. Enter the *Classical era* (1750–1820).

Toward the end of the Classical era, composers started to feel restrained by that formality and began to use a musical vocabulary that better expressed their innermost feelings, yearnings, and desires. This led to music's *Romantic era* (1820–1900). By the end of the 1800s, every aspect of traditional harmony, melody, and rhythm had been explored and employed, and composers began to experiment with new kinds of scales, chords, and rhythms. The result was the *Modern era* (after 1900), whose music sounds nothing like anything that had gone before it. In this chapter we take a look at what typifies these genres of music.

The Renaissance

Because the Renaissance directly followed the Middle Ages, composers of the late 1400s and 1500s were influenced by the earlier era's music — namely, vocal music performed in church. To show respect for God, such music contained nothing ugly or jarring. So Renaissance melodies, like the tunes of the earlier period, tend to be simple (containing more stepwise motion than wide leaps), and the harmonies tend to be mostly pure and simple (three-note major and minor chords). Renaissance composers also wrote instrumental and secular (nonreligious) music, and there they pushed some limits.

Renaissance music differs from music of other eras in the scales, instruments, and textures it uses. Our modern ears are used to hearing songs and classical pieces in major and minor keys (keys based on major and minor scales), but in the Renaissance era, the system of major and minor keys had not yet been developed. Instead, music was based on special scales called *modes,* which is why Renaissance pieces sound somewhat strange and exotic to us.

If you play only the white notes of a piano keyboard step by step, from C to C, you get a major scale, and if you play from A to A you get a minor scale. But if you play only white keys from any of the other five white keys (for example, from D to D or from F to F), you get a unique-sounding scale — a mode — that's neither major nor minor. During the Renaissance, composers wrote pieces based on those unique scales as well as on major and minor scales, but to a Renaissance composer, the major and minor scales were nothing special; they were simply two of the seven possible modes.

Today we're used to hearing music played on instruments like the piano, guitar, and violin, but those weren't fully developed during the Renaissance. Instead, music was played on instruments like the harpsichord, lute (a predecessor of the guitar with a rounded back), recorder, and viol — an early cello-like instrument with frets.

Two types of Renaissance music often played on classical guitar are arrangements of traditional 16th-century melodies and arrangements of pieces originally written for the lute. The sections that follow cover both of these.

Traditional 16th-century melodies by anonymous composers

The Renaissance — the time of Christopher Columbus, Leonardo da Vinci, and William Shakespeare — happened so long ago that the authorship of many of that era's musical works is unknown. In such cases, the composer is considered anonymous, or the piece in question is said to be traditional. Some anonymous melodies from that era are well-known today because

Book V

Classical Guitar

musicians throughout the ages have continued to arrange and perform them. Such songs include "Greensleeves" (also known as "What Child Is This?"), "Scarborough Fair," "Coventry Carol," and "The Three Ravens."

"Greensleeves" has been recorded by countless modern artists, from the Chipmunks to Elvis Presley. But Figure 4-1 shows how a Renaissance musician — Francis Cutting (c. 1550–1596) — arranged the song for lute (here adapted for guitar). The melody and chords may sound a little different from how you're used to hearing them, but that's understandable when you consider that this arrangement was written more than 400 years ago.

Track 87

Figure 4-1: "Green-sleeves" arranged by Francis Cutting.

The song sounds like it's in the key of A minor, but the F♯ in measure 6 tells you that the piece is actually based on one of the Renaissance modes (in this case the so-called *Dorian* mode, which sounds minor-ish but whose 6th degree is a half step higher than that of a normal minor scale). Also note the sudden change in harmony to A major (as opposed to A minor) in the final measure. Such sudden shifts between major and minor harmonies are typical in Renaissance music.

John Dowland and other great lutenists

During the Renaissance, lute composer/performers (called *lutenists*) flourished in England, France, and Italy, but the English lutenists — including Thomas Campion, Francis Cutting, and Philip Rosseter — are best known today. The most famous of all is Englishman John Dowland (1563–1626), who in his later years served as court lutenist for King James I.

Dowland is known for both his solo lute pieces and his *lute songs,* which consist of a vocal part, a poem set to music and sung, and a lute accompaniment. But the accompaniment was generally of such intricacy that the lute part was more or less equal to the vocal part (rather than subordinate to it), and a lute song was really more like a duet (between voice and lute) than a simple melody and accompaniment.

In writing a lute song, a composer tried to reflect in his music the mood or emotion of the poem (lyric) being sung. Because many of the poems Dowland set to music concern grief and sorrow ("Flow My Tears" and "In Darkness Let Me Dwell," for example), he has a reputation for being melancholy. In fact, Figure 4-2 is an excerpt from a solo lute piece he titled "Melancholy Galliard." (A *galliard* is a dance in 3/4 time — or music written for such a dance — popular in Europe in the 1600s.)

As a compositional device, Dowland here employs *suspension,* in which a consonant tone becomes dissonant when the chord behind it changes (see beat 2 of measures 2, 4, and 8). Also note that Dowland — and Renaissance composers in general — gives an important role to the inner voice — in this case, the one featuring the aforementioned suspensions. In music of most other eras the melody and bass predominate, with the inner voices relegated to second-class status.

A bit about the lute

During the Renaissance, the most popular instrument was the lute. It resembles a modern classical guitar in that it has a body and a neck with frets, strings, and tuning pegs — but it differs from a guitar in a number of ways:

✔ The lute has a rounded back rather than a flat one. To get an idea of what a lute's body looks like, think of half a watermelon that's been cut lengthwise.

✔ The lute's neck is shorter than a classical guitar's, and the lute's body typically meets the fretboard at the 9th fret (rather than at the 12th fret, as on a modern guitar).

✔ The neck is also wider because the lute typically has more strings than a guitar. A lute can have more than six strings (seven, eight, or more), and most of the strings — all but the highest one or two — are actually sets of *double* strings that are plucked together as if single, as on a modern 12-string guitar. A single high string or a set of double strings — whether tuned in unison, as with the middle strings, or tuned in octaves, as with the low strings — is called a *course,* so you may hear of a 6-course lute or an 8-course lute (rather than a 6- or 8-*string* lute).

✔ A lute is typically tuned a little differently from a guitar. In a 6-course lute (a common configuration), the 3rd course, which corresponds to the open G string on a guitar, is tuned a major 3rd above the 4th course (the guitar's open D string), rather than a perfect 4th above it, as on a guitar. That's why music originally written for lute must be adapted (rearranged or refingered) for the guitar (unless the modern guitarist tunes his 3rd [G] string down a half step to F♯).

✔ The lute's *headstock* (the part with the tuning pegs) is angled back from the neck perpendicularly rather than being in line with the neck, as on a modern guitar.

Figure 4-2: "Melancholy Galliard" by John Dowland.

Going for Baroque

If you ask a casual music listener what his favorite kind of classical music is, he's likely to answer Baroque. And that's not surprising, because Baroque music — exemplified by such composers as Bach, Handel, Vivaldi, Scarlatti, and Telemann — has quite a bit in common with modern-day popular music. For one thing, Baroque music, like popular music, is based on major and minor keys and the chord progressions derived from those keys. For another, Baroque pieces often feature one instrument playing melody, another playing chords, and another playing a bass line — not unlike today's pop group with a singer, guitarist, and bassist. Also like today's pop music, Baroque music is known for its regular, steady rhythm.

But Baroque music is different from today's popular music in many ways, too, and not just because it sounds like, well, classical music. Baroque music often employs *imitative counterpoint,* in which a melody played in one voice is repeated a few beats later (usually from a different starting pitch) in another voice. Also, whereas popular music employs simple song structures that are usually made up of two or three short sections that sometimes repeat, Baroque music uses all sorts of complex, extended forms, such as concertos, suites, operas, and cantatas. And whereas today's popular music can be played by amateurs and professionals alike, much Baroque music was written for virtuoso performers who often added their own highly complex ornamentation as they played.

Two composers who brought Baroque music to its peak are Johann Sebastian Bach (1685–1750) and George Frideric Handel (1685–1759). The following sections explore the classical guitar music based on their compositions.

Back to Bach

Bach's music is known for its almost paradoxical combination of intricate structure and strong passion. In a way, it sounds as though it was put together mathematically, and in another way, it sounds as though it came purely intuitively, or from the heart. One of Bach's most famous pieces, popularly titled "Jesu, Joy of Man's Desiring," comes from one of his many church *cantatas* (pieces for vocal soloists, chorus, and orchestra that form part of a church service). The piece's beauty and elegance has made it a popular wedding processional, even though that wasn't what Bach intended when he wrote it, and it's performed routinely by classical guitarists.

Figure 4-3 is an excerpt from "Jesu, Joy of Man's Desiring," and you can hear that the music is both logical and beautiful at the same time. It's in a style known as *strict counterpoint,* which means that each note of one voice is played against a strictly set number of notes in another voice — in this case, each bass note has exactly three treble notes.

Track 88

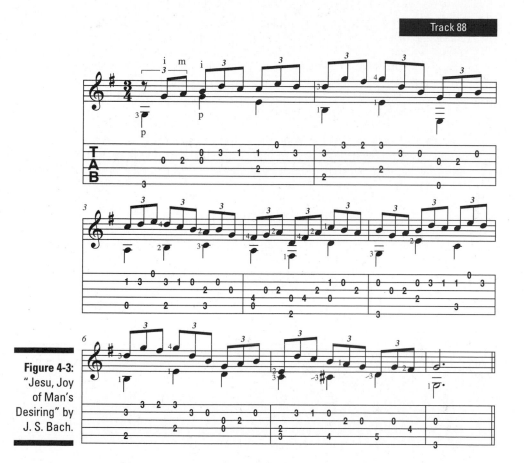

Figure 4-3:
"Jesu, Joy
of Man's
Desiring" by
J. S. Bach.

Although today Bach is the most famous Baroque composer (and among the most famous composers of all time), during his lifetime in his native Germany he was celebrated as a virtuoso organist rather than as a composer because his original works were considered too complex. The simpler pieces of fellow German composer Georg Philipp Telemann were held in higher regard. In fact, it wasn't until 79 years after his death — when 20-year-old German composer Felix Mendelssohn produced and conducted a performance of the *St. Matthew Passion* in Berlin — that Bach's music began to receive the acclaim it deserved.

Getting a handle on Handel

Along with J. S. Bach, G. F. Handel was the other giant of the Baroque era. Handel is well-known for two of his orchestral suites, *Water Music* and *Royal Fireworks,* but he's probably best known for his large-scale work for orchestra, chorus, and soloists that's now performed every Christmas — the

Messiah (even though he originally wrote it to celebrate Easter). And the most famous section of the *Messiah* is the one that audiences customarily stand up for, the "Hallelujah Chorus." (Legend has it that at the first performance of the *Messiah,* England's King George II was so roused by the music that he suddenly rose to his feet — and when the king rose, everyone in his presence was required to rise. Since then, audiences have always stood for that section of the performance.)

Figure 4-4 is an excerpt from Handel's "Hallelujah Chorus," arranged for guitar (resist the urge to stand). The piece starts with some simple major chords played in a strong, distinctive rhythm, but a suspension in measure 4 changes the mood with a bit of tension.

In this excerpt Handel uses a common compositional device known as *modulation,* in which a piece begins in one key but changes to a different key. In this case the passage begins in E major (measures 1 through 4) but ends in B major (measures 5 through 8).

Figure 4-4: "Hallelujah Chorus" by G. F. Handel.

The Classical Era: Mozart's Muse

Immersing yourself in music of the Classical era is a bit like accompanying your aunt to a formal tea party. Everything is proper and elegant and dainty — and everyone is on his or her best behavior. To put it another way, strict rules are followed.

The two most prominent composers of the Classical era were both Austrian: Franz Joseph Haydn (1732–1809), who wrote more than 100 symphonies and established the symphony as a musical form, and Wolfgang Amadeus Mozart (1756–1791), with Mozart ultimately becoming the true giant of the era.

What set Mozart apart from many other composers was his ability to write a great melody — a pretty tune. Some composers concentrate on rhythm, harmony, or texture; others create melody by taking short fragments and piecing them together. But nothing lends appeal to a composition as much as a good melody. And Mozart was particularly aware of this. In fact, he once explained, "Melody is the essence of music. A good melody writer is like a fine racehorse, but a counterpoint writer is like a horse that carries the mail."

Because Mozart's melodies are so tuneful, his music can be a delight to play on classical guitar. Figure 4-5 is an arrangement of an excerpt from an *aria* (song) from Mozart's 1787 opera *Don Giovanni.* As you play it (or listen to it on the accompanying CD), you hear that the melody is simple, playful, and quite childlike. Mozart's playfulness is another quality that sets him apart from other Classical-era composers.

Note that Mozart puts the chords on the off beats rather than on the beats, giving the song a secondary accent (or a kind of backbeat, not unlike that found in today's pop music). Also note that the piece consists of two four-bar phrases. The three double-stops that connect those phrases (at the end of measure 4) aren't part of the aria's vocal melody, and you should play them very smoothly. In contrast, you should play the two notes that finish the second phrase (also not part of the vocal melody) very short (as indicated by the *staccato* dots).

A secondary accent is different from syncopation. A *secondary accent* is a normal, natural part of a meter. For example, in 2/2 time, beat 1 gets the primary accent, and beat 2 gets a secondary accent; that is normal and expected. In *syncopation,* notes are accented in unexpected places — places that conflict with or go against a given meter.

Track 89

Figure 4-5:
Aria
from *Don
Giovanni* by
Mozart.

Beethoven, the Classical Hopeless Romantic

Starting in the early 1800s, certain composers who'd previously written in a Classical style began to make their music more emotional and colorful. This began a transition from the formality of the Classical era to the passion and intensity of the Romantic era. One such composer was Austrian Franz Schubert, who wrote more than 600 songs for voice and piano. But by far the most important of these transition-era composers was Ludwig van Beethoven (1770–1827) of Germany.

Beethoven was a pretty emotional guy — so emotional, in fact, that he had to invent a whole new style of music to express his feelings. And for that he's generally credited with initiating music's Romantic era.

At the beginning of his career, Beethoven wrote in a style similar to that of Haydn and Mozart, but by his 30s he was breaking free of his predecessors. He expanded the traditional harmonic, rhythmic, and textural vocabulary by lengthening musical forms (adding extra movements, or sections, to pieces), and by adding more instruments to his orchestral scores, such as brass and percussion.

Figure 4-6 is an arrangement of an excerpt from the second movement of Beethoven's "Piano Sonata No. 8" (the "Pathétique Sonata"), written in 1798. Though the first movement is fiery and emotional, the second movement, often played by guitarists, is in a straightforward Classical style. The piece features a pretty melody supported by arpeggios, so make sure to bring out the top line and to allow the arpeggios to ring out as long as possible.

Note that although the harmony consists of simple major, minor, and 7th chords, notes other than the chords' roots often serve as the bass notes. For example, in measure 2, the first chord, C major, has an E (rather than a C) in the bass, and the second chord, G7, has a B (rather than a G) in the bass. A chord that has a tone other than the root (namely, the 3rd, 5th, or 7th) as the bass note is said to be in *inversion*. Composers use inversions to add harmonic interest to their compositions — as Beethoven does here.

Figure 4-6: "Pathétique Sonata" by Beethoven.

Another Romantic: Brahms

As the 1800s proceeded, composers of concert music strayed farther and farther from the formal, controlled style of the Classical era. Partly, they were influenced by the new musical style of Beethoven. But they were also influenced by music that was being composed for the opera, where stories of myth and legend required bold new sounds. And they were influenced, too, by traditional tunes from their native countries (as were, for example, Hungarian Franz Liszt and Polish-born Frederic Chopin). And, like Beethoven, Romantic-era composers felt a need to express their inner feelings.

Many composers of the Romantic era are well-known today — including the aforementioned Schubert, Liszt, and Chopin, as well as Germany's Felix Mendelssohn, Robert Schumann, and Richard Wagner; France's Hector Berlioz; and Russia's Peter Ilich Tchaikovsky. But perhaps the most famous of all is Germany's Johannes Brahms (1833–1897).

Though Brahms used the complex musical vocabulary of the Romantic era, he differed from many of his contemporaries in that he wrote *absolute* music (music that exists for its own sake, as pure music) rather than *program* music (music that's meant to tell a story, evoke a mood, depict a scene, and so on).

Next to Brahms' famous "Lullaby," his rhythmically intense "Hungarian Dance No. 5" (composed in 1868 for piano duet as part of a set of 21 Hungarian dances) is probably his best-known work. Though you may not know it by name, you're sure to recognize it when you hear it, because it's been used in countless movies and cartoons.

Figure 4-7 is an arrangement of an excerpt from "Hungarian Dance No. 5." The colorful *dissonance* (lack of harmony) in measure 3 (a G♯ melody note against a D minor chord) is a Romantic-era harmonic touch; in earlier eras, such a dissonance would have been immediately resolved to a *consonance* (that is, the unharmonious tone would have been moved up or down to a tone that did blend with the background chord).

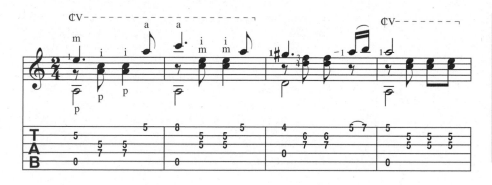

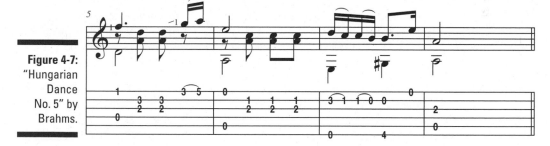

Figure 4-7: "Hungarian Dance No. 5" by Brahms.

Debussy: Music Becomes Modern

Music at the end of the 1800s was very different from, and more complex than, music at the beginning of the century — harmonically, rhythmically, and texturally. Beginning around 1900, some composers who were influenced by innovative ideas in poetry and painting — specifically, so-called *symbolist* ideas, in which reality is rejected and symbols (indirect suggestions) are used to express ideas — threw out the old rules of music and began expressing themselves using a whole new musical language. At first listeners were shocked by what they heard, but eventually, they began to find some of the work quite expressive and beautiful.

The most famous of the symbolist-influenced composers, Claude Debussy (1862–1918), developed a new musical language at the end of the Romantic era to express his ideas. His style of music, like the style of such painters as Claude Monet and Pierre Auguste Renoir, is known as *impressionism*. Impressionistic works, whether of painting or music, are meant to evoke indistinct sensory impressions rather than convey realism. As Debussy himself explained: "Every sound perceived by the acute ear in the rhythm of the world about us can be represented musically. Some people wish above all to conform to the rules; I wish only to render what I can hear."

Debussy liked to stir his listeners' imaginations by painting a mood or suggesting beautiful images of nature. He did this by employing unusual scales (the whole tone scale, for example, in which all tones are separated by a whole step), unusual chords (extended chords of the 9th, 11th, and 13th, for example), parallel intervals (such as parallel 4ths or 5ths, which earlier composers eschewed), nebulous rhythms (in which it's sometimes not clear what the basic pulse is or how it's subdivided), and ambiguous tonalities (where you can't tell what key, if any, a piece is in).

Although he was a contemporary of other late-Romantic/early-Modern composers such as Ravel (with whom he is often compared), Debussy's music was truly revolutionary in that it sounded nothing like anything heard before. It was his rejection of the traditional approach to harmony, his complete departure from the aesthetic of his forebears, and his forward-looking approach that challenged the very idea of tonality itself that paved the way for 20th-century composers such as Bartók and Stravinsky and the modern era of classical music.

Because of their often complex harmonies, many of Debussy's compositions are difficult to play on guitar; however, a few, notably his most famous work, "Clair de Lune," have found their way into the classical guitar repertoire. Figures 4-8 and 4-9 show short passages from two other Debussy works (originally for piano) that guitarists sometimes play.

In the first passage, from "The Little Shepherd" (a section of 1908's *Children's Corner Suite*), note how dissonant chords exist in their own right, with no need for resolution, and the lack of a tonal center (Figure 4-8).

The second passage is from Debussy's 1910 prelude "The Girl with the Flaxen Hair" (Figure 4-9). Note how in the first two measures he uses the interval of a *tritone* (an interval three whole steps in distance, as C to F♯ or D to G♯) to obscure the key center but how in the last three measures he changes the mood by firmly establishing the key of D (the original piano version is in G♭).

Figure 4-8:
"The Little
Shepherd"
by Debussy.

Figure 4-9:
"The Girl
with the
Flaxen Hair"
by Debussy.

Book VI

Exercises: Practice, Practice, Practice

The 5th Wave   By Rich Tennant

"This next exercise is designed to stretch my fingers and Mona's patience."

In this book . . .

We shut off the klieg lights for a second, sit you
down, and close the door to your room. It's just
you and the instrument and dozens of scales and chords.
Spending quality time firming up your technique is vital to
getting better at guitar. Consider this book a place to
come back to again and again for great ideas on making
your playing faster, nimbler, and more expressive.

Here are the contents of Book VI at a glance.

Chapter 1

Putting the Major Scales to Use in Your Playing

• •

In This Chapter

▶ Playing major scales using five patterns

▶ Performing pieces using the major scales

• •

*P*racticing scales may sound boring, but it's a discipline that guitarists use to perfect their technique, especially their right-hand technique. Think about this: Classical guitar great Andrés Segovia recommended practicing scales two hours a day! We don't ask that much, but for guitarists who use a pick, rather than their fingers and nails, these scales are an excellent medium to work on alternate picking.

Most music is based on scales. So if you learn and memorize where the scale patterns and positions are, your fingers will know what to do when you see a scale in music. Playing whole passages of notes becomes automatic.

So how do you get to such a place? By taking common scale patterns and playing them repeatedly until you know them cold. "Practice makes perfect," the saying goes, and it's true. You not only memorize the notes through repeated playings, but you gradually increase the strength and elasticity of your fingers, which allows you to play more difficult music later on. Sound like exercise? Well, it is, except that it's exercise for your fingers *and* your brain. And just like swimming, running, or biking, you need to do it several times a week to improve. For learning guitar, it's best to practice every day, even if you can manage only a little on some days.

In this chapter, you discover five patterns for playing the major scale. Each pattern has its own particular advantages, which we touch on along the way. At the end of the chapter, you get a bonus: real pieces of music to play that use the patterns.

After you memorize each fingering pattern in this chapter, simply move it up or down the neck to a different starting note to produce other major scales. The familiar *do, re, mi, fa, sol, la, ti, do* sound (think Maria von Trapp and *The Sound of Music* here) stays the same, but as you switch positions, the *key,* or letter name, of the scale changes.

Practicing Five Major Scale Patterns

You can play major scales *in position* (meaning that the left-hand fingers cover four consecutive frets and that the position is named for the fret played by the first finger) by applying five unique fingerings. So, with 12 major scales and five fingering options for each scale, you're looking at 60 major scales in position. All of these options are what make the guitar so incredibly cool. You can play a lot of music by simply memorizing five patterns, and you can play it many different ways — according to the best pattern for the situation or by changing keys easily while maintaining a pattern. These options also show why you need to practice: There's a lot to master!

As you practice, play each major scale from low to high, slowly, loudly, and deliberately at first to help develop the muscles in your hand and fingers — similar to the way athletes might lift weights. Then play it faster and lighter to more closely approach how the music is actually played in performance. Just be sure to maintain your starting tempo and *dynamic level* (loudness) throughout the scale.

Major scale pattern #1

Major scale pattern #1 starts with the second finger on the 6th string (see Figure 1-1).

Notice that the first note of the exercise has a fingering indication in the music staff. What we're talking about is the small *2* to the left of the A notehead. This indicator tells you to use your left-hand second finger to play that note. Keep in mind that the second finger is actually one fret higher than the name of the position (which is always defined as the fret number that the first finger plays). Practice this pattern as many times as you need to in order to feel comfortable playing it.

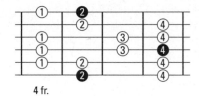

Book VI

Exercises: Practice, Practice, Practice

Track 91, 0:00

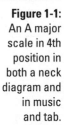

Figure 1-1: An A major scale in 4th position in both a neck diagram and in music and tab.

After you can adeptly finger this pattern in all keys, practice it in rhythm using the exercise shown in Figure 1-2. This exercise is in the key of G major in 2nd position and in ascending and descending eighth notes. Play it in a steady beat (using a metronome or a foot tap) and try to make the music flow. The exercise may be "just a scale," but you can still make it musical by employing accents (striking the string slightly harder on certain notes, usually on the beat), and varying the length of the notes from sustained (called *legato*) to crisp and clipped *(staccato)*.

Track 91, 0:35

Figure 1-2:
Practicing in the key of G major in 2nd position and in ascending and descending eighth notes.

Try major scale pattern #1 in the key of B♭ major in 5th position in ascending and descending eighth-note triplets, as shown in Figure 1-3. In actual music (versus just scales), you encounter many different types of rhythms, not just eighth notes. So playing scales in triplets helps you mix things up a bit, rhythmically speaking. Try to give your triplets a skipping or lilting feel.

Track 91, 0:54

Figure 1-3:
Pattern #1 in the key of B♭ major in 5th position.

Figure 1-4 shows major scale pattern #1 in the key of C major in 7th position in ascending and descending 16th notes. This exercise brings you back to even numbers (from the triplets of the previous exercise), but the notes now come four to the beat instead of two. So play these 16th notes a little faster than you would play eighth notes. This way you get used to playing quickly as well as moderately.

Track 91, 1:11

Figure 1-4:
Pattern #1 in
the key of C
major in 7th
position.

Major scale pattern #2

Book VI

Exercises:
Practice,
Practice,
Practice

Major scale pattern #2 starts with the fourth finger on the 6th string and includes one out-of-position note on the 4th string. An *out-of-position note* is one that doesn't fall within the four-fret span defined by the position and that requires a stretch to play. You must stretch up (higher on the neck, toward the bridge) with your fourth finger to reach this note, because it occurs one fret above where the finger naturally falls.

Wherever these patterns contain out-of-position notes, pay special attention, because these spots are where you might play a wrong note or just have trouble playing the right one correctly. If you can't perform the out-of-position note correctly, try isolating the passage with the problem note and playing it a few times by itself. Then play the whole pattern from start to finish.

Figure 1-5 shows major scale pattern #2 in the key of C major in both a neck diagram and in music and tab format. Note that in addition to the starting finger next to the first note in the music (a *4* to the left of the notehead), another fingering indication is included where an out-of-position note occurs (a *4* next to the 4th-string note B at the 9th fret). Throughout this book, we indicate fingerings for any out-of-position notes. Also, we provide the fingerings for subsequent notes if we think there's a chance you might use the wrong finger. Figure 1-5 is just such a case! Practice this pattern as many times as you need to in order to make all the notes sound smooth and effortless. When you use the correct fingerings automatically, you know you're on the right track.

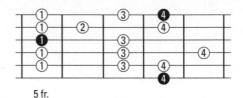

5 fr.

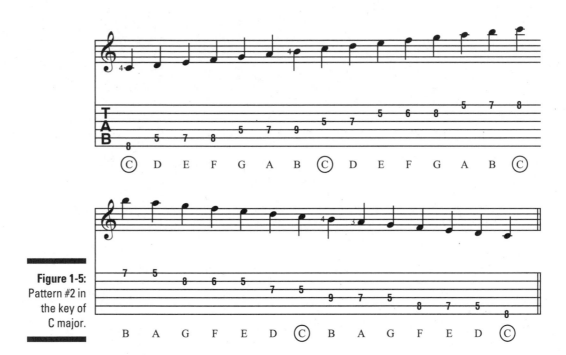

Figure 1-5:
Pattern #2 in
the key of
C major.

After you can successfully finger this pattern in all keys, practice it in rhythm. Figure 1-6 shows major scale pattern #2 in the key of B♭ major in 3rd position in ascending and descending eighth-note triplets. Don't be afraid of the flats in the key signature of this exercise. We know, usually guitar music is written in "guitar-friendly" keys, which contain sharps in the key signature. But because you're learning patterns that can be moved around and played in any key with equal ease, a flat key is no more difficult than a sharp key or a key with no flats or sharps at all!

Figure 1-6:
Pattern #2 in
the key of B♭
major in 3rd
position.

Major scale pattern #3

Patterns #1 and #2 have a range of two octaves, going from bottom to top. Major scale patterns #3, #4, and #5, on the other hand, span a bit less than two octaves. Playing just a single octave may seem a bit short, so in these patterns, as well as other patterns that span less than two complete octaves, we go as high as the position will allow.

Figure 1-7 shows major scale pattern #3, which starts on the 5th string (not the 6th as in patterns #1 and #2). The pattern is in the key of D major and is shown in both a neck diagram and in music and tab format. Notice that in addition to the starting finger next to the first note in the music (a *2* to the left of the notehead), we include the fingering for the out-of-position note (a *1* next to the 1st-string note G at the 3rd fret). In this stretch, unlike the stretch of pattern #2, you reach down (toward the nut) instead of up. This move helps you get used to stretching in both directions. Practice this pattern as many times as you need to in order to feel as confident starting a scale on the 5th string as you do on the 6th string.

Book VI

**Exercises:
Practice,
Practice,
Practice**

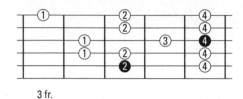

3 fr.

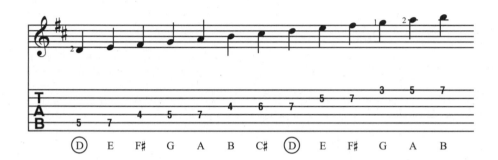

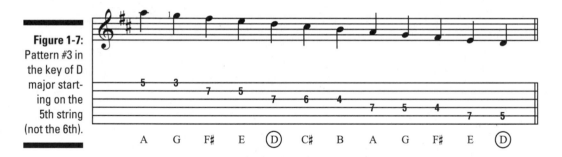

Figure 1-7:
Pattern #3 in
the key of D
major start-
ing on the
5th string
(not the 6th).

After you can confidently play this pattern starting on any 5th-string note,
practice it in rhythm with Figure 1-8 which shows major scale pattern #3 in
the key of F major in 7th position in ascending and descending 16th notes.
Because this exercise is in 16th notes (which are relatively fast compared to
eighth notes or triplets), play it slowly at first to make sure the notes come at
a steady rate. After that you can gradually speed up.

Figure 1-8:
Pattern #3 in
the key of F
major in 7th
position.

Major scale pattern #4

Book VI

**Exercises:
Practice,
Practice,
Practice**

Like pattern #3, major scale pattern #4 also begins and ends on the 5th string. This time, though, your starting finger is the fourth finger. The good news is that this position has no out-of-position notes (hooray!). So if you feel up to it, you can play the exercises using major scale pattern #4 with a little more *brio* (that's music-speak for speed) than the patterns that require stretches.

Figure 1-9 shows major scale pattern #4 in the key of F major in both a neck diagram and in music and tab format. Because this pattern is in the middle of the neck and has no out-of-position notes, you may want to jump right in and play a little faster. Whenever you try an exercise a little faster than you normally would, take a moment to prepare. Then play the entire exercise completely. Don't get into the habit of making "false starts," which is an indication that your fingers are ahead of your brain.

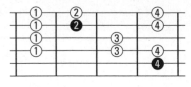

5 fr.

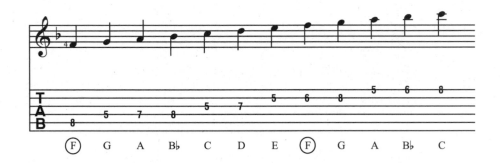

F G A B♭ C D E F G A B♭ C

Figure 1-9:
Pattern #4 in
the key of F
major.

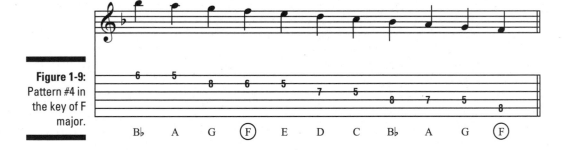

B♭ A G F E D C B♭ A G F

When you're ready, try the exercise shown in Figure 1-10 in rhythm. This figure shows major scale pattern #4 in the key of G major in 7th position. This exercise is an easy one. It's up the neck (where the frets are nicely snuggled together for comfortable playing), it's in eighth notes (which are a little easier to play than triplets or 16th notes), and there are no out-of-position notes to stretch for. So try playing this exercise fast from the get-go. You may surprise yourself by playing a lot faster than you think you can. Just be sure whenever you play fast that you don't rush (or play ahead of the tempo). When something seems easy, it's tempting to keep accelerating until you reach your limit. But you have to stay with the tempo established at the outset.

Figure 1-10: Pattern #4 in the key of G major in 7th position.

Book VI

Exercises: Practice, Practice, Practice

Major scale pattern #5

Major scale pattern #5 is a four-string pattern whose lowest note is on the 4th string. The pattern starts with the first finger on the 4th string and includes an out-of-position note that occurs on the 4th string. You have to stretch your fourth finger higher on the neck (toward the bridge) to reach this note, because it occurs one fret above where the finger naturally falls.

Figure 1-11 shows major scale pattern #5 in the key of G major in both a neck diagram and in music and tab format. The stretch for the out-of-position note comes right away — on the first string you play — so watch out for it. First practice the stretch in isolation and then try the full pattern. Play this pattern as many times as you need to in order to get it sounding as strong as the other four major scale patterns.

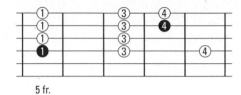

5 fr.

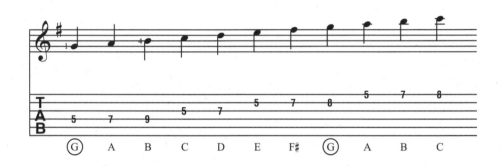

Figure 1-11:
Pattern #5 in
the key of G
major.

Figure 1-12 shows major scale pattern #5 in the key of A♭ major in 6th position in ascending and descending eighth-note triplets. Start with your first finger on the 4th string, 6th fret. Sixth position presents a moderately difficult stretch on the 4th string.

Figure 1-12:
Pattern #5 in
the key of A♭
major in 6th
position.

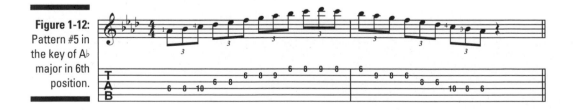

Applying Your Scale Work to Actual Pieces of Music

Okay, so you've practiced, and now you realize that playing scales on a guitar is about as interesting as watching paint dry, right? Well, don't you drop your flatpick and grab knitting needles just yet. You've made it to the fun part where you get to use your scale-playing prowess to play *actual music* — you know, songs! It's our reward to you for all the effort you've put in so far.

After you get the five major scale patterns "under your fingers" (musician lingo for knowing them cold), you can make those patterns work for you. It bears repeating that most music is made up of scales. And although you may not encounter a lot of music that runs a scale from bottom to top and back down again in eighth notes, you will play many pieces that contain passages of scale segments — the same material you practice here. When you run across a passage that's similar to a scale you've practiced, it's like the music almost plays itself. You can go into a kind of automatic pilot and enjoy listening to the music as it goes by.

Book VI

Exercises: Practice, Practice, Practice

As you practice scales more and more, you'll find that playing passages of stepwise notes becomes easier and more natural. Scales are an efficient way to practice the notes contained in a song — even if the melody doesn't lay them out in a strict, regular fashion. In fact, most music isn't laid out in a strict, regular way because it would be boring and sound like, well, scales. So while practicing scales may not prepare you for a particular piece of music, it's the best way to prepare yourself equally well for most music. The following sections include two pieces of music whose melodies are made up of primarily major scale passages.

"The First Noël"

"The First Noël" is a Christmas carol that you probably know, so you can use your familiarity with it to help ensure that you're playing the song correctly — hitting the right pitches in the correct rhythms.

You use two major scale patterns to play "The First Noël": major scale patterns #1 and #4. To begin, put your hand in 2nd position (with your left-hand first finger hovering above the 2nd fret). Then place your left-hand third finger (your ring finger) on the starting note F♯ at the 4th string, 4th fret. Now you're ready to play.

Notice in Figure 1-13 at bar 8 you switch positions, jumping up to 9th position between beats 2 and 3. Try to let that half note ring for as long as possible before making the jump, but don't be late for beat 3! This mid-measure jump allows you to play the chorus of the second phrase an octave higher. The song doesn't really do that, but we thought we'd make it more interesting for you. Plus it gives you a workout in different positions.

After playing eight bars in the upper octave, shift your hand back to 2nd position at bar 16 to finish out the last eight bars. Note that the last bar, like the first pickup bar, is incomplete. It contains two beats, which allows it to even out the one-beat bar that starts the song. You can repeat the song by mentally stitching together the first bar and the last as if the whole song were a repeatable loop.

Figure 1-13: "The First Noël" is a good song to practice scales on.

Bach's "Minuet in G Major"

J. S. Bach, a classical composer who lived and wrote during the Baroque era (1600–1750), originally wrote "Minuet in G Major" as a simple piano piece for student pianists (a group that included his wife). Despite its simplicity, the song's melody has become universal. It even made its way into pop music in the 1965 hit by The Toys, "A Lover's Concerto."

As the title notes, Bach's minuet is in the key G major. The song begins in 9th position, and the starting note is the fourth finger. To begin, place your left-hand first finger hovering above the 9th fret, and then plant your fourth finger on the starting note G on the 4th string, 12th fret.

Book VI

Exercises: Practice, Practice, Practice

Notice at the beginning of Bach's minuet (shown in Figure 1-14), you see a *repeat sign* (the combination of thick and thin vertical lines with two dots) in addition to the usual information. In a piece of music, this sign tells you that you repeat some portion of the song. So look for a corresponding repeat sign that defines the ending and outlines the passage for repeating. In Bach's minuet, the ending sign comes at the end of bar 8. But this repeat uses *first and second endings,* indicated by the lines with "1." and "2." above the music. For music with first and second endings, you play only the first ending the first time through and only the second ending the second time through.

Bach's original work has a section of music that we cut in the interest of brevity. At bar 11, the final section begins, and you switch positions so that you play major scale pattern #1 in 2nd position. The passage leads off with some string skipping, so make sure your right hand plays the correct strings. Notice that between bar 11, beat 3, and bar 12, beat 2, three notes in a row are all played on the same fret with the same finger (the fourth) but on different strings.

You have a choice of how to play these. You can do either of the following to play the 2nd-string note:

- ✔ Use the tip of your fourth finger and "hop" to the different strings
- ✔ Play the first note with the tip, as usual, and then flatten out your finger, forming a *mini-barre* (a partial barre that covers just two or three strings)

Many real-world situations call for the "flattening" approach, but in the case of Bach's minuet, the tempo is slow enough that you can play the notes comfortably by finger hopping if you'd like.

Figure 1-14:
"Minuet in G" begins in 9th position.

Chapter 2

Adding Major Scale Sequences to Your Repertoire

In This Chapter

▶ Playing major scale sequences using five major scale patterns

▶ Applying sequences to actual pieces of music

*I*f you've practiced the five major scale patterns presented in Chapter 1 in Book VI — and drilled them into your consciousness — it's time to have some fun with them, don't you think? Instead of going up and down and up and down (and up and down), in this chapter you get to mix things up by playing sequences. *Sequences* are musical patterns — not finger patterns like the ones you memorized to learn your scales (uh, you *did* memorize these, didn't you?).

Playing sequences not only makes practicing more interesting and less predictable, but it also makes you feel like you're playing real music — that is, pattern-based songs with repeated gestures. Many melodies get their "memorableness" from their sequences, which make them different enough to be interesting, but predictable enough to become recognizable. It's a delicate balance, but all great melodies have some repetition to them in the form of sequences, which you can explore in this chapter.

Just as you did in your scale work in Chapter 1 in Book VI, familiarize yourself with the sequences in this chapter and then move them up and down the neck to produce other major scale sequences in different keys. If you aren't sure how the notes lay out on the fretboard, take a look at the guitar neck diagram on the Cheat Sheet at the front of this book. It shows the letter names of all the frets on all six strings.

Practicing Major Scale Sequences

Unlike scales, which run in the same direction for long stretches, *sequences* change direction often and may at first seem a little trickier than scales. But you can make them more manageable by discovering the *scheme* (or pattern), which reveals itself in the first few notes you play. Learning the pattern can help you better anticipate the direction changes and find the starting note of the new sequence. You may have to start off practicing sequences a little slower than you would scales, but you'll soon find that learning the sequence helps your brain keep up with your fingers, allowing you to play faster.

You should always play the ascending and descending sequences as a pair. In other words, always begin the descending sequence immediately after you finish the ascending one. Doing so will help you maintain a sense of ascending and descending symmetry in your music.

Major scale sequences using pattern #1

Major scale pattern #1 is an ascending two-octave scale that starts on the 6th string and contains no *out-of-position notes* (notes that don't fall within the four-fret span defined by the position and that require stretches by the first or fourth finger to play). Even though you have no stretches to contend with, you still may want to start out slowly as you play this pattern. After all, the notes change direction often and are quite different from the "one-way" motion (all up and then all down) of scale playing.

Figure 2-1 features ascending and descending four-note sequences. In the ascending version, between bars 5 and 6, you must use the same finger (the fourth in this case) to play two notes in a row, across two strings. This may feel awkward at first, so feel free to supply your own alternate fingering in these cases. For example, try flattening out your fourth finger into a *mini-barre* (a partial barre that covers just two or three strings), or try substituting your third finger for the note played on the 3rd string. Just be sure to get back into position as soon as you can after employing an alternate fingering. And remember the old saying, "You can break the rules as long as you know the rules first."

Track 92, 0:00

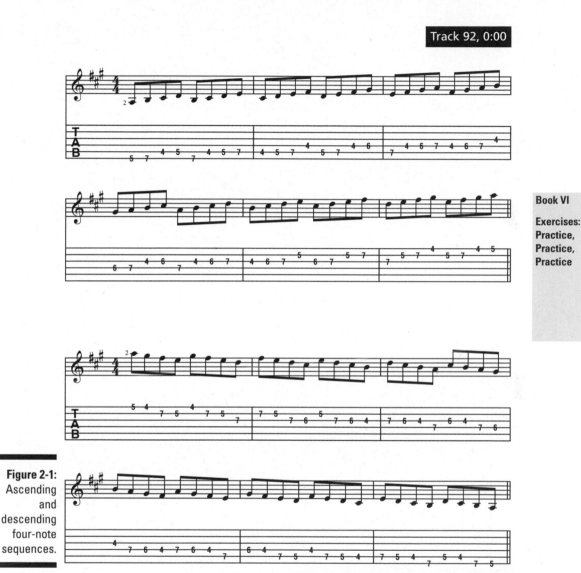

Book VI

Exercises: Practice, Practice, Practice

Figure 2-1: Ascending and descending four-note sequences.

Figure 2-2 shows ascending and descending sequences in the key of G in 2nd position. This exercise includes a wide skip after every sixth note, sometimes requiring you to jump over a string in the process. Practice these wide skips across two strings so you can play them with the same smoothness as you play a step on the same string. One trick that helps ensure smooth skip execution is to look ahead in the music slightly to help you anticipate the next interval.

Track 92, 0:53

Figure 2-2:
Ascending
and
descending
sequences
in the key
of G in 2nd
position.

Major scale sequences using pattern #2

Major scale pattern #2 starts with the fourth finger on the 6th string and
includes an out-of-position note on the 4th string. Stretch your fourth finger up
(toward the bridge) to play this note, because it occurs one fret above (higher

on the neck) the note the fourth finger would normally play. Be sure to play stretch notes with the same smoothness as you play the in-position notes.

Figure 2-3 shows ascending and descending sequences in the key of C in 5th position. The sequences are three notes in one direction followed by a change in the opposite direction of one step. These frequent changes of direction require you to glue your eyeballs to the page to make sure you handle the twists and turns of the melodic line.

Book VI

**Exercises:
Practice,
Practice,
Practice**

Figure 2-3:
Ascending
and
descending
sequences
in the key
of C in 5th
position.

Note that in bar 2 of this figure we indicate the fingering for notes 3, 4, and 5 as *4, 3, 4* — as dictated by major scale pattern #2. In reality, however, most guitarists would play this passage with fingers 4, 2, 4. That fingering is a little easier on your hand with regard to stretching, but you have to be careful not to get out of position. When you find other opportunities in this book for alternate fingerings, you're welcome to use them. Just be sure you can get back on track for the rest of the sequence using the correct fingers according to the scale pattern.

Figure 2-4 shows ascending and descending sequences in the key of B♭ in 3rd position. These sequences contain no skips and are in 16th notes, so try playing them at a fairly brisk clip. Just because you're *practicing* these sequences doesn't mean you shouldn't be playing fast — even if the music is still new or unfamiliar to you. Real music is often played fast, so at times you should practice fast, too.

Figure 2-4:
Ascending and descending sequences in the key of B♭ in 3rd position.

Major scale sequences using pattern #3

Major scale pattern #3 starts with the second finger on the 5th string and includes an out-of-position note, which occurs on the 1st string. Play this note by stretching down (toward the nut) with your first finger.

Practice the following ascending and descending sequences, which are in the key of D in 4th position. The exercise in Figure 2-5 starts with a skip right out of the gate — so watch out. Isolate the skip, if necessary. Beyond that, these exercises have a healthy amount of skip activity in and around the stepwise motion. It may help to memorize this pattern quickly. Then you can focus on the fretboard, which can help you play the mixture of skips and steps more accurately.

Figure 2-5:
Ascending
and
descending
sequences
in the key
of D in 4th
position.

Figure 2-6 shows ascending and descending sequences in the key of F in 7th position. There's only one skip in this sequence, which occurs immediately at the beginning. So work on speed and smoothness by playing at brighter tempos. In the ascending version in bar 2, consider an alternate fingering, such as flattening out your fourth finger to play both notes 13 and 14 at the 10th fret. In the descending version, try the same approach at bar 1 between notes 13 and 14.

Figure 2-6:
Ascending
and
descending
sequences
in the key
of F in 7th
position.

Major scale sequences using pattern #4

Major scale pattern #4 starts with the fourth finger on the 5th string and contains no out-of-position notes. So feel free to play these exercises with a swift and light feel, if you like.

In Figure 2-7 you see ascending and descending sequences in the key of F in 5th position. Because of the way the guitar's strings are tuned (in 4ths, mostly), this sequence has many same-fret hops between strings (first seen in the ascending version between notes 4 and 5). So you have plenty of opportunities to swap out mini-barres for these cases. You have permission to use them at will.

Figure 2-7: Ascending and descending sequences in the key of F in 5th position.

Figure 2-8 shows ascending and descending sequences in the key of G in 7th position. Only the last note of each sequence is approached by a skip (and a small one at that, a 3rd). So try playing these up to (or nearly up to) tempo right from the get-go. Playing new music fast and accurately is a skill you can develop, and this is a good sequence to try that approach on.

Book VI

**Exercises:
Practice,
Practice,
Practice**

Figure 2-8:
Ascending
and
descending
sequences
in the key
of G in 7th
position.

Major scale sequences using pattern #5

Major scale pattern #5 starts on the 4th string and includes an out-of-position note on the 4th string. Remember, this stretch comes right away — on the first string you play, and you have to reach up (toward the bridge) with your fourth finger to play the out-of-position note.

Figure 2-9 includes ascending and descending sequences in the key of G in 5th position. These sequences are fairly easy sequences to play for three reasons:

✔ The same-direction nature of the melody

✔ The absence of skips

✔ As luck would have it, the lack of any same-fret string-hopping situations

Put your metronome on *presto* — if you dare.

Figure 2-9:
Ascending and descending sequences in the key of G in 5th position.

Figure 2-10 shows ascending and descending sequences in the key of B♭ in 8th position. This sequence has just one skip, but it occurs immediately — between the first and second notes. You can breathe easy after that, however, because the remaining notes are stepwise, including the note that connects one sequence to the next.

Figure 2-10:
Ascending and descending sequences in the key of B♭ in 8th position.

Putting Your Sequence Skills to Work with a Few Songs

The two pieces in the following sections feature melodies that are based on sequences. In these songs, you'll also see scalar passages. After all, most music that contains sequences also includes scale-like material. But don't think of these songs as exercises or sequences. They're songs! Sure you're supposed to practice them, but the idea is to have fun while doing it. Simply recognizing that these songs are made up of sequences will increase your appreciation of them, deepen your understanding of their structure, and make them easier to play.

"Oh, Them Golden Slippers"

When you look at the beginning of "Oh, Them Golden Slippers," notice the elements that give you clues to the song's character: tempo marking, time signature, key signature, and dynamics. (Refer to Chapter 4 in Book I if any of these elements are unclear to you.)

"Oh, Them Golden Slippers" has two parts, and you may recognize the first part as the melody to the children's song "Polly Wolly Doodle All the Day." Yes, this children's song actually derives its melody from the early American folk song about valuable footwear.

"Oh, Them Golden Slippers" is played in A major, starting with major scale pattern #2 in 2nd position. (If you need a refresher on any of this information, refer to Chapter 1 in Book VI.) This song (shown in Figure 2-11) uses two scale patterns, one for each section. Use major scale pattern #2 for the first section, and remember that it has one out-of-position note occurring on the 4th string. Use pattern #1 (and enjoy the fact that it contains no out-of-position notes) for the second section, which begins after the second ending. Also, note that because "Oh, Them Golden Slippers" is played down the neck (in the lower frets), the frets are wider, making stretches a little more difficult.

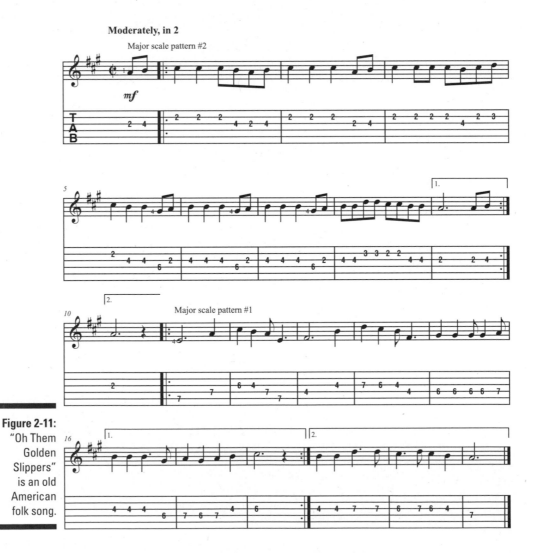

Figure 2-11: "Oh Them Golden Slippers" is an old American folk song.

A difficult stretch occurs in bar 5, beat 4, where you have to reach out of position to play the 4th string, 6th fret (G♯). Just make sure you can get back into position for the next note — the 3rd string, 2nd fret (A) — which is the last note of the bar.

At the second ending of the first section, the music has a quarter rest at the end of the bar. You can use this rest as a way of silently switching positions for the next section, which is played using major scale pattern #1 in 4th position.

"We Wish You a Merry Christmas"

Book VI

Exercises: Practice, Practice, Practice

We didn't choose "We Wish You a Merry Christmas" because we're in a holiday mood, but rather because it's such a great example of a sequential melody. The sequences present themselves in neat little two-bar phrases right from the beginning.

"We Wish You a Merry Christmas" (shown in Figure 2-12) is played in the key of F, using major scale pattern #5 in 3rd position. From bars 3 to 4 and in bar 8, there's some first finger string hopping, but the real challenge occurs at bars 5 and 6, where the third finger really has to leap around.

At the position change in bar 9 (to major scale pattern #4 in 5th position), you may notice that you don't actually have to release your fourth finger to play the first note dictated by the new position's fingering (the C at the 3rd string, 5th fret). So you can actually change positions after the text in the score tells you to. Little tricks like these help guitarists to play more *legato* (smoothly) where the notes connect or blend into one another slightly (versus *staccato,* where the notes sound separated and slightly choppy). These tricks also help musicians find economy in their hand movements that may not always be written into the music.

Brightly

Figure 2-12:
"We Wish
You a Merry
Christmas"
is a good
song for
practicing
sequences.

Chapter 3

Tackling the Three Minor Scales

In This Chapter

▶ Practicing natural, melodic, and harmonic minor scales using five patterns

▶ Performing pieces using the three minor scales

*E*ven though major scales rule the cosmos (see Chapters 1 and 2 in Book VI), life would be pretty dull without their darker counterparts: minor scales. Minor scales and minor keys are sometimes described as "sad," "foreboding," "mysterious," "haunting," and even "creepy." But minor scales can also be quite beautiful, and most music — even if it's in a major key — uses some minor material to convey a richer message.

As a guitar student studying and perfecting scales, you have three different versions of minor scales that you must tackle. With the major scale, you have only one. The three minor scale flavors are called *natural, melodic,* and *harmonic.* They all have the characteristic "mournful" quality, which is characterized by the flatted 3rd degree (meaning, the third note of the scale is a half-step lower than in the major scale). However, some of their other notes are altered (namely, the 6th and 7th degrees of the scale), depending on the musical context. The three pieces at the end of this chapter each explore a different minor scale. For now, though, don't worry about altered degrees and such; just focus on getting the notes under your fingers. This chapter helps you do exactly that.

If you're looking for even more practice, remember that after you memorize each scale's fingering pattern you can simply move it up or down the neck to different starting notes to produce and practice other minor scales. That way, you can hear how the minor scale sounds in all 12 keys using just one pattern — instead of learning 11 new ones.

Familiarizing Yourself with Natural Minor Scales

Even though a minor scale produces a decidedly different musical mood than a major scale, you treat it the same way when you sit down to practice. It's not like you have to be nicer to a minor scale because it seems so gloomy. Approach minor scales with the same vigor and positive attitude as major scales; they can take it.

As far as placing your fingers on the frets and playing your right hand in rhythm, minor scales are no different from major scales. The only wrinkle is that there are three types of minor scales (compared to just one major scale), so you have more information to keep track of. And that means you may have to spend a little more time memorizing them.

Compared to the major scale — the familiar *do, re, mi, fa, sol, la, ti, do,* or playing from C to C using all white notes on the piano — the natural minor scale has three notes that are different: the 3rd, the 6th, and the 7th degrees. These notes are *flatted,* or lowered a half-step. So a C natural minor scale would be C, D, E♭, F, G, A♭, B♭, C.

Play each of the following natural minor scale patterns slowly, loudly, and deliberately at first to build strength and confidence in your fingers. Then try playing it faster and lighter to better simulate how you'll play minor scales in actual pieces of music. Just be sure to maintain your starting tempo and dynamic level (loudness) throughout each scale.

Natural minor scale pattern #1

Natural minor scale pattern #1 starts with the first finger on the 6th string. As you play this scale pattern, watch for the out-of-position note that occurs on the 4th string. (An *out-of-position note* is a note that doesn't fall within the four-fret span defined by the position and that requires a stretch by the first or fourth finger to play it.) You must stretch up (toward the bridge) with your fourth finger to reach this note, because it occurs one fret above (higher on the neck) where the finger naturally falls.

Figure 3-1 shows an A natural minor scale in 5th position in both a neck diagram and in music and tab format. Take a look at the standard notation for a
moment to see that we indicate both the starting finger (a *1* at the first note
for the first finger) and the fingering for the out-of-position note (a *4* next
to the B on the 4th string, 7th fret). Use the figure to memorize this scale's
fingering pattern, and then practice it until you feel comfortable playing it.
Practice this pattern several times slowly to make sure you can hear the
notes that produce the minor quality as well as to get your fingers comfortable with playing a new scale.

Book VI

**Exercises:
Practice,
Practice,
Practice**

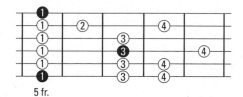

5 fr.

Track 93

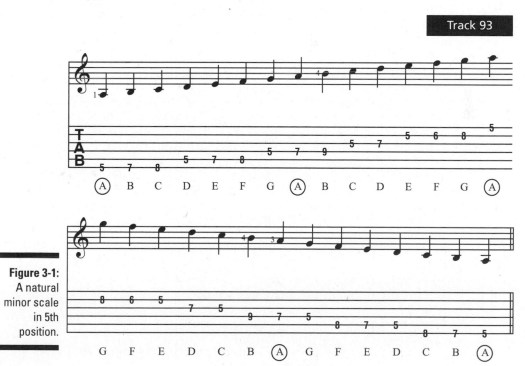

Figure 3-1:
A natural
minor scale
in 5th
position.

Now try your hand at the exercise in rhythm shown in Figure 3-2, which is in the key of B minor in 7th position.

Figure 3-2:
A rhythm exercise in the key of B minor in 7th position.

Be sure not to unduly emphasize the out-of-position note (4th string, 11th fret). Some guitar players fall into the bad habit of musically stressing the difficult parts, such as stretches and position shifts. The out-of-position note here is like any other note in the scale and should blend in. The listener shouldn't be aware that the guitarist is doing something difficult.

Natural minor scale pattern #2

Natural minor scale pattern #2 starts with the fourth finger on the 6th string and includes an out-of-position note on the 1st string. Because this note occurs one fret below (lower on the neck) where the finger naturally falls, you must stretch down (toward the nut) with your first finger to reach it.

In Figure 3-3 you find the neck diagram and corresponding music and tab for natural minor scale pattern #2 in the key of C minor. Notice that in the standard notation we include both the starting finger (fourth finger) and the fingering where the out-of-position note occurs (a *1* next to the A♭ on the 1st string, 4th fret). Practice this pattern so you can play the out-of-position note as smoothly as you play the other notes of the scale.

When you're ready, try playing this pattern in rhythm. The exercise in Figure 3-4 is in the key of A minor in 2nd position. Notice that the out-of-position note occurs on the F on the 1st string, 1st fret. Because this stretch occurs low on the neck, where the frets are wider, you really have to have your left hand warmed up. Try isolating the passage that occurs between bar 1, beat 4, and bar 2, beat 2, and play it eight times, or until you get used to the stretch.

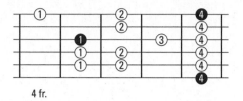

4 fr.

C D E♭ F G A♭ B♭ C D E♭ F G A♭ B♭ C

Book VI

Exercises: Practice, Practice, Practice

Figure 3-3:
Minor scale pattern #2 in the key of C minor.

B♭ A♭ G F E♭ D C B♭ A♭ G F E♭ D C

Figure 3-4:
A rhythm exercise in the key of A minor in 2nd position.

Natural minor scale pattern #3

Natural minor scale pattern #3 starts with the first finger on the 5th string (not the 6th, as in the previous two patterns) and includes no out-of-position notes. Sometimes it takes a little more "aim" to place a finger on the 5th string because it's an inside string (that is, not on the edge of the neck like the 6th string, which is easier to find by feeling your way around). So just before you're ready to put your finger down, make sure you're eyeballing that 5th string.

In Figure 3-5, you see the neck diagram and corresponding music and tab for natural minor scale pattern #3 in the key of D minor. Because this pattern includes no out-of-position notes — which can slow you down because they take extra effort — you can try taking this pattern a little faster than you normally would. Be careful not to rush it and make mistakes, though. Practice this pattern until you feel you know it well enough to play it in a steady tempo with no mistakes.

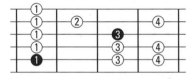

5 fr.

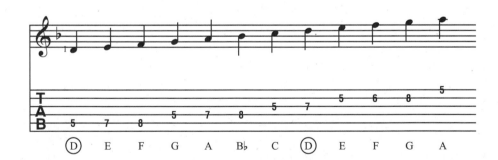

Figure 3-5:
Minor scale pattern #3 in the key of D minor.

Now try the rhythm exercise in Figure 3-6, in the key of E minor in 7th position. Be sure to play the 16th notes evenly and smoothly at first. Then, if you like, try *accenting* (striking slightly harder) the first note of each beat group. Applying accents helps to delineate the beat, which adds drive to your music.

Figure 3-6:
A rhythm exercise in the key of E minor in 7th position.

Book VI

Exercises: Practice, Practice, Practice

Natural minor scale pattern #4

Natural minor scale pattern #4 starts on the 5th string with the fourth finger and includes an out-of-position note on the 1st string. In Figure 3-7, you can see the neck diagram and corresponding music and tab for natural minor scale pattern #4 in the key of F minor. Notice that in the standard notation, in addition to the starting finger (fourth finger), we put in the fingering where the out-of-position note occurs (a *1* next to the A♭ on the 1st string, 4th fret).

You may find it difficult at first to lead off a scale with the fourth finger, because it's traditionally a weaker and "less confident" finger than the first or second finger (the fingers that begin natural minor scale patterns #1 and #3). So practice the beginning of this pattern (just the first three or four notes) a few times to make sure you kick it off steadily and confidently before playing the rest of the pattern.

When you're ready to try this pattern in rhythm, check out Figure 3-8, which is in the key of D minor in 2nd position. In this rhythm exercise, notice that an out-of-position note occurs on the F on the 1st string, 1st fret.

A stretch to the 1st fret is a wide one, so try measuring it first by placing your fourth finger on the 2nd string, 5th fret. While still holding your fourth finger down, reach up and place your first finger on the 1st string, 1st fret, and hold that down, too. That's the span your hand will have to make when you encounter the reach in bar 2. This measuring routine should help you remember how far to stretch when the time comes, and it's a little quicker than isolating the passage containing the stretch.

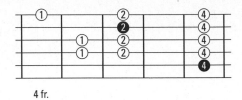

4 fr.

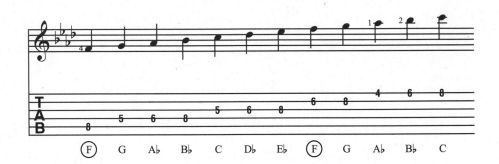

Ⓕ G A♭ B♭ C D♭ E♭ Ⓕ G A♭ B♭ C

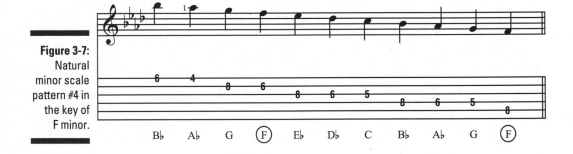

Figure 3-7:
Natural
minor scale
pattern #4 in
the key of
F minor.

B♭ A♭ G Ⓕ E♭ D♭ C B♭ A♭ G Ⓕ

Figure 3-8:
A rhythm
pattern in
the key of D
minor in 2nd
position.

Natural minor scale pattern #5

Natural minor scale pattern #5 starts with your first finger on the 4th string and includes no out-of-position notes. Figure 3-9 shows a neck diagram and corresponding music and tab for natural minor scale pattern #5 in the key of G minor. Because this pattern begins on an inside string (away from the easily accessible edges of the guitar), you may want to practice placing your first finger quickly on the starting note. The good news is that you're back to beginning a scale with a strong finger — the first. Practice grabbing the starting note at different points on the neck, naming each starting note as you do, and then play through the pattern at least four times to memorize the fingering.

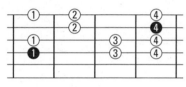

5 fr.

Figure 3-9: Natural minor scale pattern #5 in the key of G minor.

Figure 3-10 provides a rhythm exercise in the key of A minor in 7th position. To help emphasize the sound of a triplet, play the first note in each group of three with a slight accent — that is, strike it a little harder than you do the surrounding notes.

Figure 3-10:
A rhythm
exercise in
the key of A
minor in 7th
position.

Raising the Bar with Melodic Minor Scales

Compared to the major scale (for example, C, D, E, F, G, A, B, C in the key of C), the ascending melodic minor scale has only one note that's different: the 3rd, which is flatted. So an ascending C melodic minor scale would be C, D, E♭, F, G, A, B, C. The descending melodic minor is the same as the natural minor scale, and so it has three notes that are different: the 3rd, 6th, and 7th degrees. These are flatted, so a descending C melodic minor scale would be C, B♭, A♭, G, F, E♭, D, C.

The raising of the notes on only the ascending version is said to make the scale more elegant. Much Baroque and Classical music — undoubtedly elegant — often includes melodic minor scales.

Because the 6th and 7th notes are sometimes raised and sometimes not, the melodic minor scale can be somewhat tricky to memorize. But that difficulty is also what makes it interesting. After all, you simply have more notes available than with the other major and minor scales. Practice the melodic minor scale as you would the natural minor scale, but do be aware of the two scale degrees that are different (the 6th and 7th) on the ascending version. Don't make these notes obvious by hitting them harder, either. Give the raised and unraised notes equal emphasis.

Melodic minor scale pattern #1

Melodic minor scale pattern #1 begins on the 6th string with the first finger. Figure 3-11 shows the neck diagram and corresponding music and tab for the pattern. Because the melodic minor scale has two forms — one for ascending and one for descending — we include two neck diagrams side by side.

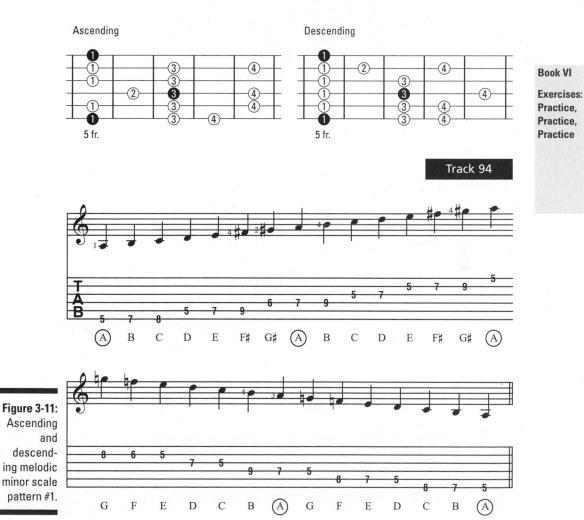

Book VI

Exercises:
Practice,
Practice,
Practice

Track 94

Figure 3-11:
Ascending
and
descend-
ing melodic
minor scale
pattern #1.

The ascending form of the melodic minor scale pattern #1 includes out-of-position notes on the 5th, 4th, and 2nd strings. The descending form includes just one out-of-position note, on the 4th string. We indicate the fingerings for these notes in the standard notation. Between the ascending and descending versions you have a fair amount of stretching to do here, so make sure you're limbered up before trying this one.

Because only the top part of the scale (between the 6th and octave notes) presents the raised and unraised notes, you need to isolate the passage from the high E (2nd string, 5th fret) to the high A (1st string, 5th fret), ascending and descending. Play the passage eight times in a row at a slow tempo before trying the exercise from the beginning. As you memorize the scale, make sure your fingers don't get confused as to which notes they're supposed to play on the ascent versus the descent. Practice this pattern both up and down so you memorize the difference between the two versions of the scale.

Figure 3-12 shows an exercise in rhythm in the key of G minor in 3rd position. Play the eighth notes with a light and quick feel, just as you would with the natural minor scale, and work so you can negotiate the altered notes here with equal ease.

Figure 3-12:
A rhythm exercise in the key of G minor in 3rd position.

The melodic minor scale is different on the way down. So if you've become used to coasting on the descending versions of other scales, you'll have to pay more attention here!

Melodic minor scale pattern #2

Melodic minor scale pattern #2 starts with the fourth finger on the 6th string and includes two out-of-position notes. One of these notes occurs when ascending (on the 4th string) and one occurs when descending (on the 1st string).

Figure 3-13 shows the neck diagrams in ascending and descending forms along with the corresponding music and tab for melodic minor scale pattern #2 in the key of C minor. Notice that in the standard notation, in addition to the starting finger (fourth finger), we put in the fingerings where the out-of-position notes occur. So not only is the scale different depending on the direction you're going, but the out-of-position notes change as well. Melodic minor scales are really two scales under one name. That means two times the effort to learn, but two times the possibilities for musical variety! Practice this pattern along with natural minor scale pattern #1, if you want; they're identical in their descending versions.

Book VI

Exercises: Practice, Practice, Practice

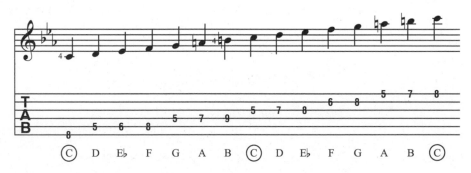

(continue)

(continue)

Figure 3-13:
Melodic minor scale pattern #2 in the key of C minor.

After you have the pattern down pat, use the rhythm exercise shown in Figure 3-14 as practice. This exercise is in the key of B minor in 4th position.

Figure 3-14:
A rhythm exercise in the key of B minor in 4th position.

Melodic minor scales require you to think, stretch, and keep track of where the different out-of-position notes fall. Are you staying relaxed through this process? Don't tense up, even if you have to stretch your fingers and think fast to ensure correctly played notes. And whatever you do, keep breathing!

Melodic minor scale pattern #3

Melodic minor scale pattern #3 starts with the first finger on the 5th string. The ascending form contains an out-of-position note on the 4th string. You must stretch up (toward the bridge) with the fourth finger to play this note. The descending form, which is the same as natural minor scale pattern #3, contains no out-of-position notes.

In Figure 3-15 you find the neck diagrams as well as the corresponding music and tab for this scale pattern in the key of D minor in both ascending and descending forms. Note the unusual stretch here: You play the out-of-position note with the fourth finger, but the next note is played with the second finger (not the first, as you may expect). Stretching between the fourth and second fingers is a little more difficult than between the fourth and first fingers, so practice the move from the 4th to the 3rd string two or three times before playing the entire pattern.

Ready to put this pattern into play? If so, check out the exercise in Figure 3-16, which is in the key of F♯ minor in 9th position. Playing this scale higher up the neck ensures that the stretch you encounter from playing the out-of-position notes is made a little easier because the frets are closer together. So if you have any say in the matter, always opt to head north to play this scale. Your fingers will thank you for it.

Book VI

**Exercises:
Practice,
Practice,
Practice**

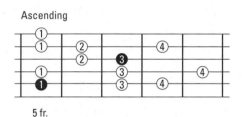

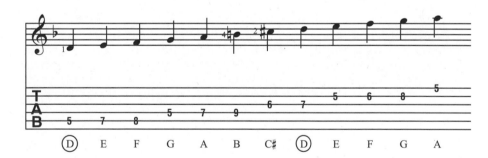

Figure 3-15: Ascending and descending scale pattern #3 in the key of D minor.

Figure 3-16:
A rhythm
exercise in
the key of F♯
minor in 9th
position.

Melodic minor scale pattern #4

Melodic minor scale pattern #4 starts with the fourth finger on the 5th string and includes an out-of-position note on the 1st string in both the ascending and descending forms.

To see the neck diagrams and corresponding music and tab (in ascending and descending forms) for melodic minor scale pattern #4 in the key of F minor, check out Figure 3-17. Because the stretch occurs in the same place in both the ascending and descending versions, do a quick hand-span measurement (which is discussed in the earlier "Natural minor scale pattern #4" section) between the 2nd and 1st strings at the 8th and 4th frets, respectively. Then you can jump into the pattern. Watch out for the notes on the 3rd and 2nd strings, though. They're different, depending on which direction you're traveling. Practice this pattern a few times, or until you can play the ascending version as easily as the descending version (which is the same as natural minor scale pattern #4, a scale we discuss earlier in this chapter).

Now take a look at Figure 3-18, which provides a rhythm exercise in the key of E minor in 4th position. Notice that an out-of-position note occurs on the G on the 1st string, 3rd fret. As melodic minor scales go, this pattern is relatively accessible because its stretch occurs in only one spot (on the 1st string). Practice the stretch first to get your fingers limbered up, and then focus on the differences between the ascending and descending version, which requires a limber brain.

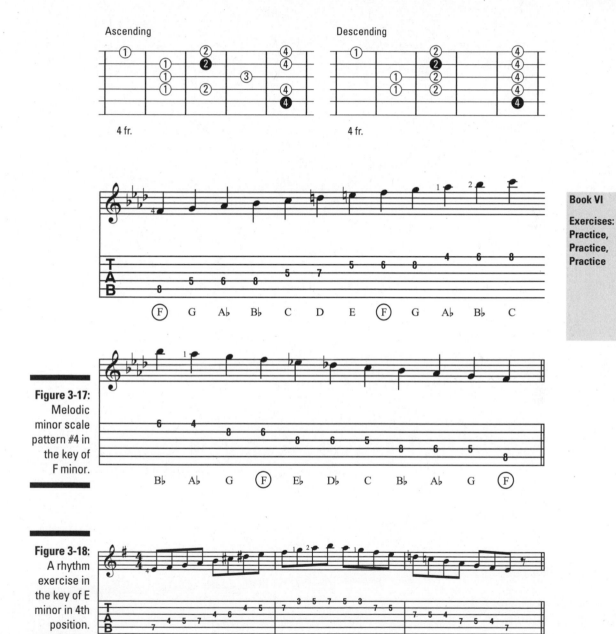

Ascending

Descending

4 fr.

4 fr.

F G Ab Bb C D E F G Ab Bb C

Figure 3-17:
Melodic
minor scale
pattern #4 in
the key of
F minor.

Bb Ab G F Eb Db C Bb Ab G F

Figure 3-18:
A rhythm
exercise in
the key of E
minor in 4th
position.

Book VI

**Exercises:
Practice,
Practice,
Practice**

Melodic minor scale pattern #5

Melodic minor scale pattern #5 begins with the first finger on the 4th string and includes no out-of-position notes in either the ascending or descending versions. In Figure 3-19, you can see the neck diagram and corresponding music and tab in ascending and descending form for melodic minor scale pattern #5 in the key of G minor. Use the figure to memorize this scale's fingering pattern, and practice it several times to ensure that the notes are equally smooth and even in either direction.

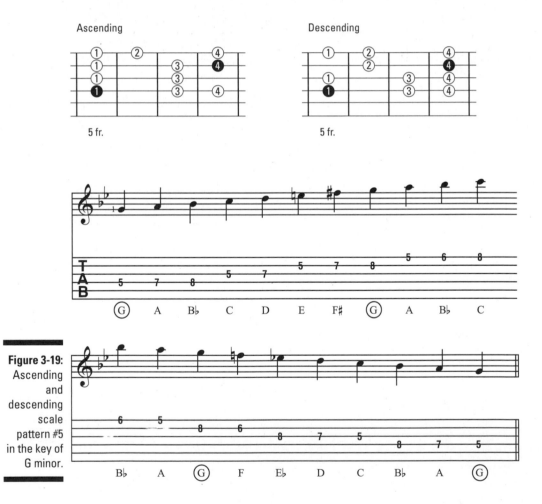

Figure 3-19: Ascending and descending scale pattern #5 in the key of G minor.

When you have pattern #5 memorized, use Figure 3-20 to practice it in rhythm. This exercise is in the key of B♭ minor in 8th position.

Figure 3-20: Rhythm exercise in the key of B♭ minor in 8th position.

B♭ minor is an unusual key for the guitar, because it contains five flats. Guitarists generally find themselves in sharp keys (such as G, D, A, and E), which are considered more favorable to the instrument. (This relates to the open strings of the guitar being the *tonics,* or starting notes, of sharp keys.) And when guitar players do have to play in flat keys, they're more comfortable with keys that have only a few flats (such as F, B♭, and E♭, which have one, two, and three flats, respectively). But one of the advantages of movable scale patterns is that they let you explore uncharted territory (including keys with lots of flats) without having to learn any new patterns.

Note: The ascending version of the melodic minor is sometimes used in both directions, especially in jazz, but examples can be found in Bach as well.

Harmonizing with Harmonic Minor Scales

Compared to the major scale, the harmonic minor scale has two notes that are different: the 3rd and the 6th degrees. These are flatted, so a C harmonic minor scale would be C, D, E♭, F, G, A♭, B, C.

Consider the harmonic minor scale alongside its other minor scale brethren. The harmonic minor is different from the natural minor in that the 7th degree is raised a half-step. This is true whether the scale is ascending or descending. This raising of the 7th degree gives the scale's melody a strong pull from the 7th degree to the top of the scale. It also allows for the formation of a dominant 7th chord in the harmony (for example, an E7 chord in the key of A minor). For these reasons, the scale is called the "harmonic" minor. After all, it allows more desirable chords to be formed from it.

Raising the 7th degree produces a colorful "skip" in the melody between the unraised 6th and the raised 7th. Some people think this skip isn't very scale-like, but the harmonic minor has a tart flavor and sounds Middle Eastern (think snake-charmer music). The harmonic minor scale is the same ascending and descending, so it should be a little easier to memorize. Practice all five patterns of the harmonic minor scale until you can play them as smoothly — skip and all — as you do the natural and melodic minor scales.

Harmonic minor scale pattern #1

Harmonic minor scale pattern #1 is an A harmonic minor scale in 5th position, starting with the first finger on the 6th string.

Figure 3-21 shows the neck diagram as well as the corresponding music and tab. This pattern has out-of-position notes on the 4th and 2nd strings. We include fingerings for these notes in the standard notation. The stretch that occurs on the 2nd string, between the second and fourth fingers, is unusual, so practice playing just the 2nd string notes two or three times before playing the rest of the pattern. Keep in mind that you have another stretch to contend with, too — on the 4th string between the third and fourth fingers. But this is the kind of stretch you're used to, so it shouldn't present an additional problem, as long as you're prepared for it.

Try the rhythm exercise in Figure 3-22, which is in the key of C minor and in 8th position. Before you begin playing, notice where the out-of-position notes fall, and be sure to observe the fingering indications.

As an option, you can play fingers 1, 2, and 4 on the 4th string (instead of fingers 2, 3, 4). This eliminates the stretch that occurs between the third and fourth finger, which some people find uncomfortable.

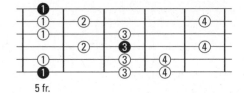

5 fr.

Track 95

A B C D E F G# A B C D E F G# A

Book VI

**Exercises:
Practice,
Practice,
Practice**

Figure 3-21:
The A harmonic minor scale in 5th position.

G# F E D C B A G# F E D C B A

Figure 3-22:
A rhythm exercise in the key of C minor in 8th position.

Harmonic minor scale pattern #2

Harmonic minor scale pattern #2 starts with the fourth finger on the 6th string, and it includes out-of-position notes on the 4th and 1st strings. You stretch up (toward the bridge) with the fourth finger to reach the out-of-position note on the 4th string, and you stretch down (toward the nut) with the first finger to reach the out-of-position note on the 1st string.

Figure 3-23 shows the neck diagram and corresponding music and tab for harmonic minor scale pattern #2 in the key of C minor. In the standard notation, in addition to the starting finger (fourth finger), we put in the fingerings where the out-of-position notes occur. Use these figures to familiarize yourself with the fingering pattern, and then play it until you know it cold.

To practice this pattern in rhythm, check out Figure 3-24, which is in the key of D minor in 7th position. Accent the first note of each triplet to help keep your place in the measure.

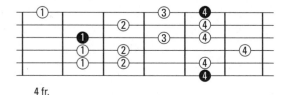

Figure 3-23:
Harmonic
minor scale
pattern #2 in
the key of C
minor.

Figure 3-24:
A rhythm
exercise in
the key of D
minor in 7th
position.

Harmonic minor scale pattern #3

Harmonic minor scale pattern #3 starts with the first finger on the 5th string
and includes no out-of-position notes. Lucky you!

Take a look at Figure 3-25, which shows the neck diagram and corresponding
music and tab for harmonic minor scale pattern #3 in the key of D minor. Be
careful that you don't overemphasize the note that's played with the second
finger on the 3rd string (the raised 7th). In trying to memorize the sound and
fingering of the three different minor scales, it's pretty obvious that the 7th
note of the scale is the one that adds the "flavor." But you should work to
make the attack as even as the rest of the notes of the scale. To ensure that
you aren't applying undue emphasis to any particular note, practice this
pattern in its entirety every time you play it (without isolating specific passages), and work to make each note equal in volume.

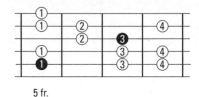

5 fr.

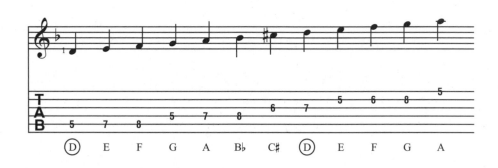

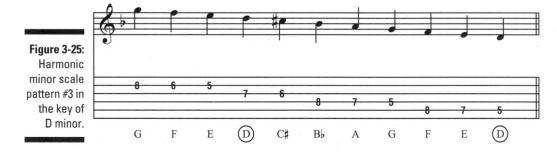

Figure 3-25:
Harmonic
minor scale
pattern #3 in
the key of
D minor.

When you have pattern #3 under your belt, practice it in rhythm. To do so, consult Figure 3-26, which is in the key of B minor in 2nd position. Playing a pattern that has no stretches and is the same ascending as descending sounds like an opportunity to give it the gas. Practice this exercise at a bright tempo, but be careful that you don't flub the notes because your fingers are going too fast for your brain. Just because you find a scale to be technically easy doesn't mean you won't make a mistake due to a lapse in concentration.

Figure 3-26:
A rhythm
exercise in
the key of B
minor in 2nd
position.

Harmonic minor scale pattern #4

Harmonic minor scale pattern #4 starts with the fourth finger on the 5th string and includes an out-of-position note on the 1st string. You must stretch down (toward the nut) with the first finger to play it.

Figure 3-27 shows the neck diagram and corresponding music and tab for harmonic minor scale pattern #4 in the key of F minor. The first-finger note on the 1st string creates a two-fret stretch between the first and second fingers. Be aware of this unusual stretch as you approach the 1st string. To limber up for the out-of-position note before you encounter it in rhythm, try practicing this pattern descending (from the top note down) first. After you do that a couple of times, practice the scale in the normal ascending approach four times, or however many times you need to memorize the fingering and feel comfortable playing the notes.

When you're ready for some practice, try your hand at the exercise in Figure 3-28, which is in the key of G minor in 7th position. When playing eighth notes in 4/4 time, the most important beat is beat 1. The next most important is beat 3, followed by beats 2 and 4. Can you play a right-hand articulation approach that reflects that? *Tip:* Don't make the changes in volume between the accented notes and the unaccented ones too drastic, or it becomes harder to play an even, steady rhythm.

Book VI

Exercises: Practice, Practice, Practice

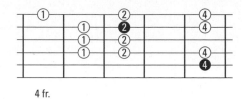

4 fr.

F   G   Ab   Bb   C   Db   E   F   G   Ab   Bb   C

Figure 3-27:
Harmonic minor scale pattern #4 in the key of F minor.

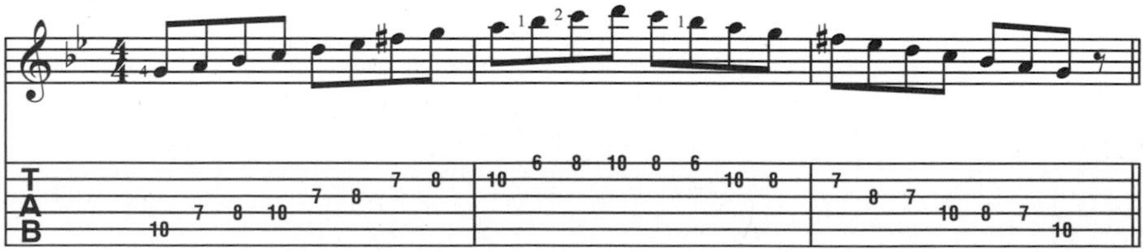

Bb   Ab   G   F   E   Db   C   Bb   Ab   G   F

Figure 3-28:
A rhythm exercise in the key of G minor in 7th position.

Harmonic minor scale pattern #5

Harmonic minor scale pattern #5 starts with the first finger on the 4th string and includes no out-of-position notes.

To see the neck diagram and corresponding music and tab for harmonic minor scale pattern #5 in the key of G minor, refer to Figure 3-29. Because this pattern has no stretches to contend with, it's rather easy to play. So try doing something different: Focus on your right hand. If you normally use a flatpick, try playing the notes smoothly and evenly by alternating your right-hand index and middle fingers. Conversely, if you play fingerstyle, try picking up a flatpick for this one. (Come on, it won't kill you to do it! And your classical guitar teacher doesn't even have to know.) In either case, approaching an exercise from a different perspective often helps you solidify your own internal rhythmic sense, so when you go back to the way you would normally play, you find new confidence. Practice this pattern using different right-hand approaches as a way to see "how the other half lives."

Book VI

Exercises: Practice, Practice, Practice

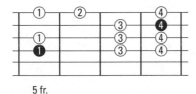

5 fr.

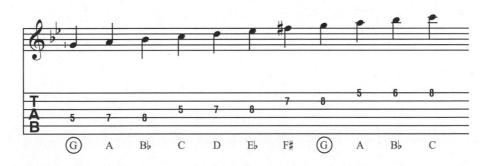

Figure 3-29: Harmonic minor scale pattern #5 in the key of G minor.

When you're ready, practice the pattern using Figure 3-30, which is in the key of F♯ minor in 4th position. Have you ever played in the dark or with your eyes closed? It's a great way to test your muscle memory, and performing this experiment on a scale with no out-of-position notes is a good place to start. It's also the acid test for seeing whether you *truly* have a pattern memorized. Try closing your eyes right now, and see how well you do going up and down one time slowly and steadily. No peeking!

Figure 3-30: A rhythm exercise in the key of F♯ minor in 4th position.

Playing Pieces Using the Three Minor Scales

Playing minor scales prepares you for the vast underworld of music that forsakes major-key optimism and chooses to express itself in darker tones. Just as you need both sunshine and rain to make your flowers grow, so too do you need a little minor among the major to make your musical garden flourish.

In this section, you get to see what minor-scale music is all about. You encounter three major-league compositions, each using a different minor scale. One piece is an old traditional carol, one is from the great Baroque composer George Frideric Handel, and one is attributed to the Renaissance. Enjoy your musical journey to the dark side!

"God Rest Ye Merry, Gentlemen"

Despite the fact that "God Rest Ye Merry, Gentlemen" is in a minor key, it's quite spirited and uplifting. The key signature has no sharps or flats, so you may think that the song is in C major. But it's actually in A minor, which shares the same key signature and notes as C major. (Now you see why A minor is known as the *relative* minor of C major). This song is composed of almost all quarter notes, so you can take it at a pretty brisk tempo. The song uses just one pattern, natural minor scale pattern #5, in 7th position, starting with the first finger.

Even though we've arranged the song using all one scale pattern, some of the intervals and direction changes can be tricky. Try playing the song by ear (close the book or look away from the music). No peeking, now! See how well you do at picking out the correct notes. Even when you know the pattern cold, "God Rest Ye Merry, Gentlemen" (Figure 3-31) can be difficult to perform completely accurately because of some of the intervals.

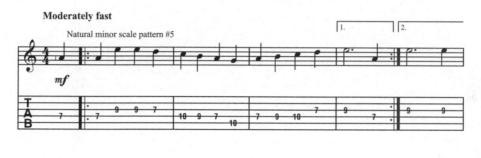

Figure 3-31: "God Rest Ye Merry, Gentlemen" may be minor, but it's lively.

Handel's "Allegro"

The opening statement in this piece is just an ascending scale. However, you may not even realize it because of the way it's disguised with different rhythms. The faster notes in bars 5 through 7 are all just descending scale segments, but do note how beautiful they sound.

Handel's "Allegro" (Figure 3-32) uses the melodic minor scale pattern #4 in 7th position, starting with the fourth finger. It's in the key of G minor and written in *cut time* (sometimes referred to as *2/2*), which is indicated with a *C* and a vertical line "cutting" it in half ₵. This symbol tells you to count the half note, not the quarter note (as you're used to doing with songs in 4/4 and 3/4), as one beat. Because you count the half note as the beat, the measure is felt in 2 (with two beats to the bar).

Brightly, in 2

Figure 3-32:
Handel's
"Allegro"
uses
melodic
minor scale
pattern #4 in
7th position.

In bar 3 of this piece, you see two accidentals in the music: an E natural and an F sharp. These accidentals indicate that those notes have been raised as the melodic minor commands. In bar 5, the melody descends, so the melodic minor scale again requires that the E♭ and F — raised on the way up to E natural and F♯ — be in their natural state, as F and E♭, which agrees with the key signature. For you music readers, we put in the natural and flat signs in bar 5 just as a gentle reminder not to play the wrong notes. The melody has a nice way of building here, using slow notes in the beginning and working up to the eighth-note passages in bars 5 through 7.

"The Three Ravens"

If you're old enough, you may recognize "The Three Ravens" (Figure 3-33) from the Peter, Paul, and Mary version of this folk song. The key signature in the music tells you that this song is in F minor, but because you're using the harmonic minor scale, every instance of the note E will be E natural, not E♭ as indicated by the key signature.

Moderately slow, in 2

Harmonic minor scale pattern #1

Book VI

Exercises: Practice, Practice, Practice

Harmonic minor scale pattern #3

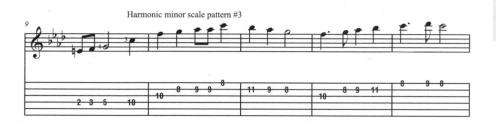

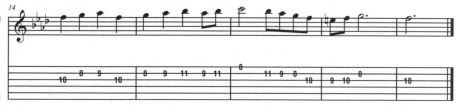

Figure 3-33:
"The Three Ravens" in F minor.

Because the harmonic scale here is in 1st position and you have some out-of-position notes to play, you have a pretty serious case of finger stretching ahead of you! So first play bars 1 and 2 in isolation. This bit of practice allows you to execute the stretch in both an ascending and descending context. Practicing these stretching parts ensures that they don't take you by surprise when you try to play the whole piece.

Chapter 4

Building Finger Independence with Chord Exercises

Chords are the rhythm guitar *yin* to the lead guitar *yang*. In most musical settings, single-note playing is supported by some sort of chord-based accompaniment. The great thing about the guitar is that it can play chords or single-note leads with equal awesomeness — try doing *that* with a flute or saxophone. But, because the guitar plays chords as well as single notes, it's important that you keep your chording and melody skills up to snuff. This chapter addresses chord playing — with all the notes of the chord sounding *together*.

As with the single-note exercises, the chord forms presented in this chapter are movable — meaning they contain no *open strings* (strings that are unfretted, with no left-hand finger touching the string at all). So after you can play a chord form comfortably, try moving it around the neck to play different chords. Doing so changes the letter name of the chord (for example, from A to C) but keeps the quality of the chord (major, minor, and so on) the same.

You can play the chords in this chapter a number of different ways with the right hand, including plucking the individual strings with your fingertips, brushing the strings with the backs of your fingernails, and striking the notes with a pick. But whether you pluck or strum with the right hand, your left-hand approach is the same. Your fingers on your left hand must fret the notes in a way that allows the strings to ring clearly, and they must be able to change chords — that is, get off the old chord and grab the new chord — quickly and imperceptibly (or close to it, anyway). And this must all be done at a performance tempo.

The exercises in this chapter are designed to help get your fingers moving independently. The bountiful number of useful examples also helps you build up strength in the process.

Practicing Inversion Patterns

Chords come in many different guises; even chords with the same name can be played in various ways. For example, you can play an F major chord on the guitar in exactly one billion and seven ways. Okay, that's a *bit* of an exaggeration. But trust us, you can find lots of chord options on the neck.

The first way you can narrow down the F major chord choices is to organize them by the low-to-high order of their notes. An F major chord is spelled F-A-C, bottom note to top. But the notes A-C-F and C-F-A are also F chords. Any chord with the combination of the notes F, A, and C constitutes an F chord, but if the lowest note of the chord is anything but an F, it's called an *inversion* of F. So we introduce you to an F (with an F on the bottom), its first inversion (with an A on the bottom), and its second inversion (with a C on the bottom).

In addition to the order of notes from bottom to top, you can also group chords by which strings they're played on. For example, you can play a chord using all six strings (as you do with a basic open E), just the top five strings, just the top four strings, or any other combination of strings.

Playing all six strings may make the guitar sound full and complete in one setting, but it's not always appropriate — especially if you're playing in a band or with other instruments. (Playing all six strings all the time can sound too full and can muddy up the texture and crowd out other instruments, such as the bass. It can be cumbersome to play, too.) Sometimes four-string chords are just right.

So here we employ two groups of four-string chords, nicknamed *outside chords* and *inside chords*.

- ✔ Outside forms refer to the top four strings that reach the outside, or edge, of the fretboard. Outside chords don't include bass notes and are good for melody playing and supplying a higher harmonic part.

- ✔ Inside forms — at least for the purposes of this chapter (the term can have other meanings) — are the 2nd, 3rd, and 4th strings (which are insulated from the outside of the neck by surrounding strings) and a 6th string for a low note. Inside chords, which include a bass note, produce a deeper, fuller sound, and are good for when there's no bass player around.

Because we start our chord explorations at the 1st fret, we chose F to name our chords. But all the forms presented in this chapter are movable, so when you practice playing them at different frets, the letter name will change. For example, if you play the chords two frets higher than where we present them in the figures, you produce G chords of various qualities. Our purpose in choosing F is that it's an efficient way to present all the different forms. But we don't favor F any more than G or B♭ or F♯. (Okay, maybe we like F a *little* more than F♯, but only because the key of F♯ has six sharps.)

As with practicing scales and arpeggios, play each chord exercise in this chapter slowly, loudly, and deliberately at first, making sure you can hear all the strings that are supposed to ring — and none of the strings that aren't! Then play the exercise faster and with a lighter touch. Just be sure to maintain your starting tempo and dynamic level (loudness) throughout each exercise.

Patterns using outside chords

Book VI

Exercises: Practice, Practice, Practice

Figure 4-1 shows the neck diagram and the corresponding music and tab for the three forms of an outside-string F major chord. Remember that when you practice these exercises, the *X*s in the chord diagrams mean that those strings aren't played. So avoid striking or plucking them with your right hand.

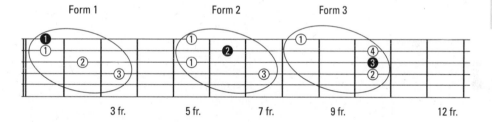

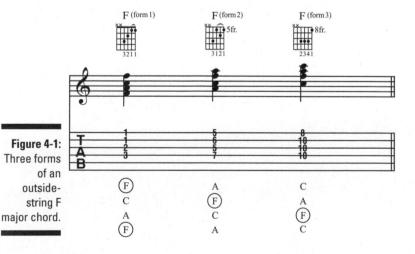

Figure 4-1: Three forms of an outside-string F major chord.

In all the rhythm examples that follow for outside chords, strum each chord lightly in quarter notes (one strum per beat) and avoid playing the lowest two strings of the guitar.

Now try the rhythm exercise in Figure 4-2, which uses the outside forms of F, played two to a bar, or two beats on each chord.

Figure 4-2:
A rhythm
exercise
for outside
F major
chords.

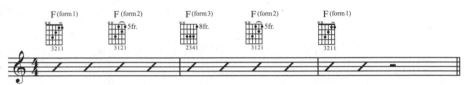

When going from the first form to the second, keep your third finger on the string as you slide up the neck. That way, you only have to reposition two other fingers (rather than all three). Apply the same "common finger" approach between the fourth and fifth chords in the exercise.

Figure 4-3 shows the neck diagram for the three forms of an outside-string F minor chord along with the corresponding music and tab. Practice this pattern as many times as you need to in order to play it smoothly — especially form 3, where you have to squeeze your fingers together a bit.

The exercise in Figure 4-4 uses the four outside forms of F minor, played two to a bar, or two beats on each chord. The common finger approach that you use in the previous exercise works like a charm here: The third finger plays the same string in all three chord forms. So keep it anchored on the 4th string as you move your hand up and down the neck.

To see the neck diagram for the four forms of an outside F7 chord, along with the corresponding music and tab, check out Figure 4-5. Practice the pattern here until you can move comfortably between the forms with no interruption in the rhythm.

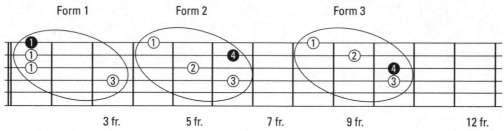

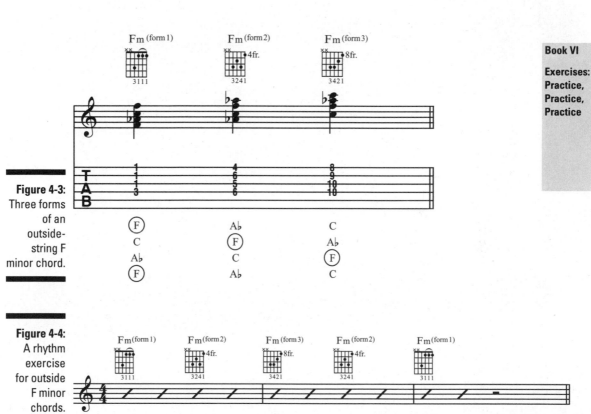

Figure 4-3: Three forms of an outside-string F minor chord.

Book VI

Exercises: Practice, Practice, Practice

Figure 4-4: A rhythm exercise for outside F minor chords.

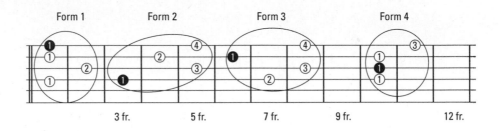

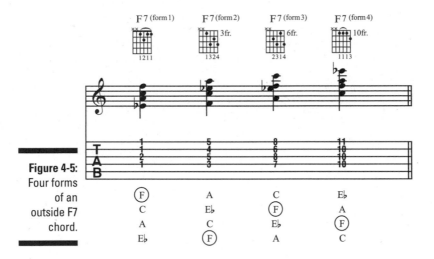

Figure 4-5:
Four forms
of an
outside F7
chord.

When you're ready, try the exercise in Figure 4-6 in rhythm. It uses the four outside forms of F7, played two to a bar, or two beats on each chord. Seventh chords are a favorite choice for blues rhythm players, so if you're interested, practice this progression with the additional blues chords of B♭7 and C7.

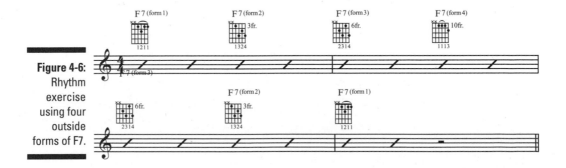

Figure 4-6:
Rhythm
exercise
using four
outside
forms of F7.

Now take a look at the neck diagram and corresponding music and tab for the four forms of an outside Fm7 chord in Figure 4-7. Try practicing this pattern in two ways: by playing it with a pick, and using just your right-hand fingers. Try to make the two approaches sound as close to each other as you can.

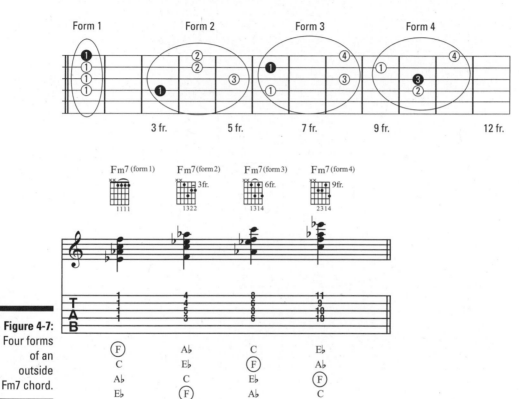

Figure 4-7:
Four forms
of an
outside
Fm7 chord.

Figure 4-8 shows an exercise using the four outside forms of Fm7, played two to a bar, or two beats on each chord. Outside minor 7th chords are quite common in the jazz guitar style known as *chord melody,* so work for a smooth, even, and mellow sound as you play these chords. Imagine yourself jamming alongside a stand-up bass and a drummer using brushes.

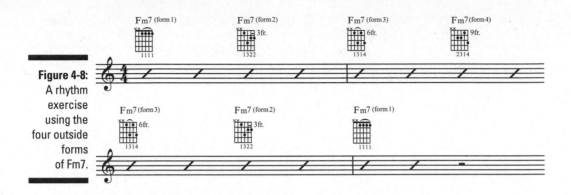

Figure 4-8:
A rhythm exercise using the four outside forms of Fm7.

Figure 4-9 illustrates the neck diagram and corresponding music and tab for the four forms of an outside Fmaj7 chord. Practice this pattern until you're completely comfortable with the four-fret spread among your left-hand fingers in form 3.

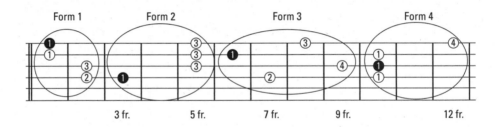

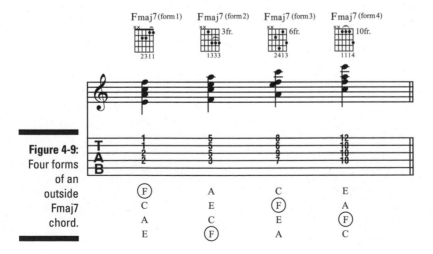

Figure 4-9:
Four forms of an outside Fmaj7 chord.

As practice, try the exercise in Figure 4-10, which uses the four outside forms of Fmaj7, played two to a bar, or two beats on each chord. Form 3 is probably the trickiest chord in this series because it requires you to stretch your fingers out over all four frets in the position, and you have a wide space between the second and third fingers. Practice grabbing this chord in isolation (by removing your hand from the chord and replaying it several times) before playing the whole exercise up to tempo.

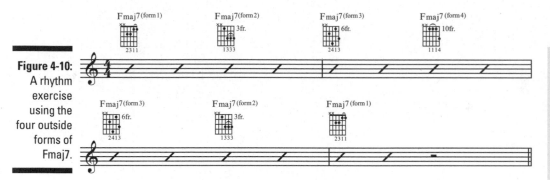

Figure 4-10:
A rhythm
exercise
using the
four outside
forms of
Fmaj7.

Book VI

**Exercises:
Practice,
Practice,
Practice**

In Figure 4-11, you see the neck diagram for the four forms of an outside F#m7♭5 chord along with the corresponding music and tab. Practice this pattern slowly at first and as many times as you need to until you have it memorized. Then, when you get "off book," work on playing it faster.

Now try your hand at the exercise in Figure 4-12, which uses the four outside forms of F#m7♭5, played two to a bar, or two beats on each chord. Except for the first and last chords, every chord in this exercise is played with a barre. Be sure to check your barre notes (by playing the individual strings one at a time, slowly) to make sure they're all ringing out clearly and with no buzzing.

To see the neck diagram and corresponding music and tab for the three forms of an outside-string F#°7 chord, check out Figure 4-13. Songs using the diminished 7th chord sometimes have you playing several forms in quick succession, so make sure you can play this at a fairly fast tempo.

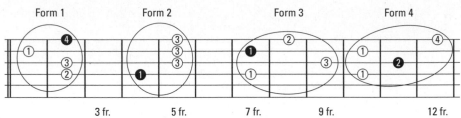

Figure 4-11: Four forms of an outside F#m7♭5 chord.

Figure 4-12: A rhythm exercise using the four outside forms of F#m7♭5.

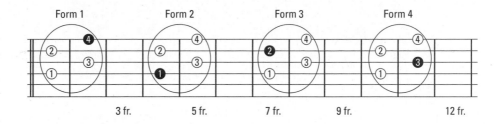

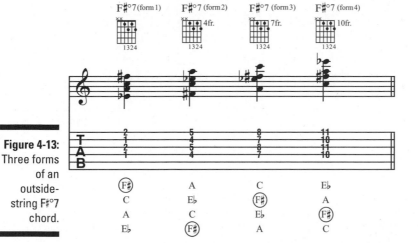

Figure 4-13: Three forms of an outside-string F♯°7 chord.

When you're ready to finish off your outside chord practice, take a look at Figure 4-14, which shows an exercise in rhythm using the four outside forms of F♯°7, played two to a bar, or two beats on each chord. The diminished chord form has the same fingering for all of its inversions. So you get a free pass here and have to learn only one form, which you can slide up and down the neck with abandon. Because your fingers don't have to switch strings, try playing this example at a brighter tempo than you normally would.

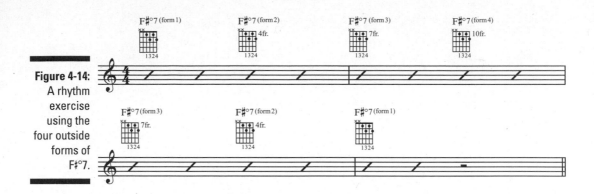

Figure 4-14: A rhythm exercise using the four outside forms of F♯°7.

Patterns using inside chords

Figure 4-15 shows the neck diagram and corresponding music and tab for the three forms of an inside F major chord. Remember that the *X*s in the chord diagrams indicate that those strings aren't played. Practice this pattern as many times as you need to in order to get it to flow smoothly and so there's no trace of that 5th string ringing through.

In the case of inside chords, it's difficult *not* to strike the 5th string when strumming (either with the backs of the fingernails or with a pick). So you should mute, or deaden, the string by allowing a left-hand finger to lightly touch it, which will prevent it from ringing out. This muting action is usually done by the finger that's fretting the 6th string. For the 1st string, simply relaxing the left hand so the underside of the fingers touch the string lightly is enough to prevent it from ringing out.

You can practice this muting technique in the exercise in Figure 4-16, which uses the three inside forms of F, played two to a bar, or two beats on each chord. Strum each chord lightly in quarter notes (one strum per beat), and avoid or mute the 5th and 1st strings of the guitar (indicated with *X*s in the chord diagrams).

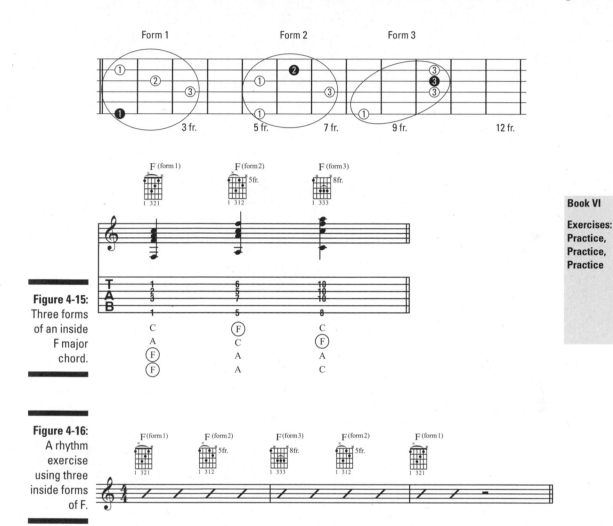

Figure 4-15: Three forms of an inside F major chord.

Book VI

Exercises: Practice, Practice, Practice

Figure 4-16: A rhythm exercise using three inside forms of F.

Figure 4-17 shows the neck diagram and corresponding standard notation and tab for the three forms of an inside F minor chord. You can practice this pattern by keeping the third and first fingers in the same basic shape as you change chords; they never leave the string they're on, and they're always one fret apart from each other.

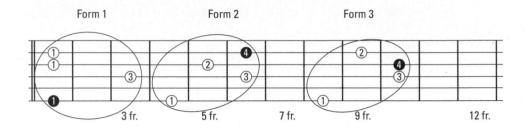

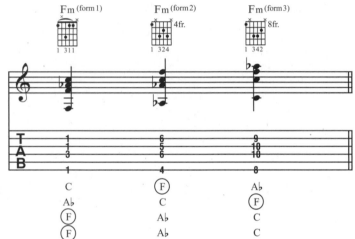

Figure 4-17:
The three forms of an inside F minor chord.

When you're ready, try Figure 4-18's exercise in rhythm, which uses the three inside forms of F minor, played two to a bar, or two beats on each chord. You may have trouble muting the 5th string (which isn't supposed to sound) on form 1. So for this exercise, try plucking the strings with your right-hand fingers rather than strumming them with a pick.

Figure 4-18:
A rhythm exercise using three inside forms of F minor.

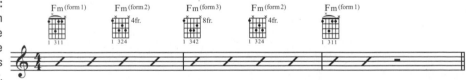

Now take a look at the neck diagram and corresponding music and tab for the four forms of an inside F7 chord, shown in Figure 4-19. Make sure that you can blend all the notes together with your right-hand attack and that no one note stands out above the rest. Practice this pattern so you can change smoothly between the chords that use barres (forms 1 and 4) and those that don't (forms 2 and 3).

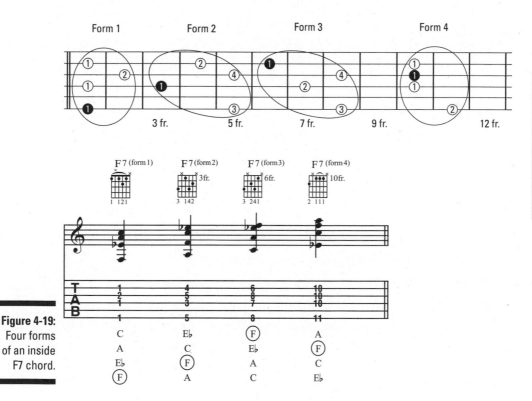

Book VI

Exercises: Practice, Practice, Practice

Figure 4-19:
Four forms of an inside F7 chord.

Give the exercise in Figure 4-20 a try. It uses the four inside forms of F7, played two to a bar, or two beats on each chord. Some guitarists, especially jazz players, like to use an alternate fingering for form 1. Try playing this chord with your first finger (not barred) on the 6th string, your second finger on the 4th string, your fourth finger on the 3rd string, and your third finger on the 2nd string. If you prefer this fingering to the barred version, you may be a jazzbo!

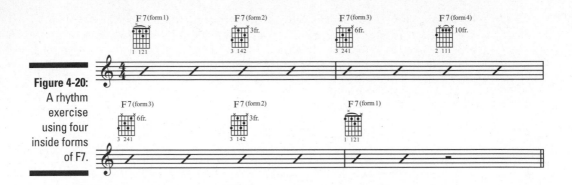

Figure 4-20:
A rhythm
exercise
using four
inside forms
of F7.

Here in Figure 4-21 is the neck diagram and corresponding music and tab for the four forms of an inside Fm7 chord. Practice this pattern using two versions of form 1: the one indicated in the pattern, and an alternate form with the second finger on the 6th string and a third-finger mini-barre for strings 4, 3, and 2.

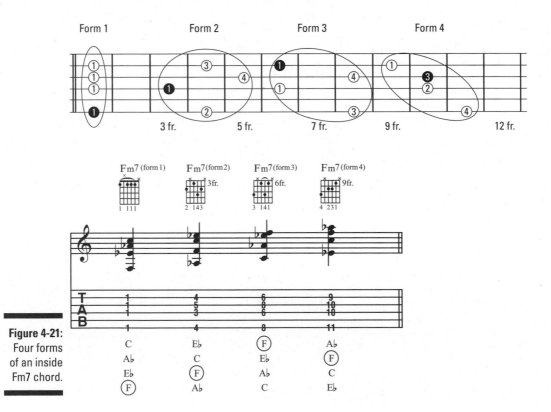

Figure 4-21:
Four forms
of an inside
Fm7 chord.

Figure 4-22 shows an exercise using the four inside forms of Fm7, played two to a bar, or two beats on each chord. Most experienced guitarists (jazz and rock players alike) play form 1 with the second finger on the 6th string and the third finger (barred) across the 4th, 3rd, and 2nd strings, described in the previous paragraph. Playing the chord this way helps you to better keep the 5th string from sounding. Try form 1 the two-finger way, and if it seems awkward at the 1st fret, move it up to the middle of the neck where it will be more comfortable.

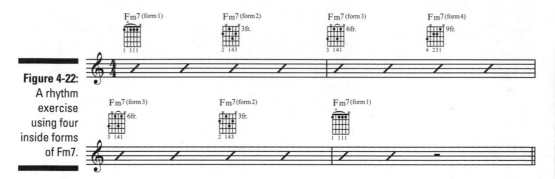

Figure 4-22:
A rhythm
exercise
using four
inside forms
of Fm7.

To see the neck diagram and corresponding music and tab for the four forms of an inside Fmaj7 chord, check out Figure 4-23. Practice form 2 first in isolation because it has a stretch between the second and first fingers. Then try the exercise in its entirety.

Figure 4-24 is an exercise using the four inside forms of Fmaj7, played two to a bar, or two beats on each chord. Between forms 3 and 4 you have an opportunity to make the chord change even smoother by leaving your third finger on the 6th string as you move up and down the neck. Just be sure to relax the third finger so it doesn't make a sliding sound on the string as you change positions.

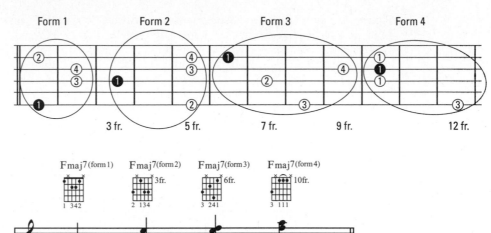

Figure 4-23: Four forms of an inside Fmaj7 chord.

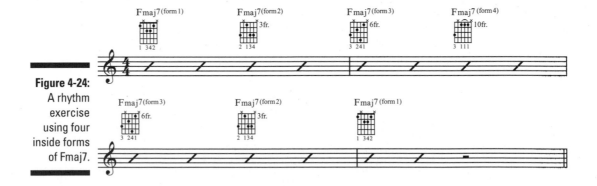

Figure 4-24: A rhythm exercise using four inside forms of Fmaj7.

Figure 4-25 shows the neck diagram and corresponding music and tab for the four forms of an inside F♯m7♭5 chord. Practice this pattern several times or until you master the three mini-barres that occur in this exercise.

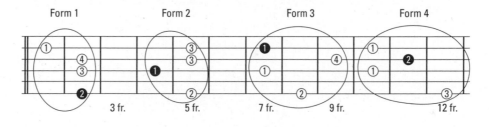

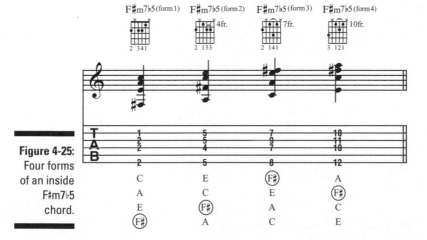

Book VI

**Exercises:
Practice,
Practice,
Practice**

Figure 4-25:
Four forms
of an inside
F♯m7♭5
chord.

As practice, try the exercise in Figure 4-26, which uses the four inside forms of F♯m7♭5, played two to a bar, or two beats on each chord. A very cool "common finger" chord change occurs between forms 2 and 3. Both the second and first fingers stay on the same strings as they move to the new form. But the first finger goes from playing a single note on the fingertip to playing a barre on the flat part. So be sure to flatten out your first finger slightly as you move. To become familiar with this efficient finger movement, try isolating these two chords (that is, practice changing between the two forms a number of times before playing the whole exercise).

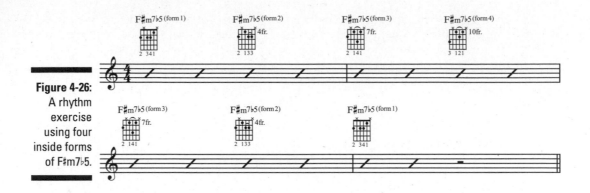

Figure 4-26:
A rhythm exercise using four inside forms of F#m7♭5.

Figure 4-27 shows the neck diagram and corresponding music and tab for the four forms of an inside F#°7 chord. Your fingering doesn't change when moving among the four forms here, so work for speed and accuracy as you shift this pattern up and down the neck in three-fret increments.

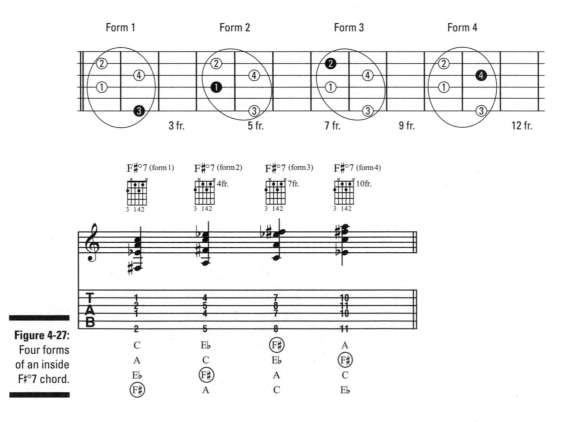

Figure 4-27:
Four forms of an inside F#°7 chord.

To practice, you can try the exercise in Figure 4-28, which uses the four inside forms of F#°7, played two to a bar, or two beats on each chord. Just as in the outside forms earlier in the chapter, the inside form of the diminished 7th chord is the same for all four forms.

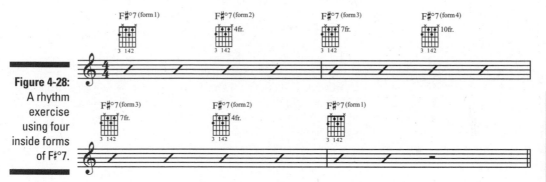

Figure 4-28: A rhythm exercise using four inside forms of F#°7.

Book VI

Exercises: Practice, Practice, Practice

As if having the same forms didn't make things easy enough, we have another tip for you. Try the alternate, three-finger version of the chord: Barre the 4th and 2nd strings with your first finger. Then play the 6th string note with your second finger and the 3rd string note with your third finger. Many guitarists find this fingering faster to grab than the one presented (especially after they become better at playing barre chords). Try both versions and decide for yourself, however.

Playing Chord Progressions

Playing chords by themselves or organized by string assignment is a good way to get your fingers in shape. But in actual musical situations, you play chords according to another organizing principle: a chord progression. A *chord progression* is merely a series of chords that go together in a musically logical fashion — to support a melody or as the framework for a jam or improvisation (such as the 12-bar blues).

The chord progressions in the following sections may sound like real and familiar songs, and they should. That's because many songs have used the following progressions either in whole or in part.

Progressions using outside chords

Outside chord forms use the top four strings of the guitar (which are the highest pitched), and they're good for rhythm parts when you have a bass player in your midst (or when you're joined by a pianist who's playing low notes in the left hand). Outside chord forms are also nice when you want the brighter sound of the higher strings to cut through — the way a mandolin sounds when it plays rhythm.

Figures 4-29 and 4-30 show two chord progressions, each of which uses nine different outside forms, played two to a bar. Play the chord progressions both *legato* (letting the strings ring out as long as possible) and *staccato* (where the strings are muted by the release of your fretting fingers) to create two different moods.

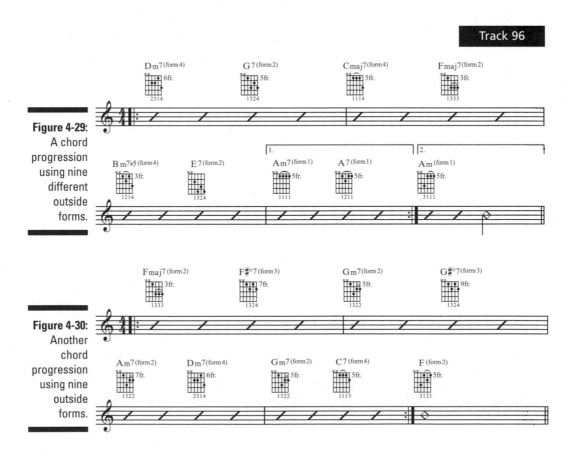

Track 96

Figure 4-29: A chord progression using nine different outside forms.

Figure 4-30: Another chord progression using nine outside forms.

Progressions using inside chords

In this book, inside chords feature the 6th string as part of the chord, separated widely from the next highest note because of the skip of the 5th string. The presence of the low note in inside chords means that the inside chords provide a nice bottom, or bass part, which is good for solo guitarists, guitarists playing with other instruments but without a bass player, or accompanists backing up a singer.

Take a look at Figures 4-31 and 4-32, which show two chord progressions, each using nine different inside forms, played two to a bar. To help get the 6th string note to ring a little more clearly, try separating it from the rest of the chord by plucking it a little harder than the rest of the strings, or by playing the bass note with your right-hand thumb and the rest of the chord with your index, middle, and ring fingers. For extra practice, try playing just the bass note on beats 1 and 3 and just the upper three strings of the chord on beats 2 and 4.

Book VI

Exercises: Practice, Practice, Practice

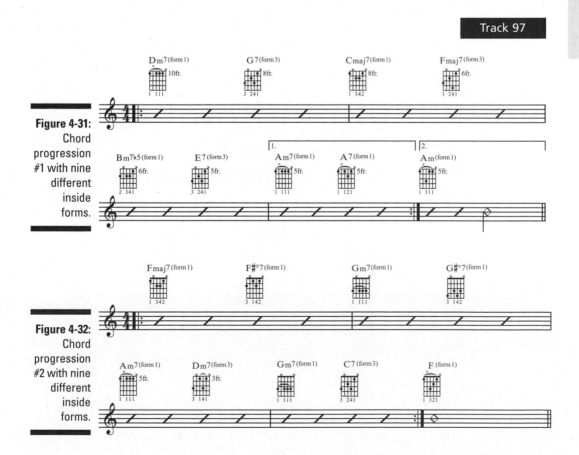

Track 97

Figure 4-31: Chord progression #1 with nine different inside forms.

Figure 4-32: Chord progression #2 with nine different inside forms.

Practicing Pieces that Use Chord Progressions

Seventh chords are great for playing jazz and jazzy types of arrangements, so we selected two songs to jazzify in the following sections: One is a traditional folk ballad, and the other is a standard by Jerome Kern. The first song has you working with outside chords, and the second one gives you an inside look at inside chords.

Putting outside chords to use with "Danny Boy"

The lovely Irish ballad "Danny Boy" is actually based on an old traditional melody called "Londonderry Air." And if you've ever checked out the *derrières* in London, you can see why they changed the title. *[Rim shot.]* But seriously. The lyrics were added later, as a poignant message from a father to his absent son.

Play "Danny Boy" (shown in Figure 4-33) slowly and gently, and try to make the one-beat chord changes (which occur in bars 8, 9, 11, 12, 14, 15, and 16) sound smooth and unrushed. Don't worry if you can't play the F chord in bar 14 cleanly at first; it takes some effort to cram three fingers onto the 2nd, 3rd, and 4th strings at the 10th fret.

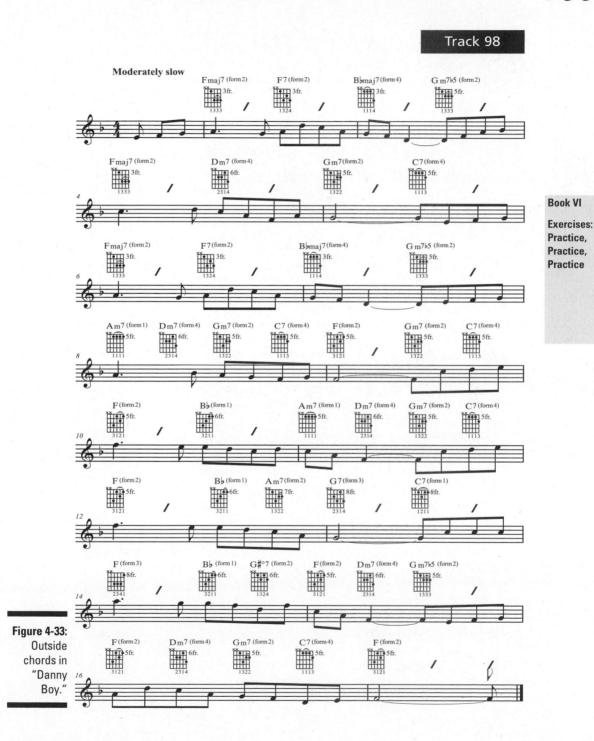

Figure 4-33: Outside chords in "Danny Boy."

You can try this alternate fingering if you're having trouble: Use your third finger to barre the 2nd, 3rd, and 4th strings at the 10th fret, lifting it just enough to allow the 1st string (fretted by the first finger) to ring. It's tricky, but you may find it easier than using four separate fingers for this form so high on the neck.

Playing inside chords in "Look for the Silver Lining"

Jerome Kern wrote "Look for the Silver Lining" for an all-but-forgotten musical called *Sally,* but most people who know this call to optimism are familiar with the versions sung by Judy Garland or jazz trumpet great Chet Baker.

Play this song (shown in Figure 4-34) moderately slowly, and try to let the chords that last only one beat (such as the Am7 and D7 chords in bar 1) sound as legato as the chords that receive two beats.

The trick to this piece is making quick and efficient motions *between* chord changes without affecting the ring-out of the chord strum itself. You need to change chords quickly, but you must also allow the chords to sound for their full duration.

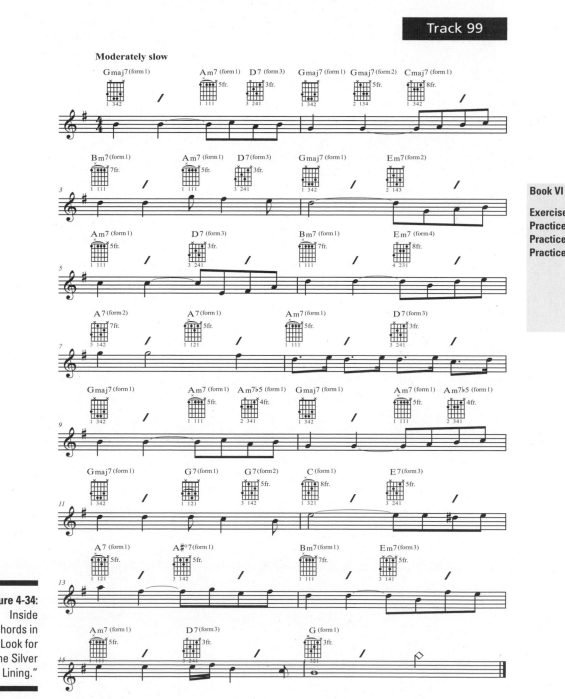

Figure 4-34: Inside chords in "Look for the Silver Lining."

Book VII
Writing Songs and Music

The 5th Wave   By Rich Tennant

"You told me to write the B flat section a whole step lower than the C section you're writing."

In this book . . .

We help you gratify your urge to share your musical vision with the world. Lots of great songs have been written on the guitar because it's such a great accompaniment for voice. Writing music and songs may sound easy, but once you try, you may find that it's not. Luckily, others who have gone before you have come back with lots of hard-earned advice on ways of doing it with increased success. This book can be your ticket to unleashing your creativity while pointing out typical beginner errors, saving you time and grief and giving you a leg up on others.

Here are the contents of Book VII at a glance.

Chapter 1

Everything You Need to Write a Song

*S*ongs — the combination of music and words (or *lyrics*) — have the power to make people laugh, cry, or even scream out in protest. They cause people to pound on their steering wheels as they're driving down the road — buttoned-down businesspeople are transformed into their favorite rockers during morning commutes. And thousands become pop divas in the privacy of their own showers. Songs can transport you to a moment 30 years in the past, and some of the songs you enjoy today will stay with you for years to come.

Given the way songs can move and inspire people, you're not alone if you're interested in writing a few songs of your own after playing a lot of guitar. Maybe you've even come up with some lyrics, or thought of a melody, but you're just not sure where to take it from there. In this chapter, you become familiar with all the facets of songwriting that you need to be aware of. Whether you're just starting out or you already have a few songs (or portions of songs) under your belt, you're at this book's beginning, and as Julie Andrews sang, that's "a very good place to start."

Understanding Why People Write Songs

People write songs for many reasons: to express their feelings, spark debate, inform their audience, push others to act. . . . There are probably as many reasons for writing songs as there are people who write them. Songs are often written by people who have a hard time verbalizing what's in their hearts — sometimes, pairing their feelings with music helps people say what they really feel. Others may write songs because they have a message to get across — a message that much of the world may not be quite ready to hear — and putting that message to music can help penetrate even the most shielded of ears.

You may want to write a song to

- Express your true self.
- Release the music inside of you that's just waiting to get out.
- Give back to your songwriting heroes some of the joy and inspiration they've given you.
- Develop the gift of expression you may have been born with.
- Gain acceptance and make new friends.
- Earn a living at something you truly love!

Whatever your motive, the goal is the same:

- To come up with words and music from the inner reaches of your imagination
- To connect with others through a song
- To create something of lasting value

Finding the Songwriter in You

Fortunately, the main requirements for writing a song are exactly the same, whether it's strictly for yourself and for your loved ones or for the music-buying public. The main ingredients are a passion for music, a need to express yourself in song, a mind receptive to the ideas that come floating your way, and a willingness to find and network with other talented individuals who can help you realize your musical vision. Ironically, many songwriters say that some of their biggest hits were never intended for mass exposure or written with success in mind. They were a personal expression of something in their hearts as a gift to themselves or for family, friends, and loved ones.

This chapter is for everyone who shares the dream of harnessing the songwriting power we all have within. You've come to the right place if your heart keeps tugging at you to write a song — but you're uncertain as to the process of the craft or what's required to create a really good one. If you know the elements that make up a great song and how the pros go about writing one, you can get on the right path to creating one of your own. Writing a song isn't rocket science, no matter what the music theory books would have you believe. Not that a little book learning isn't a great thing; it's just that complicated notions can stop you before you get started.

Songwriting is about 80 percent inspiration, 10 percent perspiration, and 10 percent implementation. So let's not get it backwards. Hopefully we can take down some of the roadblocks to writing a song and get to the heart of the matter — because that's where a song is born.

Being aware of your personal connection to songs

Book VII

Writing Songs and Music

If you are compelled to be a songwriter, you've probably gotten a great deal of enjoyment from listening to songs over the years. When you think back on your life (whether you've lived 18 years or 80), how many songs come to mind when you think of important moments? Do certain songs bring to mind sights, sounds, smells, and emotions from the places you were when you first heard them? Have certain songs become your favorites because they express exactly what you hadn't been able to put into words yourself?

If you can easily compile a soundtrack to your life, full of all the songs you've loved over the years, you're off to a good start. If you would have trouble fitting that soundtrack onto one tape or CD, that's even better! Why? Because if your life has been greatly affected by the power of music, you're in the right position to affect others through the songs *you* write.

Taking a look at your instincts

If you feel a deep connection with certain special songs throughout your life, you can be pretty sure that you have the emotional capacity to express yourself in the context of a song. Besides having that appreciation for other people's songs, check out the following list to roughly determine your S.Q. (yeah, you guessed it, your "song quotient").

You just may be a songwriter if:

- ✔ You've ever sung a melody in your shower and started gyrating wildly when you realized it was a song that didn't yet exist.

- ✔ You often find yourself lost in the industrial section of an unfamiliar town when you realize that the great lyric ideas you've been jotting down have totally obscured that little road map your friend had scribbled down for you to get to her house.

- ✔ You create a gaper's block in the freezer section of the supermarket when you take your microcassette recorder, iPhone, or digital voice recorder out of your bag and start chanting the hook of the new rap song you've created that documents the multiplicity of brands of frozen vegetables.

- ✔ You create a new angry lyric and shouted melody over the chord changes of "Muskrat Love" while performing karaoke at the local club.

- ✔ You visit friends and rudely spend most of the time in their 8-year-old son's bedroom, strumming some new chord changes on his toy guitar.

- ✔ You start haunting every club for musicians to put your latest poem to music.

- ✔ On the street, you stop everyone in a black turtleneck sweater to see if they're a poet who could supply words for your music.

- ✔ Your hands are rubbed raw from pounding out rhythms on your desktop, laptop, dashboard, dog, or garbage can.

If you can identify any aspect of yourself in this inventory list, you may be on your way to writing a song. If you haven't already done any of these things, don't despair. You can still develop your instincts and try your hand at songwriting. Who knows? You just may unlock a part of you that you never even knew existed.

Starting at the Beginning — Before You Write a Song

After you figure out why you want to write songs, and after you discover that you have what it takes to give it a shot, you're ready to dive in. But writing a song can be an intimidating process. After all, where do you begin?

Is formal music training a must?

Music training isn't a prerequisite for songwriting. However, if you don't at least have some ability on the guitar or piano to help put the ideas in your head into some tangible form, you *may* be at a disadvantage. (Notice we said "may." Funnyman Mel Brooks composed the musical score to his hit Broadway show *The Producers* by humming the melodies into a tape recorder and having someone translate that into musical notes on a page.) Musical ability, especially guitar playing, helps you with the rhythm of your words and the structure of your songs. All of this musical expertise is advantageous, but not required.

Jim Peterik, Grammy Award–winning songwriter, on songwriting

Most of what I know about songwriting, I learned by being a fan of music. Truly the best teacher is listening. I emulated the styles of songs that inspired me, and gradually, over the course of many years, integrated these influences into a style of my own. The Beatles' songwriting, to cite a notable example, was heavily influenced by the American rock 'n' roll of Chuck Berry, Carl Perkins, the Everly Brothers, and Little Richard. The Beatles created songs by absorbing those influences and adding their own unique personalities. The fact that they could barely read music hardly mattered. They had ears. Studying music theory, history, and arrangement can only enhance your abilities as a writer, but it would be a mistake to infer that formal training is a necessity to write a great song. Music appreciation classes can open your eyes and ears to what you should be listening for in songs, but you really don't need anyone to tell your foot when to start tapping or your lips to break out into a big smile when the chorus hits — that's just the power of great music. Start with your love for the songs you hear and then tap into all you have to express in your soul.

If you're still not convinced that you don't need training, consider the fact that some of the greatest songs ever written were composed by people with virtually no formal music training. Folk music, chants, Delta blues, country, and rock 'n' roll all got their start with people who had the raw talent to create songs. On the other hand, many legendary composers have extensive musical training in all forms of music, including classical composition. Just don't let the so-called "rules" hold you back or keep you frozen.

In college, my harmony teacher told me at the end of the semester, "You know all that stuff I taught you about avoiding parallel 5ths? Forget about it! If it sounds good, just do it!" By the way, that was the only formal music training I ever got, other than two years of piano and a few years of saxophone lessons. I earned a C+ in that class. It's my belief that life is the best teacher, and listening to and enjoying a good song are perhaps the best ways to learn to write songs yourself.

Book VII

Writing Songs and Music

Although songwriting is more than just an assembly line of components to be bolted together, it doesn't hurt to know what's available in the "parts bin." A song is made up of *chords* (a combination of two or more tones sounded together in harmony), *melody* (the arrangement of single tones in sequence — the part you sing), *rhythm* (the beat or pulse of the song), and words (often called *lyrics* in the context of a song). Many successful songwriters excel in one area or another. Rare individuals can do it all. Even the ones who are a songwriting "one stop" often choose to collaborate with others to create that magical song that comes from a blend of styles and personalities. It's your task at hand, if you are challenged in a given area, to find writers to complete your vision and supply the expertise you lack.

Although some songwriters do well with the trial-and-error method, the more you know about music, the better your chances are to write a great song. The more adept you can become at an instrument, the easier it will be to create and demonstrate the ideas in your head. You don't need to enroll in a college course to study music. Instructions in music theory, composition, instrument performance, and voice are available at a per-session rate. Qualified, reasonably priced private teachers can be located through your local music shop or in the back pages of the local "freebie" entertainment newspaper. Finding someone who inspires you will make songwriting a lot easier.

Being prepared when inspiration strikes

Ideas will come into your brain while you're in the strangest of places, at any time of the day or night. You've probably heard stories about how some of the greatest hits were born. Paul McCartney has said some of his best songs came to him in his dreams. Billy Joel got the song "River of Dreams" from — you guessed it — a dream. And Sting, former lead singer of the group The Police, awakened in the middle of the night, wrote a song in ten minutes, and went back to sleep. The song? "Every Breath You Take." (Makes you want to get plenty of shut-eye, doesn't it?)

When a melody or a lyrical idea pops into your head, make sure you have a way of freezing it in time. Try to carry with you, at all times, a notebook to jot down ideas and a recording device to capture your musical phrases. Never fool yourself into thinking you'll remember the ideas when you get home. And don't think that "If it's really so great of an idea, I won't forget it." Some great songs will never be heard because the songwriter couldn't reconstruct some once-in-a-lifetime moment of inspiration.

A flash of inspiration may hit you when you least expect it. Be ready to catch it — then be prepared to work hard at turning the initial idea into a finished song.

Capturing that loving feeling

In a survey based on performances, sheet music, and record sales, *Variety,* the entertainment trade paper, once named the 100 most popular songs of all time. An analysis of the themes of those 100 titles showed that about 85 percent of them were love songs. Many of those blockbuster golden oldies are still generating new recordings after 50 years.

Finding inspiration within yourself

So you aren't being awakened in the middle of the night by divine inspiration? Not to worry. You can find inspiration even if it doesn't seem to find you. The unique way you look at the world and feel about things, the mood you project in life, and all of your emotions are unmistakably projected in your song. In other words, write about what you know and feel, and you're sure to come up with something unique (because even though you thought your mother was lame when she said it, there's only one you).

Some writers, through their melodies, chord progressions, and lyrics, project a powerful optimism. Others project wonder, a bittersweet sadness, or pure anger. But few songwriters can project all emotions within a single song or even on one CD — so don't pressure yourself to cram in every possible emotion all at once.

Whatever the mood, all great songs have the ability to move people, to make them *feel* something.

Psychologists say that songs can put us in touch with our feelings. We all know what it feels like to be happy, sad, afraid, or in love. Often, a song is what puts us in touch with emotions.

Expressing your authentic feelings in a song is not only therapeutic to you as a person, but it can also be the clay from which a lasting song can be sculpted. If your audience can see a little bit of themselves in your song, if they can identify directly with what you're saying, your song just may stay in their hearts and minds (and MP3 players) long after it has dropped off the *Billboard* charts. When you feel passionate about an issue, when you are swept away by some new fad or idea, whether you are moved to tears by a movie or the passing of a loved one, or when you've recently fallen in or out of love — these are the subjects and feelings that will resonate in your song. Your own experience is perhaps more universal than you think.

Book VII

Writing Songs and Music

Words of wisdom from Johnny Van Zant, lead singer of Lynyrd Skynyrd

Whatever moves me to write a song is usually a pretty good reason. I can really only write about what I feel in my heart. On September 11, 2001, I received a call from a good friend of mine who works on the rooftops in Manhattan. He had just been witness to one of the great tragedies of our or any time, as he heard a huge explosion and watched helplessly as the first of two jet aircrafts crashed into the World Trade Center. He called me and said that when he looked around, all of his co-workers had tears streaming down their faces. I said to him, "This has got to be the day America cried."

As I watched the images of destruction all that day, I started to sing a melody that seemed to mirror my emotions at the time. The next day I called up my good buddy Jim Peterik and told him that there was a song to be written here that could possibly do some good. I sang him a piece of the melody I had in my head. The first words out of Jim's mouth were, "In the shadow of the Statue of Liberty" to which I added, "In the torchlight of the land of the free." From there, with the help of Ma Bell, digital recording, and the grace of God, a song was born.

We are proud to say that the fruits from our labor of love became the title song to *The Day America Cried* album, helped raised some money, and hopefully expressed a few emotions locked in so many hearts. That's the power of a song.

Creating the mood

It all starts with you — who you are and what feeling or mood you're able to project. The number of people who will be able to connect with and relate to the mood you're creating will determine just how successful your song will be.

In some great songs, the mood of the music matches perfectly to the lyric. For example:

- ✔ Minor chords often become the basis for sadder, deeper, and more introspective songs. Listen to "New York State of Mind" (written and sung by Billy Joel), "New York Minute" (written by Don Henley, Daniel Kortchmar, and Jai Winding; sung by Don Henley), or "Paint It Black" (written by Mick Jagger and Keith Richards; performed by the Rolling Stones).

- ✔ Major chords generally result in happier and more optimistic songs like "You Are the Sunshine of My Life" (written and sung by Stevie Wonder) or Survivor's "High on You" (written by Jim Peterik and Frankie Sullivan).

In other songs, the mood of the lyric is in direct contrast to the vibe of the music, such as in Elton John's deceptively happy ditty "I Think I'm Going to

Kill Myself" (written by Elton John and Bernie Taupin) and "I'll Never Fall In Love Again" (written by Burt Bacharach and Hal David; sung by Dionne Warwick). That bittersweet contrast between the words and the music is often what gives a song its potency.

The greatest intimacy you share with your audience as a songwriter (and your greatest responsibility) is the transference of the mood you have created in a song. Taking that idea a bit further, you're also sharing with your audience the mood you happened to be in as you were creating the song. It's a thought-provoking notion that when you respond emotionally to one of the great classics, you're actually feeling a little bit of what the composer was feeling at the moment of creation, even if it was many years ago. Such is the transcendent, timeless nature of songwriting.

Six Steps to Writing Your First Song

You have your notebook at your side, a gross of freshly sharpened pencils, your recorder in your bag, and you're just waiting for the next drip of inspiration to hit you on the head. First off, don't expect miracles right off the bat. Your first ideas may not be ready for prime time. But there's really no such thing as a bad idea, only ones that need to be refined, clarified, or made more unique and clever — and real. You've got to start somewhere. Try to find some time each day to write. Before long, those moments you set aside will become an oasis in the often dry climate of a typical day. The more you practice your craft, the better your odds of coming up with that one special song that the world wants to hear.

Songwriting takes an enormous amount of patience and hard work. Fortunately, there's a lot of fun to be had along the way. In that spirit, here are the six steps to writing your first song:

1. **Find a message you feel passionate about.** Choose a cause that resonates with you. Write about the girl you've been too insecure to ask out or that guy who you wish would take notice of you. Write about what interests you. Write about what you know. Keep it simple. If a subject is vital to you, it just might be vital to others as well. Similarly, if you don't care about a subject, don't expect others to either.

2. **Find a simple melody.** So many new songwriters get in over their heads trying to be complex to win friends and influence publishers. Songwriters are not paid by the note — you're rewarded by the connections you make in the synapses of your audiences' brains. Often the easiest melodies are the longest lasting.

Book VII

Writing Songs and Music

3. **Find a simple set of chord changes.** Search your guitar or a piano keyboard for this needed element of your song, or search the Internet or local clubs for the musicians who can furnish your words and melodies with a comfortable music bed. (Chapter 1 in Book II gets you started playing chords.)

4. **Find a place to write.** Find a quiet, pastoral setting to clear your mind, light some incense, and let the melodies and emotions flow. If this isn't possible, any chaotic subway station will do. Other key areas to write: supermarkets, flea markets, soccer matches, PTA meetings, in the car, and anywhere else where the distractions merge to zero.

5. **Be inspired by your guitar or other instrument.** Pick up any old instrument that's lying around the house and see if you can coax some sound out of it. It's really all about what you're hearing *in your head.* If you can imagine what the finished song will sound like, you can write it on your late Uncle Louie's banjo.

6. **Find the confidence within yourself to put your heart and soul on the line and share your song with others.** It's through this loop of constant feedback that you discover how to improve your songs. Resist the urge to discount everything but positive reaction. Resist the urge to devalue the positive reactions. Breathe in the accolades and weigh the brickbats. Take it all in, but before making any changes, always check it against your heart for the truth.

Chapter 2

Whipping Your Song into Shape: Song Forms

*W*hen the average listener hears a new song on the radio, she probably doesn't turn to her friend and say, "Wow, awesome pre-chorus — I love how it sets up the hook!" Nonetheless, every song is built upon a structure. The framework can follow any of several tried-and-true patterns, or it can break the mold and go where no song has gone before.

Knowing basic song *forms* (or *formats*) helps guide you as you're constructing a song. It also helps identify what you're doing instinctively. It's important to understand the basics of song structure even if you choose to stray from it in certain instances. There is, however, something reassuring to the ear about the use of familiar song organization that can help a songwriter sound immediately more professional and commercial.

In this chapter you take a look at many of the most commonly used and successful song forms. You see how a song is broken down to its basic modular components and how the various sections can be organized to create a synergy that is greater than the sum of its parts.

Talking the Talk

Before you look at song forms, it's important to understand the terminology songwriters use when they're talking shop. Here are the main terms for the various sections of a song:

- ✔ **Intro:** This section, which starts out the song, is typically an abbreviated instrumental form of the chorus or sometimes the verse. Its purpose is to get the ear ready and introduce all that is to come. Listen to any radio station. The majority of the songs you hear will have some form of intro, and your "tune-out factor" will be directly affected by how effective the writers and arrangers are at catching your attention right off the bat.

- ✔ **Verse:** The purpose of the verse is to reveal the storyline of the tune. It helps propel the listener to the chorus while conveying the song's basic mood and message. The words, or lyrics, of the verse, tend to expand from verse to verse with new information added to move the story along. The melody and chord pattern of the verse is usually the same from verse to verse, except for minor variations in melody usually to make a lyric fit.

- ✔ **Pre-chorus:** This section, also known as the "B" section and the set-up, among other nicknames, is the optional section preceding the chorus that provides a little fresh terrain both lyrically and chordally before pressing on to the chorus. It's usually no more than eight bars in length and sometimes contains the identical lyric each time it comes around. The decision to use a pre-chorus is strictly on a "need-to-use" basis. If a song is propelled sufficiently to the chorus without it, then you don't really need the extra baggage.

- ✔ **Chorus:** The chorus is the "money section" of a song — which is to say that if you've done your job well, this is the part that people will go around singing as they plunk down their hard-earned money to own a copy for themselves. This section usually contains the title or *hook* of the song either at the beginning or end of the chorus. The chorus features a signature phrase or musical figure that's repeated throughout the song and serves as the main identifying portion of the song. Musically and lyrically, choruses tend to be identical except for minor variations. (One exception to this generality is the song, often a country song, that saves the surprise lyrical payoff for the last chorus and is therefore very different.) In most cases, songwriters like to keep their choruses identical so it's harder for the audience to muff a line in the big sing-along.

- ✔ **Bridge:** The bridge, sometimes called the *release, channel, special,* or *middle 8* (referring to the eight musical measures that the bridge tends to occupy), comes after the second chorus in the majority of pop songs.

It's not a necessity in all songs. It can either contain lyrics or be instrumental in nature. Whether the bridge contains words or not, its main function is to give the ear some fresh real estate to land on.

✔ **Coda:** A special ending section, also called an *outro* or a *tag,* that can be added to the end of a song. It's typically a kind of grand finale.

Now that you see the various components that make up a song, take a look at the various ways of organizing them in the following sections. Again, there's no right or wrong way, only what *sounds* right or wrong to the ear. The sections of the song are each designated by a letter, the first melodic section you hear (generally the verse) is "A." The second melodic section you hear is designated "B," and the third section is called "C." The fourth section (usually the bridge) is then called "D." If you repeat a melodic section, even if the words are different, it's still assigned the same letter.

Dealing with Verses

The basic fundamental section for any song is the verse. Some songs consist of nothing *but* verses.

Book VII

Writing
Songs and
Music

The verse form: AAA

The *verse form* is often referred to as the *AAA form.* This is when different lyrics are placed over the same music and are repeated in close succession. Because the chorus and bridge are often eliminated in this form, the title will often appear in the first or last line of the verse. This form is often used when a story is being told, using each verse to propel the action forward. Church hymns usually fall into the AAA category, as do many folk songs. Many of the songs of Joni Mitchell, Joan Baez, and Judy Collins use the AAA form as well.

It's especially important for your melody to be interesting in this form so it can withstand the repetition of identical sections. Often a musical section can come between verse sections to add interest. Sometimes a writer can throw in a sort of *faux chorus* (that's a section that is chorus-like, but doesn't contain the title hook of the song). Songs like this are generally considered a variation of the AAA in form.

The number of verses in a song written in the AAA form varies widely. Jimmy Webb's song "By the Time I Get to Phoenix" (Glen Campbell's breakthrough hit) only takes three verses to tell the story. There are three well-crafted verses, and each presents a location that the singer is thinking about as he embarks upon his journey away from his former girlfriend in California. The song is about what she'll be doing when the singer arrives at each of three destinations: Phoenix, Albuquerque, and Oklahoma.

The title of the song is only mentioned once, in the first line of the first verse. That's because each verse describes a different location, which Webb has cleverly shown in his first lines. Webb also has a clever use of lyric elsewhere in the song — for example, "She'll just hear that phone keep on ringin' off the wall" is followed by a simple "That's all." True to the verse form, the song tells a story that progresses from verse to verse.

For another example, check out "All Along the Watchtower" by Bob Dylan and made famous by Jimi Hendrix. It consists of three verses and is a good example of the style of lyric writing that Bob Dylan introduced during the 1960s. If you listen carefully to these well-crafted words, you'll hear that there's no hook in the song at all: The title, "All Along the Watchtower," is introduced in one place only, as the first line of Verse 3. Notice, however, that it's probably the best candidate in the song for a title. Dylan could have called the song "Two Riders Were Approaching" or "There Must Be Some Way Out of Here," but neither of these phrases comes close to "All Along the Watchtower" as a great title. Look up some (or all) of the songs in Table 2-1 for more help with this form.

Table 2-1	AAA Song Examples	
Song title	*Songwriter(s)*	*Singers/Performers*
"Amazing Grace"	John Newton	Judy Collins and many others
"Born in the U.S.A."	Bruce Springsteen	Bruce Springsteen
"On Broadway"	Barry Mann, Cynthia Weil, Mike Stoller, Jerry Leiber	The Drifters
"Subterranean Homesick Blues"	Bob Dylan	Bob Dylan, Red Hot Chili Peppers
"Turn, Turn, Turn"	Pete Seeger	The Byrds, Pete Seeger

The two-verse form: AA

In the classic songs that were written by American composers for film and Broadway, a type of form called the *two-verse form,* or *AA form,* arose and became very popular. This form was very common from the 1940s through the 1960s and is the form of choice for many standards. Because of its lack of chorus, it hasn't been used much in the pop music of the 1970s and beyond, but songwriter Lionel Ritchie did use an extended two-verse form for his hit 1980s song "Hello."

This form consists of, as its name implies, only two verses, but in these two verses, a complete and tidy story is told. Each verse is traditionally 16 measures, or *bars,* long. The second verse is usually a musical repeat of the first, but in some songs the second verse resembles the first, beginning the same way, but wraps up differently musically.

If you want to study the AA form in more detail, take a look at the list of other songs to pick from in Table 2-2.

Table 2-2	AA Song Examples	
Song title	*Songwriter(s)*	*Singers/Performers*
"In My Life"	John Lennon, Paul McCartney	The Beatles
"Moon River"	Johnny Mercer, Henry Mancini	Henry Mancini, Stevie Wonder, more than 1,000 recordings by various artists
"Stardust"	Hoagy Carmichael, Mitchell Parish	Willie Nelson and many others
"Walk On By"	Burt Bacharach, Hal David	Dionne Warwick
"White Christmas"	Irving Berlin	Many, made popular by Bing Crosby

Book VII

Writing Songs and Music

The AABA Form

The form known as AABA was *the* form of choice in the first half of the 20th century. It's still used today in songwriting, but has fallen off in popularity. However, it's good to know this form because you never know when it'll be the perfect fit for the song you're writing.

The basics of the AABA form

In the *AABA form,* the A sections are the verse sections, and the B section is a *bridge.* In other forms, B represents whatever section comes second in the song. The title is usually placed either in the first or the last line of each verse and is in the same place each time it comes around.

The *bridge* is a section that provides a contrast to the verse sections by using different chords, a different melody, and sometimes a shift in the focus in the lyrics. It provides an interlude between verses, which can be very effective if it's done well.

In the classic AABA song, the A sections are usually eight bars in length and constitute the main melody of the song. Each of the three A sections has a different set of words, although the last verse section can be a repeat of the first, as is the case in the song "Monday, Monday" performed by The Mamas and The Papas (written by John Phillips). In fact, all three verses can be the same, as in John Lennon and Paul McCartney's "Do You Want to Know a Secret?" But these are exceptions to the rule and you won't find many songs that repeat verses like that. Songwriters usually compose three separate sets of lyrics for the verse sections of the AABA form.

The AABA form continues to be used today in many styles of music — country, gospel, Christian, pop, jazz, theatre, and film — but not as often as it once was. The form can be used to provide a very effective emotional satisfaction: The first two verses establish the main melody of the song, and then when the bridge is sung, it provides a different feeling because of its contrasting quality. Thus, the return to the last verse provides an emotionally satisfying return to what was presented before.

There are always exceptions to every rule — that's what makes life (and songs) interesting. Some AABA songs don't introduce the title in the first or last line of each verse. "The Christmas Song" (written by Mel Torme and Robert Wells) is an example of this. Everyone knows this song ("Chestnuts roasting on an open fire . . ."), but the title, "The Christmas Song," doesn't appear in the lyrics at all because the title describes what the song is about and it's not a phrase that would sound good in the song itself.

Another example of a different placement for the title is George and Ira Gershwin's famous song "I Got Rhythm." The title appears at the beginning of the first verse, and then gets transformed in the next two verses. In the second verse it becomes "I got daisies," and in the third verse, it's "I got starlight." This is a great trick, the same one used by songwriter Jimmy Webb in "By the Time I Get to Phoenix." Take note of it — you may want to do the same thing in a song of your own someday.

A real classic, "Over the Rainbow," was sung by Judy Garland in the film *The Wizard of Oz*. This is a great example of an AABA song with an added section at the end called a *coda*. The verses have a flowing feeling to them with the expansive quality of the words ("Somewhere over the rainbow, bluebirds fly"). This is perfectly contrasted by the quick movement of words in the bridge ("Where troubles melt like lemon drops away above the chimney tops"). The bridge provides a perfect interlude between the second and third verses.

Table 2-3 shows some great AABA songs for you to explore in order to discover more about the form.

Table 2-3	AABA Song Examples	
Song title	*Songwriter(s)*	*Singers/Performers*
"Blue Moon"	Richard Rodgers, Lorenz Hart	Chris Issak, Willie Nelson, and many others
"Just the Way You Are"	Billy Joel	Billy Joel
"Save the Last Dance for Me"	Doc Pomus, Mort Shuman	The Drifters
"Something"	George Harrison	The Beatles
"Will You Still Love Me Tomorrow?"	Carole King, Gerry Goffin	The Shirelles

The extended AABA form: AABABA

Beginning in the 1960s, some songwriters began using an extended version of the AABA form, called the *AABABA*. This is merely the AABA form with an additional bridge and a final verse. This final verse may be a repeat of a previous verse or even just a part of one of the previous verses.

John Lennon and Paul McCartney's song "Yesterday" uses an extended AABA form. The title appears as the first line in each verse except for Verse 2, where the word *suddenly* is used instead. The title also appears in the last line of each verse, and in the last line of the bridge, and the final verse is just a repeat of Verse 3.

This AABABA form is also used in other Beatles songs (written by John Lennon and Paul McCartney), including the following:

- "I'll Follow the Sun"
- "I Want to Hold Your Hand"

✔ "Hey Jude"

✔ "Hard Day's Night"

✔ "Long and Winding Road"

✔ "I Call Your Name"

Things get a little more complicated in a few of McCartney's songs. "Michelle," for example, has a form of AABABABA. The fourth verse is not sung but is instead played as an instrumental. The words in the second verse are repeated in the third and fifth verses, so all of these verses are the same. All three bridges have different words, however. This is a very unusual and innovative formal structure. Because the formal structures in *many* of the songs written by McCartney and Lennon are very advanced, you can get a lot out of studying them. (Don't you wish your studies in school were this much fun?)

The Verse-Chorus Form: ABAB

The verse-chorus form is the most common in today's pop, rock, gospel, R&B, and country music. In the *verse-chorus form,* or *ABAB form,* verses alternate with a chorus section. The chorus is always the same except, perhaps, at the end, where you can extend it to make a really great ending for the song.

The story that the song unfolds is contained within the verses. When the chorus is sung, it usually proclaims the title as the hook. Pop or rock songs that work well usually start out right away with a line that people relate to; then the words of the verse pull the listeners in, get them hooked. But the power comes when the chorus is sung. A good chorus is something that listeners really take notice of; and because it's repeated over and over, if it's a great chorus, the song will imprint itself in listeners' minds.

The basic version

Here's an example of a basic ABAB song: "Goodbye Yellow Brick Road" by Elton John and Bernie Taupin has two verses that tell the story about a person who is tired of the high life and wants to return to his life on the farm. The chorus emphasizes his feelings, bidding farewell to the "yellow brick road" and stating that he's going back to his former life on the farm. No matter how many verses there are in the song, the chorus will always apply because it describes the main topic of the song. Notice that it starts and ends with the title, which helps it stick in the listener's mind as the song's hook.

The best place to put a title in a verse-chorus song is in the first line of the chorus. Some songwriters place the title in both the first line and the last line (as in "Goodbye Yellow Brick Road").

Another great verse-chorus song comes from Alicia Keys, the first artist to be released on legendary producer and Arista Records founder Clive Davis's new label, J Records. Her song "Fallin'" is a great example of a very simple verse-chorus song elevated to high art by a smoldering vocal and a brilliant arrangement. Two chords make up the entire song — the basic blues progression that you've heard in the classic song "I Put a Spell on You" by Screamin' Jay Hawkins (covered by The Animals in the '60s — and note the Hawkins song does eventually resolve to a third chord, unlike Ms. Keys's). The progression in "Fallin'" that toggles between E minor and B minor has never sounded more elegant. The structure is the verse-chorus form with a very simple chorus. The song gains its momentum through repetition and the swelling of strings and background vocals in the arrangement. The song begins with a gospel-drenched *a cappella* (group or solo singing without musical accompaniment) opening line: "I keep on falling in and out of love with you" and then continues with the verse supported by piano:

"Fallin'" written and sung by Alicia Keys

Verse 1 (A)

I keep on falling in and out with you
Sometimes I love ya, sometimes you make me blue
Sometimes I feel good, at times I feel used
Lovin' you, darlin', makes me so confused

Chorus (B)

I keep on falling in and out of love with you
I never loved someone the way that I love you

Verse 2 (A)

Oh I never felt this way
How do you give me so much pleasure
Cause me so much pain
Just when I think I'm takin' more than would a fool
I start fallin' back in love with you

Chorus (B)

I keep on falling in and out of love with you
I never loved someone the way that I love you

Coda

I'm, I'm, I'm, I'm fallin'
I, I, I, I'm fallin'

Fallin', Fallin'
I keep on fallin' in and out of love with you
I never loved someone the way that I love you
I'm fallin' in and out of love with you
I never loved someone the way that I love you
I'm fallin' in and out of love with you
I never loved someone the way that I love you

Words and Music by Alicia Keys ©2000 EMI April Music, Inc., and Lellow Productions (ASCAP)

"Goodbye Yellow Brick Road" and "Fallin'" stick to the verse-chorus form exactly. Sometimes, however, a verse-chorus song will present two verses before the first chorus is sung. This form variation would be described as AABAB, and you can look up the lyrics to some (or all) of the songs listed in Table 2-4 to learn about two verses before the chorus. This approach is sometimes an effective way to get into the feel of the song before the chorus arrives.

Table 2-4	AABAB Song Examples	
Song title	*Songwriter(s)*	*Singers/Performers*
"Daniel"	Elton John, Bernie Taupin	Elton John
"Did You Ever Have to Make Up Your Mind"	John Sebastian	The Loving Spoonful
"Helpless"	Neil Young	Crosby, Stills, Nash & Young

If you want more examples of verse-chorus songs in ABAB form, you may want to study songs listed in Table 2-5. As you're reading the lyrics and/or listening to these songs, pay close attention to the placement of the titles and ask yourself what title placement accomplishes.

Table 2-5	ABAB Song Examples	
Song title	*Songwriter(s)*	*Singers/Performers*
"Amazed"	Marv Green, Aimee Mayo, Chris Lindsey	Lonestar
"American Pie"	Don McLean	Don McLean, Madonna
"Foolish Games"	Jewel	Jewel
"I'll Never Break Your Heart"	Albert Manno, Ronnie Broomfield	Backstreet Boys

Song title	Songwriter(s)	Singers/Performers
"If You Ever Have Forever in Mind"	Vince Gill	Vince Gill
"The Wind Beneath My Wings"	Larry Henley, Jeff Silbar	Bette Midler

The verse-chorus form with a pre-chorus: ABC

A *pre-chorus* — a short section that leads up to the chorus — is a great device that you can use when writing a verse-chorus song. The Beatles' "Lucy in the Sky with Diamonds" is an excellent example of a song that uses a pre-chorus with great success. If you don't know the song well, listen to it while reading the words so you can get a good idea of what the pre-chorus sounds like and what it accomplishes. You'll notice that Lennon and McCartney create a pre-chorus (each with different words) before the first two times that the chorus is sung, but not before the last time it's sung.

Book VII

Writing Songs and Music

Grammy Award winner Jim Peterik on your vehicle to success

My first number one song, "Vehicle," performed by the Ides of March, is probably the simplest song I've ever written. The verse just kind of merges seamlessly with the chorus as opposed to being set up by a pre-chorus:

Verse

I'm the friendly stranger in the black sedan
Won't you hop inside my car
I got picture, got candy, I'm a lovable man
And I can take you to the nearest star

Chorus

I'm your vehicle, baby
I'll take you anywhere you wanna go
I'm your vehicle, baby
By now I'm sure you'll know

That I love you (love you),
need you (need you)
Want you, got to have you, child
Great God in heaven you know I love you

*Words and music by Jim Peterik
© 1970/1999, Bald Medusa Music (ASCAP)*

I have to write another one like that! As a songwriter, I tend to devalue the simple songs I write, but those seem to always be the ones that turn out to be the biggest hits. In this example, every section has a hook, climaxing with "Great God in heaven you know I love you." It took me years to figure out what I was doing right in my more successful songs, but it usually boils down to simplicity, relatability, and a great beat.

Think of the pre-chorus as a mini bridge, because like the actual bridge of a song, it's taking your listeners' ears and minds into some new territory. It also allows the lyricist to build the story before hitting the chorus.

The next time you're writing a song, ask yourself whether your chorus would have more impact if it were set up by a pre-chorus. Often a good pre-chorus will have some fresh chord changes that haven't been used in the verse, especially if the chorus is in the same key as the verse.

Songwriter Chad Kroeger and the band Nickleback created a very powerful hit song, using the verse-chorus with pre-chorus. What's innovative about the song "How You Remind Me" is the placement of the title in the pre-chorus instead of the chorus. The pre-chorus leads to a powerful sing-along chorus that's very effective.

In the second verse, the singer tells how he has failed in the past. The pre-chorus is restated with the title and thesis of the song, then the chorus.

The final verse is simply the first verse, but this time a completely stripped-down version using only the vocal and electric guitar, using just the first two lines. The pre-chorus is then repeated, and it leads into a full-stride version of the final chorus accentuated by dramatic breaks from the entire band. In this song, the pre-chorus, like the chorus, uses the same words each time.

The verse-chorus form with a bridge: ABABC

The purpose of a bridge is to provide an interlude between other sections. Verse-chorus songs with bridges are very much a part of today's world.

Vertical Horizon is one of those bands that took many years and multiple albums to become an overnight sensation. Released in 2000, "Everything You Want" became their big breakthrough. In a mere 4 minutes and 17 seconds, it defined what modern rock would sound like — intelligent, concise, catchy, cryptic, and extremely well crafted. The song is basically written in a verse-chorus form with the writer using two verses before hitting the chorus. Starting with a telegraphic electric guitar figure and soon joined by acoustic guitar and bass, the very "in-your-face" vocal starts the verse and immediately pulls you in.

After the first two verses, the song hits the very catchy and repetitive chorus. This is really the part you remember most when you first hear the song. Next comes the third verse, which treads some of the same emotional ground already covered but in a slightly different way. The chorus is now repeated. Following is the bridge — and it's everything a bridge should be: It blazes new ground chordally and thematically, and it raises the stakes as the singer strains for higher notes. Finally, the song enters the fourth verse — the kind of nostalgic looking back that's a perfect wrap-up for this song. Following this is a double chorus — the first a clone of the other two choruses. The repeat chorus changes into the first person, however. Weaving in and out of the song is a magical, moody guitar motif. It's probably as important an element as anything else in the song.

If you like bridges and want to know them better, check out the songs in Table 2-6 and see how they were used to create some pretty big hits.

Table 2-6	ABABC Song Examples	
Song Title	*Songwriter(s)*	*Singers/Performers*
"Hands"	Jewel	Jewel
"Here Comes the Sun"	George Harrison	The Beatles
"I Turn to You"	Diane Warren	Christina Aguilera
"I Want It That Way"	Max Martin, Andreas Carlsson	Backstreet Boys
"Un-break My Heart"	Diane Warren	Toni Braxton

The verse-chorus form with a pre-chorus and a bridge: ABCABCD

This very popular song form, sometimes referred to as *ABCABCD*, pulls out all the stops to convince the listener a song means business. The form includes not only a pre-chorus before every chorus, but also a formal bridge at the center of the song, usually after the second chorus, before the *out chorus* (as the final chorus is sometimes called). The truly daring can further test the audiences' attention span by adding a third verse after the bridge, before the out chorus.

This form expands your chances of getting your lyrical point across, gives you the opportunity to make additional musical statements, and challenges the programming directors at radio stations across the country with songs longer than their formats allow. When using this form, make sure that it doesn't collapse under the weight of too many sections.

A prime example

"Hold on Loosely," the top-ten hit by 38 Special (written by Jim Peterik, Don Barnes, and Jeff Carlisi), is an example of a song that just flat out works in this form, as validated by its continued airplay. Take a look at how the song builds as you sing along and you'll see why it has become a staple at classic rock radio:

"Hold on Loosely" written by Jim Peterik, Don Barnes, and Jeff Carlisi

Verse 1 (A)

You see it all around you
Good lovin' gone bad
And usually it's too late when you
Realize what you had

Pre-chorus (B)

My mind goes back to the girl I met
Long years ago, who told me

Chorus (C)

Just hold on loosely
But don't let go
If you cling too tightly
You're gonna lose control
Your baby needs someone to believe in
And a whole lotta space to breathe in

Verse 2 (A)

It's so damn easy
When your feelings are such
That you overprotect her
That you love her too much

Pre-chorus (B)

My mind goes back to the girl I met
Long years ago, who told me

Chorus (C)

Just hold on loosely
But don't let go
If you cling too tightly
You're gonna lose control
Your baby needs someone to believe in
And a whole lotta space to breathe in

Bridge (D)

Don't let her slip away
Sentimental fool

Don't let your heart get in the way
Yeah, yeah, yeah

Verse (A)

You see it all around you
Good lovin' gone bad
And usually it's too late when you
Realize what you had

Chorus (C)

So hold on loosely
But don't let go
If you cling too tightly
You're gonna lose control
Your baby needs someone to believe in
And a whole lot of space to breathe in

As you may have noticed, the last verse bypasses the pre-chorus and heads right to the final chorus. By this time in the song, the writers felt it was no longer necessary and more important to get to the main hook.

Some variations of the form

One of Jim's favorite songs that he's ever co-written is "I Can't Hold Back," a hit for his band, Survivor, in 1985. It starts with an intricately picked guitar intro figure, then hits the first verse, "There's a story in my eyes . . .", then into the pre-chorus, "I can feel you tremble when we touch . . .", and into the chorus, "I can't hold back — I'm on the edge . . .". From there it goes unexpectedly into an instrumental version of the pre-chorus and then slides into a spacey bridge, "Another shooting star goes by . . .", and then glides straight into the pre-chorus. Next, instead of going into a chorus, the song returns to a reprise of the verse, "There's a story in my eyes. . . .", and then it skips the pre-chorus and goes directly to the out chorus. Whew-boy! When Jim and his writing partner, Frankie Sullivan, were sitting at the piano at the Record Plant recording studio in Los Angeles with the producer, Ron Nevison, throwing around ideas, Jim wasn't sure this unorthodox structure was going to work,

Book VII

Writing Songs and Music

but the next day when they recorded it, it was magic. The experience taught Jim to not be afraid to play around with song structure. Take a look:

"I Can't Hold Back" written by Jim Peterik and Frankie Sullivan

Verse 1 (A)

There's a story in my eyes
Turn the pages of desire
Now it's time to trade those dreams
For the rush of passion's fire

Pre-chorus 1 (B)

I can feel you tremble when we touch
And I feel the hand of fate
Reaching out to both of us

Verse 2 (A)

I've been holding back the night
I've been searching for a clue from you
I'm gonna try with all my might
To make this story line come true

Pre-chorus 2 (B)

Can ya feel me tremble when we touch
Can you feel the hand of fate
Reaching out to both of us
This love affair can't wait

Chorus (C)

I can't hold back, I'm on the edge (I can't hold back)
Your voice explodes inside my head
I can't hold back, I won't back down
Girl it's too late to turn back now

Bridge (D)

Another shooting star goes by
And in the night the silence speaks to you and I
And now the time has come at last
Don't let the moment come too fast

Pre-chorus 3 (B)

I can feel you tremble when we touch
And I feel the hand of fate
Reaching out to both of us

Verse 3 (A)

There's a story in my eyes
Turn the pages of desire
Now it's time to trade those dreams
For the rush of passion's fire

Chorus (C)

I can't hold back, I'm on the edge (I can't hold back)
Your voice explodes inside my head
I can't hold back, I won't back down
Girl it's too late to turn back now

Pre-Chorus 4 (B)

I can see you tremble when we touch
Oooh, and I feel the hand of fate
Reaching out to both of us
This love affair can't wait

I can't hold back, I can't hold back
I can't hold back, I can't hold back

Words and music by Jim Peterik and Frankie Sullivan III © 1984 EMI Virgin Music Inc., Easy Action Music and Rude Music. All rights for Easy Action Music controlled and administered by EMI Virgin Music Inc. All rights reserved. International Copyright secured. Used by permission.

Listen to the songs of John Lennon and Paul McCartney and the various Motown writers. It's a great way to learn about the variations of song structure.

Even though the songs in Table 2-7 are older, they set the template for much of the new music you currently hear every day and demonstrate some non-standard song forms.

Book VII

Writing Songs and Music

Table 2-7	Structure Variations	
Song Title	*Songwriter(s)*	*Singers/Performers*
"I'm Looking Through You"	John Lennon, Paul McCartney	The Beatles
"My Girl"	Smokey Robinson, Ronald White	The Temptations
"Standing in the Shadows of Love"	Holland/Dozier/Holland	The Four Tops
"We Can Work It Out"	John Lennon, Paul McCartney	The Beatles

"Drops of Jupiter" (written and performed by Train) is one of those songs that makes an immediate impression. Usually with brilliant songs like this, you remember where you were and what you were feeling when it first hit your ears. It's an example of a song that takes a standard tried-and-true song form and twists it here and there to make it sound unusual and fresh — a pop/rock masterpiece. The song starts with the piano figure of the verse. The first verse contains the only reference to the song's title. So much for the traditional wisdom of driving the hook into the ground — but that didn't seem to hurt sales.

By the way, the music charts, such as *Billboard, Radio and Records,* and so on, have taken to putting the words ("Tell Me") after the song's title for those of us who can't identify it by its cryptic title, "Drops of Jupiter."

The chorus comes next, although it's not a traditional type of chorus in that the title is never stated. After the chorus, a significant instrumental signature is created by a string section. We now hit the second verse. It follows the same structure of the first verse, except that the last line before the second chorus is extended for extra impact. The song cleverly uses modern-day references such as "tae-bo" and later on, "soy latte." What's unusual in the second chorus is that although the rhythm of the words and melody stay the same, practically all the words are different. The hook "Tell me" is about all that stays the same. Moving the action along in a chorus as opposed to marking time is unique.

A bridge follows the second chorus, although not in the traditional sense in changing keys and mood. It's more chant-like and modifies the action by changing up the rhythm of the words. The arrangement then breaks down to just piano and voice again, and the song enters the final chorus. Again, the writers break form by combining elements of both earlier choruses into one. The song ends with the infectious "Na, na, na" refrain with alternating vocal ad libs lifted from various sections of the song. The last line is a brand-new variation on an earlier passage. The lyrics in this song are very open to interpretation. The majestic tone of the music matches perfectly the broad scope of the lyrics.

There are some great songs out there that don't play by the rules. The writers have ignored the standard forms to create something truly unique. "Drops of Jupiter" by Train can be corralled, kicking and screaming, into some kind of traditional form but it's really a maverick. As an experiment, try challenging the listener by shifting your sections around to make your song stand out from the pack of cookie-cutter tracks. If your song becomes confusing and unfocused when playing it for others, it's time to go back to the drawing board.

Practice Makes Perfect

Often the best way of learning a craft is taking the best examples you can find and start tearing them apart to see what makes them tick. Pick five of your favorite songs, which could be anything from a 1940s standard to the latest by Radiohead. Listen to the song and analyze its structure by writing out the lyrics (you can find accurate transcripts of lyrics on many music sites on the Internet or printed on the CD label). It should then be easy to note the song's various sections by verse, pre-chorus, chorus, bridge, out chorus, and whatever other spare parts you may encounter. See if the songs you like the most follow any particular pattern — if so, you may want to pattern your song after that form.

When analyzing the structure of your favorite songs, notice the various ways in which the great ones push the boundaries of song craft to the max. As you listen and make notes, take an especially close look at the following areas:

✔ **What is it about each section that sets it apart from the rest of the song?** For instance, notice how the story builds verse to verse as the song unfolds, how the chorus lifts the song to new heights, how the bridge does its job by giving the listener some fresh chord changes and some new emotional ammunition.

✔ **What is truly unusual or original in the songs you love the most?** Most songs you encounter that have survived to make a difference in this world have one or more elements that elevate it above the pack. "We Built This City" (written by Bernie Taupin, Peter Wolf, Martin Page, and Dennis Lambert), the '80s hit for Jefferson Starship, starts right out with the sing-along chorus. Certain songs defy logic by shifting their key signature down on the last chorus instead of up. Find those special elements in the songs that really get your attention.

✔ **Where do the titles appear in your favorite songs?** The traditional practice of placing the title at the beginning of the chorus is often disregarded by daring writers. Notice songs that position their title at the end of the chorus, in the verse or pre-chorus, or that dispense with it altogether.

Book VII

Writing Songs and Music

Chapter 3

Scales and Modes, Moods and Melodies

. . . .

. . . .

Sometimes you have more of an idea about the direction you want your melody to move in than which notes you're going to use to create your melody. You probably have an idea of the mood you want to convey with your music, without thinking about whether the melody should rise, fall, or take on any specific shape. If you're writing with a sense of directional movement — that is, up and down the staff — there are times you can benefit from limiting yourself to notes within a *scale* or *mode*.

There are 12 different pitches in the Western *chromatic scale*. That's the total number of notes that are available in any one octave. But there are many other combinations of those notes — other scales — and if you don't know at least several of them frontward and backward, you should work on that, because it can benefit your composing tremendously. The other scales have fewer than 12 notes, boiling them down to as few as five or as many as seven.

✔ Diatonic scales have seven different pitches in them.

✔ Pentatonic scales have five different pitches in them.

In this chapter, the words *scale* and *mode* mean pretty much the same thing: a particular selection of successive notes within an octave. You will encounter both terms, so both appear here, too.

Major and Minor Modes and the Circle of Fifths

Different modes and scales can evoke different moods. Major scales are good for happy, lively, calming moods. The minor ones are great communicators of sadness, seriousness, and introspection.

Figures 3-1 and 3-2 show two examples of nearly identical melodies in terms of directional movement. Figure 3-1 is in a major mode, and Figure 3-2 is in a minor mode.

Figure 3-1:
This simple melody is in major mode.

Figure 3-2:
Here's the same melody in minor mode.

Play those pieces on a guitar, and you can easily hear the difference in mood between these two examples without even knowing what written key they're in (we deliberately left out the key signature). The melody in Figure 3-1 is actually in the key of F major, and the one in Figure 3-2 is in F minor. Note that even though the directional shape of the notes on the staffs is identical, the pieces sound different because the first example is in a major mode and the second example is in a minor mode.

Figures 3-3 and 3-4 show the melodies with their proper key signatures.

Getting moody

It's no big secret that playing a good song is an easy way to set the mood of a room. For some reason, that's doubly true in film. How many times have you watched a film with a wall-to-wall soundtrack of busy, unconnected pop songs and had it spoil the picture for you? But how long does it take to get the creepy but incredibly simple soundtracks of films like *Halloween* or *Friday the 13th* out of your head after watching them?

The connection between music and mood isn't even confined to the human realm, either: Birds, bees, and four-legged animals of all sizes modulate their vocal utterances to try to attract mates or scare away competition. And if you think dogs barking isn't musical, take one more listen to the Jingle Dogs' *Christmas Unleashed.*

The ancient Greeks believed that not only did music itself invoke mood and even provoke certain behaviors, but that the *modes* the songs were written in were just as responsible. The original name for the Greeks' set of seven musical scales was *échos,* later renamed *modus* by the Romans who adopted the system.

Plato himself recommended that soldiers preparing for war should listen to music written in Dorian and Phrygian modes (more on these modes later in this chapter). In a modern context, that would mean that before heading off for any great confrontation, one should listen to songs like The Doors' "Light My Fire," Steppenwolf's "Born to Be Wild," Jefferson Airplane's "White Rabbit," and Yngwie Malmsteen's "Heavy E Phrygian." On the other hand, Plato discouraged these same soldiers from listening to songs in the Lydian or Ionian modes because it would interfere with their bloodlust. Therefore, putting on R.E.M.'s "Man on the Moon" is not a good idea before going off to war.

Plato and Aristotle also believed that an affinity toward certain musical modes were insights into a person's character, and that people who were fond of music in the Ionian, Aeolian, and Locrian modes were too relaxed and easygoing to do well in high-power political or military positions. After reading this chapter, you may want to take a look at the sort of music you prefer listening to and see what musical modes most often pop up in your personal CD collection.

Book VII

Writing Songs and Music

Figure 3-3:
The melody in major mode is shown with the F major key signature.

Figure 3-4:
The same melody in minor mode is shown with the F minor key signature.

The Circle of Fifths (Figure 3-5) is a handy tool when thinking about scales, moods, and keys. Each position on the circle contains two keys: the major key and its relative minor, which share the same key signature. The major keys are given capitalized letters here, and the minor keys are in lowercase. In the Circle of Fifths, every time you move one letter clockwise from the C major/A minor position at the top, you add a sharp to the key signature. And at every point counterclockwise from C major/A minor, you add a flat. The number of sharps or flats in a key corresponds to the number of fifths away from C that key is located. For example, the key of D is located two fifths above C and, interestingly enough, has two sharps.

Here are a couple of tips for using the Circle of Fifths when you're composing:

✔ When you're writing something in a particular major key and you want to change the mood a little (maybe make it a little sadder or darker), you can use the relative minor scale of the key. For example, if your original melody was in G major, you could change to E minor for the sad parts. Doing this makes it unnecessary to change the key signature, though you may have to use a few *accidentals* (sharping or flatting individual notes) here and there. Figure 3-5 shows you at a glance which major keys coordinate with which minor keys.

✔ Another common practice in composition is to write the darker, sadder bits in the minor key of the original major. For example, go from a G major scale to a G minor. As you can see from the Circle of Fifths chart in Figure 3-5, the parts written in G major would be written with the key signature for G, which has a single sharp (F♯). The parts in G minor, then, would require the signature from *its* relative major, which is B♭. The key signature for B♭ has two flats: a B♭ and an E♭.

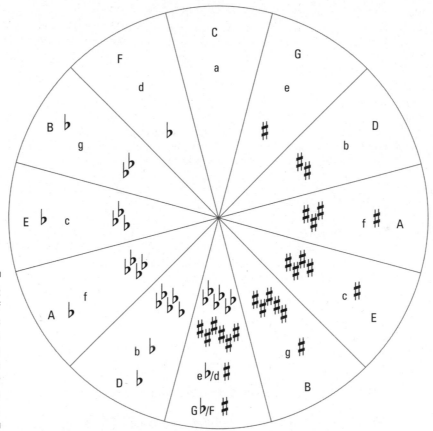

Figure 3-5:
The Circle of Fifths shows the relation between major keys and their relative minors.

Book VII

Writing Songs and Music

Moods à la Modes

Just playing a mode or scale without any particular melody in mind can inspire you to come up with a melody. An easy way to start experiencing a few different modes is to play scales on all white piano keys, but starting on the different notes within the C scale. There are seven modes (often called *church modes*, although they're really ancient Greek) that you can make this way because there are seven unique white piano keys in an octave.

For example: Play a scale from F to F using only the white keys. Note that you will play the B natural instead of the B flat that is found in the key of F major. It turns out, you just played a scale in the *Lydian* mode, and it sounds a little different from the old *do re mi* that you learned as a kid.

There are seven modes, just as there are seven white keys on a piano. You can try all seven modes by starting and finishing on other notes using only the white keys. Can you hear the interesting mood possibilities lurking in these modes? You can gain a lot of ideas by sampling the different modes and deciding which mode evokes which moods.

We look at all seven modes a little more closely in the following sections. It's true that for simplicity's sake we're illustrating the modes using only the white keys on the piano keyboard. But of course, each mode can be based on any note, and the notes work the same on guitar. It's the different pattern of the intervals between the notes that defines each mode.

A half step is the musical interval equivalent to a fret on a guitar. One fret is one half step. A whole step is two frets.

Quite a few other scales and modes aren't used much at all in Western music — and by *Western* we don't mean cowboy campfire songs, we mean European music and its descendents. Some non-Western scales have pitches between half steps called *quarter tones*. Some use intervals that sound odd or even out of tune to the Western ear. The subject of modes and scales is a huge one, but if you intend to compose music where a keyboard of some kind is involved, you probably won't have any way of conveying pitches in some of the more exotic modes.

Ionian (the major scale)

When you play seven ascending white keys starting with C, you get the Ionian mode (Figure 3-6). To build an Ionian scale on another note besides C, you use the whole-step (W), half-step (H) pattern: WWHWWWH.

Figure 3-6:
The Ionian mode should sound famil-iar, because it's the major scale.

Notice something familiar about this? You're right — this is the same pattern used to build major scales today.

Dorian

Figure 3-7 shows the D Dorian mode. To build a Dorian mode on another note besides D, you would use the pattern WHWWWHW.

Figure 3-7:
The Dorian mode sounds melancholy and full of bittersweet longing.

The Dorian mode is most commonly heard in Celtic music and early American folk songs derived from Irish melodies. Songs written in Dorian mode sound melancholy and soulful because the final note of the scale doesn't quite resolve itself, so it feels almost like a question left unanswered. One of the most famous pieces based on the Dorian mode is "So What" by Miles Davis, from his famous 1959 recording, *Kind of Blue*.

Phrygian

Figure 3-8 shows the E Phrygian mode. To build a Phrygian mode on another note besides E, you would use the pattern HWWWHWW.

Figure 3-8:
The Phrygian mode can give your music a bit of exotic spice.

Most flamenco music is written in the Phrygian mode, which has a bright, Middle Eastern sound to it that works well with folk and traditional dance music. Many modern composers and guitarists commonly use Phrygian

Book VII

Writing Songs and Music

modes with major scales (instead of minor scales) because it sounds brighter and less melancholic than the minor scale.

Lydian

Figure 3-9 shows the F Lydian mode. To build a Lydian mode on another note besides F, you would use the pattern WWWHWWH.

Figure 3-9:
The Lydian mode has something of a surprising, jazzy feel to it.

The Lydian mode is the complete opposite of the Ionian mode/major scale, so it feels as solid and bright as a major scale but the intervals are surprising and unexpected. This is a popular mode among jazz musicians who enjoy using a mixture of major and minor chord progression in inventive ways.

Mixolydian

Figure 3-10 shows the G Mixolydian mode. To build a Mixolydian mode on another note besides G, you would use the pattern WWHWWHW.

Figure 3-10:
The Mixolydian mode is often used for blues and bluesy rock music.

Mixolydian is similar to Lydian in the sense of having a major-scale feel with minor intervals, and it's a great mode to work within to give a bluesy feel to your compositions. Mixolydian mode is another popular scale for solo musicians looking for a counterpoint to the Ionian key of the song.

Aeolian (the natural minor scale)

Figure 3-11 shows the A Aeolian mode. To build an Aeolian scale on another note, the pattern you'd use is WHWWHWW. This should also look familiar to you — it is the whole-step, half-step pattern used to build minor scales today.

Figure 3-11:
The Aeolian mode can convey great sorrow, regret, and despair.

The intervals of Aeolian mode create the same feel as many modern blues songs. Songs composed in Aeolian mode have a strong sense of sadness. The final note of an Aeolian scale feels resolved in a completely different sense than the final note of the Ionian. If the Dorian mode reflects melancholy, the Aeolian reflects despair. Check out Neil Young's "Cowgirl in the Sand" for a great example.

Book VII

Writing Songs and Music

Locrian

Figure 3-12 shows the B Locrian mode. To build a Locrian scale on any other note, you would use the pattern HWWHWWH.

Figure 3-12:
The Locrian mode sounds a bit twisted and wrong.

Locrian mode is considered to be so unstable that most composers declare it unworkable. Few songs are written in the Locrian mode, which has led some music theorists to label it a "theoretical" mode. You find it occasionally used in heavy metal. This mode exists because all seven notes of the Ionian scale could form it in a mathematical sense, but the relationship between intervals in the Locrian mode is difficult for many composers to work with. Music that is composed within this mode sounds unsettling, disturbing, and just a little bit off. Listen to the synthesizer melody at the beginning of Rush's "YYZ" for an example, or try playing "Three Blind Mice" in a Locrian mode — it sounds like incidental music from a Tod Browning film.

These modes are good tools for writing *tonal* music (music that conforms to a scale or mode and adheres to a tonal center or key). By limiting yourself to notes within a particular mode — that is, notes that make some harmonic sense together — you may find it easier to write something engaging for most listeners. Your composition style is partly a product of your limitations, and modes are limitations. Working within limitations can help you define your style. It's like tennis: It wouldn't be as fun without the net and the lines that define the court.

The Pentatonic Scale

There is one kind of scale that is fairly common throughout the world — despite all the other musical differences among various cultures. That would be the *pentatonic scale,* also called the *five-toned scale.* As you find out in Books III and IV, the pentatonic scale is the guitar soloist's best friend. One can refer to a major pentatonic scale or a minor pentatonic scale, but the notes of the major scale are shared with the relative minor key.

For example, Figure 3-13 shows a G major pentatonic scale, and Figure 3-14 shows the pentatonic scale of its relative minor, E minor.

Figure 3-13:
The pentatonic scale is found all over the world.

Figure 3-14:
The E minor pentatonic scale, G's relative minor.

Notice that although these two scales have a different *tonic* note, they share the same five notes: G, A, B, D, and E (which are the first, second, third, fifth, and sixth tones of the major scale). Many of the other scales and modes around the world seem to revolve around this simple scale formula. Every rock 'n' roll guitar soloist on the planet should be able to play a pentatonic scale without even thinking about it.

The Harmonic Minor and Melodic Minor Scales

Two commonly used scales that aren't listed with the preceding modes and scales are the *harmonic minor* and the *melodic minor* scales. These scales differ from the *natural minor* scale (Aeolian mode) — which is basically a scale taken directly from a relative major — in small, but important ways.

- Harmonic minor sharps the 7th note in the scale (Figure 3-15). This note brings the scale a little closer to the A major scale, but other notes in the scale prevent it from sounding too happy.

- The melodic minor scale has different notes when the scale ascends than it does when the scale descends (Figure 3-16). It's like a major scale with a flatted 3rd on the way up, and it's a natural minor on the way down.

Book VII

Writing Songs and Music

Figure 3-15: The A harmonic minor scale contains a G sharp, unlike the A natural minor scale.

Figure 3-16:
The A
melodic
minor scale
is differ-
ent going
up than it
is coming
down.

Melody Writing Exercises

Here are some suggestions of exercises to do while waiting to be inspired to write your song. And who knows? These exercises could well lead to songs.

1. **Try to write a melody using notes from the C major scale while playing a G major chord underneath.**

   The scale from G to G is G Mixolydian mode now. If you want, you could add a flat 7th (F natural) to the chord you're playing for a more playful-sounding combination.

2. **Write a short melody in a major mode (it could be your own or someone else's).**

3. **Rewrite Step 2's melody in a minor mode.**

4. **Write a short melody in a minor mode.**

5. **Rewrite Step 4's melody in a major mode.**

6. **Improvise using notes in the C major scale while playing an F major chord.**

   Sound mysterious? You're in the Lydian mode.

7. **Pick a different mode among the ones discussed in this chapter, one that sounds interesting to you, and try to write a melody that fits its mood.**

8. **Find the pentatonic scales for all major and minor keys.**

   Hint: After you find the major, you can apply it to the relative minor.

Chapter 4

Composing with Chords

· ·

In This Chapter

▶ Getting moody with chords

▶ Making progress with chord progressions

▶ Ending up with cadences

▶ Getting harmony from melody

▶ Exercising your chord harmonization

· ·

The *key signature* of a piece of music governs the main notes within that piece. When you want to escape the key signature within that piece of music, you have to use *accidentals* (sharps, flats, and naturals) to indicate notes outside the key.

You have several octaves' worth of notes on a guitar, but only the notes allowed by the key signature can be used without accidentals in that piece of music. The *scale* of the piece governs the music's tonality — which means breaking free from the original key is a good way to add spice.

Therefore, if you have a song written in C major, the main eight notes that will appear in the song are C natural, D natural, E natural, F natural, G natural, A natural, and B natural. If your song is written in A major, the only notes appearing in that song will be A natural, B natural, C sharp, D natural, E natural, F sharp, and G sharp. In either of these keys, the chords are also made of some combination of the seven notes in each key.

In this chapter, you discover the basics of composing with chords: the moods of various chords, combining chords, creating rhythmic movement, using chord progressions and cadences, and putting together chords and melodies.

Chords and Their Moods

There are two types of major chords:

- **Diatonic chords** are built from the seven notes of a major key signature. The letter name of a diatonic chord (such as A major, A minor, or A augmented) comes from the major scale the chord is built on.

- **Chromatic chords** are built from notes *outside* the major key signature, such as chords built on minor scales. Chords found within minor keys are a little trickier, because nine notes potentially can fit under a single minor key signature when you take the melodic and harmonic minor scales into consideration. (See Chapter 3 in Book VII for more information about the melodic and harmonic minor scales.)

Because the natural, melodic, and harmonic scales are taught as separate scales for musicians to practice, there's a misconception that you have to stick to *one* of these types of minor scales when composing music. But really, you can draw from all three types of minor scales within the same piece of music.

You can let your melodic ideas suggest different chords, for example. This can be a very good way to open up possibilities — by suggesting departures from your key center and adding color to your work. But you could just as easily start with a chord progression and build a melody from there. Thousands of compositions began with a sense of harmonic movement first, followed by melody.

Here's an opportunity for your Muse to step in. Or maybe you could just put your hands on your guitar and listen for the possibilities. To excel at chordal composition you should have a strong knowledge of chords. You should, at the very least, have a working familiarity with following chord qualities in every key, which you get to explore in the following sections:

- Major and minor
- Major and minor 7th
- Dominant 7th
- Major and minor 6th
- Suspended 4th
- 9th and minor 9th
- Diminished
- Augmented
- Minor 7th, flat 5th (also known as half-diminished)

No matter which key you're in, each of those specific chords comes with its particular sonic character, called its *mood,* or quality. Therefore, if you know how minor chords are constructed, and you pick up the guitar and play some minor chords, chances are the sound that comes from that set of chords is closer to what you're looking for than if you just started playing random chords.

Certain chords express certain moods. It's really up to you what sort of mood is to be implied by each chord, but in the following sections we include a short list of our own observations, based on asking students to describe the feelings conveyed by these chords. There are many, many more chord configurations than just these, but the ones that follow are a good start. You have to decide for yourself how each of these chords makes you feel.

A *root* is the main note of the chord and gives the chord it's name. In a C chord, for example, C is the root. A *half step* is the smallest interval in Western music — conveniently, and not coincidentally, each fret on a guitar represents change in pitch of a half step. A whole step is two half steps, or two frets. And when we say *flat* we mean the note one half step lower in pitch; likewise, *sharp* means the next higher half step.

Major

Major chords are happy, simple, honest, bold. They're made from the 1, 3, and 5 tones of the major scale. To build a major chord using half and whole steps, remember: root + 4 half steps + 3 half steps (check out Figure 4-1).

Figure 4-1:
C major.

Minor

Minor chords are sad or serious. They're made from the 1, flat 3, and 5 tones of the major scale. To build a minor chord using half and whole steps, remember: root + 3 half steps + 4 half steps (see Figure 4-2).

Book VII

Writing Songs and Music

Figure 4-2:
C minor.

Major 7th

Major 7th chords are pretty, delicate, sensitive, thoughtful. They're made from the 1, 3, 5, and 7 tones of the major scale. To build a major 7th chord using half and whole steps, remember: root + 4 half steps + 3 half steps + 4 half steps (see Figure 4-3).

Figure 4-3:
C major 7th.

Minor 7th

Minor 7th chords are pensive, moody, introspective. They're made from the 1, flat 3, 5, and flat 7 tones of the major scale. To build a minor 7th chord using half and whole steps, remember: root + 3 half steps + 4 half steps + 3 half steps (take a look at Figure 4-4).

Figure 4-4:
C minor 7th.

Dominant 7th

Dominant 7th chords are sassy, outgoing, strong. They're made from the 1, 3, 5, and flat 7 tones of the major scale. To build a dominant 7th chord using half and whole steps, remember: root + 4 half steps + 3 half steps + 3 half steps (see Figure 4-5).

C7

Figure 4-5:
C dominant
7th.

Major 6th

Major 6th chords are playful. They're made from the 1, 3, 5, and 6 tones of the major scale. To build a major 6th chord using half and whole steps, remember: root + 4 half steps + 3 half steps + 2 half steps (see Figure 4-6).

C6

Figure 4-6:
C major 6th.

Book VII

Writing Songs and Music

Minor 6th

Minor 6th chords are dark, sensuous, troubled. They're made from the 1, flat 3, 5, and 6 tones of the major scale. To build a minor 6th chord using half and whole steps, remember: root + 3 half steps + 4 half steps + 2 half steps (see Figure 4-7).

Cm6

Figure 4-7:
C minor 6th.

Suspended 4th

Suspended 4th chords are regal or martial. They're made from the 1, 4, and 5 notes of the major scale. To build a suspended 4th chord using half and whole steps, remember: root + 5 half steps + 2 half steps (check out Figure 4-8).

Csus4

Figure 4-8:
C sus-
pended 4th.

9th

Ninth chords are energetic and lively. They're made from the 1, 3, 5, and 9 tones of the major scale. To build a 9th chord using half and whole steps, remember: root + 4 half steps + 3 half steps + 3 half steps + 3 half steps (see Figure 4-9).

C9

Figure 4-9:
C 9th.

Minor 9th

Minor 9th chords are sad, tender, complex. They're made from the 1, flat 3, 5, and 9 tones of the major scale. To build a minor 9th chord using half and whole steps, remember: root position + 3 half steps + 4 half steps + 3 half steps + 4 half steps (take a look at Figure 4-10).

Figure 4-10: C minor 9th.

Diminished

Diminished chords are dark, strained, complex. They're made from the 1, flat 3, and flat 5 tones of the major scale. To build a diminished chord using half and whole steps, remember: root + 3 half steps + 3 half steps (see Figure 4-11).

Figure 4-11: C diminished.

Book VII

Writing Songs and Music

Augmented

Augmented chords are anticipatory and full of movement. They're made from the 1, 3, and sharp 5 tones of the major scale. To build an augmented chord using half and whole steps, remember: root position + 4 half steps + 4 half steps (see Figure 4-12).

Figure 4-12:
C aug-
mented.

Minor 7th, flat 5th (also known as half-diminished)

The minor 7th, flat 5th chord is also called the half-diminished chord. No matter what you call them, these chords are despairing, sorrowful, difficult, and deep. They're made from the 1, flat 3, flat 5, and flat 7 tones of the major scale. To build a minor 7th, flat 5th chord using half and whole steps, remember: root + 3 half steps + 3 half steps + 4 steps (see Figure 4-13).

Figure 4-13:
C minor 7th,
flat 5th.

It's important to note that the character of a chord is strongly dependent upon its surroundings. For example, a dark and dissonant chord like a minor 7th, flat 5th sounds dark and dissonant when out there on its own (see Figure 4-14), but if used to pass from one chord to another, it doesn't have the same feeling (see Figure 4-15).

Figure 4-14:
A dissonant
chord all on
its own.

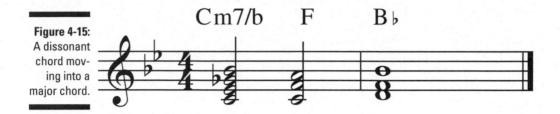

Figure 4-15:
A dissonant chord moving into a major chord.

Putting Chords Together

After you've decided on a chord progression for a section of your piece, you may find it useful to experiment with different chord *voicings,* or all the different ways the same chord can be put together. A simple *triad* (a chord with three different pitches in it) has three different arrangements of its notes within an octave.

A chord's voicing can be arranged in the following ways:

- ✔ Root voicing has the root as the lowest note: C (root), E, G
- ✔ First inversion has the 3 tone as the lowest note: E, G, C
- ✔ Second inversion has the 5 tone as the lowest note: G, C, E

The examples in Figures 4-16 through 4-18 use the C major chord to illustrate.

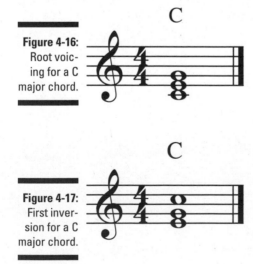

Figure 4-16:
Root voicing for a C major chord.

Figure 4-17:
First inversion for a C major chord.

Figure 4-18:
Second
inversion for
a C major
chord.

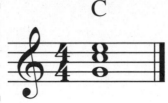

If you already have a melody, you'll find it useful in determining your chord voicings (the arrangement of the notes in the chord). Most often you'll want the melody to represent the top notes in your chords. This will dictate which voicings sound best. If you don't have a melody yet, choosing your chord voicings can help you write one. Try a few chord voicing changes and have your melody grab the top notes. If you don't like the results, invert some chords and try again.

Creating Rhythmic Movement

When composing with chords, determining a rhythmic movement for your chord changes may help. What this means is that you'll decide how often, and on which beats or accents, your chords will generally change. You could have a chord change every measure, every four measures, every two beats, or even every beat within a measure. The choice is yours, but remember that fast-moving melodies can sound awkward if the chords change too quickly. A general rule is that more frequent chord changes work better with slower melodies, but this, like most rules, can be broken from time to time.

Of course, the rhythmic movement of your chord changes can vary as your composition moves along (as shown in Figure 4-19). You don't need to keep the chords changing at the same rate throughout the section of your piece.

Figure 4-19:
Different
melodic
rhythms in
the same
piece of
music.

Writing chord changes out first is just one way to create some underlying structure for your composition. You may want to find some locations in the rhythmic structure of your composition that lend themselves to pivoting your chords out of the key center. It's not difficult to hear in your head where a surprise or a change harmonically would be good. Just don't overdo the surprises and departures. If you're driving down a bumpy road and you hit another bump, it doesn't mean much. Lead the listener into your changes. Build drama, tension, and release.

"Rules" for Major and Minor Chord Progressions

One way to easily build tension and release in your music is to follow some of the simple rules already laid out for you hundreds of years ago by people like Christiaan Huygens and Nicola Vicentino. According to them — and the thousands of musicians who followed — certain sequences of chords, called *chord progressions,* sound nicer than others. Over time, a consensus about the "rules" of chord progressions has come about.

In the following lists, capital Roman numerals indicate major chords, and lowercase Roman numerals stand for minor chords. The numeral itself stands for the note on the major scale the chord is built on. For example, in C major, the I is the C major chord, the ii is D minor, the iii is E minor, the IV is F major, and so on. The ° symbol indicates a diminished chord, and the + symbol is used for augmented chords. (You can find out more about diminished and augmented chords earlier in this chapter.)

"Rules" for major chord progressions include the following:

- I chords can appear anywhere in a progression.
- ii chords lead to I, V, or vii° chords.
- iii chords lead to I, ii, IV, or vi chords.
- IV chords lead to I, ii, iii, V, or vii° chords.
- V chords lead to I or vi chords.
- vi chords lead to I, ii, iii, IV, or V chords.
- vii° chords lead to I or iii chords.

Book VII

Writing Songs and Music

"Rules" for minor chord progressions include the following:

- ✔ i chords can appear anywhere in a progression.
- ✔ ii° or ii chords lead to i, iii, V, v, vii°, or VII chords.
- ✔ III or III+ chords lead to i, iv, IV, VI, ♯vi°, vii°, or VI chords.
- ✔ iv or IV chords lead to i, V, v, vii°, or VII chords.
- ✔ V or v chords lead to i, VI, or ♯vi° chords.
- ✔ VI or ♯vi° chords lead to i, III, III+, iv, IV, V, v, vii°, or VII chords.
- ✔ vii° or VII chords lead to the i chord.

As far as these rules go, they just mean (in the case of major chord progressions) that a ii chord (such as D minor if you're playing in the key of C major) sounds most natural when it leads to I (C major), V (G major), or vii° (B diminished). However, there's absolutely no reason why you can't go from a ii chord to a IV chord, for example — but bear in mind that it won't be what listeners are expecting.

When it comes to departing from the rules, a little goes a long way. You may have to back off after using a couple of unconventional chord changes and play more conventional ones to satisfy your audience. Pop music especially adheres to the rules regarding chord progressions, and is even more didactic than classical music about what sounds "good" and what sounds "strange."

Try the chord progressions with an added 7th to the triads to see if they sound acceptable to you. You'll probably find that some sound good — and some, not so good.

Coming Home with Cadences

An important part of making your music (and audience) breathe is through the use of *cadence,* or a return to the I/i chord from a iv or a V chord. The longer you take to reach this point of cadence, the more tension you can build in your music.

This section covers the four main types of cadences:

- ✔ Authentic
- ✔ Plagal
- ✔ Deceptive or interrupted
- ✔ Half-cadence

A musical phrase can come to an end by simply stopping, of course, but if that stopping position doesn't make "sense" to the listeners, they may not be very happy with you. Ending your song on the wrong note or notes is like ending a conversation with a non sequitur, and you may leave your listeners a little uncomfortable. Some audiences are absolutely delighted to hear music that confounds their expectations, however, and this may be exactly the audience you're trying to reach.

Authentic cadences

Authentic cadences are the most obvious-sounding cadences and are therefore considered the strongest. In an authentic cadence, the harmonic goal of the phrase is the 1 chord via the 5 chord (V or v, depending on whether the piece is in a major or minor key). The cadence occurs when you move from that V/v chord to a I/i chord, as shown in Figure 4-20.

Figure 4-20: Authentic cadences are the most common, obvious-sounding ones.

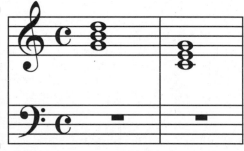

Plagal cadences

The harmonic goal of a *plagal cadence* is ultimately the 1 chord via the 4 (IV or iv) chord, with cadence occurring when the 4 chord moves to the 1 chord. The progressions IV-I, iv-i, iv-I, and IV-i are all possibilities.

The plagal structure originated with Medieval Church music, which was mostly vocal, and is therefore often referred to as the *Amen cadence*. If you're familiar with Gregorian chants at all, or even many modern hymns, then you've heard the Amen cadence in action. It usually happens (no surprise here) at the point where the chanters sing the two-chord "A-men."

Plagal cadences are usually used within a song to end a phrase, and not at the very end of a song, because they're not as decisive-sounding as a perfect cadence (Figure 4-21).

Figure 4-21: Plagal cadences are not as conclusive as authentic cadences.

Deceptive or interrupted cadences

A *deceptive cadence,* or *interrupted cadence,* essentially reaches an ultimate point of tension on a V/v chord, just like the authentic cadence, but it resolves to something *other* than the tonic (I/i) chord — hence, the name *deceptive.* The most common deceptive cadence out there, used 99 times out of 100, is the V/v chord that moves up to a VI/vi chord. The phrase looks and feels like it's about to end and close with the I chord, but instead it moves up to the VI instead, as shown in Figure 4-22.

Other deceptive/interrupted cadences include moving from the V chord to the IV chord, the V chord to the ii chord, and the V chord to the V7.

Deceptive cadences are considered one of the weakest cadences because they invoke a feeling of incompleteness.

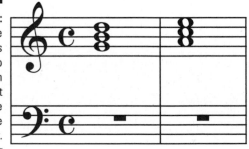

Figure 4-22: Deceptive cadences are nice to use when you want to fake the audience out.

Half-cadences

Half-cadences are a little more confusing than other cadences. The authentic, plagal, and deceptive cadences all occur in musical phrases that resolve before the phrase is complete. In other words, with the other cadences the phrase starts at a point of rest (I/i) and moves through a series of chords to reach either a iv/IV or a v/V chord. It could be as easy as the I/i chord going straight to the V/v chord and back to the I/i, or it could spend 20 hours circling like a plane in a holding pattern between those points, but authentic, plagal, and deceptive will all musically release to the point of rest: the I/i chord.

Half-cadences are the only ones that don't end this way. With a half-cadence, the musical phrase ends at the point of tension — the V/v chord itself. It basically plays to a chord that's not the I/i and stops, resulting in a musical phrase that feels unfinished. Examples would be a V-IV progression, a V-vi progression, a V-ii progression, and a V-V7 progression. It's called a half-cadence simply because it just doesn't feel like it's done yet.

Fitting Chords and Melodies Together

Book VII

Writing Songs and Music

Often, when you're working with just a melody, the basic accompanying harmony is already there in your subconscious. The melody lends itself to the harmony so obviously that accompanying the melodic line is the easiest part of writing the music. You may be aware of which note in your melody represents the tonic note right away, and you may even be aware of very specific chord movements that are screaming out at you from your melody.

Likewise, that cool chord progression you came up with last night is eager to provide you with *structural tones* (also sometimes called *chord tones*) from which a melody can magically emerge.

In the following sections, you find out how to pull harmonies out of melodies and discover the power of chord changes.

Extracting harmony from melody

If you take a simple major scale and consider only the I chord (also called the *tonic*), the IV chord (the *subdominant*), and the V chord (the *dominant*), you can hear fairly simple and obvious suggestions of relationship between notes in the given key that might be used to accompany them. There are, of course, many other possibilities and substitutions, but here we stick with the I, IV, and V chords in the example shown in Figure 4-23.

Figure 4-23: Seeing the scale in I, IV, and V chords.

You can use tones from within the chords (called, as we mentioned, chord tones) and string these tones together in various ways using *non-chord tones*.

First, Figure 4-24 is an example of a simple chord progression that you can use to extract some structural tones from.

Figure 4-24: Seeing structural tones in a simple chord progression.

Now you can extract a melody from these chords using only notes from within each chord — the chord tones (check out Figure 4-25).

Figure 4-25: Extracting chord tones from a chord progression.

Now you can add some passing tones. *Passing tones* close the gaps between structural tones. They make *disjunct* melodies more *conjuct.* Passing tones go in steps and end up stepping into the next structural tone (take a look at Figure 4-26).

Figure 4-26:
Adding passing tones to fill in the structural tones.

If you step away from the tone before stepping back to it, it's called a *neighboring tone* (see Figure 4-27).

Figure 4-27:
Having a little visit with neighboring tones.

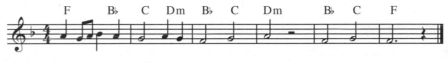

Using chord changes

A chord change is a powerful thing. It's hard to take a chord change lightly. That's why you need to be picky about the choices you make regarding where in the rhythm of your music the chords change.

If your chords change every measure on beat one, that beat will be strengthened. If instead you place the chord changes on beats four *and* one, both of those beats will gain some gravity. A chord change brings some attention to any rhythmic subdivision. It's a good idea to place chord changes strategically to emphasize the rhythmic feel, or groove, of your piece.

Often your music will benefit from adding more chords in between the structural chords you started off with. For this you can go back to your non-chord tones, as shown in the previous section. Some of the non-chord tones you

Book VII

Writing Songs and Music

added while stringing together your chord tones may provide rhythmic accents. Or maybe you just like these notes and want the listener's attention drawn to them. So why not add chord changes at those same moments? You can call these *passing chords*.

Figure 4-28 shows the example again with all the non-chord tones that were added.

Figure 4-28: Adding all the non-chord tones.

Now add some passing tones to go along with the non-chord tones (see Figure 4-29).

Figure 4-29: Adding passing tones again.

That makes for a richer, more colorful phrase, doesn't it? The possibilities are limitless. You could have a chord change every beat, every half beat, or whatever suits your intentions. This would be a good time to study the earlier lists regarding "rules" for major and minor chord progressions. Knowing which chords flow into which can be helpful here. And don't forget about the moods you evoke with your choices. A study of jazz can provide you with some ideas about chord substitutions as well.

On the other hand, there are times when a chord change is distracting and pulls away from the hypnotic, trancelike mantra of your groove. As an example, Ravel's *Boléro* (which was written intentionally as a piece with no structural development) pulls listeners along and drives them deeper and deeper into its feel. When Ravel exhausts the dynamic headroom of his orchestra, he surprises us and wakes us up into a new realm by changing the chord and the tonality all at once, near the very end. This alerts us that the climax is on its way (it also puts the orchestra in a range where there is some additional dynamic power to be tapped into). It's totally unexpected and somewhat disconcerting, but he had to launch an ending somehow.

You're okay when you can use an unexpected wake-up chord change as powerfully as Ravel, but in the meantime be careful not to loosen your hold on the listener with too many chord changes if you've got a good groove on.

You can have more than one musical idea going on at the same moment in the same piece. Three or more are perhaps too many, because confusion ensues and the listener doesn't know where to turn. You always want to retain a sense of focus, even when your music gets chaotic.

You could have your chords change in one rhythmic pattern and have the melody move in another pattern. Mixing it up like that would convey two different rhythmic statements. You might think of it as keeping the non-chord tones and the chord structure and throwing out some of the structural chord tones in your piece. Figure 4-30 shows an example with a tiny bit of polishing.

Book VII

Writing Songs and Music

Figure 4-30:
Melody and harmony, together in perfect . . . well, harmony.

From what you've read in this chapter so far, it should be easy enough to reverse these processes if you had a melody to start with and were looking for the right chords to go along with it. You have to decide which notes in your melody are structural. Then you can determine the key of your piece and where you feel you need to accentuate your melody with chords. The challenge here is to be aware of the many harmonic possibilities available to you for harmonizing your melody. There are more harmonic possibilities in a single note than there are melodic possibilities in a chord.

Exercises for Composing with Chords

This chapter covers a lot of ground. The following exercises are designed to help you distill and apply the information in this chapter to begin your own compositions.

1. **Harmonize an ascending 5th (one letter name clockwise around the Circle of Fifths; see Chapter 3 in Book VII for more on the Circle of Fifths).**

   Find chords that fit with a D note held for two beats followed by an A above held for two beats. Ideas:

   • Start with a D major chord.

   • Start with a B flat major chord.

   • Start with an E minor 7th, flat 5th chord.

   • Start with a G major chord.

2. **Try chord progressions at random.**

   Write the names of a dozen or so chords on small pieces of paper. Make sure you include some of the ones that sound strange to you. You can use any chord in any key. Put them in a hat and shake them up. Pick out four or five of them and write them down in the order you picked them on some staff paper. Compose a melody that makes sense of this chord progression. You can add some passing chords if you like.

3. **Lead Exercise 2 to a perfect cadence.**

   Add chords and melody where needed. Give it a key signature.

4. **Take any two notes and explore the chord combinations available.**

5. **Take any two chords and explore the melodic possibilities between them.**

6. **Listen to some familiar music and see if you can identify the non-chord tones by ear.**

7. Write a chord progression and extract the structural tones.

8. See how many different non-chord tones you can add and determine which ones work well for your style of music composition.

9. Invent a whole new melody by removing some of the original structural tones and leaving the non-chord tones.

Book VII

Writing Songs and Music

Book VIII

Appendixes

"First you play a G7 diminished, followed by an augmented 9th, then a perverted 32nd chord ending with a mangled 11th with a recovering 3rd."

In this book . . .

We give you a colossal chord chart that contains far more chords than you'll ever likely play — but if and when you need to form an obscure chord, you can feel secure that it's in the chart. You also find a handy guide on how to use the CD that accompanies this entire book.

Here are the contents of Book VIII at a glance.

Appendix A

The Mother of All
Guitar Chord Charts

· ·

*T*his appendix functions as a quick reference to chords on the guitar. It covers all the keys and shows each key's chords to the 7th degree.

The tricky thing about diagramming guitar chords is that the same chord can be built in many ways, in many different places on the neck. To make things easier, we only included chords that don't go beyond the upper seven frets of the guitar neck.

Big black dots show where to put your fingers on the frets. An X above a string means you don't play that string. An O above a string stands for "open," meaning you play the string but don't fret it. Also, for each diagram, the pitches for each open (non-fretted) string are, from left to right, (low) E, A, D, G, B, (high) E.

AM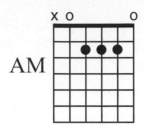

Am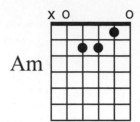

Aaug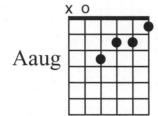

Adim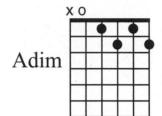

AM7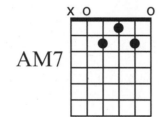

Am7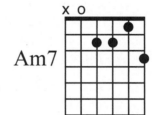

A7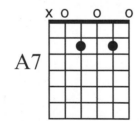

Am7(♭5)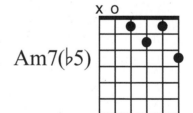

Adim7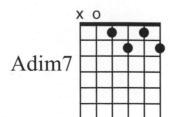

AmiMA7

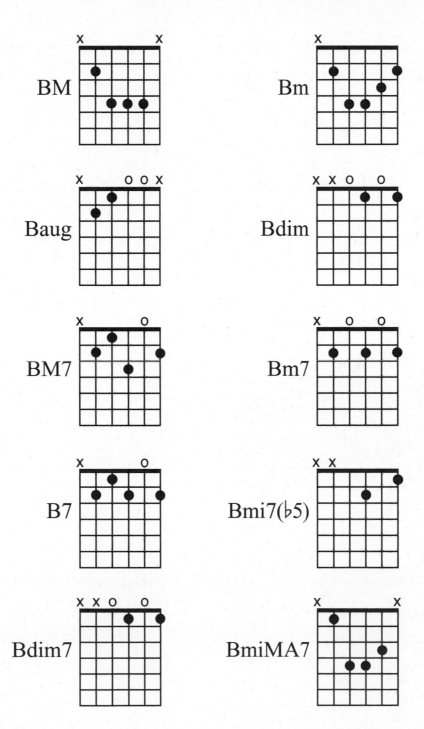

Book VIII

Appendixes

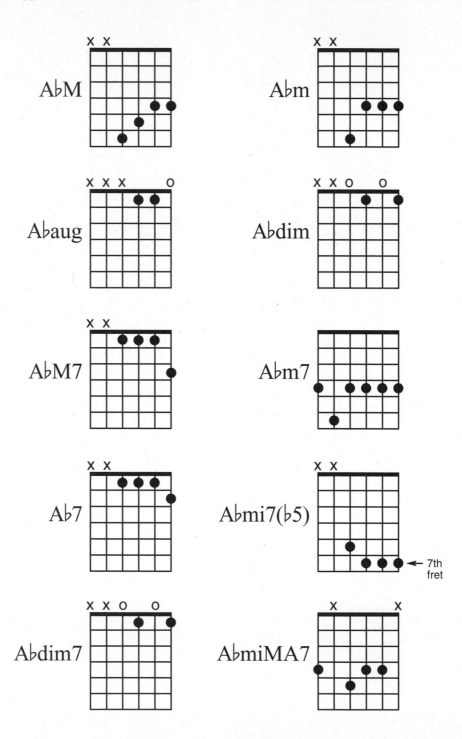

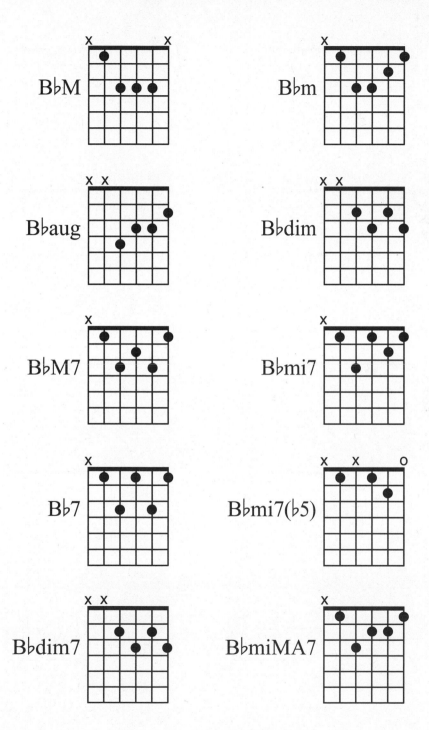

B♭M

B♭m

B♭aug

B♭dim

B♭M7

B♭mi7

B♭7

B♭mi7(♭5)

B♭dim7

B♭miMA7

Book VIII

Appendixes

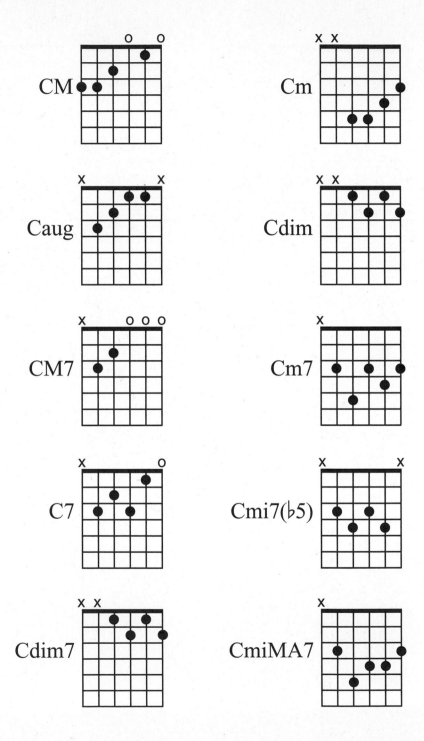

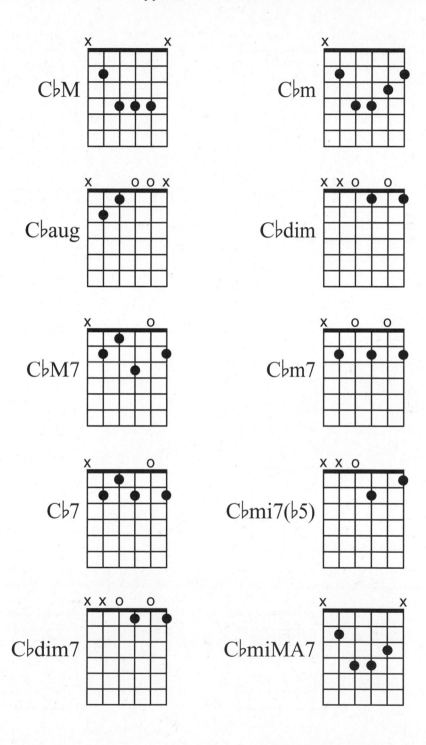

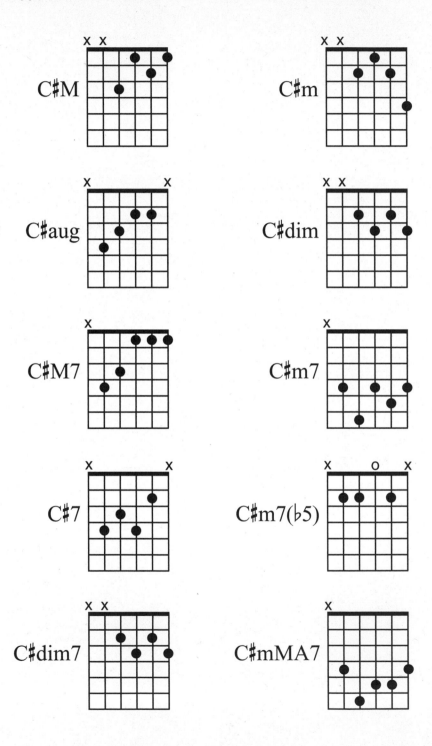

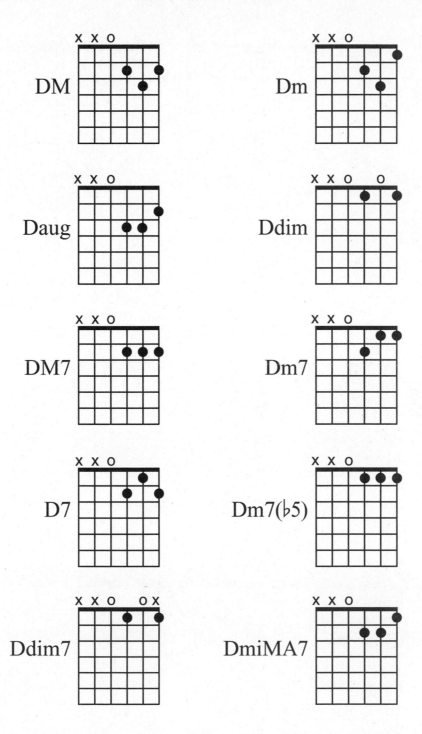

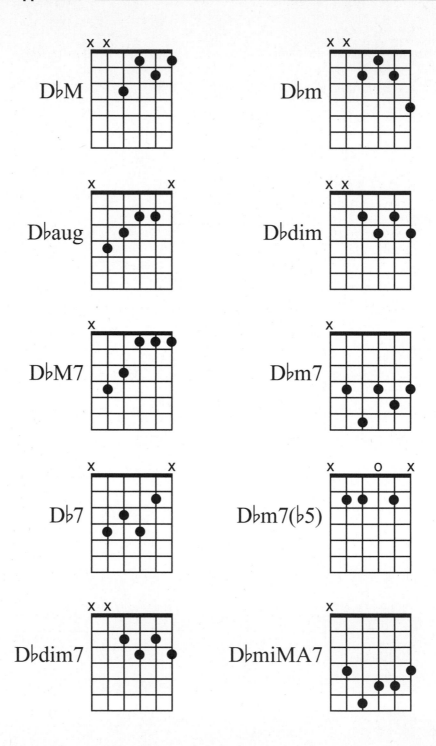

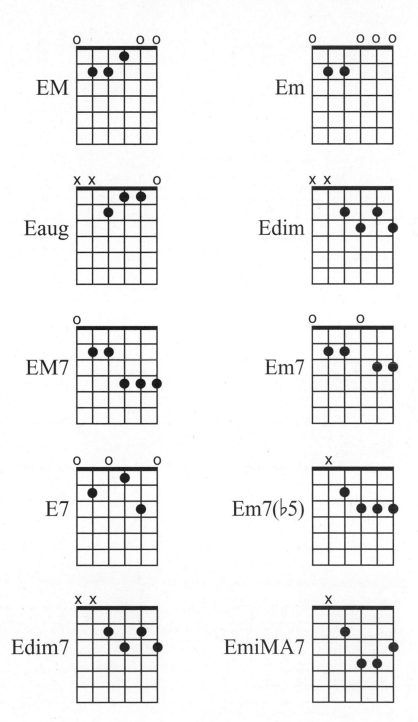

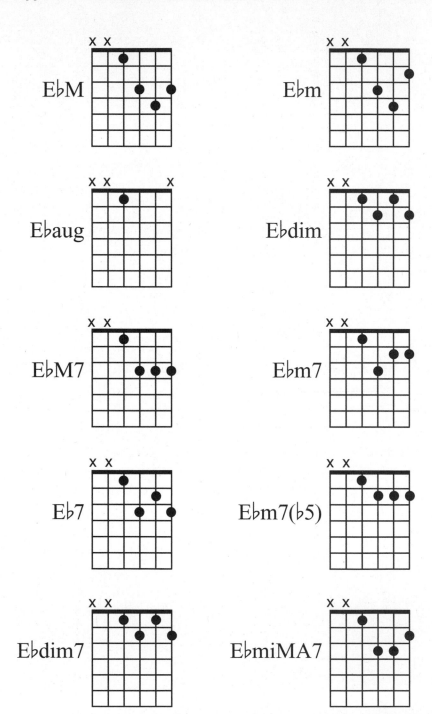

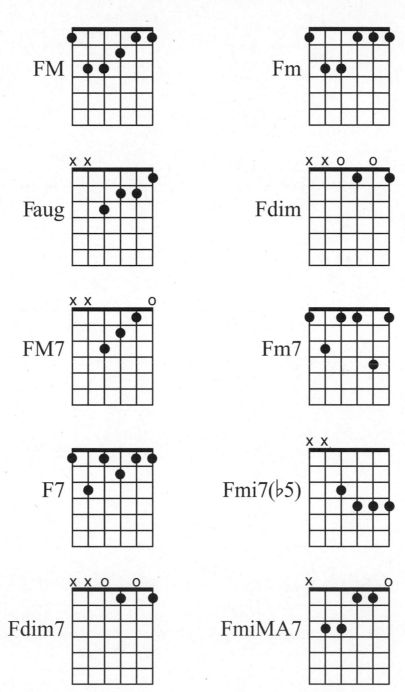

Book VIII

Appendixes

F#M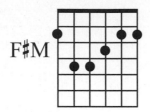

F#m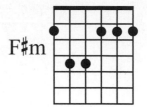

F#aug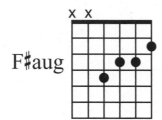

F#dim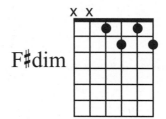

F#M7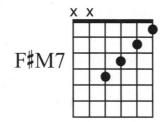

F#m7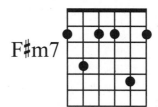

F#7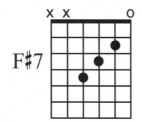

F#m7(♭5)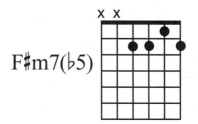

F#dim7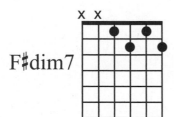

F#miMA7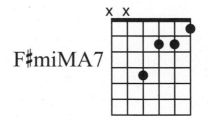

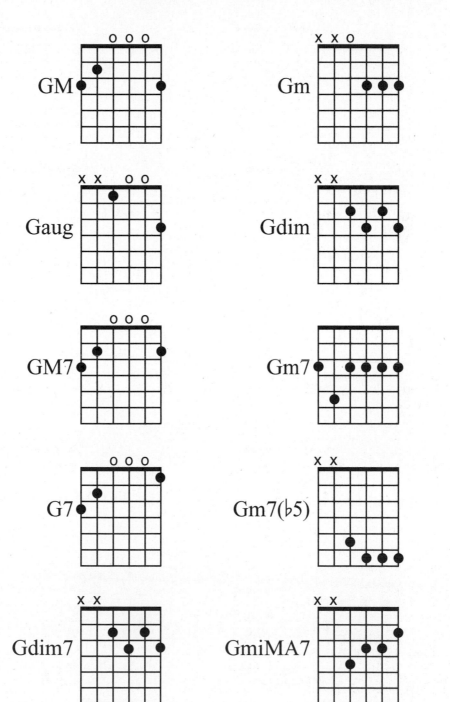

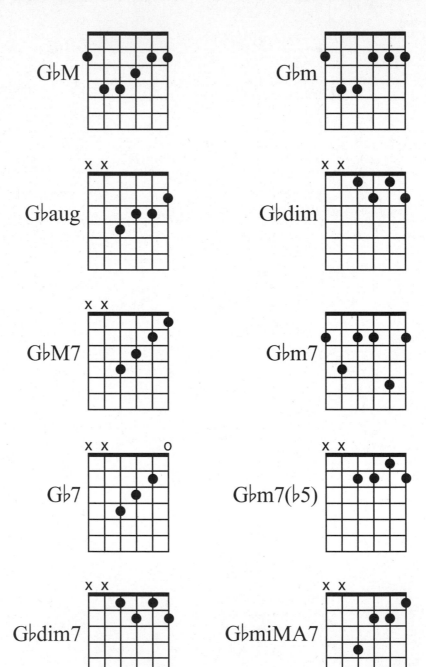

Appendix B

How to Use the CD

Many music examples in *Guitar All-in-One For Dummies* are performed on the CD that comes with this book — 99 of them in fact — making the book something of a multimedia experience. In many cases, you see the music notation and/or tablature in a figure along with a pointer to the track number. The tracks on the CD are in audio CD format, so just stick it in your CD player, find the track you want, and press "Play." You can also rip the tracks to your computer and play them on your portable music player.

The CD is especially helpful when you're not yet reading music well, or when you're just not sure how something is supposed to sound. Table B-1, later in this appendix, lists all track numbers, figure references, and track times (in minutes and seconds).

Keep the CD in its sleeve in the back of the book, rather than in your rack of CDs. Whenever you want to refer to *Guitar All-in-One For Dummies* (the book), the CD will always be right where you expect it. Also, try to get in the habit of following along with the printed music whenever you listen to the CD, even if your sight-reading skills aren't quite up to snuff. It really does help. You absorb more than you expect just by moving your eyes across the page in time to the music, associating sound and sight.

Relating the Text to the CD

Whenever you want to hear what written music in the text sounds like on the CD, refer to the box in the upper right-hand corner, which tells you the track number and start time in minutes and seconds. Use the track skip control to go to the desired track number, and then use the cue button of the cue/review function (also known as the "fast forward/rewind" control) to go to the specific time within that track. When you get on or near the start time, release the cue button, and the example plays.

If you want to play along with the CD, cue up to a spot a few seconds before the start time. Giving yourself a few seconds head start allows you to put down the remote and place your hands in a ready position on the guitar.

Many of the music examples are preceded by a *count-off,* which is a metronome clicking in rhythm before the music begins. This tells you what the tempo is, or the speed at which the music is played. It's like having your own conductor going, "A-one, and a-two . . ." so you can hit the *downbeat* (first note of music) in time with the CD.

Some examples are recorded in what's known as a *stereo split.* In certain pieces, the backing, or accompanying, music appears on the left channel of your stereo, while the featured guitar appears on the right. If you leave your stereo's balance control in its normal position (straight up, or 12:00), you'll hear both rhythm tracks and the featured guitar equally — one from each speaker. By selectively adjusting the balance control (turning the knob to the left or right), you can gradually or drastically reduce the volume of one or the other.

Why would you want to do this? If you've practiced the lead part to a certain example and feel you've got it down good enough to where you want to try it "along with the band," take the balance knob and turn it all the way to the left. Now only the sound from the left speaker comes out, which is the backing tracks. The count-off clicks are in both channels, so you'll always receive your cue to play in time with the music. You can reverse the process and listen to just the lead part, too, which means you play the chords against the recorded lead part. Good, well-rounded guitarists work on both their rhythm *and* their lead playing.

System Requirements

Here's what you need to know to play the CD on different equipment.

Audio CD player

The CD included with this book will work just fine in any standard CD player. Just put it into your home stereo system or boom box. Check out Table B-1 in the section "Tracks on the CD" later in this appendix for track descriptions.

Computer CD-ROM drive

If you have a computer, you can pop the accompanying CD into your CD-ROM drive to play the CD. Make sure that your computer meets the minimum system requirements shown here:

- ✔ A computer running Microsoft Windows or Mac OS
- ✔ Software capable of playing CD audio tracks (for example, iTunes or Windows Media Player)

- A CD-ROM drive
- A sound card for PCs (Mac OS computers have built-in sound support)

Follow these steps to play the CD on your computer:

1. **Put the CD in your computer's CD-ROM drive.**
2. **Rip the tracks to your hard drive as you normally do with an audio CD.**
3. **If you have a digital music player such as an MP3 player or iPod, transfer the tracks to it as you normally do.**

The specific steps you go through to transfer tracks to your hard drive and/ or digital music player depend on your computer platform and software. See your software documentation for help.

Tracks on the CD

Here is a list of the tracks on the CD along with the figure numbers, where applicable, that they correspond to in the book. Use this as a quick reference to finding more about interesting-sounding tracks on the CD.

Table B-1			Tracks on the Book's CD
Track	*(Time)*	*Figure Number*	*Description*
1		N/A	Tuning reference
2	(0:00)	Book II, 1-2	Chord progression using A-family chords
	(0:16)	Book II, 1-4	Chord progression using D-family chords
	(0:43)	Book II, 1-6	Chord progression using G-family chords
	(1:10)	Book II, 1-8	Chord progression using C-family chords
3		N/A	"Kumbaya"
4		N/A	"Swing Low, Sweet Chariot"
5		N/A	"Auld Lang Syne"
6		N/A	"Michael, Row the Boat Ashore"
7		N/A	"Home on the Range"
8		N/A	"All Through the Night"
9		N/A	"Over the River and Through the Woods"
10		N/A	"It's Raining, It's Pouring"
11		N/A	"Oh, Susanna"

Book VIII

Appendixes

(continued)

Table B-1 *(continued)*

Track	(Time)	Figure Number	Description
12		Book II, 3-5	Strummed E chord
13		Book II, 3-13	Progression using power chords
14		Book II, 3-15	Progression using alternating forms
15		Book II, 4-1	E chord in one bar of four quarter notes
16		Book II, 4-2	Eighth-note progression using downstrokes
17		Book II, 4-3	4/4 eighth-note strum using down- and upstrokes
18		Book II, 4-4	Strumming to convey different levels of intensity
19		Book II, 4-5	Medium-tempo progression using 16th notes
20		Book II, 4-6	Eighth-note shuffle in G
21		Book II, 4-7	Bass-chord pattern in a country-rock groove
22		Book II, 4-10	Rock figure using eighth-note syncopation
23		Book II, 4-12	Rhythm figure with palm mutes and accents
24		Book II, 4-13	Eighth-note 5-6 progression
25		Book II, 4-14	Fingerstyle arpeggios played with right-hand fingers
26	(0:00)	Book II, 5-4a	1-2-3-1 permutation exercise
	(0:10)	Book II, 5-4b	1-3-2-4 permutation exercise
	(0:20)	Book II, 5-4c	15-14-13 permutation exercise
27	(0:00)	Book II, 5-5	C major up-the-neck double-stop scale
	(0:11)	Book II, 5-6	C major across-the-neck double-stop scale
28		N/A	"Turkey in the Straw"
29		N/A	"Aura Lee"
30	(0:00)	Book III, 3-1	Quarter-note melodies on each of the guitar's six strings in open position
	(1:12)	Book III, 3-2	Quarter-note melody played across different strings
31	(0:00)	Book III, 3-7	Rocking low-note melody
	(0:11)	Book III, 3-8	Low-note melody in moving eighth notes
	(0:26)	Book III, 3-9	High-note melody in open position
32		Book III, 3-11	Classic walking-bass/boogie riff

Track	(Time)	Figure Number	Description
33		Book III, 3-12	Neck diagram showing pentatonic scale in 5th position
34	(0:00)	Book III, 3-13	Descending eighth-note C pentatonic major scale
	(0:11)	Book III, 3-14	Solo in C major over a medium-tempo 4/4
	(0:35)	Book III, 3-15	Minor solo over a heavy backbeat 4/4 groove
	(0:52)	Book III, 3-16	Blues solo over an up-tempo shuffle in A
35		Book III, 3-17	Slow blues shuffle in A
36	(0:00)	Book III, 4-1	Powerful-sounding riff using only half notes and whole notes
	(0:11)	Book III, 4-2	Quarter-note riff, with one eighth-note pair
	(0:19)	Book III, 4-3	Eighth-note riff, with one quarter note on beat 2
	(0:27)	Book III, 4-4	Boogie shuffle in quarter notes
	(0:37)	Book III, 4-5	Steady-eighth-note riff in E minor with chromatic notes
	(0:45)	Book III, 4-6	Two-bar riff in steady eighth notes
	(0:57)	Book III, 4-7	Riff that steps through quarter, eighth, and 16th notes
	(1:12)	Book III, 4-8	Heavy metal gallop riff
	(1:23)	Book III, 4-9	Fast 16th-note-based riff in a hard-rock style
	(1:33)	Book III, 4-10	Eighth-note riff with beat 1 anticipated, or tied over
	(1:46)	Book III, 4-11	Eighth-note riff with anticipations on beats 1 and 3
	(1:58)	Book III, 4-12	Highly syncopated eighth-note riff
37	(0:00)	Book III, 4-13	Moving double-stop figure used as a chordal device
	(0:13)	Book III, 4-14	Double-stop figure on nonadjacent strings
38		Book III, 4-15	Hard rock progression mixing chords and single notes
39	(0:00)	Book III, 5-1	Open position chord forms
	(0:13)	Book III, 5-2	Moving double-stops over an A pedal
40	(0:00)	Book III, 5-8a	Melodic figure that shifts on the 5th string
	(0:08)	Book III, 5-8b	Shifting melodic figure on the 2nd string

Book VIII

Appendixes

(continued)

Table B-1 *(continued)*

Track	(Time)	Figure Number	Description
	(0:16)	Book III, 5-9	Lateral and longitudinal motion
41		Book III, 5-11	Pentatonic melody in all five positions
42	(0:00)	Book III, 5-12	Short blues lick in 5th position and 7th position
	(0:09)	Book III, 5-13	Lick that dips down from 5th to 2nd position
	(0:18)	Book III, 5-14	Ascending line with three position shifts
43	(0:00)	Book III, 5-15	Riff in 7th-position G major pentatonic
	(0:08)	Book III, 5-16	F major lick with an added flat 3 in 7th position
	(0:18)	Book III, 5-17	Low riff in 1st-position F minor pentatonic
44		Book III, 6-1	The Bo Diddley beat
45		Book III, 6-3	5-to-6 rhythm figure in 12-bar blues
46		Book III, 6-4	Progression using all open-position chords
47		Book III, 6-5	Dynamic all-chord rhythm part
48		Book III, 6-7	Blues-based lead solo in the style of Eric Clapton
49		Book III, 6-8	Jimi Hendrix–style lead featuring bent notes and whammy bar moves
50		Book III, 6-9	Heavy low-note riff followed by a blues-based riff
51		Book III, 6-11	Stevie Ray Vaughan–style rhythm figure and lead
52		Book III, 6-12	Arpeggiated rhythm figure in the style of U2's The Edge
53		Book III, 6-15	Two-handed tapping lick in Van Halen style
54		Book III, 6-16	Straight-ahead blues rock
55		Book III, 6-17	Bluesy lick placed within a progressive format
56		Book IV, 2-4	Bass-and-chord pick-strum pattern for country blues
57		Book IV, 2-5	Two-beat or cut shuffle feel
58		Book IV, 2-6	Pick-strum pattern in a slow 12/8 feel
59	(0:00)	Book IV, 2-8	Straight-eighth progression in A with syncopation
	(0:16)	Book IV, 2-9	Shuffle in A with syncopation

Track	(Time)	Figure Number	Description
	(0:32)	Book IV, 2-10	Strumming pattern that employs left-hand muting to simulate syncopation
60		Book IV, 2-12	Fingerstyle blues with a quarter-note bass
61		Book IV, 2-13	Shuffle feel is the most common groove in the blues
62		Book IV, 2-14	Straight-four feel is used for a more driving sound
63		Book IV, 2-15	12/8 feel is used for slow-tempo blues
64		Book IV, 2-16	16 feel for funky-sounding blues grooves
65	(0:00)	Book IV, 3-2	12-bar blues in E
	(0:37)	Book IV, 3-3	Quick-four change in E blues
66		Book IV, 3-5	Slow blues in 12/8 with added chords
67		Book IV, 3-7	Straight-four progression with a variation
68		Book IV, 3-8	Jimmy Reed move in E
69		Book IV, 3-10	Minor blues progression using minor 7th chords
70		Book IV, 3-21	High moves in a 12-bar blues in E
71	(0:00)	Book IV, 4-11	Triplet-based intro riff in E
	(0:11)	Book IV, 4-12	Double-stop intro riff in E
	(0:21)	Book IV, 4-13	Melodic intro riff based in all triplet eighth notes
	(0:30)	Book IV, 4-14	Descending double-stop turnaround riff in A in the style of Robert Johnson
72	(0:00)	Book IV, 4-15	Turnaround riff in E featuring contrary motion
	(0:12)	Book IV, 4-16	Turnaround riff in C with gospel flavor
	(0:22)	Book IV, 4-17	Triplet-based ending riff
	(0:33)	Book IV, 4-18	Low-note ending riff in E
73		Book IV, 4-19	Rhythm groove over a 12-bar blues in E
74		Book IV, 5-1	12-bar blues in the Delta blues style
75		Book IV, 5-3	Bouncy Piedmont passage
76		Book IV, 5-5	Country blues with a melody on top of an alternating bass
77		Book IV, 5-7	Slide lick in open E
78		Book IV, 5-10	Lick in the style of Elmore James's "Dust My Broom"

Book VIII

Appendixes

(continued)

Table B-1 *(continued)*

Track	(Time)	Figure Number	Description
79		Book IV, 5-12	Classic Texas shuffle
80		Book V, 2-1–2-5	Texture exercises
81		N/A	"Minuet in G"
82		N/A	"Air in A Minor"
83		Book V, 3-1	Arpeggio exercise with melody in the bass
84		Book V, 3-3	Arpeggio exercise with melody in the treble
85		Book V, 3-5	Arpeggio exercise with melody alternating between treble and bass
86		N/A	"Romanza"
87		Book V, 4-1	"Greensleeves"
88		Book V, 4-3	"Jesu, Joy of Man's Desiring" by Bach
89		Book V, 4-5	Aria from *Don Giovanni* by Mozart
90		Book V, 4-6	"Pathetique Sonata" by Beethoven
91		Book VI, 1-1–1-4	Major scale pattern #1
92		Book VI, 2-1–2-2	Major scale sequences using pattern #1
93		Book VI, 3-1	Natural minor scale pattern #1
94		Book VI, 3-11	Melodic minor scale pattern #1
95		Book VI, 3-21	Harmonic minor scale pattern #1
96		Book VI, 4-29	Outside chord progression #1
97		Book VI, 4-31	Inside chord progression #1
98		Book VI, 4-33	"Danny Boy"
99		Book VI, 4-34	"Look for the Silver Lining"

Troubleshooting

If you have trouble with the CD that came with this book, please call the Wiley Product Technical Support phone number: 877-762-2974. Outside the United States, call 317-572-3994. You can also contact Wiley Product Technical Support at www.wiley.com/techsupport. Wiley Publishing will provide technical support only for installation and other general quality control items.

Index

• *O* •

● *P* ●

Wiley Publishing, Inc.
End-User License Agreement

READ THIS. You should carefully read these terms and conditions before opening the software packet(s) included with this book "Book". This is a license agreement "Agreement" between you and Wiley Publishing, Inc. "WPI". By opening the accompanying software packet(s), you acknowledge that you have read and accept the following terms and conditions. If you do not agree and do not want to be bound by such terms and conditions, promptly return the Book and the unopened software packet(s) to the place you obtained them for a full refund.

1. **License Grant.** WPI grants to you (either an individual or entity) a nonexclusive license to use one copy of the enclosed software program(s) (collectively, the "Software") solely for your own personal or business purposes on a single computer (whether a standard computer or a workstation component of a multi-user network). The Software is in use on a computer when it is loaded into temporary memory (RAM) or installed into permanent memory (hard disk, CD-ROM, or other storage device). WPI reserves all rights not expressly granted herein.

2. **Ownership.** WPI is the owner of all right, title, and interest, including copyright, in and to the compilation of the Software recorded on the physical packet included with this Book "Software Media". Copyright to the individual programs recorded on the Software Media is owned by the author or other authorized copyright owner of each program. Ownership of the Software and all proprietary rights relating thereto remain with WPI and its licensers.

3. **Restrictions on Use and Transfer.**

    (a) You may only (i) make one copy of the Software for backup or archival purposes, or (ii) transfer the Software to a single hard disk, provided that you keep the original for backup or archival purposes. You may not (i) rent or lease the Software, (ii) copy or reproduce the Software through a LAN or other network system or through any computer subscriber system or bulletin-board system, or (iii) modify, adapt, or create derivative works based on the Software.

    (b) You may not reverse engineer, decompile, or disassemble the Software. You may transfer the Software and user documentation on a permanent basis, provided that the transferee agrees to accept the terms and conditions of this Agreement and you retain no copies. If the Software is an update or has been updated, any transfer must include the most recent update and all prior versions.

4. **Restrictions on Use of Individual Programs.** You must follow the individual requirements and restrictions detailed for each individual program in the "How to Use the CD" appendix of this Book or on the Software Media. These limitations are also contained in the individual license agreements recorded on the Software Media. These limitations may include a requirement that after using the program for a specified period of time, the user must pay a registration fee or discontinue use. By opening the Software packet(s), you agree to abide by the licenses and restrictions for these individual programs that are detailed in the "How to Use the CD" appendix and/or on the Software Media. None of the material on this Software Media or listed in this Book may ever be redistributed, in original or modified form, for commercial purposes.

5. **Limited Warranty.**

   (a) WPI warrants that the Software and Software Media are free from defects in materials and workmanship under normal use for a period of sixty (60) days from the date of purchase of this Book. If WPI receives notification within the warranty period of defects in materials or workmanship, WPI will replace the defective Software Media.

   (b) WPI AND THE AUTHOR(S) OF THE BOOK DISCLAIM ALL OTHER WARRANTIES, EXPRESS OR IMPLIED, INCLUDING WITHOUT LIMITATION IMPLIED WARRANTIES OF MERCHANTABILITY AND FITNESS FOR A PARTICULAR PURPOSE, WITH RESPECT TO THE SOFTWARE, THE PROGRAMS, THE SOURCE CODE CONTAINED THEREIN, AND/OR THE TECHNIQUES DESCRIBED IN THIS BOOK. WPI DOES NOT WARRANT THAT THE FUNCTIONS CONTAINED IN THE SOFTWARE WILL MEET YOUR REQUIREMENTS OR THAT THE OPERATION OF THE SOFTWARE WILL BE ERROR FREE.

   (c) This limited warranty gives you specific legal rights, and you may have other rights that vary from jurisdiction to jurisdiction.

6. **Remedies.**

   (a) WPI's entire liability and your exclusive remedy for defects in materials and workmanship shall be limited to replacement of the Software Media, which may be returned to WPI with a copy of your receipt at the following address: Software Media Fulfillment Department, Attn.: *Guitar All-in-One For Dummies*, Wiley Publishing, Inc., 10475 Crosspoint Blvd., Indianapolis, IN 46256, or call 1-877-762-2974. Please allow four to six weeks for delivery. This Limited Warranty is void if failure of the Software Media has resulted from accident, abuse, or misapplication. Any replacement Software Media will be warranted for the remainder of the original warranty period or thirty (30) days, whichever is longer.

   (b) In no event shall WPI or the author be liable for any damages whatsoever (including without limitation damages for loss of business profits, business interruption, loss of business information, or any other pecuniary loss) arising from the use of or inability to use the Book or the Software, even if WPI has been advised of the possibility of such damages.

   (c) Because some jurisdictions do not allow the exclusion or limitation of liability for consequential or incidental damages, the above limitation or exclusion may not apply to you.

7. **U.S. Government Restricted Rights.** Use, duplication, or disclosure of the Software for or on behalf of the United States of America, its agencies and/or instrumentalities "U.S. Government" is subject to restrictions as stated in paragraph (c)(1)(ii) of the Rights in Technical Data and Computer Software clause of DFARS 252.227-7013, or subparagraphs (c)(1) and (2) of the Commercial Computer Software - Restricted Rights clause at FAR 52.227-19, and in similar clauses in the NASA FAR supplement, as applicable.

8. **General.** This Agreement constitutes the entire understanding of the parties and revokes and supersedes all prior agreements, oral or written, between them and may not be modified or amended except in a writing signed by both parties hereto that specifically refers to this Agreement. This Agreement shall take precedence over any other documents that may be in conflict herewith. If any one or more provisions contained in this Agreement are held by any court or tribunal to be invalid, illegal, or otherwise unenforceable, each and every other provision shall remain in full force and effect.

BUSINESS, CAREERS & PERSONAL FINANCE

Accounting For Dummies, 4th Edition*
978-0-470-24600-9

Bookkeeping Workbook For Dummies†
978-0-470-16983-4

Commodities For Dummies
978-0-470-04928-0

Doing Business in China For Dummies
978-0-470-04929-7

E-Mail Marketing For Dummies
978-0-470-19087-6

Job Interviews For Dummies, 3rd Edition*†
978-0-470-17748-8

Personal Finance Workbook For Dummies*†
978-0-470-09933-9

Real Estate License Exams For Dummies
978-0-7645-7623-2

Six Sigma For Dummies
978-0-7645-6798-8

Small Business Kit For Dummies, 2nd Edition*†
978-0-7645-5984-6

Telephone Sales For Dummies
978-0-470-16836-3

BUSINESS PRODUCTIVITY & MICROSOFT OFFICE

Access 2007 For Dummies
978-0-470-03649-5

Excel 2007 For Dummies
978-0-470-03737-9

Office 2007 For Dummies
978-0-470-00923-9

Outlook 2007 For Dummies
978-0-470-03830-7

PowerPoint 2007 For Dummies
978-0-470-04059-1

Project 2007 For Dummies
978-0-470-03651-8

QuickBooks 2008 For Dummies
978-0-470-18470-7

Quicken 2008 For Dummies
978-0-470-17473-9

Salesforce.com For Dummies, 2nd Edition
978-0-470-04893-1

Word 2007 For Dummies
978-0-470-03658-7

EDUCATION, HISTORY, REFERENCE & TEST PREPARATION

African American History For Dummies
978-0-7645-5469-8

Algebra For Dummies
978-0-7645-5325-7

Algebra Workbook For Dummies
978-0-7645-8467-1

Art History For Dummies
978-0-470-09910-0

ASVAB For Dummies, 2nd Edition
978-0-470-10671-6

British Military History For Dummies
978-0-470-03213-8

Calculus For Dummies
978-0-7645-2498-1

Canadian History For Dummies, 2nd Edition
978-0-470-83656-9

Geometry Workbook For Dummies
978-0-471-79940-5

The SAT I For Dummies, 6th Edition
978-0-7645-7193-0

Series 7 Exam For Dummies
978-0-470-09932-2

World History For Dummies
978-0-7645-5242-7

FOOD, GARDEN, HOBBIES & HOME

Bridge For Dummies, 2nd Edition
978-0-471-92426-5

Coin Collecting For Dummies, 2nd Edition
978-0-470-22275-1

Cooking Basics For Dummies, 3rd Edition
978-0-7645-7206-7

Drawing For Dummies
978-0-7645-5476-6

Etiquette For Dummies, 2nd Edition
978-0-470-10672-3

Gardening Basics For Dummies*†
978-0-470-03749-2

Knitting Patterns For Dummies
978-0-470-04556-5

Living Gluten-Free For Dummies†
978-0-471-77383-2

Painting Do-It-Yourself For Dummies
978-0-470-17533-0

HEALTH, SELF HELP, PARENTING & PETS

Anger Management For Dummies
978-0-470-03715-7

Anxiety & Depression Workbook For Dummies
978-0-7645-9793-0

Dieting For Dummies, 2nd Edition
978-0-7645-4149-0

Dog Training For Dummies, 2nd Edition
978-0-7645-8418-3

Horseback Riding For Dummies
978-0-470-09719-9

Infertility For Dummies†
978-0-470-11518-3

Meditation For Dummies with CD-ROM, 2nd Edition
978-0-471-77774-8

Post-Traumatic Stress Disorder For Dummies
978-0-470-04922-8

Puppies For Dummies, 2nd Edition
978-0-470-03717-1

Thyroid For Dummies, 2nd Edition†
978-0-471-78755-6

Type 1 Diabetes For Dummies*†
978-0-470-17811-9

* Separate Canadian edition also available
† Separate U.K. edition also available

Available wherever books are sold. For more information or to order direct: U.S. customers visit www.dummies.com or call 1-877-762-2974.
U.K. customers visit www.wileyeurope.com or call (0)1243 843291. Canadian customers visit www.wiley.ca or call 1-800-567-4797.

INTERNET & DIGITAL MEDIA

AdWords For Dummies
978-0-470-15252-2

Blogging For Dummies, 2nd Edition
978-0-470-23017-6

Digital Photography All-in-One Desk Reference For Dummies, 3rd Edition
978-0-470-03743-0

Digital Photography For Dummies, 5th Edition
978-0-7645-9802-9

Digital SLR Cameras & Photography For Dummies, 2nd Edition
978-0-470-14927-0

eBay Business All-in-One Desk Reference For Dummies
978-0-7645-8438-1

eBay For Dummies, 5th Edition*
978-0-470-04529-9

eBay Listings That Sell For Dummies
978-0-471-78912-3

Facebook For Dummies
978-0-470-26273-3

The Internet For Dummies, 11th Edition
978-0-470-12174-0

Investing Online For Dummies, 5th Edition
978-0-7645-8456-5

iPod & iTunes For Dummies, 5th Edition
978-0-470-17474-6

MySpace For Dummies
978-0-470-09529-4

Podcasting For Dummies
978-0-471-74898-4

Search Engine Optimization For Dummies, 2nd Edition
978-0-471-97998-2

Second Life For Dummies
978-0-470-18025-9

Starting an eBay Business For Dummies, 3rd Edition†
978-0-470-14924-9

GRAPHICS, DESIGN & WEB DEVELOPMENT

Adobe Creative Suite 3 Design Premium All-in-One Desk Reference For Dummies
978-0-470-11724-8

Adobe Web Suite CS3 All-in-One Desk Reference For Dummies
978-0-470-12099-6

AutoCAD 2008 For Dummies
978-0-470-11650-0

Building a Web Site For Dummies, 3rd Edition
978-0-470-14928-7

Creating Web Pages All-in-One Desk Reference For Dummies, 3rd Edition
978-0-470-09629-1

Creating Web Pages For Dummies, 8th Edition
978-0-470-08030-6

Dreamweaver CS3 For Dummies
978-0-470-11490-2

Flash CS3 For Dummies
978-0-470-12100-9

Google SketchUp For Dummies
978-0-470-13744-4

InDesign CS3 For Dummies
978-0-470-11865-8

Photoshop CS3 All-in-One Desk Reference For Dummies
978-0-470-11195-6

Photoshop CS3 For Dummies
978-0-470-11193-2

Photoshop Elements 5 For Dummies
978-0-470-09810-3

SolidWorks For Dummies
978-0-7645-9555-4

Visio 2007 For Dummies
978-0-470-08983-5

Web Design For Dummies, 2nd Edition
978-0-471-78117-2

Web Sites Do-It-Yourself For Dummies
978-0-470-16903-2

Web Stores Do-It-Yourself For Dummies
978-0-470-17443-2

LANGUAGES, RELIGION & SPIRITUALITY

Arabic For Dummies
978-0-471-77270-5

Chinese For Dummies, Audio Set
978-0-470-12766-7

French For Dummies
978-0-7645-5193-2

German For Dummies
978-0-7645-5195-6

Hebrew For Dummies
978-0-7645-5489-6

Ingles Para Dummies
978-0-7645-5427-8

Italian For Dummies, Audio Set
978-0-470-09586-7

Italian Verbs For Dummies
978-0-471-77389-4

Japanese For Dummies
978-0-7645-5429-2

Latin For Dummies
978-0-7645-5431-5

Portuguese For Dummies
978-0-471-78738-9

Russian For Dummies
978-0-471-78001-4

Spanish Phrases For Dummies
978-0-7645-7204-3

Spanish For Dummies
978-0-7645-5194-9

Spanish For Dummies, Audio Set
978-0-470-09585-0

The Bible For Dummies
978-0-7645-5296-0

Catholicism For Dummies
978-0-7645-5391-2

The Historical Jesus For Dummies
978-0-470-16785-4

Islam For Dummies
978-0-7645-5503-9

Spirituality For Dummies, 2nd Edition
978-0-470-19142-2

NETWORKING AND PROGRAMMING

ASP.NET 3.5 For Dummies
978-0-470-19592-5

C# 2008 For Dummies
978-0-470-19109-5

Hacking For Dummies, 2nd Edition
978-0-470-05235-8

Home Networking For Dummies, 4th Edition
978-0-470-11806-1

Java For Dummies, 4th Edition
978-0-470-08716-9

Microsoft® SQL Server™ 2008 All-in-One Desk Reference For Dummies
978-0-470-17954-3

Networking All-in-One Desk Reference For Dummies, 2nd Edition
978-0-7645-9939-2

Networking For Dummies, 8th Edition
978-0-470-05620-2

SharePoint 2007 For Dummies
978-0-470-09941-4

Wireless Home Networking For Dummies, 2nd Edition
978-0-471-74940-0

OPERATING SYSTEMS & COMPUTER BASICS

iMac For Dummies, 5th Edition
978-0-7645-8458-9

Laptops For Dummies, 2nd Edition
978-0-470-05432-1

Linux For Dummies, 8th Edition
978-0-470-11649-4

MacBook For Dummies
978-0-470-04859-7

**Mac OS X Leopard All-in-One
Desk Reference For Dummies**
978-0-470-05434-5

Mac OS X Leopard For Dummies
978-0-470-05433-8

Macs For Dummies, 9th Edition
978-0-470-04849-8

PCs For Dummies, 11th Edition
978-0-470-13728-4

Windows® Home Server For Dummies
978-0-470-18592-6

Windows Server 2008 For Dummies
978-0-470-18043-3

**Windows Vista All-in-One
Desk Reference For Dummies**
978-0-471-74941-7

Windows Vista For Dummies
978-0-471-75421-3

Windows Vista Security For Dummies
978-0-470-11805-4

SPORTS, FITNESS & MUSIC

Coaching Hockey For Dummies
978-0-470-83685-9

Coaching Soccer For Dummies
978-0-471-77381-8

Fitness For Dummies, 3rd Edition
978-0-7645-7851-9

Football For Dummies, 3rd Edition
978-0-470-12536-6

GarageBand For Dummies
978-0-7645-7323-1

Golf For Dummies, 3rd Edition
978-0-471-76871-5

Guitar For Dummies, 2nd Edition
978-0-7645-9904-0

**Home Recording For Musicians
For Dummies, 2nd Edition**
978-0-7645-8884-6

**iPod & iTunes For Dummies,
5th Edition**
978-0-470-17474-6

Music Theory For Dummies
978-0-7645-7838-0

Stretching For Dummies
978-0-470-06741-3

Get smart @ dummies.com®

- **Find a full list of Dummies titles**
- **Look into loads of FREE on-site articles**
- **Sign up for FREE eTips e-mailed to you weekly**
- **See what other products carry the Dummies name**
- **Shop directly from the Dummies bookstore**
- **Enter to win new prizes every month!**

* Separate Canadian edition also available
† Separate U.K. edition also available

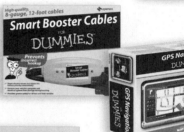